Events Management

Events Management

G. A. J. Bowdin, I. McDonnell, J. Allen and W. O'Toole

OXFORD AMSTERDAM BOSTON LONDON NEW YORK PARIS
SAN DIEGO SAN FRANCISCO SINGAPORE SIDNEY TOKYO

Butterworth-Heinemann
An imprint of Elsevier Science
Linacre House, Jordan Hill, Oxford OX2 8DP
225 Wildwood Avenue, Woburn, MA 01801-2041

First published in Australia by John Wiley & Sons Australia Ltd
33 Park Road, Milton Q 4064 1999
First published in Great Britain 2001
Reprinted 2002

British Library Cataloguing in Publication Data
A catalogue record for this book is available from the British Library

ISBN 0 7506 4796 5

For information on all Butterworth-Heinemann publications visit our website
at www.bh.com

Composition by Genesis Typesetting, Rochester, Kent
Printed and bound in Great Britain MPG Books Ltd, Bodmin, Cornwall

Contents

List of figures

Hospitality, Leisure & Tourism Series

List of tables

About the authors

Glenn A. J. Bowdin, BA (Hons), MPhil, MHCIMA, is Senior Lecturer in Events Planning at the UK Centre for Events Management, Leeds Metropolitan University, and specializes in the area of planning and management of events and quality costing. Over the past five years, he has been actively involved in developing the BA (Hons) Events Management degree programme and more recently the HND Events Management programme. He is responsible for various areas of the courses, including dissertations research. Glenn is co-ordinator of the event-management list-serve (http://www.jiscmail.ac.uk/lists/event-management.html), set up to promote the sharing of research and experience within events management education, and owns/manages WorldofEvents.net, designed to support event industry professionals, educators, students and researchers. Glenn is on the editorial board of Event Management (formerly Festival Management and Event Tourism).

Ian McDonnell, MA, MHEd is a lecturer at the University of Technology, Sydney's School of Leisure and Tourism Studies, and specializes in the management and marketing of tourism and leisure studies. Prior to becoming an academic, Ian held a managerial position for many years with Qantas. In this position he lived and worked in northern and western Australia, south-east Asia, the south Pacific and Europe.

Johnny Allen's lifelong career in events ranges from being co-director of 'a major counter-cultural youth festival' at Nimbin in northern New South Wales in 1973, to events manager for Sydney's Darling Harbour, and devising an events strategy for the New South Wales government as Special Events Manager for Tourism New South Wales. Johnny currently teaches events management at the University of Technology, Sydney, where he has established the Australian Centre for Events Management focusing on education, training and research.

William O'Toole, BSc, has been creating and managing events for over twenty years. His company, EPMS.NET, advises on risk and project management to major festivals, and provides a free resource for event managers. The website (www.epms.net) is used both for teaching and managing events around the world. Currently he trains event managers in project management methodology at the University of Technology, Sydney, and teaches event project management on line at the University of Sydney (www.pmoutreach.usyd.edu.au). His latest text, *Corporate Event Project Management*, written with the event manager from Xerox, is available through John Wiley & Sons.

Hospitality, Leisure & Tourism Series

Preface

Each year, events occur throughout the United Kingdom. They dominate the media, fill transport systems, hotels and venues, meet business objectives, motivate communities and create positive and negative impacts. For example, the Notting Hill Carnival can trace its origins back to 1964 when, established as a festival, it provided an opportunity for West Indians to celebrate and commemorate their ancestors' freedom from slavery. Over the years, the event grew slowly, from 200 visitors, to some 3000 in the early 1970s. The turning point for the Carnival came in 1975, when it was promoted by Capital Radio, resulting in 150 000 people from the West Indian community attending. Today, the Carnival boasts an audience of an estimated 2.5 million people from all communities – attracting attention from Greater London Authority, the police and others who fear for the safety of visitors.

Until relatively recently, events have been seen as part of the hospitality, tourism, leisure and recreation industries, or as a support service to businesses. However, the environment is changing and many believe that the events industry now exists in its own right. The UK events industry is wide ranging, incorporating many different sectors from the smallest of exhibitions, conferences and parties, through to large-scale sport and entertainment events. Although definitive data are not available, due to the complex nature and diversity of the industry, figures suggest that the economic impact of business tourism alone (e.g. conferences, exhibitions, incentive travel) is £12 billion and expected to grow to £16 billion within the next ten years (Business Tourism Forum, 1999). This suggests that the industry offers significant income to the UK economy. This income has not gone unnoticed by local and national government and other public sector bodies. Increasingly, they are using events as a means of serving a host of policy objectives – from delivering tourists, regenerating communities and celebrating moments in time (such as the extensive range of events during the Millennium) to arousing civic pride, inspiring the arts and stimulating regional economies. Alongside this, the industry is seeking to increase professionalism, illustrated by the development of qualifications, education and training programmes within the industry and academia, supported by a range of professional associations.

The UK has developed an enviable programme of events, including The Championships (known the world over as simply Wimbledon), Notting Hill

Carnival, The Open Championship, Glastonbury Festival, Royal Ascot, Edinburgh International Festival, the British Grand Prix, and the FA Cup – together with many others that cover the full spectrum of business and community interests. These events and others, which are discussed in this book, illustrate in various ways the power they have to raise the profile of their host cities, attract visitors, deliver economic benefits and create jobs. They also show the various origins of events, ranging from community celebrations growing out of protest, to international events supported for political and economic needs. They raise issues of the costs, benefits and impacts on their host communities and serve as models for event management, development and marketing.

Events Management examines these and other aspects of events from the UK perspective. Specifically, the book aims to:

- Present the study of events management within an academic environment
- Introduce students and practitioners to the concepts of event planning and management
- Develop an understanding of key areas required for planning and managing events, including management, logistics, legal considerations, budgeting, staging, marketing, promotion, and evaluation
- Increase the student's understanding of the events industry within its broader business context.

The first part of the book deals with the context for events – the reasons human societies create events – and the events culture that has evolved are examined, as are the range and types of events and their impacts on their host communities, environment and economy. Next, a methodology for the strategic management of events is illustrated by an examination of the processes involved in developing, planning, implementing, marketing and sponsoring events. Finally, the event project is explored, discussing budgeting and control, legal and risk management, logistics, staging and the process of monitoring and evaluating events and reporting back to stakeholders.

The book is conveniently divided into twelve chapters, which may be used to structure teaching sessions. Each chapter commences with clear objectives and ends with review questions in order to assess the student's understanding. The book is also amply illustrated throughout with case studies, which assist the reader to relate the theory of events management to the real world of events practice, with all its challenges, frustrations and rewards. The book provides the reader with both a tool for greater understanding of events management and a framework for planning and implementing events.

By its very nature, events management is a creative process, and by drawing on the body of knowledge in the field, it is hoped that the reader will in turn contribute to the future of this young and exciting industry.

Events Management is supported by a Web site (http://em.worldofevents.net), which includes updates, downloadable figures from the book to enhance assignments and an online 'history of events', together with links to Web sites and other useful resources for both students and lecturers. Further, for lecturers adopting the book, a companion site is available that includes Microsoft PowerPoint slides and associated teaching aids.

Acknowledgements

Glenn A. J. Bowdin wishes to thank the following people/organizations for their assistance with the production of this text: Ian McDonnell (planning, leadership and human resources, marketing and sponsorship), Johnny Allen (event history and typologies, impacts, conceptualizing events and evaluation) and William O'Toole (control and budgets, legal and risk management, logistics and staging), Sally Bentley and team (Theme Traders Ltd), Carolyn Chan (International Confex), Edinburgh International Festival, Bill Egan (GE Energy Rentals Ltd), Roger Foley (Fogg Productions), Peter Haywood and Dirk Mischendahl (Logistik), David Hill (The Open Championship), Glastonbury Festival of Contemporary Arts, Claire Holder (Notting Hill Carnival), Caroline McKinnes (formerly of Cheltenham Festivals), SMMT Ltd (British International Motor Show), Randle Stonier (Skybridge Group plc), Rebecca Wilson (ESP Recruitment), Keith Wrighton, Graham Keene and David Hurst (World Event Management). Special thanks and appreciation to colleagues and students from the UK Centre for Events Management, Leeds Metropolitan University, for their ideas and input, and the publishing team at Butterworth-Heinemann for all their support, advice and assistance. Finally, to Eileen Bowdin, for a year of lost evenings and weekends.

The authors and publishers wish to thank the following people and institutions for permission to reproduce material covered by copyright.

Figures
p. 16 (Figure 1.1): Fletcher, Mike (2000), Calling time on the gender gap. *Marketing Event*, October, pp. 23–24. © Haymarket Business Publications Ltd/Marketing Event; p. 34 (Figure 2.1): Xerox Corporation, *Guide to Waste Reduction and Recycling at Special Events*, 1998, reproduced with permission of Xerox Corporation, New York; p. 76 (Figure 4.4) *Management*, 6th edn by Stoner, Freeman & Gilbert Jr., 1995. © 1995 by Prentice Hall, Inc., reprinted with permission of Pearson Education, Inc., Upper Saddle River, NJ; p. 97 (Figure 5.2), p. 98 (Figure 5.3) Bradner, J. (1995) Recruitment, orientation, retention. In: Connors, T. ed., *The Volunteer Management Handbook*, New York, John Wiley and Sons; p. 101 (Figure 5.4) Buckler, B. (1998), Practical steps towards a learning organization: applying academic knowledge to improvement and innovation in business performance, *The Learning Organization*, 5(1), pp. 15–23, reproduced by permission of MCB University Press, Bradford; p. 102 (Figure 5.5)

Peach, E. and Murrell, K. (1995), Reward and recognition systems for volunteers. In: Connors, T. ed., *The Volunteer Management Handbook*, New York, John Wiley & Sons; p. 128 (Figure 6.3) Brassington, F. and Pettitt, S. (2000) *Principles of Marketing*, 2nd edn. © Pearson Education Limited, 1997, 2000, reproduced with permission of Pearson Education Limited; p. 133 (Figure 6.6), reprinted by permission of Harvard Business Review. [Exhibit] From 'Strategies for diversification' by Ansoff, I., September–October, 1957. Copyright © 1957 by the Harvard Business School Publishing Corporation, all rights reserved; p. 121 (Table 6.2), p. 134 (Figure 6.7), p. 138 (Figure 6.10), p. 145 (Figure 6.12) Morgan, Michael (1996) *Marketing for Leisure and Tourism*, © Prentice Hall Europe, reprinted by permission of Pearson Education Limited; p. 153 (Figure 7.1) Crompton, J. (1994), Benefits and risks associated with sponsorship of major events, *Festival Management and Event Tourism*, 2(2), pp. 65–74, reproduced by permission of Cognizant Communications Corporation, New York; p. 156 (Figure 7.2) Geldard, E. and Sinclair, L., *The Sponsorship Manual, 1996*. Victoria, Australia, The Sponsorship Unit, reproduced by permission of The Sponsorship Unit, Victoria; p. 157 (Figure 7.3) Sunshine, K., Backman, K. and Backman, S. (1995), An examination of sponsorship proposals in relation to corporate objectives, *Festival Management and Event Tourism*, 2(3/4), pp. 159–166, reproduced by permission of Cognizant Communications Corporation, New York; p. 191 (Figure 9.1) Allen, K. and Shaw, P. (2001) *Festivals Mean Business: The Shape of Arts Festivals in the UK*, reproduced by permission of British Arts Festivals Association, London; p. 193 (Figure 9.2) Chris Hannam, Stagesafe Limited; p. 200 (Figure 9.5), p. 204 (Figure 9.6): Crown copyright material is reproduced with the permission of the Controller of HMSO and the Queen's Printer for Scotland; p. 228 (Figure 10.8) Slice Communications, London; p. 253 (Figure 11.3) Roger Foley, Fogg Productions; p. 285 (Figure 12.6) Media Release on Economic Impact of 1998 Network Q Rally. Reproduced by permission of the Motor Sports Association.

Text
p. 9 (Table 1.1) PSI (1992), Arts festivals, *Cultural Trends*, 15, reproduced by permission of Policy Studies Institute, London; p. 106 (Table 5.1) Peach, E. and Murrell, K. (1995), Reward and recognition systems for volunteers. In: Connors, T. ed. *The Volunteer Management Handbook*. New York, John Wiley & Sons; p. 127 (Table 6.5) Getz, D. (1997), *Event Management and Event Tourism*, reproduced by permission of Cognizant Communications Corporation, New York.

Every effort has been made to trace ownership of copyright material. Information that will enable the publisher to rectify any error or omission in subsequent editions will be welcome. In such cases please contact the Permissions Department at Butterworth-Heinemann.

CHAPTER 1

What are events?

After studying this chapter, you should be able to:

- define special events, mega-events, hallmark events and major events

- demonstrate an awareness of why events have evolved in human society

- describe the role of events in the UK, and the UK tradition of events

- describe the rise and effect of the community arts movement on events

- understand the growth and emergence of an events industry

- distinguish between different types of events

- discuss the attributes and knowledge requirements of an events manager

- describe the consolidation of the events industry in the UK.

Introduction – events as benchmarks for our lives

Since the dawn of time, human beings have found ways to mark important events in their lives: the changing of the seasons; the phases of the moon; the eternal cycle of birth, death and the miraculous renewal of life each spring. In Britain, the early folk festivals were associated with Plough Monday, May Day, Midsummer Day and Harvest Home, the latter celebrating the final gathering of the grain harvest (Oxford Interactive Encyclopedia, 1997). From the Chinese New Year to the Dionysian rites of ancient Greece and the European carnival tradition of the Middle Ages, myths and rituals have been created to interpret cosmological happenings. To the present day, scratch the surface of the archetypes of Old Father Time on New Year's Eve, Guy Fawkes on 5 November Bonfire Night, Hallowe'en, or Father Christmas on 25 December, and remnants of the old myths and celebrations will be found underneath.

Both in private and in public, people feel the need to mark the important happenings in their lives, to celebrate the key moments. Coming of age, for example, is marked by rites of passage, such as initiation ceremonies, the Jewish bar mitzvah and the suburban twenty-first birthday party. At the public level, momentous events become the milestones by which people measure their private lives. We talk about things happening 'before the new millennium', in the same way that an earlier generation talked of marrying 'before the Depression' or being born 'after the War'. Occasional events – the 1966 World Cup, the new millennium, and the Manchester 2002 Commonwealth Games – help to mark eras and define milestones.

Even in the high-tech era of global media, when people have lost touch with the common religious beliefs and social norms of the past, we still need social events to mark the local and domestic details of our lives.

This chapter traces the historical development of events, exhibitions and festivals within the UK through to the establishment of the events industry that is seen today. It ends by defining and classifying events, which then provides the focus for further study.

The rich tradition of events

The UK, and the various countries and cultures within it, have a rich tradition of rituals and ceremonies extending over thousands of years. These traditions, influenced by changes within society, including urbanization, industrialization and the increasingly multicultural population, have greatly influenced many events as they are celebrated today. Palmer and Lloyd (1972) highlight that Britain has many customs and traditions that are tied in with the changing seasons and country life. In addition, they note that with developing immigration, particularly after the war, settlers brought their own customs and traditions that have now become part of Britain's heritage. In the cultural collision with the first migrants from the former colonies of India, Pakistan and the Caribbean, new traditions have formed alongside the old. However, many events which people take for granted today have been taking place in one form or another for hundreds of years. These include fairs, festivals, sporting events, exhibitions and other forms of public celebration.

The Lord Mayor's Show provides an example of this – originating from 1215 when King John granted a Charter confirming the citizens of London's right to choose their own mayor. One of the conditions of the Charter was that the man chosen as mayor must be presented to King John for approval and had to swear an oath of allegiance. This was the basis for the original show – literally the mayor has to go to Westminster to be shown to the king. The Lord Mayor's Show is now the largest parade of its kind in the world, with 6000 participants, 2000 military personnel, 200 horses, 220 motor vehicles, 56 floats, 20 marching bands, and the state coach involved in the procession that is nearly 2.5 miles long, yet travels a route of less than 2 miles (Lord Mayor's Show, 2000).

The term 'festival' has been used for hundreds of years and can be used to cover a multitude of events. The Policy Studies Institute (PSI, 1992, p. 1) note:

> A festival was traditionally a time of celebration, relaxation and recuperation which often followed a period of hard physical labour, sowing or harvesting of crops, for example. The essential feature of these festivals was the celebration or reaffirmation of community or culture. The artistic content of such events was variable and many had a religious or ritualistic aspect, but music, dance and drama were important features of the celebration.

The majority of fairs held in the UK can trace their ancestry back to Charters and privileges granted by the Crown. The original purpose of the fairs was to trade produce, much the same as exhibitions operate today. For example, the famous Scarborough Fayre dates back to 1161. The first recorded Charter granted to King's Lynn was 1204, with the Charter for the Valentine's Day fair granted by Henry VIII in 1537. Cambridge Fair dates back to 1211 and provides an excellent example of a fair that started out as a trade fair, run under the auspices of the local religious community, but continues today as a pleasure fair. Hull Fair, the largest travelling fair in Europe, dates back to 1278 and Nottingham Goose Fair to 1284 (Toulmin, 1995).

Britannica.com (2001) notes that the term 'festival', as commonly understood today, was first used in England in 1655, when the Festival of the Sons of the Clergy was first delivered at St Paul's Cathedral, London. Established as an annual charity sermon, it assumed a musical character in 1698. Other examples of early festivals include the Three Choirs Festival (1713), the Norfolk and Norwich Festival (1789) and the Royal National Eisteddford of Wales (revived in 1880 although it originates from 1176) (PSI, 1992). Festivals of secular music started in the eighteenth century – the first devoted to Handel took place in Westminster Abbey in 1784 – with many of these continuing well into the twentieth century (Britannica.com, 2001).

Industrialization, festivals and the sporting event calendar

Exhibitions and trade shows have taken over much of the traditional purpose of the fairs. the Exhibition Liaison Committee (1995, pp. 2–3) noted:

> Since pre-Biblical times producers and merchants have displayed their wares at fairs. However the present UK exhibition industry can trace its origin back to the first industrial exhibitions held in London in 1760 and 1791. These were organised by the Royal Society of Arts and culminated . . . in the Great Exhibition of 1851 which was housed in the impressive 'Crystal Palace' erected in Hyde Park.

Dale (1995) highlights that the Great Exhibition was a triumphant success, with over 6 million visitors – around 25 per cent of the population. It proved to be an excellent promotional tool for Britain, British industry and related trades, and was the first international trade show (Cartwright, 1995). The exhibition generated profits of over £180 000 (Exhibition Liaison Committee, 1995). The following years saw the development of many exhibition facilities that are in existence today, including Alexandra Palace and the Royal Agricultural Hall (1862), Olympia (1886) and Earls Court (originally opened 1887, current structure from 1936).

Sport provides many of the UK's most significant and enduring events. As well as attracting large crowds and media attention, they help to create a national identity and are important to the country's tourism appeal. As the origin of most team sports, Britain has an international reputation for sport and stages many international world-class events each year, drawing in large numbers of visitors and providing major benefits for local economies (English Tourism, 1999). Many of the most famous UK sporting events have their origins in the eighteenth and nineteenth centuries, including equestrian events such as Royal Ascot (1711), the Epsom Derby (1780) and the Aintree Grand National (1839, name adopted 1847), water-based events such as Cowes Week (1826), Henley Royal Regatta (established 1839, named Henley Royal Regatta from 1851) and the first Americas Cup race off the Solent, Isle of Wight (1851). Other major events from this period include The Open Championship (Golf) (1860), the FA Cup (1872), The Championship (Wimbledon) (1877) and Test cricket (England vs Australia, 1882).

During the eighteenth and nineteenth centuries, mostly choral festivals were developed in cities across England, including Leeds. However, further trends included local singing competitions in taverns in the eighteenth century, and amateur singing and brass band competitions in the nineteenth century (Britannica.com, 2001).

Wood (1982) observed that due to the dual forces of industrialization and Christianity in the mid-nineteenth century, many of the traditional festivities that developed alongside folklore were lost. In the emerging climate of industrialization, the working classes had little time for traditional celebrations, with the new National Police Force disciplining the working classes through criminalizing many of the traditional festivities. The middle of the nineteenth century saw at least forty saint days per year, although not all were public holidays in all areas. However, the Victorians believed that it was uneconomical for workers to have so much free time and, as a result, they abolished a number of festivals and tidied up the public holidays to control this. Later, they introduced a week's paid holiday to replace the lost Bank holidays (Harrowven, 1980). Wood (1982, p. 13) noted:

> The assumed irrationality of festivity underlay the bourgeois social order of industrial life and for the working classes this meant that old ways of thinking about the future, steeped in folklore and superstition, were slowly obliterated. The emerging morality of industrialism insisted that personal security could only be gained by thrift, diligence and abstinence from the pleasures of the flesh. There was little place for riotous assembly in this code of ethics until far sighted [sic] commercial entrepreneurs began to discover in the frustrated needs of the working class a whole new sector of the industrial market. Celebration was then resurrected as the Leitmotif of the emerging leisure industry and has remained a key element of mass entertainment ever since.

Palmer and Lloyd (1972) acknowledge that weakening community life and the increasing pace of progress lead to folk festivities that had lasted hundreds of years being changed, a trend which they note will continue with the rapid change in civilization. However, they highlight that British resolve has prevented the complete extinction of these celebrations, with many too deep-rooted in communities to completely disappear. Although many do not take place as spontaneously as previously, the folk rituals continue to survive or be revived, with some of the modern revivals adding new energy to old traditions. They explain:

> It is said that if you scratch civilisation you find a savage. If you scratch the owner-occupier of a desirable semi-detached residence you will find a man who is unconsciously seeking something safe and familiar, something with roots deep in the forgotten past. He may call Morris dancers 'quaint' . . . and refuse to appear as St. George in a mummer's play, but he will still eat hot cross buns on Good Friday, hang up mistletoe at Christmas, and give a Hallowe'en party . . . Modern man is what history has made him, and one facet of history lies in the popular customs that have their beginnings in cults almost as old as man himself. (Palmer and Lloyd, 1972, pp. 9–10)

Records of amateur festivals taking place across Britain date from as early as 1872. The 1870s witnessed the spontaneous birth of local competition festivals alongside developments of intense competition in industry. The first recorded festival was Workington Festival, which is still running today (BFF, 2001). Perhaps one of the most famous music events in the world, the Last Night of the Proms, originates from this period, with the first Proms concert taking place in 1895.

Birth of an events industry?

Wood (1982) highlighted the birth of what is now becoming known as the events industry. She identified that commercializing popular celebrations required wealth for people to participate and therefore meant selecting suitable elements of the traditional festivities and adapting them for 'vicarious consumption'. Consequently, celebrations that were traditionally seen as indecent or immoral were restricted. The Hoppings, in Newcastle (now one of Britain's biggest fairs), provides a good example of one approach, founded in 1882 as a Temperance Festival, in conjunction with race week. The idea of using a fair to advise people to act morally and not drink was in contrast to the London Council and the Fair Act in 1871, which asserted fairs were places of ill repute and dangerous for residents. The purpose of fairs has changed over time to what are seen today as events that mainly operate for enjoyment, with rides, sideshows and stalls (Toulmin, 1995).

With the increase in work through industrialization, the practicalities of celebration meant that people were too tired to celebrate as they had done previously. Thus, celebration, and commercial celebration, provided the opportunity to relax from working life and, from a government perspective, it provided the basis for ensuring that celebration and traditional pleasure culture did not interfere with work. Wood (1982, p. 15) noted:

> In order to remove the guilty feelings attached to the pursuit of 'sinful pleasure' by the legacy of the Protestant Work Ethic, it became necessary

to firstly earn the material means of acquiring product of the entertainment industry and secondly, to ornate the rituals of mass celebration with an aura of professionalism and beneficient spectacle strong enough to dispel the appeal of popular home-spun amateur entertainment and pleasure seeking.

In 1871 bank holidays were made lawful, with the days dictated by the government and the monarch. Since that time, the monarch has retained the power to proclaim additional holidays, with the approval of Parliament, as illustrated by the extra bank holidays given for the 1977 Silver Jubilee and the 2002 Golden Jubilee celebrations (Harrowven, 1980).

Speak to any international visitor, and it is likely that comments relating to Britain's rich history will emerge. The monarchy and anniversaries of major historic events have played a key role in public celebrations and the traditions, image and culture of Britain for hundreds of years. Royal events encourage patriotic fervour and serve not only to involve the general public in celebrating the monarchy itself, they have also contributed much to the UK's position as one of the leading international tourist destinations, attracting millions of tourists each year. Judd (1997) notes that Queen Victoria's Diamond Jubilee celebrations in June 1897 were staged mainly to display the achievements of Britain and the British Empire. Patriotic sentiment, lavish receptions and balls, street parties with flags and bunting, shows, and military and naval displays marked the festivities – similar displays have been witnessed since, for example, at the Coronation of Queen Elizabeth in 1953 and the Queen's Silver Jubilee in 1977.

According to Rogers (1998), the origins of the UK conference industry lie in political and religious congresses, and trade and professional association conventions in America in the late nineteenth century. However, Shone (1998) notes that although the emergence of the conference industry dates from the last thirty years, and to some extent, the past 250 years, this would ignore the development that took place for the preceding thousands of years. He goes on to discuss the development of meeting places for trade, supported by the growth in appropriate facilities, from public halls (first century AD), churches (tenth and eleventh centuries), market towns (thirteenth century), and guildhalls (fourteenth century), through inns and coffee houses (seventeenth century), assembly rooms, town halls and universities (eighteenth century), to the growth in specialist banqueting and assembly facilities such as the Café Royal and Connaught Rooms in London, and meeting rooms within hotels (nineteenth century).

Some of the leading exhibitions today have their origins in the early part of the twentieth century. The Daily Mail Ideal Home Show is a prime example. The show was launched in 1908. Since that time, it has mirrored changes in Britain's social and lifestyle trends. The show is dedicated to setting and reflecting trends, from the 1930s when plastics and stainless steel made their first appearance, through the 1960s with the introduction of American-style kitchens as an international dimension was introduced, to the twenty-first century when the exhibits continue to be at the forefront of innovation and still include the 'House of the Future' – one of the show's most famous features. Who would have thought in 1908 that technological concepts showcased at the exhibition as futuristic and innovative could become part of everyday life?

Significance of events established

In 1915, the British government realized the value of exhibitions to the country and held the first British Industries Fair at the Royal Agricultural Hall (now the Business Design Centre), London. The event proved to be a great success and grew rapidly over the following years, to the stage where it ran in Earls Court, Olympia and Castle Bromwich (Birmingham) simultaneously. However, due to the increasing demand from trade associations and exhibitors for more specialized events, the final British Industries Fair took place in 1957 (Cartwright, 1995). The period is also notable for the 1938 Empire Exhibition at Bellahouston in Glasgow, which attracted 12.6 million paying customers (Dale, 1995).

Following the world wars, the promotion of popular celebration became a thriving sector of the new industrial economy. The Policy Studies Institute (PSI, 1992) notes that, since 1945, arts festivals have become a prominent feature in the UK. It adds that over 500 festivals now take place each year, plus hundreds more one-day community festivals and carnivals. Some of the most famous festivals, including Cheltenham (1945), the Edinburgh International Festival (1947) and the Bath Festival (1948 – then named Bath Assembly), were developed by arts practitioners following the two world wars as a means of encouraging contact between European countries (PSI, 1992). Although some arts festivals have been in existence for hundreds of years, over half of all festivals have been established since 1980, with only six festivals within the PSI research established before the twentieth century and a small number held before the end of the Second World War. Those taking place before 1945 tended generally to be music festivals, for example, Glyndebourne Festival (1934) which focuses on opera, as arts festivals are more contemporary.

The 1951 Festival of Britain was held at South Bank Centre, London, to celebrate the centenary of the Great Exhibition and to provide a symbol for Britain's emergence from the Second World War. It proved to be a great success, yet it underlined the fact that Britain had lost its early lead in staging international exhibitions (Cartwright, 1995). As a result, in 1959 the Pollitzer Committee inquiry identified that the shortage of quality exhibition space was damaging the UK's ability to compete in the global marketplace and recommended that further developments were required. Rogers (1998) identifies that since the 1960s significant investment has taken place in the infrastructure to support conferences, meetings and related events, illustrated by the developments in Birmingham (International Convention Centre) and Glasgow (Scottish Exhibition and Conference Centre).

Emergence of professional events

The 1950s and 1960s were also notable for other factors that shaped events as they appear today. First, the period saw the rapid increase in communities from the West Indies and South Asia, and the establishment of events to celebrate these cultures. For example, the Notting Hill Carnival was established in 1964 by the West Indian community to celebrate their ancestors freedom from slavery (see the case study in Chapter 12). Second, the period saw the emergence of festival culture that is still around today. McKay (2000) highlights that, contrary to popular belief, festival culture was established in the 1950s, rather than the 1960s. He states:

The early roots of British festival culture in the jazz festivals run by Edward (Lord) Montagu at Beaulieu (1956–1961) and in Harold Pendelton's National Jazz Federation events at Richmond then Reading (from 1961 on) indicate the perhaps surprising extent to which the trad and modern jazz scenes of the 1950s and early 1960s blazed the trail for the hippy festivals of the later 1960s and beyond.

This period saw the appearance of a number of popular music festivals, including the Bath Blues Festival (1969), the Pilton Festival (1970, forerunner of the Glastonbury Festival), and the Isle of Wight Festival (1968, 1969, 1970). The Isle of Wight Festival 1970 is believed to be the largest ever UK festival, when over 600 000 people are believed to have attended. This event illustrated the need for professional organization and control, as the organizers ended up making the event free when they lost control of admissions. The promoters, Fiery Creations, are said to have made this their last festival on the island owing to concerns over the festival's size, claiming that it had become unmanageable.

The 1970s and 1980s saw a range of multipurpose venues being built that were funded predominantly by local authorities, including the National Exhibition Centre (NEC) in Birmingham (1976) and the Wembley Exhibition Centre (1977) (Exhibition Liaison Committee, 1995). Since then, the pace of development has continued, with the addition of exhibition space alongside or within football stadia, an increasing number of multipurpose indoor arenas (e.g. Sheffield, Manchester, Newcastle, London and Birmingham), additional exhibition space at the NEC and Earls Court (Greaves, 1999), plus the launch of Excel in London (2000), yet demand still outstrips supply.

The growth in community festivals in the 1970s allowed professional artists to measure their skills against ordinary working people, and provided a means of harnessing community spirit by focusing attention away from social deprivation and unrest. Funding for such celebrations came through art associations, with the events developed within an umbrella of social welfare and community development. Thus, community festivals and festivities were used by governments to provide a focus for society, in order to rejuvenate communities and provide the basis for social and economic regeneration (Wood 1982). Festivals had become part of the cultural landscape, and had become connected again to people's needs and lives. Every community, it seemed, had something to celebrate, and the tools with which to create its own festival.

Closely allied to sporting events is the area of corporate entertainment and hospitality. Crofts (1992) observes that Britain has one of the most sophisticated corporate hospitality markets, due in part to the concentrated summer social season that includes many of the distinguished events highlighted earlier. Peter Selby, of Keith Prowse Hospitality, noted that corporate hospitality in the UK is believed to originate from the early 1970s, when the Open Golf Championship let Gus Payne erect a catering tent at the event. Other events saw this as a means of generating revenue and keeping control of their events, by limiting their reliance on sponsors, and quickly followed suit. Further, in the mid to late 1970s, Keith Prowse Hospitality was established. Initially selling incentive packages, clients began asking to use the facilities for entertaining their customers as well – at this point, it is believed, a new industry was born (Crofts, 1992). Greaves (1996, p. 46) notes, 'with the blip of the recession putting a stop to the spiralling extravagance of the 1980s, a more targeted and cost efficient display of corporate entertainment has had to step into the shoes of the last decade, refashion them and then carry on walking down a different path'.

Through the 1980s and 1990s certain seminal events set the pattern for the contemporary events industry as we know it today. The Olympic Games in Los Angeles in 1984 demonstrated that major events could be economically viable, and blended the media mastery of Hollywood with sport and events in a manner that was destined to be prophetic. The production and marketing skills of the television industry brought the Olympics to a wider audience than ever before, and demonstrated the power of a major sporting event to bring increased profile and economic benefits. The 1980s saw a rapid increase in the use of spectator sports for corporate hospitality, with international sporting events such as the Open Golf Championship, Wimbledon, Royal Ascot, the British Grand Prix and rugby events at Twickenham still popular today. Roger de Pilkyngton, marketing director of Payne & Gunter, noted that the focus changed from entertaining for the sake of it, to a more strategic use of hospitality. The mid to late 1980s saw an expansion of teambuilding and multiactivity events (Greaves, 1996), the market growth continuing into the twenty-first century.

In 1985, Live Aid introduced the era of the telethon, followed by the BBC's Children in Need and Comic Relief's Red Nose days (Bear Necessities of Golf, 1998). Live Aid was a unique television event – it was a direct plea to the audience of 1.5 billion people in 160 countries to give Ethiopia famine relief. It resulted in £200 million being raised (Younge, 1999).

Table 1.1 illustrates the origin dates of arts festivals. It shows particularly that the 1980s benefited from significant expansion, due to success observed in established festivals, supported by increased funding from the Arts Council and regional arts associations (now boards). New Leisure Markets (1995) note that as a result of festival development and redevelopment in the 1970s and 1980s, the typical festivals are modern events. Further, the 1980s saw increasing links with local authorities as they recognized the role of the arts in regeneration and tourism.

These festivals gave the cities and towns a sense of identity and distinction, and became a focus for community groups and charity fundraising. It is a tribute to their

Year of origin	Percentage of total
Pre-1940	4
1940s	4
1950s	3
1960s	12
1970s	21
1980s	51
1990/1	5

Source: PSI, 1992, p. 14.

Table 1.1 Year of origin of UK arts festivals

Hospitality, Leisure & Tourism Series

place in the lives of their communities that many of these festivals still continue a century later.

During 1995, extensive VE Day and VJ Day commemorations, parades and celebrations marked the fiftieth anniversaries of the end of the Second World War in Europe and Japan. A series of events was staged not only to celebrate victory and to thank those that fought for their country, but also to look forward to the future and meet former enemies in a spirit of reconciliation. The finale to the VE celebrations was the biggest celebration of reconciliation in European history. Taking place in Hyde Park, London, it was attended by the Queen and members of the royal family, leaders and representatives of fifty-four countries touched by the war, and a crowd of 150 000 people (Hardman, 1995).

The UK has enjoyed success throughout the twentieth century, hosting some of the world's major international sporting events. These have become more than the particular sport – many are 'festivals of sport', reflecting the package of events taking place alongside the main event, and also the increasing crossover between sport, leisure, festivals and public events. These develop interest in the event, encouraging festive spirit and community involvement, and enhancing the image of the event in the host community. For example, during the twentieth century, the UK has hosted the 1908 and 1948 Olympic Games in London, the 1966 World Cup in London, the 1986 Commonwealth Games in Edinburgh, the 1991 Rugby Union World Cup in England and the 1991 World Student Games. In the past ten years alone, the UK has hosted in quick succession the UEFA European Football Championships (1996), the Rugby Union World Cup (1999), the Cricket World Cup (1999), the Rugby League World Cup (2000) and Ryder Cup (2001). The UK also spent £10 million bidding for the FIFA Football World Cup in 2006, a bid subsequently awarded to Germany, will be hosting the Manchester 2002 Commonwealth Games and have successfully bid for the 2005 IAAF World Athletics Championships. The pursuit of major events such as these forms part of government strategy, implemented through UK Sport (discussed further in Chapter 2). Speaking at the Second UK Sport Major Events Conference in June 2000, Sir Rodney Walker, Chairman of UK Sport, commented on the success achieved so far:

> The World Class Events Programme has already helped to secure the World Athletics Championships in 2005 – one of the world's sporting crown jewels. Along with the Commonwealth Games in 2002 we have now secured two out of four of our strategic priorities. This programme works alongside the World Class Performance Programme to provide a national showcase for our elite sportsmen and women. UK Sport is uniquely placed to ensure that the UK genuinely pulls together and uses experience from all events to ensure that we continue to be a world player in major sporting events. (UK Sport 2000a)

The spirit of Live Aid was rejuvenated in 1999, with the NetAid fundraising concerts. Using modern technology not available at Live Aid in 1985, the NetAid concerts took place simultaneously in London, Geneva and New Jersey, with a combined live audience of 110 000. However, the difference with this event was that 2.4 million people watched the live Internet broadcast of the event in one day, setting a new world record, and worldwide television, radio and Internet coverage has so far generated over 2 billion impressions on the NetAid.org website. NetAid illustrates the potential use of the Internet as a medium for social change, through using the Internet to provide a global resource against extreme poverty. NetAid has also been credited with helping to secure $27 billion in US debt relief by U2's Bono (NetAid.org, 1999).

Into the new millennium

The trend in local authority funding for arts festivals has continued into the twenty-first century. Allen and Shaw (2001) found that, of the 137 festivals responding to their study, 82 per cent received part of their funding in 1998/9 from local authorities, with 51 per cent gaining grants from arts councils and 42 per cent from the English Regional Arts Boards. New Leisure Markets (1995, p. 4) identifies that festivals are attractive to local authorities for a number of reasons. They provide:

- visitors/tourists and spending
- commercial sponsorship for visual arts, thereby taking the strain off arts authorities
- cultural experiences for local residents, thus taking arts to some visitors who would never normally attend museums or art galleries
- a focal point for staff to work towards and to motivate contributions from local professional and amateur artistes, especially children.

Commenting on the study (BAFA, 2000), Tim Joss, Chair of BAFA and Director of the Bath Festivals Trust highlights the modern role of festivals. He comments:

> It's time for many people – in the arts, in national and local government, and elsewhere – to change their attitude to festivals. The old view that festivals are flashes in the pan contributing nothing to long-term development must go. This valuable research paints a very different picture. It makes an impressive case for arts festivals as flexible, efficient, contemporary enterprises rooted in their local communities. And thanks to their special freedom to collaborate with artists, venues, and artistic and other partners, they are proving themselves valuable catalysts for cultural, social and economic development. (BAFA, 2001)

Across the UK, the new millennium brought an unprecedented level of funding for community projects, including events, and firmly focused the spotlight on the events industry. North West Arts Board (1999) note that community festivals and events such as melas, Chinese New Year and carnivals are extremely important, providing not only the opportunity for communities to celebrate their identity and presence in the UK, but also a stage for creative expression within the context of their cultural heritage. The year-long Millennium Festival, supported with £100 million from the National Lottery funded Millennium Commission, saw communities take part in around 2000 events across the UK, including major celebrations in twenty-two towns and cities on New Year's Eve 1999, a further thirty-two events closing the year in 2000 and over 370 large-scale festivals. Steve Denford, Senior Festival Manager at the Millennium Commission Press Office (2000), noted: 'The Millennium Festival is the largest programme of year-long celebrations ever mounted in the UK with an opportunity for all communities to come together and celebrate the year 2000.

Throughout the year the diverse programme of events is offering something for everyone and something happening everywhere.'

One of the largest combined events was the Beacon Millennium Project, whereby 1400 beacons were lit across the UK on 31 December 1999, providing the focal point for community-level celebrations. Further initiatives included investment of over £1.3 billion in around 200 new buildings, environmental project, visitor attractions, and a total of £200 million provided as 40 000 grants, or 'Millennium Awards' for individuals to put their ideas into action for their communities (Millennium Commission, 2000).

The Millennium Festival caused communities across Britain to pause and reflect on identity and the past, and to look forward to the future. It also changed forever the nature of our public celebrations, as a new benchmark has been created against which all future events will be measured. The millennium also left a legacy of public spaces dedicated to celebrations and events, and government, both local and central, supportive of their social and economic benefits. For example, the Millennium Square in Leeds opened on 31 December 2000 as a multipurpose event and leisure space in the heart of the city – purpose-built to provide a relaxing leisure space for the people of Leeds, yet incorporating a range of services to reflect the needs of event organizers.

Consolidating the events industry

The growth of events that serve a wide variety of purposes and agendas has led to the emergence of an events industry with its own body of knowledge, job opportunities and career paths.

Further indications of the emergence of an events industry are the formation of industry associations and the establishment of training courses, education programmes and accreditation schemes. The UK has a multitude of industry associations that represent the various sectors within the industry, with some serving more than one sector and others competing for members within the same sectors. Indeed, some argue that there is a need for consolidation of associations to ensure that the industry can move forward and its needs be effectively lobbied to government. Event managers should identify the association(s) that best suits their individual situation and the needs of their organization, as some associations promote individual membership, whilst others promote membership on an organizational basis. Some of the main associations covering the events industry are listed below:

- *Conference/meetings*: Association for Conferences and Events (ACE), Meetings Industry Association (MIA), Association of British Professional Conference Organizers (ABPCO), British Association of Conference Destinations (BACD). UK/European chapters of international associations, for example Meeting Professionals International (MPI) and Professional Convention and Meetings Association (PCMA).
- *Exhibitions*: Association of Exhibition Organizers (AEO), Exhibition Venues Association (EVA), British Exhibition Contractors Association (BECA), National Exhibitors Association (NEA).
- *Incentive travel*: The Incentive Travel and Meetings Association (ITMA), UK chapter of the Society of Incentive Travel Executives (SITE).

- *Festivals*: British Art Festivals Association (BAFA), Association of Festival Organizers (AFO), British Federation of Festivals for Music, Dance and Speech (BFF), International Festival and Events Association (IFEA) Europe.
- *Corporate hospitality*: Corporate Hospitality and Events Association (CHA), Hotel, Catering and International Management Association (HCIMA).
- *Event (other)*: National Outdoor Events Association (NOEA), The Event Services Association (TESA), Society of Event Organisers (SEO), International Special Events Society (ISES), International Visual Communications Association (IVCA), Institute of Leisure and Amenity Management (ILAM).
- *Music events/event production*: Production Services Association (PSA), Professional Light and Sound Association (PLASA), Concert Promoters Association (CPA).
- *Miscellaneous/suppliers*: Made-Up Textiles Association (MUTA), Mobile Outdoor Catering Association (MOCA), National Arenas Association (NAA), Society of Ticket Agents and Retailers (STAR).

An extended list of associations is available on the website, Worldofevents.net.

The Travel, Tourism Services and Events National Training Organisation (TTENTO) was established in 1997 to help support the industry and to further the agenda toward a fully trained workforce. This has included industry research, encouraging communication between education providers, employers and industry associations, and encouraging the development of National Vocational Qualifications (NVQs) for the events industry, together with the Events Sector Industry Training Organization (ESITO). Many of the associations provide training courses for the industry and are beginning to recognize the benefits that these, together with the developments in formal education, can have to address the shortfall in qualified professionals that some areas of the industry are experiencing. For example, ISES offers an examination-based accreditation as a Certified Special Events Professional (CSEP), the Meetings Industry Association (MIA) provides training courses for the industry and also runs a general industry accreditation programme (Hospitality Assured Meetings), and the ITMA is in the process of developing a specific education programme under the ITMA Institute banner. Other developments include the PSA offering production-related courses, and the AEO offering a range of training courses to both exhibition companies and exhibitors, including health and safety, sales and exhibiting. Thus, each area of industry is increasingly investing in training and education in order to ensure that there is a sufficient qualified staffing base to support the developing industry.

Dedicated courses in events management are being delivered at colleges and universities across the UK, including the Higher National Diploma (HND) in Promotions and Events Management at Fife College, the BA (Hons) Events Management degree and HND Events Management at the UK Centre for Events Management (Leeds Metropolitan University) and the European Masters in Convention Management at Sheffield Hallam University. These courses focus on providing education and training for future event professionals, and cover areas such as event planning and management, marketing, human resource management and operations. Other universities, such as the University of North London, are delivering combined honours degrees with, for example, leisure management and events management (for a full list of events-related qualifications, please visit http://education.worldofevents.net). Modules in event management are also included in many tourism, leisure, recreation and hospitality qualifications in universities and colleges around the country. In order to support these develop-ments, an increasing number of books by UK authors have been written, such as Cartwright, (1995), Rogers (1998), Shone (1998), Watt (1998) and Shone with Parry (2001), to supplement the established body of knowledge from internationally recognized authors such as Goldblatt (1997) and Getz (1997). The industry is served by two dedicated journals, *Event Management* (formerly *Festival Management and Event Tourism*) and the *Journal of Convention and Exhibition Management*, which aim to develop the research base to support the new professionals. Finally, this wealth of knowledge is enhanced with a range of periodicals providing contempo-rary articles and industry news, such as *Access All Areas*, *Conference and Exhibition Factfinder*, *Conference and Incentive Travel*, *Exhibition Bulletin*, *Live!*, *Marketing Event* and *Meetings and Incentive Travel*.

Research for the Institute of Management (Coulson and Coe, 1991) identified the qualities that future managers should possess. These included the ability to communicate, flexibility, adaptability, a broad perspective on organization goals, a balanced perspective overall and an understanding of the business environment. Further, nine out of ten believed that managers should have an ability to assume greater responsibility, contribute to teams, handle uncertainty and surprise, be aware of ethics and values, and have a commitment to ongoing learning. Later research by Pedler, Burgoyne and Boydell (1994, cited in Mullins, 1999) identified the qualities possessed by successful managers compared with unsuccessful managers, which they grouped under the headings of basic knowledge and information, skills and attributes, and meta-qualities. Mullins (1999) notes that many are interconnected, with possession of one contributing to possession of another. The three areas include the following qualities:

- *Basic knowledge and information*: includes a command of basic facts and relevant professional understanding.
- *Specific skills and attributes*: includes continuing sensitivity to events, analytical, problem-solving and decision/judgement-making skills, social skills and abilities, emotional resilience and proactivity.
- *Meta-qualities*: includes creativity, mental agility, balanced learning habits and skills, and self-knowledge.

Limited research has been conducted within the events industry to identify the skills, qualities and attributes of successful event managers, particularly in the UK. The Business Tourism Forum and the Business Tourism Advisory Committee (1999, p. 36) found that the conference and event industries required enhanced negotiation skills, higher client management skills and a detailed knowledge of specific venues. In addition, the industry requires people with an informed understanding of, and ability to anticipate, client needs and to suggest solutions to problems and improvements to plans. Further research, conducted in Australia, provides a useful insight into the attributes and knowledge required specifically by event managers. Perry, Foley and Rumpf (1996) described the attributes and knowledge required by event managers resulting from their survey of 105 managers attending the Australian Events Conference in Canberra in February 1996. Seven attributes were frequently mentioned, of which vision was listed as the most important, followed closely by leadership, adaptability, and skills in organization, communications, marketing and people management. Knowledge areas considered most important

Typical male	Typical female
Has worked in the industry for six years or more	Has held her job for less than six years
About 35 years old	Under 35 years old
Educated to HND standard	Educated to degree or postgraduate level
Likely to be a manager with aspirations to be director	Likely to have a junior role (for now)
Motivated by the commission he makes by winning new business	Enjoys the social and logistical aspects of the job
Often works more than 40 hours a week	Works a 40-hour week
Uses the Internet at home and at work	Uses the Internet at work more than at home
Will move jobs for a better financial package	Will move jobs for a better overall package

Source: Fletcher, 2000, p. 24.

Table 1.2 Event industry stereotypes

were project management, budgeting, time management, relating to the media, business planning, human resources and marketing.

Another development is a gradual shift within the make-up of the workforce. The annual Salary and Lifestyle Survey 2000, undertaken by Marketing Event with ESP Recruitment and Vivid Interface, found that although men still dominate the most senior positions within event and exhibition industries, the trend shows that women will increasingly gain senior-level responsibility within the next few years (Fletcher, 2000). Further, a number of stereotypes were identified from the survey, illustrated in Table 1.2.

The emerging events industry with its needs, challenges and opportunities will be examined in the following chapters.

What are special events?

The term 'special events' has been coined to describe specific rituals, presentations, performances or celebrations that are consciously planned and created to mark special occasions and/or to achieve particular social, cultural or corporate goals and objectives. Special events can include national days and celebrations, important civic occasions, unique cultural performances, major sporting fixtures, corporate functions, trade promotions and product launches. It seems at times that special events are everywhere; they have become a growth industry. The field of special events is now so vast that it is impossible to provide a definition that includes all varieties and shades of events. In his groundbreaking work on the typology of events, Getz (1997, p. 4) suggests that special events are best defined by their context. He offers two definitions, one from the point of view of the event organizer, and the other from that of the customer, or guest:

1 A special event is a one-time or infrequently occurring event outside normal programmes or activities of the sponsoring or organizing body.
2 To the customer or guest, a special event is an opportunity for a leisure, social or cultural experience outside the normal range of choices or beyond everyday experience.

Among the attributes that Getz believes create the sense of specialness are festive spirit, uniqueness, quality, authenticity, tradition, hospitality, theming and symbolism.

Types of events

Events are often characterized according to their size and scale. Common categories are mega-events, hallmark events and major events, though definitions are not exact and distinctions become blurred. This is illustrated in Figure 1.1. Events are also classified according to their purpose, or the particular sector to which they belong, for example, public, sporting, arts, festivals, tourism and business/corporate events. In this text, the full range of events that are produced by the events industry will be examined, and the term 'events' will be used to cover all categories.

Mega-events

Mega-events are those events that are so large that they affect whole economies and reverberate in the global media. These events are generally developed following

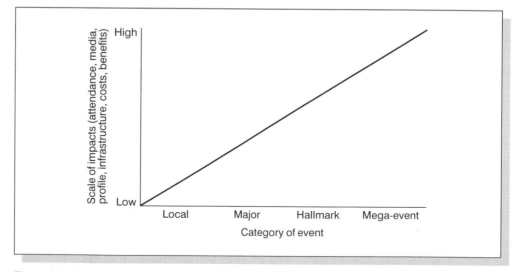

Figure 1.1 Categorization of events

competitive bidding. They include the Olympic Games, the Paralympic Games, the FIFA World Cup, the IAAF World Championships and World Fairs, but it is difficult for many other events to fit into this category. Getz (1997, p. 6) defines them: 'Mega-events, by way of their size or significance, are those that yield extraordinarily high levels of tourism, media coverage, prestige, or economic impact for the host community or destination . . . Their volume should exceed 1 million visits, their capital costs should be at least $500 million, and their reputation should be of a 'must see' event.

Hall (1997, p. 5), another researcher in the field of events and tourism, offers this definition:

> Mega-events such as World Fairs and Expositions, the World Soccer Cup Final, or the Olympic Games, are events which are expressly targeted at the international tourism market and may be suitably described as 'mega' by virtue of their size in terms of attendance, target market, level of public financial involvement, political effects, extent of television coverage, construction of facilities, and impact on economic and social fabric of the host community.

In relative terms, by these definitions the Great Exhibition in London in 1851 was perhaps the UK's first mega-event. Although belonging to an era of less encompassing media, other early examples may include the 1908 and 1948 London Olympics, the 1938 Empire Exhibition in Glasgow, the 1951 Festival of Britain and the 1966 World Cup. Modern events such as the 1991 World Student Games in Sheffield and the Euro '96 football championships would struggle to meet all of Getz's criteria. However, the UK Millennium Festival in 2000, if taken as a national event, would probably qualify, as may the Manchester 2002 Commonwealth Games, with the associated national Spirit of Friendship Festival.

Hallmark events

The term 'hallmark events' refers to those events that become so identified with the spirit or ethos of a town, city or region that they become synonymous with the name of the place, and gain widespread recognition and awareness. Tourism researcher Ritchie (1984, p. 2) defines them as: 'Major one time or recurring events of limited duration, developed primarily to enhance awareness, appeal and profitability of a tourism destination in the short term or long term. Such events rely for their success on uniqueness, status, or timely significance to create interest and attract attention.'

Classic examples of hallmark events are Carnival in Rio, known throughout the world as an expression of the Latin vitality and exuberance of that city, the Tour de France, the Oktoberfest in Munich, Germany, and the Edinburgh Festival in Scotland. These events are identified with the very essence of these places and their citizens, and bring huge tourist revenue as well as a strong sense of local pride and international recognition. Getz (1997, pp. 5–6) describes them in terms of their ability to provide a competitive advantage for their host communities:

> The term 'hallmark event' is used to describe a recurring event that possesses such significance, in terms of tradition, attractiveness, image, or

publicity, that the event provides the host venue, community, or destination with a competitive advantage. Over time, the event and destination become inseparable. For example Mardi Gras gives New Orleans a competitive advantage by virtue of its high profile . . . Increasingly, every community and destination needs one or more hallmark events to provide the high levels of media exposure and positive imagery that help to create competitive advantages.

Examples in the UK might include the Notting Hill Carnival, the Grand National at Aintree, the FA Cup Final (until recent redevelopment this was clearly associated with Wembley Stadium) and The Championships at Wimbledon, all of which have a degree of international recognition. Commenting on the value of The Championships, John Barrett, author, and Senior BBC Commentator, stated: '"Wimbledon", as The Championships are universally known, has become over the years an established part of the fabric of British life. It is more than a tradition, more than just the world's most important and historic tennis tournament. It is a symbol of all that is best about sport, royal patronage, and social occasion that the British do so well, a subtle blend that the rest of the world finds irresistible' (Barrett, 2000).

Major events

Major events are events that, by their scale and media interest, are capable of attracting significant visitor numbers, media coverage and economic benefits. The Isle of Man hosts the TT Races and Silverstone has the British Formula One Grand Prix, both significant annual major events. Cowes Week, hosted on the Isle of Wight each year, provides a focus on maritime pursuits as well as attracting international prestige and media. The Open Championship, staged at different links golf courses each year, attracts strong destination promotion around the world for the host region. Many top international sporting championships fit into this category, and are increasingly being sought after, and bid for, by national sporting organizations and governments in the competitive world of international major events. UK Sport consider that three elements are required to be classed as a major sporting event:

- It involves competition between teams and/or individuals representing a number of nations.
- It attracts significant public interest, nationally and internationally, through spectator attendance and media coverage.
- It is of international significance to the sport(s) concerned, and features prominently on their international calendar (UK Sport, 1999a, p. 4).

Sporting events

It is interesting to note that UK Sport classify the sporting calendar into four groups within the overall umbrella of major events, including mega, calendar, one-off and showcase events. There is some duplication with the points discussed earlier. However, the categories are included, together with the elements above, in order to illustrate the need to clarify terminology before commencing a study into events or bidding, and provide a useful illustration of potential objectives and means of attracting these types of events.

1 *Mega events*: awarded after competitive bidding. Includes the Summer Olympics, the Paralympic Games, the FIFA World Cup and the IAAF World Athletic Championships.
2 *Calendar events*: no bidding required, commercially successful events, play a regular part in the international calendar for that sport, e.g. The Championships (Wimbledon), the British Formula One Grand Prix, The Open Championship, Test Series in cricket, Rugby Union Internationals.
3 *One-off events*: generally awarded after competitive bidding, substantial television rights interest nationally and internationally, e.g. the Rugby League and Union World Cups, the Cricket World Cup and European Football Championships.
4 *Showcase events*: generally awarded after competitive bidding, these events have the potential to boost sport development, provide the UK with a good chance of winning medals and can improve the UK's image overseas and/or involve regions in UK, e.g. the World Judo Championships, the World Disability Championships and the European Showjumping Championships.

Cultural events

Cultural events can also be contenders as major events. For example, major musicals such as *Phantom of the Opera*, *Miss Saigon* and *Cats* reap considerable tourism revenue for London's West End. Edinburgh Council and related organizations, supporting both private and public sector initiatives, have developed an enviable reputation and tourism bonanza through staging a wide range of nine festivals that cater to different market needs. As discussed later in this text, Cheltenham has developed the International Jazz Festival, the International Festival of Music and Festival of Literature, Bath and North East Somerset have developed the Bath International Music Festival and Glyndebourne has the developed the world-famous opera festival. Each has an eye to positioning itself in the tourism markets as well as in the arts world. Some local authorities are taking these initiatives one stage further, by developing an event-focused arts strategy (e.g. Bath and North East Somerset Council), using events to deliver the cultural strategy (e.g. Brighton and Hove, Newham Council) or developing a specific event and festival strategy (e.g. Edinburgh District Council).

Arts festivals share a number of characteristics, including intense artistic output, and a clear time-specific programme delivered with a clear purpose and direction (Rolfe, 1992). South East Arts (1998, p. 2) have developed seven categories for festivals within their region based on the overall purpose and size, which can usefully be applied to classify festivals in other regions. These are:

1 *High-profile general celebrations of the arts*: these address an ambitious agenda and a multitude of aims – to reach the highest standards, to achieve a high media profile, to reach a broad audience, to generate high levels of income.
2 *Festivals that celebrate a particular location*: from small villages to large towns, these festivals aim to bring people together to celebrate their local area, often featuring a large number of local groups. These festivals subdivide into those run by voluntary groups and those run by local authorities. Festivals run by voluntary groups tend to be smaller.

3 *Art-form festivals*: focused on a specific art form, offering unique opportunities for audiences to see particular kinds of work, and may also address the development of that artform by providing a focus for critical debate, master classes, commissions of new work etc.

4 *Celebration of work by a community of interest*: these festivals highlight work by specific groups of people, e.g. disabled people, young people or women and often contain a large proportion of participatory workshops.

5 *Calendar*: cultural or religious festivals. Indigenous traditions of large-scale assembly have largely died away in England, but the Asian and Caribbean communities have brought carnival and melas to enhance the cultural mix of festivals in the UK.

6 *Amateur arts festivals*: a large but low-profile sector that involves thousands of people. Many of these festivals are competitive.

7 *Commercial music festivals*: a hugely popular phenomenon, some local authorities also run outdoor pop music festivals that adopt a similar model.

New Leisure Markets (1995) identify that UK festivals are divided between single-theme and multi-theme events. The main themes for single-theme festivals are folk (35 per cent), classical music (15 per cent), jazz (15 per cent), literature (5 per cent) and film (5 per cent). Mintel (2000) note that the live music market, which includes commercial music festivals, is estimated to be worth £361 million in 2000, of which rock/pop account for 76 per cent.

Business events

Research undertaken by RS&M, on behalf of event agency McMenemy Hill, estimated that UK companies spend £330 million annually on events. Their survey of seventy-seven companies found that exhibitions are the most frequently held event (36 per cent), followed by sporting events (14 per cent), corporate hospitality (11 per cent), road shows (9 per cent), trade shows (9 per cent) and product launches (8 per cent). Further, the main reason for holding events was to maintain relationships (55 per cent) and raise brand awareness (47 per cent) (Cook, 2000). Further research suggests that conferences, exhibitions, incentive travel, corporate hospitality and business travel combined account for 25 per cent of total inbound tourism to the UK and 29 per cent of all inbound tourism expenditure. This equates to an economic impact of £12 billion and is forecast to increase to £16 billion over the next decade (Business Tourism Forum and The Business Tourism Advisory Committee, 1999). As a result, business events are sometimes discussed in the broader context of business tourism, or referred to as MICE (meetings, incentives, conventions and exhibitions).

The conference sector is largely characterized by its business and trade focus, though there is a strong public and tourism aspect to many of its activities. Conferences can be very diverse, as revealed by the definition of the Convention Liaison Committee and the Joint Industry Council 'International Meetings Industry Glossary' (1993, cited in Rogers, 1998, p. 18): 'An event used by any organisation to meet and exchange views, convey a message, open a debate or give publicity to some area of opinion on a specific issue. No tradition, continuity or periodicity is required to convene a conference. Although not generally limited in time, conferences are usually of short duration with specific objectives.'

The conference and exhibition market is worth an estimated £6 billion per annum (Business Tourism Forum and the British Tourism Advisory Council, 1999). One major event alone – the Rotary International World Convention – brought 24 000 big-spending delegates to Glasgow in 1997. Another example is when the Bournemouth International Centre hosted the biggest political conference so far in the UK – around 20 000 delegates, journalists, exhibitors and technicians attended the Labour Party Conference in September 1999 (Barnes, 1999).

Another lucrative aspect is incentive travel, defined by the Society of Incentive Travel Executives (1997, cited in Rogers, 1998, p. 47) as 'a global management tool that uses an exceptional travel experience to motivate and/or recognise participants for increased levels of performance in support of organisational goals'. The UK's unique locations and international popularity as a tourism destination make it a leading player in the incentive travel market, with the inbound incentive travel market alone estimated to be worth between £140 million and £150 million in 1994 (Business Tourism Forum and the British Tourism Advisory Council, 1999).

Last, but by no means least, exhibitions are a considerable and growing part of business events. Research by the Incorporated Society of British Advertisers suggests that marketing spend on exhibitions has increased 18 per cent over the past decade and is expected to reach £964 million by 2002, an increase of 22 per cent on 1997 (McLuhan, 2000). Exhibitions bring suppliers of goods and services together with buyers, usually in a particular industry sector. The British International Motor Show, the Ideal Home Show and the International Boat Show are three of the largest exhibitions in the UK, each generating tens of thousands of visitors. The Exhibition Liaison Committee (1995, p. 8) identified that there are four main categories of exhibition in the UK:

- *Agricultural shows*: held in the countryside on open sites (including purpose-built show grounds). Normally occur once a year, with attendance ranging from 5000 to 200 000 at the largest events within a period of one to five days. Examples include the Royal Show (180 000) and the Newbury and Royal Berkshire Show (70 000).
- *Consumer shows*: aimed mainly at the general public, although may have a trade element. Include subjects such as gardening, home interiors, motoring and fashion. Extensively promoted by the media, for example, the Ideal Home Show (established in 1908), the British International Motor Show or Clothes Show Live.
- *Specialized trade shows and exhibitions*: the product emphasis and target buying audience are generally defined and controlled by the organizer. For example, International Confex at Earls Court, Event Expo at London Arena and the Showmans Show at Newbury Showground all focus on various aspects of the developing events industry.
- *Private exhibitions*: includes product launches, in-store and concourse displays, which are exclusive to one or a defined group of manufacturers. The audience is normally by direct invitation.

The modern exhibition industry is clearly structured, taking in venue owners, exhibition organizers and contractors from the supply side, and exhibitors and visitors generating the demand. Major conference and exhibition centres in the main cities and many regional centres now vie for their share of the thriving business event market. In addition, the Live Events Survey in 1998 found that the audiovisual productions needed to support conference, exhibitions and road shows represented an industry sector worth more than £300 million (Anon., 1998).

Summary

Events perform a powerful role in society. They have existed throughout human history in all times and all cultures. British cultures have a rich tradition of rituals and ceremonies. The events tradition in modern Britain began to take off towards the end of the nineteenth century, with industrialization reducing spontaneous celebration and increasing professionally organized events. The ruling elite often decided the form and content of public celebrations, but an alternative tradition of popular celebrations arose from the interests and pursuits of ordinary people. Many nineteenth-century leisure pursuits such as race meetings have survived to the present day. Through the twentieth century, the changes in society were mirrored by changes in the style of public events. A tradition of city and town festivals evolved in the post Second World War years, and was rejuvenated by the social movements and cultural changes of the 1970s. Notions of high culture were challenged by a more pluralistic and democratic popular culture, which reinvigorated festivals and community events. With the coming of the 1980s, the corporate sector began to recognize the economic and promotional value of events.

The 1990s saw the events industry emerge, with various sectors, particularly those focused on business-related events, pushing forward the claim for an industry to be recognized, supported by dialogue with government and for an increase in training and support for the industry-related NVQs. Further, the period saw the growth in events-related education in colleges and universities, with dedicated courses and modules being developed to support the emerging industry. Events vary in their size and impact, with terms such as special events, mega-events, hallmark events and major events used to describe and categorize them. Events are also categorized according to their type and sector, such as public, cultural, festivals, sporting, tourism and corporate events. The business events sector (including meetings, incentives, conventions and exhibitions) is one of the fastest growing areas of events. With increasing corporate involvement, events are now seen as an industry with considerable economic and job creation benefits.

Questions

1 Why are events created, and what purpose do they serve in society?

2 Do events mirror changes in society, or do they have a role in creating and changing values? Give examples to illustrate your answer.

3 Why have events emerged so strongly in recent years in the UK?

4 What are the key political, cultural and social trends that determine the current climate of events in the UK? How would you expect these to influence the nature of events in the coming years?

5 Identify an event in your city or region that has the capacity to be a hallmark event. Give your reasons for placing it in this category.

6 What characteristics define an industry, and using these criteria do you consider that there is an events industry in the UK?

7 Do you agree with the attributes and knowledge areas required by events managers listed in this chapter? Do an inventory of your own attributes and skills based on these listings.

Case Study

Manchester 2002 Commonwealth Games

The XVII Commonwealth Games, to be held in Manchester in July 2002, will be the largest multi-sport event ever hosted in England. Alongside sporting excellence, the Games provide the opportunity to celebrate Her Majesty the Queen's Golden Jubilee Year and modern multicultural Britain at the start of the new millennium.

Manchester's objectives are to host a superb sporting event, to promote a national celebration of sport and culture and to secure a lasting legacy for the North West and for Britain. The Games will play a crucial role in the continued physical, economic and social regeneration of Manchester, will bring proven regional economic benefits and provide a boost to national claims to host future world-class sporting events. For example, 40 hectares of land is being reclaimed for the Sportcity development (including the City of Manchester Stadium, Indoor Tennis Centre and National Squash Centre) which will act as the catalyst for the major regeneration of East Manchester, and 15 000 volunteers will be trained, leaving skilled and motivated people in the North West region.

Manchester is fully committed to promoting and staging an 'inclusive Games', with equality of opportunity for competitors, spectators, volunteers and employees, irrespective of race, nationality, ethnic origin, gender, religion, age, or disability. For the first time at a major event elite athletes with a disability are fully integrated into the sports programme with 200 sportsmen and women participating in eight events over five sports.

A national Spirit of Friendship Festival will be organized alongside the Games, embracing the Golden Jubilee celebrations. Led by a series of high-profile events supported by Commonwealth Games' sponsors, the arts, cultural, sporting and education festival will take place across the UK from Commonwealth Day (11 March 2002) to 10 August 2002 – with the carnival atmosphere peaking during the period of the Games (25 July to 4 August 2002).

The Games are predicted to produce longer-term benefits, including world-class sports facilities, an increase in visitor numbers (business and leisure) and the creation of a pool of talent within public and private sector organizations. With an expected global television audience of over 1 billion watching from 1500 hours of broadcasting within 110 countries, together with 1 million spectators, 5250 athletes, teams and officials, and 4500 accredited media personnel, the Games will provide an excellent opportunity to showcase Manchester and the North West.

The Games have been seized as a catalyst to set new standards for the hosting of international events, ensuring lasting benefits are generated for all those involved. It is on course to be both a commercial and a popular success, and will be a proud testament to global excellence centred on the UK at the start of the new millennium.

For further details on the Manchester 2002 Commonwealth Games, please visit www.commonwealthgames.com.

Source: adapted from Manchester 2002 (2000a, 2000b, 2000c).

Questions

1 What type of event are the Commonwealth Games? Explain your answer.

2 Running festivals alongside sporting events is becoming increasingly popular. What can these bring to the event?

3 Using other materials at your disposal, for example, the official website, conduct research into the Manchester 2002 Commonwealth Games. What facts can be ascertained from this material regarding the size, nature and management of the event?

4 How would you expect the experience of organizing the Manchester 2002 Commonwealth Games to influence bidding for and management of large-scale events within the UK in the future? Explain your answer.

CHAPTER 2

The impacts of events

After studying this chapter, you should be able to:

- identify the major impacts which events have on their stakeholders and host communities
- use events to strengthen community pride and values
- anticipate the social impact of events and plan for positive outcomes
- understand the management of crowd behaviour
- describe the physical and environmental impacts of events
- understand the political context of events
- use events to increase tourist visits and length of stay
- balance the economic costs and benefits of staging an event
- demonstrate an understanding of the role of the event manager in balancing the impacts of events.

Introduction – balancing the impacts of events

Events have a range of impacts – both positive and negative – on their host communities and stakeholders. It is the task of the event manager to identify and predict these impacts and then to manage them to achieve the best balance for all parties, so that in the balance the overall impact of the event is positive. To achieve this, all foreseeable positive impacts must be developed and maximized, and negative impacts countered. Often negative impacts can be addressed through awareness and intervention – good planning is always critical. Ultimately, the success of the event depends on the event manager achieving this positive balance sheet and communicating it to a range of stakeholders.

Great emphasis is often placed on the financial impacts of events, partly because of the need of employers and governments to meet budget goals and justify expenditure, and partly because such impacts are most easily assessed. However, the event manager should not lose sight of the full range of impacts resulting from the event, and the need to identify, describe and manage them. It is also important to realize that different impacts require different means of assessment. For example, social and cultural benefits play a vital role in calculating the overall impact of an event, but describing them may require a narrative rather than a statistical approach. Some of the complex factors that need to be taken into account when assessing the impacts of events are summarized in Table 2.1 and discussed in this chapter.

Social and cultural impacts

All events have a direct social and cultural impact on their participants, and sometimes on their wider host communities as outlined by Hall (1997) and Getz (1997). This may be as simple as a shared entertainment experience, as is created by a sporting event or concert. Other impacts include increased pride, which results from some community events and celebrations of national days, and the validation of particular groups in the community, which is the purpose of many events designed for senior citizens and disabled people. Some events leave a legacy of greater awareness and participation in sporting and cultural activities. Others broaden people's cultural horizons, and expose them to new and challenging people, customs, or ideas. For example, the melas held in Bradford, Leeds, Manchester, East London (Newham) and Edinburgh each summer have introduced Asian tradition with its strong religious and cultural associations to wider audiences. The City of Bristol illustrated the benefits to be gained through social inclusion, from hosting the West Indies cricket team during the Cricket World Cup 1999. The council in partnership with Gloucester County Cricket Club and First Group developed a range of events targeted at schoolchildren and the local Afro-Caribbean community, including free access to warm-up sessions, coaching clinics and school visits (Select Committee on Culture, Media and Sport, 1999). In 1997, the ceremonies for the handover of Hong Kong from Britain to China had great symbolic importance for both countries. World media coverage of the ceremonies provoked emotions ranging from pride to sadness, jubilation to apprehension.

Events have the power to challenge the imagination and to explore possibilities. For example, the installation of the Ice Cube outdoor ice-skating rink at Millennium Square in Leeds and similar events in Edinburgh and Somerset House in London illustrate the trend in finding innovative alternative uses for city centre space.

Sphere of event	Positive impacts	Negative impacts
Social and cultural	Shared experience Revitalizing traditions Building community pride Validation of community groups Increased community participation Introducing new and challenging ideas Expanding cultural perspectives	Community alienation Manipulation of community Negative community image Bad behaviour Substance abuse Social dislocation Loss of amenity
Physical and environmental	Showcasing the environment Providing models for best practice Increasing environmental awareness Infrastructure legacy Improved transport and communications Urban transformation and renewal	Environmental damage Pollution Destruction of heritage Noise disturbance Traffic congestion
Political	International prestige Improved profile Promotion of investment Social cohesion Development of administrative skills	Risk of event failure Misallocation of funds Lack of accountability Propagandizing Loss of community ownership and control Legitimation of ideology
Tourism and economic	Destinational promotion and increased tourist visits Extended length of stay Higher yield Increased tax revenue Job creation	Community resistance to tourism Loss of authenticity Damage to reputation Exploitation Inflated prices Opportunity costs

Source: adapted from Hall, 1989.

Table 2.1 The impacts of events

Events can form the cornerstone of cultural strategies. For example, Newham Council have developed a local cultural strategy, entitled 'Reasons To Be Cheerful', at the heart of which is the vision that people choosing to live and work in Newham by 2010. In order to achieve this, events are used in a number of key areas. The strategy includes the following themes, with selection key points from the action plan:

- *New governance arrangements*: work with the Mayor and the Greater London Authority (GLA) to ensure Newham plays a full part in London's Cultural Strategy and in bids for major events such as the Olympics.
- *Showcase developments and a strengthened economy*: establish Three Mills as a major centre for creative industries, a regional performance venue and a visitor destination.
- *An environment which supports a good quality of life*: establish mechanisms to attract major events to the area.
- *Local area strategies*: planning celebrations of local cultures which will increase community cohesion (Newham Leisure Services, 2000).

Research suggests that local communities often value the 'feel-good' aspects of hallmark events, and are prepared to put up with temporary inconvenience and disruption because of the excitement which they generate, and the long-term expectation of improved facilities and profile. The Flora London Marathon provides the opportunity each year for professional and amateur athletes to participate in a great international sporting event. For the professionals, this is an opportunity for them to prove their sporting excellence against the world's elite. For others, it provides an opportunity to prove to family, friends and relatives their endurance. However, for 76 per cent of the runners, it provides an opportunity to raise funds for their favoured charity. Charities benefit each year from the millions of pounds raised through sponsorship. A survey after the 2000 marathon found that £24 million had been raised for good causes (London Marathon, 2000), an achievement placing this as the largest fundraising event in the UK resulting in an entry in the Guinness World Records (2000).

A study of Leeds residents' and visitors' views of Euro '96 for Leeds City Council, indicated that the success of the tournament nationally and regionally had impressed people who traditionally had little to do with football, leading to civic pride. For a proportion of Leeds residents, the football stadia would be associated with the spectacle of the France vs Spain game rather than the long-held association with hooliganism (Tourism Works, 1996). However, the same support was not received from Leeds residents for Leeds Love Parade or the Leeds Festival, with the result that the former did not gain approval for 2001 and moved to an alternative city.

Wimbledon Tennis Club and the Lawn Tennis Association attempt to take a socially aware attitude to the organization of the championships, using the event to encourage junior interest and participation in tennis. In addition to the proceeds of the tournament being ploughed back into tennis development each year, and 10 000 tickets being distributed for dedicated junior tickets, specific local benefits include:

- local schools and tennis clubs offered use of the covered courts
- financial assistance to Merton Borough's tennis development programme

- renewal of 15 tennis courts in Wimbledon Park in 1986 and provision of floodlighting
- Raynes Park Sports Ground facilities (football, cricket, hockey, athletics and tennis) offered to schools and sports clubs
- Merton Youth Concert Band and Jazz Orchestra play on both semi-final days of the championships
- Ball boys and girls drawn solely from local schools since 1969 and 1977, respectively.

A public opinion study by UK Sport (1998) found that 87 per cent of the public believe it important that the UK host major events, with 88 per cent believing that success on the world sporting stage creates a national 'feel-good' factor. In developing a UK strategy for major events, UK Sport highlight the role that events play in sport, and as a result, society as a whole. They state, 'Events matter . . . because they are the heart and soul of the experience for everyone involved in sport – athletes, coaches, officials, volunteers, media, sponsors and fans. Our attitude to events is ultimately our attitude to sport: the hosting of major events should therefore be a key part of any sports system which aims to be a world leader' (UK Sport, 1999a, p. 4).

However, such events can have negative social impacts. Bath and North East Somerset Council conducted a resident survey to canvass opinion on the local impact of events staged at Royal Victoria Park. The survey found that of the 303 returned questionnaires (27 per cent response rate), a significant number (almost 25 per cent) said they had planned time away from home to coincide with events to avoid noise or disruption. Further, although over 75 per cent of the sample had attended some of the events in the last twelve months, including Bath Festival Opening Night, the Spring Flower Show and the Fringe Festival, respondents considered the Festival Opening Night, the Fringe Festival and the Funfair to be the most intrusive events in terms of both amplified music and general disturbance. As a result of these disruptions, most respondents considered that finishing times for events between 10.00 p.m. and midnight would be most appropriate (Howey, 2000).

The larger and more high profile the event, the more potential there is for things to go wrong, and to create negative impacts. A study into the impact of the Network Q Rally 1999 on Lanidloes and the forest of mid-Wales found that 48 percent of respondents had a negative attitude towards spectators, with main reasons being the spectators driving recklessly, imitating rally drivers and their lack of respect for locals (Blakey et al., 2000). In 1997, the bomb scare at the Aintree Grand National, one of Britain's most popular sport events, had an unforeseen impact on the local community, when 60 000 racegoers were evacuated. Due to the security alert, thousands of people were left stranded with 20 000 cars and hundreds of coaches trapped inside the grounds overnight. With all hotels fully booked, Merseyside Emergency Committee was convened and schools, leisure centres, church halls, together with generous local families, providing emergency accommodation (Henderson and Chapman, 1997).

Events, when they go wrong, can go very wrong indeed. Consider the impact of gatecrashers on Glastonbury 2000 – immediately, the pressure placed on facilities, food and other resources, and in the long term, the cancellation of Glastonbury Festival in 2001 amid worries of crowd safety and prosecution of the organizer for breach of the entertainment licence. More seriously, the tragic death of ninety-six Liverpool fans at Hillsborough in 1989, the bombing incident at the Atlanta Olympics in 1996 and the death of eight fans at Roskilde Festival in 2000 shocked the world. Such events have far-reaching negative impacts, resulting not only in bad press but damage or injury to participants, stakeholders and the host community.

Managing crowd behaviour

Major events can have unintended social consequences such as substance abuse, bad crowd behaviour and an increase in criminal activity (Getz, 1997). If not managed properly, these unintended consequences can hijack the agenda and determine the public perception of the event. In recent years, English football clubs have successfully implemented strategies to manage alcohol-related bad crowd behaviour in order to protect their reputation, football's image and future. However, the image was tarnished by the alcohol-fuelled violence of fans abroad during the World Cup 1998 and European Championships in Holland and Belgium in 2000, which some believe to be a main factor in England losing their bid to host the World Cup in 2006. It should be remembered that football is not the only sport to suffer, with the 'yobbish' behaviour spreading into the summer Test cricket programme and Royal Ascot. For example, in the 1998 Test cricket series between England and South Africa, Old Trafford Cricket Ground banned non-members from bringing alcohol into the games and, bizarre as it would seem to some, the wearing of novelty clothing, as a result of 'rowdyism' at the previous match at Edgbaston. Deeley (1998) noted:

> At Edgbaston there were many complaints about the behaviour of groups of bizarrely dressed young men in the cheapest seating on the Rea Bank stand, chanting football fashion, shouting obscene remarks and dancing in the aisles. At Old Trafford people wearing dress deemed offensive and 'full body suits' (pelicans, teddy bears and the like) will be refused admission. The county say hats, wigs and head-dress restricting the view of others will not be tolerated.

He goes on to investigate the possible causes, as similar behaviour was not demonstrated at either Lords or the Fosters Oval grounds. He found that availability of alcohol could have a significant affect if the grounds did not have an effective bar management policy (either leaving bars open or unnecessarily closing could influence the mood of the crowd). The other issue, so called 'rowdyism' could be managed through strictly limiting tickets to avoid large groups sitting together (for example, Lords limited tickets to four per person) and banning or ejecting those that turn up in eccentric costumes, or those causing a disturbance to others through chanting or taking part in congas. However, this may take away from the atmosphere at games. Other events such as the Notting Hill Carnival, the summer music festivals (e.g. Glastonbury and Reading) and dance events have in some years been tainted by a perceived drug culture, which some believe is encouraged by tolerant policing.

Crowd behaviour can be modified with careful planning. Sometimes this is an evolutionary process. Managing New Year's Eve in London and in Edinburgh have seen a series of modifications and adjustments. In 1999, at the launch of the Millennium Festival year, around 3 million people partied along the banks of the

River Thames and around Trafalgar Square to witness the largest firework display ever staged in Britain. An estimated 2 million of these used the London Underground to access Central London between midday and midnight, with only a temporary closure of Underground stations to alleviate safety fears. Police made ninety-nine arrests (more than half for drunkenness) and three police officers were attacked in two separate incidents, but generally the celebrations passed off without serious incident (Harrison and Hastings, 2000). However, Londoners were to be disappointed in 2000 when Greater London Authority cancelled celebrations due to a clash between crowd safety management and commercial viability. The main issue raised was a fear that the transport system would be dangerously overcrowded as seen the previous year, which lead to Underground and train operators proposing a restricted service, and transport unions threatening industrial action unless safety concerns were addressed. A strategy proposed to manage this – restricting transport, cancelling the midnight firework display and moving an earlier display from 7 p.m. to 5 p.m. – proved unpopular with sponsors due to the reduced audience, leading to the largest sponsor, Yahoo, withdrawing their £350 000 offer and, ultimately, cancellation of the event (O'Neill, 2000). The Royal Bank of Scotland Street Party, Edinburgh's Hogmanay, had its capacity reduced from a record 200 000 in 1999 to 100 000 for New Year 2000 in order to increase safety. As a result of better crowd management and improved strategies, global celebrations of the New Millennium were largely reported as good spirited and peaceful.

Community ownership and control of events

Badly managed events can also have wider effects on the social life and structure of communities. These can include loss of amenity owing to noise or crowds, resentment of inequitable distribution of costs and benefits, and cost inflation of goods and services that can upset housing markets and impact most on low-income groups as outlined by Getz (1997). It follows that communities should have a major say in the planning and management of events. For example, at the time of writing, the Greater London Authority is reviewing the operation and management of Notting Hill Carnival, together with longer-term trends and opportunities for the event's development. This will include the views of stakeholders, including relevant community organizations (GLA, 2000, GLACRE, 2001). However, Hall (1989, p. 32) concludes that the role of communities is often marginalized:

> In nearly every case study of hallmark events the most important decision of all, whether to host an event or not, is taken outside of the public arena and behind the closed doors of a private office or city hall. Indeed, often government may have no initial say as to whether to host an event or not, as with the winning of the America's Cup by Alan Bond in 1983. Therefore, public participation usually becomes a form of placation in which policy can only be changed in an incremental fashion and then only at the margins. The substantive policy decision, that of hosting the event, still remains. In this situation, public participation within the planning process becomes reactive rather than proactive. Instead of a discussion of the advantages and disadvantages of hosting events, public participation becomes a means to increase the legitimacy of government and developers' decisions regarding the means by which events should be held.

This makes it all the more important for governments to be accountable through the political process, for the allocation of resources to events. Hall (1997) maintains that political analysis is an important tool in regaining community control over hallmark events, and ensuring that the objectives of these events focus on maximizing returns to the community.

Allegations of corruption within the International Olympic Committee (IOC), the scandal over ticketing strategies by the Sydney Organizing Committee for the Olympic Games (SOCOG) and the outrage over a loan from the English Football Association to the Welsh Football Association, allegedly in return for their support of the England 2006 World Cup bid, are examples of the increasing pressure for transparency and public accountability in the staging of major events.

Physical and environmental impacts

An event is an excellent way to showcase the unique characteristics of the host environments. Hall (1989) points out that selling the image of a hallmark event includes the marketing of the intrinsic properties of the destination. However, host environments may be extremely delicate and great care should be taken to protect them. A major event may require an environmental impact assessment to be conducted before council or government permission is granted for it to go ahead. Even if a formal study is not required, the event manager should carefully consider the likely impact of the event on the environment. This impact will be fairly contained if the event is to be held in a suitable purpose-built venue, e.g. a stadium, sports ground, show ground, conference or exhibition centre. The impact may be much greater if the event is to be held in a public space not ordinarily reserved for events, such as a park, town square or street. For example, Birmingham city centre was brought to a standstill in 1993 when an unforeseen number of residents turned up to witness the relaunch of local radio station, BRMB, leading to a reprimand for organizers from police and the council. Another example is the 13 tonnes of litter left after the Oasis concert in the Haymarket, Roseburn and Murrayfield areas. Not only did Edinburgh Council arrange the cleanup from this event, which they acknowledged was only one-third of the litter created by New Year/Hogmanay celebrations, disturbingly, their cleanup staff came under attack from people throwing bottles and their vehicles had to be escorted off site by police (City of Edinburgh Council, 2000a). Aspects such as crowd movement and control, noise levels, access and parking will be important considerations. Other major issues may include wear and tear on the natural and physical environment, heritage protection issues and disruption of the local community.

Good communication and consultation with local authorities will often resolve some of these issues. In addition, careful management planning may be required to modify impacts. In Liverpool, organizers of the Martell Grand National have worked over several years to progressively reduce the traffic impact of visitors to the event by developing a park-and-ride system of fringe parking and shuttle buses to the event area. A similar park-and-ride system is operated at the Royal Show held at the National Agricultural Centre in Stoneleigh, Warwickshire. Many festivals have reduced their impact on the environment by banning glass bottles, which can break and get trodden into the ground, and implementing effective waste management strategies.

When staging large events, the provision of infrastructure is often a costly budget component, but this may result in an improved environment and facilities. Many of

London's landmark venues have been the legacy of major events, including Crystal Palace (1851 Great Exhibition), Earls Court/Olympia (1887 to 1890 American, Italian, French and German Exhibitions), Royal Festival Hall and South Bank (1951 Festival of Britain) and more recently the Millenium Dome (1999/2000 Millennium Festival) (Evans, 1996). Similarly, Sheffield profited from an investment of £139 million in the development of state-of-the-art facilities for the 1991 World Student Games, including Ponds Forge International Swimming Pool, the Sheffield Arena and the Don Valley Stadium (Select Committee on Culture, Media and Sport, 1999) and Manchester will benefit from investment in facilities for the Commonwealth Games 2002 for years to come.

Waste management and recycling

Governments are increasingly using public education programmes and legislation to promote the recycling of waste materials and reduce the amount of waste going to landfill sites. Events are targeted as opportunities to demonstrate best practice models in waste management, and to change public attitudes and habits. The Commonwealth Games 2002 will provide Manchester with sporting facilities to take it well into the twenty-first century, as well as major infrastructure improvements in accommodation, transport and communications. However, the development of facilities for events such as this raises major environmental issues that are magnified by the scale and profile of the project. In order to address these concerns, UK Sport clearly identifies the need for environmental sensitivity in all aspects of bidding for and staging major events. It states:

> Major events and the environment are inextricably linked, and without due care events can impact adversely on the environment, directly or indirectly. Major events also have a very positive role to play in fostering under-standing of environmental issues, raising awareness and generating resources . . . Particular attention will be paid to the environmental issues raised by very large numbers of people coming together for a short period of time, with subsequent problems of safety, congestion, consumption, and waste. Areas of particular attention will include: access; infrastructure; energy consumption; energy renewal; sustainability; minimising resource requirements; the use of natural products; and innovative design and technology that reduces both operating and maintenance costs and greatly extends the lifetime of sports facilities and new event venues. (UK Sport, 1999a, p. 10)

For the event manager, incorporating a waste management plan into the overall event plan has become increasingly good policy. Community expectations and the health of our environment require that events demonstrate good waste management principles, and provide models for recycling. The environmentally conscious event manager will reap not only economic benefits, but also the approval of an increasingly environmentally aware public. For example, Glastonbury Festival effectively reduce their impact on the environment through an effective waste management and recycling strategy, using hundreds of volunteers as part of their dedicated Recycling Crew. Their role includes collecting litter, separating recyclable items, giving out litter bags and working with the 'Reclammator' to help

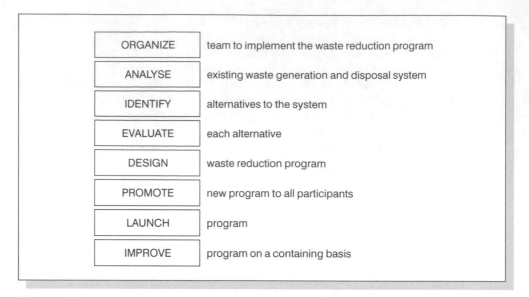

ORGANIZE	team to implement the waste reduction program
ANALYSE	existing waste generation and disposal system
IDENTIFY	alternatives to the system
EVALUATE	each alternative
DESIGN	waste reduction program
PROMOTE	new program to all participants
LAUNCH	program
IMPROVE	program on a containing basis

Figure 2.1 Eight-stage process for waste reduction and recycling
Source: Xerox Corporation, 1998, *Guide to Waste Reduction and Recycling at Special Events*. New York, Xerox Corporation, p. 1.

Glastonbury become the greenest festival (Glastonbury Festivals Ltd, 2000). With increasing concern for the atmosphere, events such as the Brit Awards and Glastonbury are also beginning to take part in schemes such as 'Carbon Neutral'. This involves an assessment of the energy used by the event – as a result, sufficient trees are then planted to absorb the carbon dioxide produced.

Based on experience gained at the 1996 Summer Olympics in Atlanta, the Xerox Corporation (1998) present an eight-step model for waste reduction and recycling at events, illustrated in Figure 2.1.

The Sydney Olympic Games and the environment

The Sydney Olympic Games have provided Sydney with sporting facilities that will take it well into the twenty-first century, as well as major infrastructure improvements in accommodation, transport and communications. However, the preparation of the site and the building of the Olympic Village raised major environmental issues, which were magnified by the scale and profile of the project. The Sydney Olympic Games' Environmental Guidelines were based on principles adopted at the United Nations Earth Summit. They were expressed in ecologically sustainable development policies, which included commitments to energy conservation, water conservation, waste avoidance and minimization, air, water and soil quality and the protection of significant natural and cultural environments.

In the planning and construction of Olympic facilities and the running of the Games, the guidelines committed Sydney to initiatives including:

- conduct of environmental and social impact studies
- minimization of adverse impacts on Olympic sites and nearby residents
- protection of the natural environment or threatened eco-systems

- enforcement of Environmental Guidelines on suppliers and contractors
- concentration of venues in compact zones
- placement of all venues and the majority of training venues within 30 minutes' travel from the Olympic Village
- use of energy efficient design and materials
- maximum use of renewable sources of energy
- water conservation and recycling
- best practice in waste reduction and avoidance
- use where practicable of non-toxic substances
- use of recyclable packaging and non-disposable cutlery and crockery at food outlets where possible
- use of recycling bins at all Games venues
- information transferred electronically where possible to conserve paper, supplemented by paper recycling procedures
- public transport being the only means of access by spectators to events at Olympic sites.

Although threatened at times by the practicalities of their implementation, the guidelines provide an excellent model that will have a profound impact on the staging of major events in the future.

Political impacts

Politics and politicians are an important part of the equation that is contemporary event management. Ever since the Roman emperors discovered the power of the circus to deflect criticism and shore up popularity, shrewd politicians have had an eye for events that will keep the populace happy and themselves in power. No less an authority than Count Nicolo Machiavelli, adviser to the Medicis in the sixteenth century, had this to say on the subject:

> A prince must also show himself a lover of merit, give preferment to the able and honour those who excel in every art . . . Besides this, he ought, at convenient seasons of the year, to keep the people occupied with festivals and shows; and as every city is divided into guilds or into classes, he ought to pay attention to all these groups, mingle with them from time to time, and give them an example of his humanity and munificence, always upholding, however, the majesty of his dignity, which must never be allowed to fail in anything whatever. (Machiavelli, 1962, pp. 112–13)

The Royal House of Windsor took this advice to heart, providing some of the most popular events of the last century with the Coronation of Queen Elizabeth II and the fairytale-like wedding of Prince Charles and Lady Diana Spencer. Following the tragic death of Diana in 1997, more recent royal events have attempted to reflect the modernization of the monarchy and the mood of the people, with the wedding of Prince Edward and Sophie Rhys-Jones, and the one-hundredth birthday of the Queen Mother. Plans are already being made for the Queen's Golden Jubilee in 2002, which coincides with the Commonwealth Games in Manchester, with an extra bank holiday announced in anticipation of the celebrations. Successive British politicians have continued to use the spotlight of events to build their personal profile and gain political advantage. Commenting on the Great Exhibition of 1851, Asa Briggs noted how criticism of the project disappeared as the crowds flocked to see the event – crowds that were encouraged to attend through the equivalent of a Travelcard (Carling and Seeley, 1998). In 1951, Foreign Secretary Herbert Morrison received significant criticism due to his enthusiasm for the Festival of Britain project, leading an opposition MP to label him 'Lord Festival' a title that stuck (Carling and Seeley, 1998). Former Prime Minister John Major was frequently seen at major cricket matches during his term in office. In 1997, his first year in office, the Prime Minister, Tony Blair, continued with the Conservative government planned Millennium Dome project, attempting to use the Dome as a symbol of 'New Labour, New Britain', and of himself as a visionary and enlightened leader. When details of the Dome's contents were first published, he summarized the aim of the festival:

> In this Experience I want people to pause and reflect on this moment, about the possibilities ahead of us, about the values that guide our society . . . It will be an event to lift our horizons. It will be a catalyst to imagine our futures . . . As we approach the Millennium we can boast that we have a richness of talent in this country that is unparalleled: the finest artists, authors, architects, musicians, designers, animators, software makers, scientists . . . so why not put it on display? (Carling and Seeley, 1998, p. 5)

Arnold et al. (1989, pp. 191–2) leave no doubt as to the role of events in the political process: 'Governments in power will continue to use hallmark events to punctuate the ends of their periods in office, to arouse nationalism, enthusiasm and finally, votes. They are cheaper than wars or the preparation for them. In this regard, hallmark events do not hide political realities, they are the political reality.'

Governments around the world have realized the ability of events to raise the profile of politicians and the cities and areas that they govern. They have also realized the ability of events to attract visitors, and thus create economic benefits and jobs. This potent mixture has led to governments becoming major players in bidding for, hosting and staging major events. The UK government has undertaken two major inquiries into the staging of major events. In 1995, the National Heritage Committee ran an inquiry into 'Bids to Stage International Sporting Events' which identified how bidding for and staging international events could be improved. They found that, 'unless Britain does coordinate the multitudinous and sometimes apparently conflicting organisations that are involved, and is given a clear focus, then our country is unlikely to be successful in any bid for which there is fierce competition' (House of Commons National Heritage Committee Report, 1995, cited in UK Sport, 1999b, p. 5). This led to the GB Sports Council (the forerunner of UK Sport) being given the responsibility for sport event development in the UK (English Sports Council, 1999).

In 1998 a second Select Committee was established to investigate all aspects of staging international sporting events, from bidding through to economic, environmental and regeneration legacies of these events (Select Committee on Culture, Media and Sport, 1999). The committee took comprehensive evidence from associations and groups representing all major sports, government ministers and tourism bodies, together with information from organizations with experience of hosting major events (including fact-finding trips to Australia and Malaysia). The ensuing report detailed thirty-two principal conclusions and recommendations, including:

- the need for further research into economic benefits and impacts, and incorporation of an independent assessment as a requirement for future funding
- support for the proposed UK Sport Major Event Strategy
- the need to vet qualifications and ability of suitable candidates for committee posts of international sporting events, in order to ensure the effective representation of British interests
- the need for central government to partner local authorities in order to gain the national benefits from the event, including the Manchester 2002 Commonwealth Games
- the need for a 'Minister for Events' with responsibility for an events strategy incorporating sport and non-sport events (Select Committee on Culture, Media and Sport, 1999, s. IX).

The outcomes of the committee have been reviewed to monitor performance, with generally positive feedback gained (see Select Committee on Culture, Media and Sport, 2001).

Established in 1997, UK Sport includes the aim to, 'promote the UK or any part of it as a venue for international sports events and to advise, encourage and assist bodies in staging or seeking to stage such events'. It aims to provide a one-stop shop for event advice and support. In keeping with this, it established a Major Events Steering Group in 1999 which includes members with a range of experience including legal issues, media, marketing, sponsorship, event management, local authority involvement and the international politics of sport (UK Sport, 1999a). Elsewhere, the Northern Ireland Events Company has been established. This 'aims to support the promotion of major events in Northern Ireland which have the potential to reflect a positive image of Northern Ireland, create opportunity for greater social cohesion and bring economic benefits'.

Edinburgh has built up a strong international reputation as a festival city, with an extensive programme of major events including Edinburgh International Festival, Edinburgh Fringe, and Edinburgh's Hogmanay.

This involvement of governments in events has politicized the events landscape as pointed out by Hall (1989, p. 236):

> Politics is paramount in hallmark events. It is either naïve or duplistic to pretend otherwise. Events alter the time frame in which planning occurs and they become opportunities to do something new and better than before. In this context, events may change or legitimate political priorities in the short term and political ideologies and socio-cultural reality in the longer term. Hallmark events represent the tournaments of old, fulfilling psychological and political needs through the winning of hosting over other locations and the winning of events themselves. Following a hallmark event some places will never be the same again, physically, economically, socially and, perhaps most importantly of all, politically.

It is important to acknowledge that events have values beyond just tangible and economic benefits. Humans are social animals, and celebrations play a key role in the well-being of the social structure – the common wealth. Events have the ability to engender social cohesion, confidence and pride. Therein lies the source of their political power and influence, and the reason why events will always reflect and interact with their political circumstances and environment.

Tourism and economic impacts

Governments are increasingly turning to tourism as a growth industry capable of delivering economic benefits and job creation. Events in turn are seen as catalysts for attracting visitors, and increasing their average spend and length of stay or repeat visits. They are also seen as image-makers, creating profile for destinations, positioning them in the market and providing competitive marketing advantage. For example, the World Masters Athletics Championships 2000 in Gateshead were expected to lead to an estimated 150 000 additional bednights, adding a minimum of £12 million to the local economy (Select Committee on Culture, Media and Sport, 1999). This has led to the creation of a new field, known as Event Tourism, which Getz (1997, p. 16) defines as:

1 The systematic planning, development and marketing of events as tourist attractions, catalysts for other developments, image builders, and animators of attractions and destination areas; event tourism strategies should also cover the management of news and negative events.
2 A market segment consisting of those people who travel to attend events, or who can be motivated to attend events while away from home.

Government tourism and arts bodies often consciously use events to position their destinations in the market and deliver tourism, culture and art strategies. For example, Hampshire County Council noted that, 'festivals can provide high profile opportunities to celebrate communities, to promote artistic excellence and innovation, and to improve the image, identity and competitiveness of particular localities' (Fuller, 1998). The Events Unit within the Belfast City Development Department aims to 'promote and develop a high quality, sustainable, inclusive programme of public access events, in a safe enjoyable environment, in order to help raise the profile of Belfast in support of regeneration' (Belfast City Council, 2000a, p. 2). Key objectives of the Events Unit Strategy, mapped into the Development Department Strategy are:

- Develop and promote a high-quality, sustainable, inclusive programme of public access events to raise the profile of Belfast and utilize the common Belfast branding to ensure Belfast is an attractive and welcoming city.
- Work in partnership with the Tourism Development Unit and the Arts Unit to ensure the development, packaging and promotion of events which will enhance Belfast's reputation.
- Ensure that all promotional tools including literature, advertisements, press releases provide an appropriate range of information for residents and visitors to the city.
- Work in conjunction with the Tourism Unit and the Belfast Visitor and Convention Bureau (BVCB) to ensure that the common branding of the city is adopted appropriately (Belfast City Council, 2000b).

Another example is the key role that events play within the arts strategy of Bath and North East Somerset Council (B&NES) for 2001 to 2004 (B&NES, 2001). The strategy aims 'to increase the number of residents and visitors to B&NES experiencing high-quality arts events and activities'. To achieve this, B&NES have set the following objectives:

1 To increase the number of admissions to existing arts events and activities by 5 per cent by 2004 (audience building).
2 To develop opportunities for new audiences to access the arts (audience development) by:
   (a) increasing the amount of arts events and activities taking place or located in community and public settings by 20 per cent by 2004
   (b) enhancing the facilities and services in B&NES for the presentation and production of the Arts (to be audited in 2004 and compared to the 1999 research)
   (c) increasing the amount of effective community and education arts activity by 20 per cent
   (d) increasing the range of arts events and activities in the area (to be audited in 2004 and compared to the 2000 Arts Impact Assessment)
   (e) spreading the availability of arts events and activities more evenly throughout the year and the area (to be audited in 2004 and compared to the 2000 Arts Impact Assessment)(B&NES, 2001)

It is notable that these objectives meet the SMART objective principles discussed in Chapter 4.

The Wales Tourist Board undertook a major marketing and promotional campaign in relation to the Rugby World Cup in Wales in 1999. Its overall aim was to use the tournament as an opportunity to attract additional visitors, in order to raise the profile of the host nation and to secure lasting tourism benefits. Over 330 000 people were estimated to have visited Wales as a result of the event. In a survey of international rugby fans conducted before and after the Rugby World Cup, fewer than 20 per cent had visited Wales. Of those who had, almost 70 per cent thought it likely that they would return on holiday. Amongst those who had seen coverage of the event on television, 25 per cent thought that they would be much more likely to visit Wales on holiday as a result. Research indicated that around 135 000 trips may be generated from the UK over the next five years, potentially worth around £15 million (Anon., 2000).

If events are to be effective in positioning their destinations in the market, they must strive for authenticity and the expression of the unique characteristics of their communities. Visitors want to do what the locals do, and experience what the locals enjoy. The UK government report 'Tomorrow's Tourism' (DCMS, 1999, p. 7) argues that:

> Tourism is based largely on our heritage, culture and countryside and, therefore, needs to maintain the quality of the resources upon which it depends. Tourism can provide an incentive and income to protect our built and natural environment and helps to maintain local culture and diversity. Where tourism is popular, it underpins local commercial activity and services and it can help to regenerate urban and rural areas.

Conversely, destinations that produce events for the tourists rather than events that have meaning for their own communities, run the danger of producing inauthentic, shallow events. Exploitative or badly run events with inadequate management or facilities can damage the reputation of a destination.

Events and seasonality

A strong advantage of event tourism is the ability to attract visitors in the low season, when airline and accommodation providers often have surplus capacity. Attracting visitors to use what would otherwise be underutilized tourism infrastructure derives additional economic benefit. Getz describes the way that events can overcome seasonality by capitalizing 'on whatever natural appeal the off-season presents, such as winter as opposed to summer sports, seasonal food and produce, and scenery or wildlife viewed in different places and under changing conditions'. He also notes that 'in many destinations the residents prefer the off-season for their own celebrations, and these provide more authentic events for visitors' (Getz, 1997, p. 53).

Many UK destinations have developed events to enliven off-season periods. Within 'A Tourism Strategy for Wales' (WTB, 2000, p. 53) the Wales Tourist Board note the benefit that events can bring to Wales, highlighting that, 'Festivals and event . . . can play a key role in attracting larger numbers of overseas visitors and in developing new markets within the UK throughout the year'. However, they go on to note that due to a previously uncoordinated approach to developing the event programme, the best known events within Wales are in the main summer months, which reinforces seasonality. As a result, the tourism strategy recommends the development of an events/festival strategy to distribute events throughout the year and a more co-ordinated approach to marketing in order to gain full benefit from business tourism (including meetings, incentives, conferences and exhibitions). A further example is Edinburgh, which in 2000 launched the new Capital Christmas winter festival to extend the traditional New Year Hogmanay celebrations and attract visitors in the off-season winter months. Donald Anderson, Leader of the Council, noted, 'Edinburgh attracts thousands of visitors all year round and our world renowned festivals play a major part in this. Capital Christmas and Edinburgh's Hogmanay together offer the best winter festival programme in the world and I know of no other city that hosts a full month of family entertainment throughout the festive season' (City of Edinburgh Council, 2000b).

Events enhance the tourism experience

Events can provide newness, freshness and change, which sustain interest in the destination for locals, and enhance its attraction for visitors. Tourist attractions and theme parks incorporate events as a key element in their marketing programmes. Bradford Museum of Film, Television and Arts, Alton Towers in Staffordshire and Blackpool Pleasure Beach all use extensive event programmes to increase market profile and attract repeat visits. Getz (1997, p. 55) notes the use of events by a wide variety of tourism attractions to animate and interpret their products:

> Resorts, museums, historic districts, heritage sites, archaeological sites, markets and shopping centers, sports stadia, convention centers, and theme parks all develop programs of special events. Built attractions and facilities everywhere have realized the advantages of 'animation' – the process of programming interpretive features and/or special events that make the place come alive with sensory stimulation and appealing atmosphere.

Events as catalysts for development

Events can enhance the quality of life, and thus add to the sense of place and the residential amenity of neighbourhoods. Millennium Square, a £12 million project funded by Leeds City Council and the Millennium Commission, is used for events but also provides traffic-free leisure space for residents to enjoy. Leeds' annual multicultural programme of events is the envy of many cities, ranging from Opera in the Park and Party in the Park, through to the Irish and Chinese festivals.

Large events can also act as catalysts for urban renewal, and for the creation of new or expanded tourism infrastructure. The Sheffield World Student Games in 1991 provided major facilities, including Ponds Forge International Pool, the Sheffield Arena and the Don Valley Stadium that have contributed to Sheffield's reputation as a sporting city. The Commonwealth Games 2002 are leading to the regeneration of East Manchester, including development of the City of Manchester Stadium, which will be home to Manchester City Football Club following the Games to ensure a legacy and long-term after-use. Other examples include the Millennium Dome and surrounding area in Greenwich (East London) as the focal point for the Millennium Festival celebrations, and the Festival Hall and South Bank Centre developed for the Festival of Britain in 1951, all of which gained infrastructure development stemming from hosting large-scale events. Hotel and facilities development, better communications and improved road and public transport networks are some of the legacies left by these events. One of Edinburgh International Festival's founders, Henry Harvey Wood, noted in 1947 the role that the festival could play in regenerating the economy. He stated, 'If the Festival succeeds, Edinburgh will not only have scored an artistic triumph but laid the foundations of a major industry, a new and exciting source of income' (EIF, 2000, p. 2). The festival has succeeded and his prediction has come true. Edinburgh International Festival continues to be of substantial economic importance. In 1997 alone Edinburgh's festivals generated an estimate £125 million for the economy, sustaining the equivalent of 4000 jobs (EIF, 2001).

Economic benefits

Events have a wide range of economic impacts. The expenditure of visitors is spread over travel, accommodation, restaurants, shopping and other tourism-related services. This is part of a general trend in the UK economy away from an industrial product base to a more service-based economy. The construction industry – witness the construction boom resulting from the Commonwealth Games 2002 in Manchester and the redevelopment of Wembley National Stadium – is often stimulated by the need for new or improved facilities required to stage a major event. Employment and the local economy are temporarily boosted by the expenditure involved in staging an event. Thus whole mini-economies surround and work off the events industry.

The expenditure generated by events also circulates in the wider economy. For example, the meal consumed by the event visitor results in further business for the companies that supply and transport food produce. Further, sales of goods at exhibitions result in jobs being supported elsewhere, for example, at the International Spring Fair at Birmingham NEC in 1997, it was estimated that over £1.6 billion of orders were taken. This indirect or induced expenditure is known as the multiplier effect, and while there is considerable disagreement on the calculation of multipliers, it is generally agreed that event expenditure does have a flow-on effect on the economy (further discussed in Chapter 12). This generalized benefit to the wider economy provides the impetus for governments to become involved in bidding for and staging events.

A survey of 1000 tourism-related businesses was conducted in relation to the Rugby World Cup in Wales in 1999 (Anon., 2000). The accommodation sector fared best, with two-thirds of accommodation providers experiencing improvements in business performance, and a 7.5 per cent increase in room rates by operators in Cardiff and the south-east of Wales. Around half of food and drink outlets reported increased performance. This sector also reported having made considerable investment in promotional activities and small-scale product development. However, over half of those who responded from the retail sector thought that, despite improvements in average spend, the event had impacted negatively on their overall performance.

An impact review commissioned by the Motor Sport Association on the Network Q Rally, one of the largest spectator sports in the UK with 134 921 paying spectators, found that it pumped £11.1 million into the local economy, 60 per cent of which was from outside the area. Those to benefit included local accommodation providers, restaurants, retail outlets and transport providers. They noted that the event also generates an additional £17 million from tourism stimulated by the television coverage (Lilley III and DeFranco, 1999a). Impacts could indeed be greater, as later research by Blakey et al. (2000) indicates that in 1999 there were over 1 million live spectators and 11 000 volunteer officials, which would make it the largest sporting event in the UK. The British Grand Prix, seen by many to be one of the showcase UK events, has an economic impact of £28 million, £25 million from outside the local area (Lilley III and DeFranco, 1999b). British International Motor Show, held at Birmingham NEC in October 2000, played host to an estimated 600 000 visitors, or over 1 million if the 'Internet visitors' were included, bringing an additional £30 million into the local economy. The organizers noted that they are the first international motor show in the world to have an independently audited attendance, conducted by the Audit Bureau of Circulations (ABC) (SMMT, 2000).

Table 2.2 summarizes the economic benefits of a number of recent events in the UK. The results are not strictly comparable, as the methodologies for evaluating events vary widely. However, the table does demonstrate the considerable tourism and economic benefits that flow from major events. UK Sport is attempting to address comparability issues through proposing a standard methodology, discussed in Chapter 12.

Events have the potential to provide niche development opportunities for city and regional governments. Research conducted on behalf of the Society of London Theatre demonstrated that theatre can have a major impact on tourism and the economy, with the 1997 West End theatre season worth £1075 million to the city of London, supporting 41 000 jobs (Travers, 1998). Birmingham is maximizing the benefits of successfully staging the G8 Birmingham Summit, the Eurovision Song Contest and the Lions Clubs International Conference in 1998, which had a combined impact of £35.65 million additional spend and highlighted the city's ability to successfully stage international conferences. Following these high-profile events, a national telephone survey of 1000 people, by Birmingham Marketing Partnership (BMP), found that 68 per cent believed Birmingham had improved as a city, 55 per cent thought it was a friendly city and 70 per cent considered Birmingham to be a leading event city. Further research by the City Council and

Event	Total attendance	Total visitors from outside local area	Total expenditure from outside local area (£m)	Total economic impact (£m)
European Football Championships (Euro '96), UK 1996		280 000	120.0	195.0
1st Cornhill Test Match England vs Australia 1997	72 700	66 900 (92%)	4.6	9.0
World Badminton Championships and Sudirman Cup 1997	21 700	13 500 (62%)	0.386	1.9
British Grand Prix 1997	170 000	136 000 (80%)	25.0	28.0
Weetabix Women's British Open Golf Championship, Sunningdale 1997	50 000		0.207	2.1
Network Q Rally of Great Britain 1998	135 000	81 000 (60%)	6.7	17.0
Leeds Love Parade, 2000	250 000	165 000 (66%)		12.8
Motor Show 2000	600 000		30.0	

Sources: Lilley III and DeFranco, 1999a, 1999b; Tourism Works, 1996; UK Sport, 2000b; Yorkshire Tourist Board, 2000.

Table 2.2 Comparative table of economic benefits of events

BMP established that the media impact was eight times greater than could be expected for major news stories, equating to approximately £1.8 million of media coverage. Birmingham has continued to capitalize on its image as a major event city, through promoting itself as 'Europe's meeting place' and expanding the NEC complex, the UK's largest exhibition space, which generated £441 million impact, of which £141 million was retained locally – supporting 12 400 jobs (Notman, 1999). Birmingham NEC have successfully bid to host ITMA 2003 (the International Exhibition of Textile Machinery) – the world's largest exhibition. This is the first time the event will take place in the UK since its launch in 1951. Taking over 160 000 square metres of stand space, with 1400 exhibitors from forty countries, an audience of 150 000 is expected (ITMA, 2000). Independent research by KPMG forecasts that the event will result in £291 million expenditure, equivalent to 1300 full-time equivalent jobs (ITMA, 1999).

Cost-benefit analysis

Money spent on events represents an opportunity cost of resources that may have been devoted to other needs in the community. This has caused governments to look at the cost-benefit analysis of events, and has given rise to a specialized branch of economic study. As discussed earlier, Edinburgh has developed a year round strand of economic activity based on its positioning as the festival capital of Europe. For example, City of Edinburgh Council (2000c) note that Edinburgh's Hogmanay is now in the same league as the Edinburgh International Festival in terms of both its image and the impact it has on the city's economy. For an outlay of around £1.4 million the event generates an economic return in the region of £30 million.

An extensive evaluation commissioned in 1990 by the Department of the Environment of the Liverpool International Garden Festival (1984), Stoke National Garden Festival (1986) and Glasgow Garden Festival (1988) found that Liverpool and Stoke cost in the region of £40 million to stage, with an additional local impact of £21 million (1985 prices). Costs of staging the Glasgow festival were higher at around £69 million, due in part to the greater sponsorship and franchising. Benefits generated fit under three broad headings of reclamation (increased speed and higher-quality reclaiming of the site), environmental gains (visual impact during and after the festival, image-building for the cities) and economic impact (1400–2500 jobs) (PA Cambridge Economic Consultants, 1990).

Monitoring long-term impacts

Impacts that are calculated during the actual timeframe of an event tell only part of the story. In order to form a full picture of the impact of the event, it is necessary to look at the long-term effects on the community and its economy. The case of the 1991 World Student Games give some indication of the aftershock of the event. Bramwell (1997) notes that there is a temptation to evaluate mega-events too soon after an event, before the full impact can be assessed. He points out that, despite the debt incurred by the city during the event, five years after the games the city had been designated a City of Sport and had benefited from an extensive programme of national and international events, and the development of a further £20 million private leisure scheme next to the Arena. The city was left with a legacy of infrastructure and quality tourism developments that were either initiated or speeded up by the event. On a wider level, an event-led city strategy grew out of the games (Destination Sheffield, 1995). With a brief to attract or initiate events each year that would profile the city, it has already hosted 160 national, 19 European, 10 world championships and 48 other international events (KRONOS, 1997).

The methodology for evaluating the economic impact of events will be treated in more detail in Chapter 12.

Summary

All events produce impacts, both positive and negative, which it is the task of the event manager to assess and balance.

Social and cultural impacts may involve a shared experience, and may give rise to local pride, validation or the widening of cultural horizons. However, social problems rising from events may result in social dislocation if not properly managed. Events are an excellent opportunity to showcase the physical characteristics of a destination, but event environments may be very delicate, and care should be taken to safeguard and protect them. Events may involve longer-term issues affecting the built environment and the legacy of improved facilities. Increasingly, environmental considerations are paramount, as shown by the environmental guidelines that have been developed by UK Sport to be considered when bidding for and staging events, to manage their environmental impact.

Political impacts have long been recognized by governments, and often include increased profile and benefits to the host community. However, it is important that events fulfil the wider community agenda. Governments are attracted to events because of the economic benefits, job creation and tourism that they can provide. Events act as catalysts for attracting tourists and extending their length of stay. They also increase the profile of a destination, and can be designed to attract visitors out of season when tourism facilities are underutilized. Large events also serve as catalysts for urban renewal, and for the creation of new tourism infrastructure. Events bring economic benefits to their communities, but governments need to weigh these benefits against costs when deciding how to allocate resources.

Questions

1 Describe some examples of events where the needs have been perceived as being in conflict with those of their host communities. As the event manager, how would you resolve these conflicting needs?

2 Describe an event with which you are familiar and which has been characterized by social problems or bad crowd behaviour. As the event manager, what would you have done to manage the situation and improve the outcome of the event? In your answer, discuss both the planning of the event and possible on-the-spot responses.

3 Select a major event that has been held in your region, and identify as many environmental impacts as you can. Evaluate whether you think the overall environmental impact on the host community was positive or negative, and recommend what steps could be taken to improve the balance.

4 Describe an event that you believe was not sufficiently responsive to community attitudes and values. What steps could be taken in the community to improve the situation?

5 Identify an event in your region which has a significant tourism component, and examine the event in terms of its ability to:
   (a) increase tourist visits and length of stay
   (b) improve the profile of the destination
   (c) create economic benefits for the region.

6 Select an event in which you have been involved as a participant or close observer, and identify as many impacts of the event as you can, both positive and negative. Did the positive impacts outweigh the negative?
   (a) What measures did the organizers have in place to maximize positive impacts and minimize negative impacts?
   (b) As the event manager, what steps could you have taken to balance the impacts and improve the outcome of the event?

Hospitality, Leisure & Tourism Series

Case Study

British International Motor Show

Organized by Britain's leading motor industry trade association, the Society of Motor Manufacturers and Traders (SMMT), the British International Motor Show 2000, the seventy-third to be organized by SMMT, took place from 19 to 29 October at the NEC, Birmingham. The first SMMT Motor Show was held at Crystal Palace in London in 1903 and around 10 000 visitors came to look at the new models on display. Interestingly, at that time, there were just 8000 cars on the road in the whole of the UK! The Motor Show soon became a major event in the UK and by the 1970s, the exhibition had grown too big for London. The decision was made to move the show to the National Exhibition Centre in Birmingham to allow for a multi-halled exhibition in 1978. The Show runs every two years, overseen by the International Organization of Motor Vehicle Manufacturers (OICA) which sanctions the international status of motor shows, based on that country's market size, manufacturing and sales presence.

The Show is now the single biggest consumer exhibition in the country, equivalent to an area seventeen times the size of Wembley's pitch or 2.5 Wembley stadiums. In order to operate the event, around 22 000 people were involved in the Show's build-up and running, with the NEC providing up to 2000 extra staff during the event. Exhibition space in 2000 covered 66 815 square metres – over 2000 square metres larger than the 1998 Show, with a total of 326 exhibitors exhibiting sixty-nine new cars (out of over 1000) at the Show, including fifteen world debuts, four European debuts and fifty UK debuts.

The Show attracts visitors from far and wide – 709 422 visitors attended in 1998 (roughly broken down as 55 per cent men, 35 per cent women and 10 per cent children) and the 2000 Show looked set to break the 750 000 barrier. However, due to the significant problems on the UK railways, with a 50 per cent fall in visitors travelling to the NEC by train, the overall number of visitors to the Motor Show reduced to approximately 600 000. This will be confirmed when the final audited numbers are released by Audit Bureau of Circulations (the British International Motor Show 2000 was the first international motor show in the world to have an independent attendance audit). During the Show, visitors consumed an estimated 350 000 sandwiches and baguettes, 150 000 hot dogs and burgers, 400 000 cups of tea, 100 000 pints of beer, 4500 bottles of wine. Ninety thousand self-service and 12 000 waitress-served meals were eaten.

It was a record-breaking Show for attendance too, as the Internet boosted overall attendance to well over 1 million for the first time in the history of the Motor Show. The true extent of the information superhighway was unveiled at the show, reflecting an incredible rise in on-line communications. Since the 1998 show, the Internet has transformed the way business is conducted right from the moment the materials are dug from the ground to the point of sale. The first Motor Show of the new millennium highlighted ground-breaking innovations, which enable customers to see the latest products designed and delivered using the World Wide Web. Show organizers also unveiled the first-ever Virtual Media centre, available twenty-four hours a day at http://www.motorshow-mediacentre.co.uk. Registered media users unable to make it to the Show could log on to the facility and download news, pictures, information and comment.

The British International Motor Show 2000 set new records despite the disruption caused to visitors who travelled by train. For the first time ever, exhibitors and visitors added more than £30 million to the economy in the West Midlands, as Britain's biggest consumer show also employed more than 20 000 local people to stage this record-breaking event.

In addition, intangible benefits were gained such as boosting the area's international profile. Philip Jones, head of exhibitions at the SMMT said:

> Once again, Birmingham and the NEC have demonstrated an ability to stage a major international event. Many of the senior executives of the motor industry have been fulsome in their praise for both the venue and the facilities in and around the city. These not only stand comparison but often exceed those on offer at other leading international motor shows such as Frankfurt, Detroit or Geneva.

Businesses throughout the West Midlands were boosted by the continuing success of this year's International Motor Show in Birmingham, according to Barry Cleverdon, chief executive of the NEC Group. He noted during the Show:

> The British International Motor Show is once again proving one of the highlights of the busy calendar at the NEC. With its massive national and international profile, the show brings enormous benefits to the region, including millions of pounds in visitor and business spending. Activity at this show is helping to sustain many businesses in a variety of sectors throughout the region. In response, the region is once again proving how well it can deliver for major events. It's this level of impact that is one of the key factors driving our future development plans at the NEC, which focus on further enhancing all aspects of the visitor experience.

Exhibitors smashed their own targets too, with record levels of orders taken and interest in their products at all-time highs. For example, in just the first ten days of the Show the new Mini generated over 20 000 serious sales leads and more than 200 orders, while Toyota has registered more than 15 000 serious enquiries about its cars.

Motor Show chief executive Christopher Macgowan said: 'This has been the most successful British International Motor Show on record and has generated high levels of new business both in the West Midlands and for companies across the whole motor industry.'

For further details about the British International Motor Show, please visit www.motorshow.co.uk.

By the Society of Motor Manufacturers and Traders.

Questions

1 From the case study, identify the main stakeholders in the British International Motor Show.

2 In evaluating the impacts, what are the long-term benefits to Birmingham of hosting the Show?

3 What factors contribute to the continuing success of the Show?

4 The case illustrates the impact of the external environment on the event itself with rail disruption causing a reduction in target numbers and a change in transportation. What other issues from the external environment may impact on the Show? What strategies could event managers implement to minimize the impact of such issues?

Hospitality, Leisure & Tourism Series

CHAPTER 3

Conceptualizing the event

After studying this chapter you will be able to:

- identify the range of stakeholders in an event

- describe and balance the overlapping and conflicting needs of stakeholders

- describe the role of government, corporate and community sectors in events

- discuss trends and issues in society that affect events

- understand the role of sponsorship in events

- develop partnerships with sponsors and the media

- identify the unique elements and resources of an event

- understand the process of developing an event concept.

Introduction – who are the stakeholders?

With increased regulation and the growth of government and corporate involvement in events, the environment in which events are staged has become much more complex. Event managers are now required to identify and service a range of stakeholders in the event, and to balance their needs and objectives. The prime stakeholder is the host organization, or the body putting on the event. This may be a local government department often staging the event as part of its charter or service delivery programme. It may be a corporate organization, staging the event in order to raise its profile, increase market share or promote the sale of goods or services. Or it may be a community organization staging the event in order to serve the social, cultural or sporting needs of its members. Whatever the host organization, it is important for the event manager to identify clearly and aim to satisfy its objectives in staging the event. The host community is also an important stakeholder. It is vital for the event manager to understand the values and trends in the host community, and how these impact on its reactions and expectations of the event. The combined forces of globalization and technology are exposing events to wider influences and enabling them to reach larger audiences. Event managers face the challenge of operating in this increasingly global environment, whilst maintaining the local relevance and authenticity of events. They must involve the host community in the planning of the event, consulting with community leaders and public authorities to identify likely event impacts and devise strategies to manage them. Establishing good community relations and word-of-mouth communication can contribute greatly to the success of the event.

Sponsors are another important stakeholder as the amount and importance of sponsorship of events increases, and as companies develop more sophisticated sponsorship strategies. The event manager must clearly identify the objectives of individual sponsors, and form partnerships with them in order to achieve 'win-win' outcomes for both the event and its sponsors. Technical innovations and global networking of the media have vastly expanded its significance in recent years, making the media coverage of some events just as important, if not more so, than the live event. The media is influencing the style and presentation of events, and gives them much of the added value vital to host organizations and sponsors. The event manager needs to consider carefully the needs of media organizations, and work with them to optimize the coverage and impact of the event. Another important stakeholder is the event team – the co-workers who implement the event plan and contribute to the myriad of details that comprise its success. The event manager must lead and inspire the event team, enabling its members to share the vision of the event, appreciate that their efforts can make a difference and be rewarded for their contribution to the event. The last stakeholders, but certainly not the least, are the event participants and spectators. It is the responsibility of the event manager not only to look after their physical needs and comfort, but also to ensure the quality of their event experience.

In developing the event concept, the event manager should ask and explore several key questions – why is the event being held? Who are the stakeholders? When and where will the event be staged? What is the event content or product? An important part of this process will be the identification and development of unique elements that make the event special. A useful technique to assist in this process is brainstorming, whereby a number of key stakeholders are brought

Hospitality, Leisure & Tourism Series

together to explore and develop creative concepts for the event. The synergy arising from this process can often give rise to high-quality ideas and a shared vision for the event.

Relationship of stakeholders to events

Events are increasingly attracting the support of local government and the corporate sector. One aspect of this growth and increasing professionalization of events is that they are now required to serve a multitude of agendas. It is no longer sufficient for an event to meet just the needs of its audience. It must also embrace a plethora of other requirements including local government objectives, regulations, media requirements, sponsors needs and community expectations. The successful event manager must be able to identify the range of stakeholders in an event (Figure 3.1), and manage their individual needs that will sometimes conflict and overlap. As with event impacts, the success of the event will be judged in terms of balancing the competing needs and interests of a diverse range of stakeholder expectations. For example, UK Sport (1998) identify that a list of key stakeholders for major sporting events would include athletes, the British Olympic Association, broadcasters, coaches, event organizers, the general public, international federations, local authorities, the media, national government, national sports governing bodies, officials, sponsors, sports councils and volunteers.

Mal Hemmerling, architect of the Adelaide Grand Prix and former Chief Executive of SOCOG, describes the task as follows (Hemmerling, 1997):

> So when asked the question 'what makes an event successful?', there are now numerous shareholders that are key components of modern major events that are looking at a whole range of different measures of success. What may have been a simple measure for the event organiser of the past,

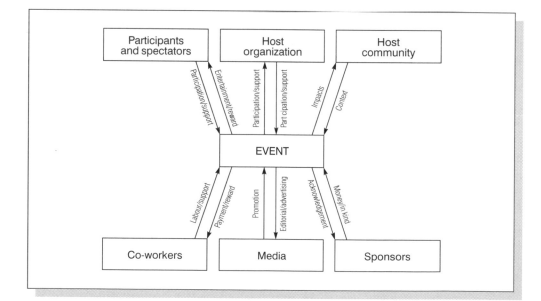

Figure 3.1 The relationship of stakeholders to events

which involved the bottom line, market share, and successful staging of the event are now only basic criteria as the measures by other investors are more aligned with increased tourism, economic activity, tax revenues, promotional success, sustained economic growth, television reach, audience profiles, customer focus, brand image, hospitality, new business opportunities and investment to name but a few.

The host organization

Events have become so much a part of our cultural milieu that they can be generated by almost any part of the government, corporate and community sectors, as illustrated in Table 3.1. Governments create events for a range of reasons, including the social, cultural, tourism and economic benefits generated by events. Some government departments have an events brief as part of their delivery of services, for example, the Department of Culture, Media and Sport and the government-appointed Millennium Commission. Others, including 'arms-length' government organizations, generate events as a means to achieve other objectives – the British Tourism Authority to increase and extend tourist visits, the Arts Council and Regional Arts Boards to preserve cultures and encourage tolerance and diversity, and Department for Trade and Industry (DTI) to assist industry and generate jobs. Many other departments are involved in one-off events to promote specific goods and services such as health promotions, Age Concern Week and National Science Week. Such events may celebrate special days such as Remembrance Sunday, St Patrick's Day, or World AIDs Day. These events are often characterized by free entry and wide accessibility, and form part of the public culture.

The corporate sector is involved in events at a number of levels. Companies and corporations may sponsor events in order to promote their goods and services in the marketplace. They may partner government departments in the presentation of events that serve common or multiple agendas. On other occasions, companies may create their own events in order to launch new products, increase sales or enhance their corporate image. These events, although they may still be characterized by free entry, may be targeted at specific market segments rather than at the general public.

Within the corporate sector there are also entrepreneurs whose business is the staging or selling of events. These include sports or concert promoters who present ticketed events for profit, and conference organizers/event management companies or industry associations mounting conferences or exhibitions for the trade or public, for example, wine shows, equipment exhibitions or medical conferences. Media organizations often become partners in other people's events, but also stage events for their own promotional purposes or to create programme content. Examples are radio stations promoting their identity through concerts, newspapers promoting fun runs, or television networks presenting New Year celebrations live to air.

Still other events emanate from the community sector, serving a wide variety of needs and interests. These may include service club fundraisers, car club meets, local arts and craft shows – the spectrum is as wide as the field of human interest and endeavour. All these sources combine to create the wonderful tapestry of events that fill our leisure time and enrich our lives.

Whether events emanate from the corporate, government or community sectors will determine the nature of the host organization. If the host is from the corporate

Event generators	Types of events
GOVERNMENT SECTOR Central government, e.g. Millennium Commission	Civic celebrations and commemorations
Public space authorities, e.g. National Trust, National Park Authorities	Public entertainment, festivals, leisure and recreation events
Tourism, e.g. British Tourism Authority (BTA), English Tourism Council, Scottish Tourist Board, Wales Tourist Board, Northern Ireland Tourist Board	Festivals, special interest and lifestyle events, destination promotions
Visitor and convention bureaus	Meetings, incentives, conferences and exhibitions
Arts, e.g. Arts Council of England, Scottish Arts Council, Arts Council of Northern Ireland, Arts Council of Wales, Regional Arts Boards	Arts festivals, cultural events, touring programmes, theatre, themed art exhibitions
Sport, e.g. UK Sport, Sport England, Scottish Sports Council, Sports Council for Northern Ireland, Sport Council for Wales	Sporting events, hosting of national and international events
Economic development e.g. Northern Ireland Events Company	Focus on events with industry development and job creation benefits
Local government, e.g. city councils	Community events, local festivals and fairs
CORPORATE SECTOR Companies and corporate organizations	Promotions, product launches, incentives, corporate hospitality, corporate entertainment and image-building sponsorships
Industry associations	Industry promotions, trade fairs/exhibitions, seminars, training, conferences
Gaming and racing, e.g. Racecourse Holdings Trust (owners of Aintree, Epsom, Newmarket)	Race meetings and carnivals
Entrepreneurs	Ticketed sporting events, concerts and exhibitions
Media	Media promotions, e.g. concerts, fun runs, appeals
COMMUNITY SECTOR Clubs and societies	Special interest groups, e.g. flower festivals, car shows, traction engine rallies
Charities	Charity events and fundraisers

Table 3.1 Event typology

sector, it is likely to be a company, corporation or industry association. The event manager may be employed directly by the host organization, or on a contract basis with the organization as the client. If the host is from the government sector, the host organization is likely to be a government or council department. Again the event manager may be a direct employee, or a contractor if the event is outsourced. If the host is from the community sector, the host organization is more likely to be a club, society or committee, with a higher volunteer component in the organization.

Whatever the host organization, it is a key stakeholder in the event, and the event manager should seek to clarify its goals in staging the event. These will often be presented in a written brief as part of the event manager's job description or contract. Where they are not, it will be worthwhile spending some time to clarify these goals and put them in a written form as a reference point for the organization of the event, and a guideline for the evaluation of its eventual success.

The host community

Event managers need to have a good grasp and understanding of the broad trends and forces acting on the wider community, as these will determine the operating environment of their events. The mood, needs and desires of the community will determine its receptiveness to event styles and fashions. Actively gauging and interpreting these is a basic factor in the conceptualization of successful events.

Among the current significant forces acting on the community are globalization and technology, which are combining to make the world seem both smaller and more complex. These forces are impacting on almost every aspect of our lives, including events. Giddens (1990, p. 64) defines globalization as, 'the intensification of worldwide social relations which link distinct localities in such a way that local happenings are shaped by events occurring many miles away and vice versa'.

This process is speeded up by technology and the media, which have the power to bring significant local events to a worldwide audience, overcoming the barriers of national boundaries and cultural differences. This is exemplified by the global television coverage of major sporting events. World championships and mega-events such as the Olympic Games and World Cup Football, calendar events such as the Grand National, The Championships (Wimbledon) and the FA Cup Final, and even New Year celebrations are beamed instantly to live audiences throughout the world, giving them previously unimagined coverage and immediacy.

As global networks increasingly bring the world into our living rooms, the question arises of how local cultures can maintain their own uniqueness and identity in the face of global homogenization. International arts festivals increasingly draw from the same pool of touring companies to produce similar programmes. Local festivals and celebrations must increasingly compete with international product, and the raised expectations of audiences accustomed to streamlined television production. The challenge for many events is how to function in this increasingly global environment whilst expressing the uniqueness of local communities and addressing their specific interests and concerns.

Globalization is also impacting on corporate events as companies increasingly plan their marketing strategies, including their event components, on a global level. This has resulted in some British event companies expanding internationally – for example, World Event Management – or taking over, merging with or being bought out by overseas companies in an attempt to create networks that can serve the international needs of their clients – for example, Jack Morton Worldwide, Skybridge Group and United Business Media. This approach sometimes comes unstuck, as different markets in, say, New York, Sydney and Hong Kong reflect different event needs and audience responses. However, the forces of globalization are likely to lead to an increasing standardization of the corporate event product and market.

Simultaneously, the all-pervasive Internet and advances in information technology are increasing the availability and technological sophistication of events. For example, live broadcasts from music concerts and dance events are relayed instantly through the Internet to a global market. Madonna's concert at the Brixton Academy in November 2000 had a live audience of only 3500, but was 'webcast' to millions through the Internet, made possible by a £30 million sponsorship deal with Microsoft's MSN. Basing his forecast on projections by leading futurists and trends in the event management industry, Goldblatt (2000, p. 8) predicts '24 hour, seven day per week event opportunities for guests who desire to forecast, attend, and review their participation in an event'. He also predicts that events will eventually become 'totally automated enabling event professionals to significantly expand the number of simultaneous events being produced using fewer human staff' (Goldblatt, 2000, p. 8). As a counter-trend, Goldblatt (2000, p.3) also points out that 'with the advance of technology individuals are seeking more "high touch" experiences to balance the high tech influences in their lives. Events remain the single most effective means of providing a high touch experience'.

Event managers must be aware of these trends, and learn to operate in the new global environment. Paradoxically, live events may increasingly become the means by which communities confirm their own sense of place, individuality and cultural uniqueness.

Working with the host community

It is important to recognize the impact of the event on the host community, and for it to own and participate in the event. The host community may include residents, traders, lobby groups and public authorities such as council, transport, police, fire and ambulance services. The event manager should aim to identify community leaders and to consult them when planning of the event.

Councils have certain requirements, such as public entertainment licences. For larger-scale events, the local authorities will generally call a meeting to include emergency services, environmental health, transport and the management team to discuss such matters as street closures, special access and parking arrangements (HSE, 1999).

If the event is large enough to impact significantly beyond the boundaries of the venue, a public authorities' and residents' briefing may identify innovative ways to minimize the impact and manage the situation. Events held by Leeds City Council at Temple Newsam Park, Leeds, regularly attract upwards of 20 000 people to a wide programme of summer events, for example, Party in the Park (60 000 people) and Opera in the Park (50 000 people), in addition to commercial ventures such as the Leeds Festival that takes place over the August bank holiday. Consultation with local community groups will ensure that the event is supported and its impacts minimized. With the increasing audience, the events have received much negative publicity in recent years due to the impact that these events have on the local community, including traffic disruption, but also the effect of litter, visitors trampling gardens and damaging the local environment.

In addition to formal contact with authorities, the event manager should listen out for the all-important rumour-mill that can often make or break the host community's attitude to the event, sometimes manifesting itself in commentary within local media. In the summer of 1999, many events established to celebrate the eclipse in and around Cornwall were not as successful as predicted. Two events to be worse hit were the high-profile failure of the Lizard Festival, at a cost of £1.5 million, and the Total Eclipse Festival, which led to the subsequent bankruptcy of the event organizer, Harvey Goldsmith's Allied Entertainment Group. These events failed, according to the organizers, due to the negative publicity generated by local authorities that claimed the area would not be able to cope with the anticipated large influx of visitors. This was only heightened by the negative reports by the media and, it could be said, a lack of counter-publicity by the promoters. As a result of this, and weather forecasts predicting cloud cover for the day, many events were not as successful as planned. Initial information had predicted an influx of 5 million extra visitors to the area, however, only 450 000 eventually arrived (Gartside, 1999).

Another high-profile example of the effect that public opinion can have on events is the Love Parade, hosted in Leeds for the first time in July 2000. The event, originally planned to take place in Leeds City Centre, was at short notice transferred to Roundhay Park due to police concerns over the expected audience being higher than initially predicted. An estimated 250 000 people attended the event which was generally seen as running without major incident. However, many residents did not appreciate the effect of this number of people in the area, with the litter, broken glass and general inconvenience they caused. Campaigning by local politicians and some residents led to the event not returning to Leeds in 2001.

Sponsors

Recent decades have seen enormous increases in sponsorship and a corresponding change in how events are perceived by sponsors. There has been a shift by many large companies from seeing sponsorship as primarily a public relations tool generating community goodwill, to regarding it as an important part of the marketing mix. Successful major events are now perceived as desirable properties, capable of increasing brand awareness and driving sales. They also provide important opportunities for relationship-building through hosting partners and clients. Major businesses invest large amounts in event sponsorship, and devote additional resources to supporting their sponsorships in order to achieve corporate and sales goals.

BDS Sponsorship Ltd (2001), define sponsorship as, 'a business relationship between a provider of funds, resources or services and an individual, event or organisation which offers in return some rights and association that may be used for commercial advantage'.

In order to attract sponsorships, event managers must offer tangible benefits to sponsors, and effective programmes to deliver them. Large companies such as Coca-Cola, Vodafone and NTL will receive hundreds of sponsorship applications each week, and only those events which have a close fit with corporate objectives and which demonstrate the ability to deliver benefits will be considered.

Sponsors as partners in events • • •

It is important for event managers to identify exactly what sponsors want from an event, and what the event can deliver for them. Their needs may be different from those of the host organization or the event manager. Attendance numbers at the event, for example, may not be as important to them as the media coverage that it generates. It may be important for their chief executive to officiate, or to gain access to public officials in a relaxed atmosphere. They may be seeking mechanisms to drive sales, or want to strengthen client relationships through hosting activities. The event manager should take the opportunity to go beyond the formal sponsorship agreement, and treat the sponsors as partners in the event. Some of the best ideas for events can arise from such partnerships. Common agendas may be identified which support the sponsorship and deliver additional benefits to the event.

Barclays Bank were a major sponsor of the Ideal Home Show held at Earls Court, London, in April 2000. The sponsorship was supported with a national advertising campaign in television, radio and print media, and through branches of Barclays' Bank, with customers offered discounted tickets. The show was retitled 'The Daily Mail Ideal Home Show in Partnership with Barclays Bank', with the logo, all signage, branding, promotional material and main entrance kitted out in Barclays' corporate colour, blue (Litherland, 1997). The sponsorship helped to promote sales of mortgages for Barclays, as well as increasing the profile of the event. Likewise, in 1999, Guinness supported its sponsorship of the Rugby World Cup with a major campaign in pubs and retail outlets, a national advertising campaign through television, print media and the Internet, competitions and street sampling. The sponsorship clearly identified Guinness with the celebrations, and provided the event with an additional promotional outlet – so much so, few can remember other sponsors involved in the event.

Media

The expansion of the media, and the proliferation of delivery systems such as cable and satellite television and the Internet, have created a hunger for media products as never before. The global networking of media organizations, and the instant electronic transmission of media images and data, have made the global village a media reality. The Olympic Games were first televised on a trial basis during the 1936 Berlin Olympics, when the audience peaked at an estimated 162 000 viewers. When the 1948 London Olympics were televised, the world still relied largely on the physical transfer of film footage to disseminate the images of the Games across the UK and overseas. An estimated 500 000 people watched the sixty-four hours of coverage, mostly within 50 miles of London. This event proved to be the starting point of what is now seen as a major source of revenue – television rights fees (IOC, 2000). Indeed, only Children in Need and Red Nose Day feature multidirectional television link-ups that enable the British to experience the fundraising simultaneously from a diverse range of locations and perspectives. The Opening Ceremony of the Winter Olympic Games in Nagano in 1998 featured a world choir singing together from five different locations on five continents, with 200 singers each in Sydney, New York, Beijing, Berlin and Cape Town, singing along with a 2000-strong choir at the main stadium. Global television networks followed New Year's Eve of the New Millennium around the world, making the world seem smaller and more immediate. When the 2000 Olympic Games began, a simultaneous global audience estimated at 2.5 billion people were able to watch the event tailored to their own national perspectives, with a variety of cameras covering the event from every possible angle. Events such as the funeral of Diana, Princess of Wales, have become media experiences shared by millions as they are beamed instantly to a global audience. In Britain alone, the Princess's death attracted record media coverage.

This revolution in the media has, in turn, revolutionized events. Events now have a virtual existence in the media at least as powerful, sometimes more so, as in reality. The television audience may dwarf the live audience for a sports event or concert. Indeed, the event may be created primarily for the consumption of the television audience, what popular media refer to as 'event television' (Goldblatt, 2000). For example, the London Weekend Television *Audience with . . .* events, which feature a prominent celebrity performing and involving the audience, or the recent trend of music concerts, such as Boyzone and Phil Collins, allowing television audiences to request their favourite songs to be performed. Events have much to gain from this development, including media sponsorships and the payment of media rights. Their value to commercial sponsors is often increased greatly by their media coverage and profile. However, the media often affects directly how events are conceptualized and presented, as in the case of One Day Cricket or Super League, and can have a profound effect on the relationship of the event with its live audience. For example, note the effect on the scheduling of Premier League football matches since the increased involvement of Sky TV. So far sports events have been the main winners (and losers!) from this increased attention by the media. The range of sports covered by television has increased dramatically and some sports, such as basketball, have gone from relative obscurity in the UK to high media profile largely because of their suitability for television production and programming.

The available media technology influences the way that live spectators experience the event, for example, with instant replays available on large screens at major sporting events. Media interest in events is likely to continue to grow as their ability to provide community credibility and to attract commercial sponsors is realized. Parades, spectacles, concerts and major public celebrations are event areas of potential interest to the media, and where the need to make good television is likely to influence the direction and marketing of events. The role of the media can vary from that of media sponsors to becoming full partners, or even producers of the event.

Whatever the role of the media, it is important for the event manager to consider the needs of the different media groups, and to consult them as important stakeholders in the event. Once the media are treated as potential partners, they have much to offer the event. The good media representative, like the event manager, is in search of the good idea or unusual angle. Together they might just dream up the unique approach that increases the profile of the event and provides value in turn to the media organization. The print media might agree to publish the event programme as editorial or as a special insert, or might run a series of lead-in stories, competitions or special promotions in tandem with sponsors. Radio or television stations might provide an outside broadcast, or might involve their on-air presenters as compères or special participants in the event. This integration of the event with the media provides greater reach and exposure to the event and, in turn, gives the media organization a branded association with the event.

Co-workers

The event team that is assembled to implement the event represents another of the key stakeholders. For any event to be truly effective, the vision and philosophy of the event must be shared by all the team, from key managers, talent and publicist, right through to the stage manager, crew, stewards and cleaners. No matter how big or small, the event team is the face of the event, and each is a contributor to its success or failure.

Most people have experienced events that went well overall, but were marred by some annoying detail. There are different ways of addressing such problems, but team selection and management are always crucial. The Disney organization has a system where the roles of performer, cleaner, security, etc. are merged in the concept of a team looking after the space. The roles tend to ride with the needs of the moment – when the parade comes through, its all hands on deck! The daily bulletin issued to all staff members reminds them that customers may only ever visit Disneyland once, and their impressions will depend forever on what they experience that day. This is a very positive philosophy that can be applied to all events.

Participants and spectators

Last but not least are the 'punters' on the day – the participants, spectators, visitors or audience for whom the event is intended and who ultimately vote with their feet for the success or failure of the event. The event manager must be mindful of the needs of the audience. These include their physical needs, as well as their needs for comfort, safety and security. Over and above these basic requirements is the need to make the event special – to connect to the emotions. A skilled event manager strives to make events meaningful, magical and memorable. Hemmerling (1997) describes the criteria by which spectators judge an event:

> Their main focus is on the content, location, substance and operation of the event itself. For them the ease with which they can see the event activities, the program content, their access to food and drinks, amenities, access and egress etc., are the keys to their enjoyment. Simple factors such as whether or not their team won or lost, or whether they had a good experience at the event will sometimes influence their success measures. Secondary issues, such as mixing with the stars of the show, social opportunities, corporate hospitality and capacity to move up the seating chain from General Admission to premium seating are all part of the evaluation of spectator success.

Developing the event concept

Goldblatt (1997) suggests the 'Five Ws' as important questions to ask in developing the event concept. These are:

1 *Why* is the event being held? There must be compelling reasons that confirm the importance and viability of holding the event.
2 *Who* will be the stakeholders in the event? These include internal stakeholders, such as the board of directors, committee, staff and audience or guests, and external stakeholders such as media and politicians.

3 *When* will the event be held? Is there sufficient time to research and plan the event? Does the timing suit the needs of the audience and, if the event is outdoors, does it take the likely climatic conditions into account?

4 *Where* will the event be staged? The choice of venue must represent the best compromise between the organizational needs of the event, audience comfort, accessibility and cost.

5 *What* is the event content or product? This must match the needs, wants, desires and expectations of the audience, and must synergize with the why, who, when and where of the event.

An important part of developing the event will be identifying unique elements and resources, which can make the event special, and contribute to its imagery and branding. Millennium event celebrations in 1999 had to be special, particularly with the eyes of the world focused on locations across the globe. In London, celebrations focused along the banks of the River Thames and around Trafalgar Square. At the stroke of midnight and to the chimes of Big Ben, a live audience of over 1 million, together with a worldwide television audience of millions, watched as the river turned to flames and what was claimed to be the largest firework display ever to take place in the world, illuminated the sky above London.

Brainstorming

Once the parameters of the event have been set, it is desirable to brainstorm the concept of the event, letting the imagination soar and consulting with as many stakeholders as possible. A good way to do this is to meet with them individually at first, establishing relationships with them and allowing them to become comfortable with their role in the event. In these discussions ideas will arise, but the process should be acknowledged as exploratory, not yet seeking to reach fixed conclusions.

Once the diverse stakeholders are brought to the meeting table, the ideas will start to flow. This is a time to ignore restraints of practicality – of cost, scale or viability. That time will come. The task is to create and to dream, and no idea should be dismissed as too wild to consider. The goal is to discover the right idea, the one that resonates so that everyone recognizes it and is inspired by the challenge and the potential that it offers. This is where the skills of an event director come to the fore – the ability to draw out ideas, to synthesize content and eventually to construct a compromise. No matter how good the idea or how strong the support, eventually it must serve the objectives of the event and be deliverable within the available resources. With some good fortune, this may be achieved in a single meeting, but most often the process will take several meetings and weeks or months of patience and hard work. But the results will be worthwhile if a strong vision for the event emerges, one that is shared and supported by all stakeholders and in which they all have confidence and are committed to achieve. This process is at the very heart of creative event planning, and when it works well it is one of the joys of being in the business.

The synergy of ideas

Most good events emerge from a synergistic group process. Such a process was illustrated in 1999, when the Millennium Commission brought together a group of people to devise a programme of celebrations for the millennium.

The brief had some unusual features. The celebrations should capture the mood of the UK population, and reflect the multicultural communities within the country. It should provide an opportunity for all people, from all backgrounds, to take part. The Millennium Festival concept was born out of these discussions, with a plan for a whole year of National Lottery funded celebrations across the country. The highest profile element of the Millennium Festival was the Millennium Dome, opened on 31 December 1999. Although much criticized by the press, primarily due to the costs involved and not hitting projected attendance targets, it was still visited by over 6 million people throughout the year, with a high level of customer satisfaction achieved. With the theme 'Time to Make a Difference' and pulling on the creativity of professionals from across the country, the Dome included zones dedicated to mind, body, spirit, learning, skill and play. At the centre, a 10 000-seat auditorium hosted the Millennium Experience – a show developed by Sir Cameron Mackintosh and John Napier as a creative masterpiece, involving artists, circus acts, trapeze artists and stilt-walkers. The overall event experience, it is claimed, was to be a once in a lifetime experience, which people would talk about in years to come. Whether this was achieved, only time will tell.

Although the above may have been the highest profile element, the Millennium Festival also included a wide range of events, from small community events to major city celebrations, on New Year's Eve in 1999 and again in 2000, and throughout 2000. The First Weekend, as the 1999 celebrations were known, enabled twenty-two towns and cities to develop the scale and creativity of their traditional New Year street parties. Many city councils chose to produce firework and music spectaculars, for example, with Edinburgh's Hogmanay attracting nearly 200 000 people, and Liverpool city centre attracting an audience of around 150 000 people to a laser show highlighting in the sky moments from the city's history.

Perhaps one of the largest initiatives for the evening was the Beacon Millennium Project. Involving communities from across the UK, the project enabled 1400 beacons to be lit as the focal point of community celebrations, starting in the Scottish islands and moving down the country, taking in Edinburgh, Belfast, Cardiff and London along the way. The event included Her Majesty Queen Elizabeth II lighting the world's largest beacon, in London. With the beacon as the focal point, communities chose to celebrate in their own unique way. Some celebrated the evening in a traditional manner, focusing on the religious significance of the event with hymns, prayers and reflection, while others developed the evening into a major community occasion, with street parties, fireworks, food and drink, and a party atmosphere.

The millennium events served to illustrate festival and community celebrations not seen for some time in the UK, with events ranging from the professionally run council events, to community based, focused and organized events that allowed each to celebrate in their own unique way. The synergistic process started with funds being made available through the National Lottery funded Millennium Commission, and an underlying theme of time. Yet each company, council, committee and community chose to interpret the theme of the event and, as a result, a true sense of community spirit and celebration was developed.

Summary

With the increased involvement of governments and the corporate sector, events are required to serve a multitude of agendas. The successful event manager must be able to identify and manage a diverse range of stakeholder expectations. Major stakeholders will include the host organization staging the event, and the host community and its various public authorities whose support will be needed. Both sponsors and media are important partners, and can sometimes contribute much to the event in support and resources beyond their formal sponsorship and media coverage. The vision and philosophy of the event should be shared with co-workers, and the contribution of each should be recognized and treated as important. Ultimately it is the spectators and participants who decide the success or failure of an event, and it is crucial to engage their emotions.

Once the objectives of the event and the unique resources available to it have been identified, the next priority is to brainstorm ideas with stakeholders in order to shape and communicate a shared vision for the event. No event is created by one person, and success will depend on a collective team effort.

Questions

1 Who are the most important stakeholders in an event, and why?

2 Give examples in your region of government, corporate and community involvement in events and their reasons for putting on events

3 Focusing on an event that you have experienced at first hand, list the benefits that the event could offer a sponsor or partner.

4 Using the same event example that you have discussed in the last question, identify suitable media partners and outline how you would approach them to participate in the event.

5 What are the means by which an event creates an emotional relationship with its participants and spectators?

6 What events can you think of that demonstrate a unique vision or idea? What techniques have they used to express that vision or idea, and why do you consider them to be unique?

7 Imagine that you are planning an event in the area where you live. What are its unique characteristics, and how might these be expressed in an event?

8 Name a major event that you have attended or in which you have been involved, and identify the primary stakeholders and their objectives.

Case Study

Vodafone Ball by Skybridge

Brief

Create, produce and manage a celebratory ball for Vodafone UK's employees and their guests. The objective of the ball is to celebrate the success of the company and to thank staff for their role in the company's achievements throughout the previous year. It is also to be used as a vehicle to sensitively reinforce the Vodafone brand values; to highlight the transition from being a UK-based company to becoming a truly international business and to help create a sense of pride in now being part of a global family.

The venue has to accommodate as many people as possible due to the size of Vodafone in the UK and has to be accessible from the major employee sites of Newbury, London and Banbury.

The brief covered pre-event planning, guest management and invitation process, total creative treatment including theming and entertainment, production and all logistical considerations relating to the proposed event.

The ball had to exceed the expectations of those guests who had attended in previous years. Furthermore, guests are offered transport to and from the event (from around the UK) and are also given the opportunity to state a preference as to with whom they would like to sit at dinner! The theme had to appeal to a wide profile of guests and complement Vodafone's brand values and core messages.

Response

A feasibility study was undertaken, incorporating a SWOT analysis in conjunction with the previous year's post-event evaluation. Inevitably there is a balance to be struck between accessibility, budget, time lines and production values. The venue selected was Earls Court due to its size, flexibility and reputation as a renowned entertainment venue. In reality, there were only two viable venue options. Previous use of the venue for this event, the combined experiences and resultant success counted in Earls Court's favour.

Pre-event planning

Although the event itself lasts only a few short hours, the planning and logistics exercises required to deliver the event in a smooth and seamless manner are immense.

The event requirements were assessed, based on the experiences of the previous year's event, the post-event evaluation, wash-up reports and the anticipated additional requirements arising from the proposed uplift in guest numbers.

From this requirements specification, a project plan was developed complete with a critical path for each functional dynamic. Responsibilities were identified and a full project team created. The main functional responsibilities included overall project, venue and budgetary management, entertainment selection and management, the main stage show production and direction, catering, technical production, health and safety including crowd control, creative execution including theming, transportation management, database management, administrative management and client relationship management.

A series of status meetings were established with all stake-holders to continuously monitor and evaluate progress based on SMART principles, both internally within the agency and directly with the client's project co-ordinators, providing regular budgetary updates, status and contact reports.

Twelve thousand Vodafone employees were mailed in a three-stage mailshot. The initial mailing was in January, inviting them to apply for tickets (two per employee).

Eleven thousand requests for tickets were received. A waiting list was then compiled, as capacity was capped at 8000 guests (this rose to 9500 six weeks before the ball!).

Guests were provided with a Personal Details Form, asking if they required coach transport and asking them to record their dietary and medical details. Guests were also able to request who they sat alongside at dinner (special software was developed for this task). All responses were entered on to the database and regular reports issued to the project management team. Guests were also referred to a special event website that provided a flavour of what lay ahead, addressed frequently asked questions (FAQs) and provided photographs of the previous year's highlights with a picture caption competition.

The second mailing confirmed whether their application had been successful and also confirmed the number of tickets reserved.

The third mailing confirmed the details of number of tickets, dietary and medical requirements and any transport arrangements. This mailing also included the programme for the evening, consisting of:

- an introductory message from the Chief Executive
- the full itinerary
- useful information and numbers
- a plan of Earls Court
- the menu
- drinks vouchers.

Finally, it 'teased' the entertainment.

The theme

As this is an annual event, the theme had to exceed the previous year's expectations. The rationale of the theme took into account the growth of Vodafone in a global market and, of course, the wide profile of the potential guests.

A series of internal brainstorms took place at Skybridge involving staff, reflecting the wide profile of potential guests for the event. Particular attention was also given to the interests of the stakeholders in this event and meeting the client core objectives. Following a series of international acquisitions that saw Vodafone catapulted to being the world's largest mobile communications company, the theme 'Rocking All Over the World' was selected.

This theme was incorporated into all aspects of the event from the invitation collateral through theming and entertainment.

The event

In April, 6300 of the guests arrived at Earls Court by coach. Earls Court 2 was used as a coach park in order to comply with the local council's noise pollution rules. Other private and public transportation was also used.

The programme for the evening was:

6.30 p.m.   Doors open.

Drinks reception with entertainment from roving artists pulled from around the world, an Electric Avenue of amusement games, a funfair in Earls Court 2 with Dodgems, galloping horses, the waltzer and many more side stalls.

7.30 p.m.   Silver service dinner for 9500 served in Earls Court 1 – complete with a table plan!

Hosts, Tim Vincent and Penny Smith then introduced the Vodafone evening's entertainment. Following a welcome speech by Chief Executive, Chris Gent, the audience was treated during dinner to a glittering array of live entertainment on the main stage. This included: Kid Creole and the Coconuts; Maxine Barrie (a Shirley Bassey lookalike), Horse, one of Scotland's finest singing secrets; Supergirly, a risqué Australian duo; Stephen Gately of Boyzone and All Saints.

From 10.00 p.m. until 1.00 a.m. guests were able to enjoy a rich mix of entertainment in satellite areas including:

- Funfair
- Kitsch Attack Disco
- Comedy Zone – leading artists from various comedy clubs
- Curtain Call – stars of London's West End musical theatre
- Horse
- The Funking Barstewards – covering classic disco hits of the 1970s
- Tziganka – Russian Cossack dancing
- Cavern Club – Rock 'n' Blues
- Rawhide – live karaoke
- Hot Chocolate
- Electric Avenue with simulators, pinball machines and videos in Earls Court 1, Level 2.

The main stage entertainment continued after a two-hour break with special appearances by:

- Belinda Carlisle
- Boy George and Culture Club.

The bar remained open until 1.00 a.m. when guests were ready to depart.

The actual event was carefully co-ordinated through a series of command and control functional units, all reporting into the ultimate 'event director'.

As soon as the event was over, the process of wash-up meetings from each functional area began, with the client co-ordinators and post-event evaluation with the guests in preparation for any possible event in the following year.

Major challenges

The event required a continuous party atmosphere and seamless itinerary with heavy information technology (IT) and logistics support to provide one entertainment act after another whilst including motivational key messages, faultless hot catering and coping with the various health and safety issues as they arose. Interesting facts from the event include:

- 9500 guests consumed more than 2 tonnes of chicken, 3 tonnes of vegetables, 5700 bottles of wine, 2400 litres of water and 2000 litres of coffee.
3 kms of tablecloths were used to cover tables, with 65 000 pieces of crockery and 78 000 pieces of cutlery used.
- 130 coaches arrived on site within a 45-minute period.

As well as 9500 delegates, the event was supported by 10 production crew, 120 event crew, 400 security staff, 1500 catering staff including 1200 waiting staff, 100 chefs and 80 supervisors. The production and support teams, coach drivers and artists also had to be fed.

Managing such a large number of guests provided an interesting challenge from the point of view of logistics management, crowd control, security, health and safety and subtle 'on-brand' messages.

Achievements

The logistics exercise achieved Guinness Book of Records status for the world's largest single-service dinner event and probably the world's largest table plan. The event also attracted extensive industry-specific press coverage.

Client comment

From the client perspective, the event was hailed as the best ever Vodafone event; guests await the next one with great anticipation!

The challenge is now – how do we build from here whilst keeping it aspirational and tightly budgeted?

For further details about Skybridge Group plc, please visit www.skybridgegroup.com.

By Randle Stonier, Chief Executive, Skybridge Group plc, Wimbledon Bridge House, 1 Hartfield Road, London SW19 3RU.

Questions

1 Identify the many stakeholders in the Vodafone ball, and list the likely benefits to each.

2 From the event description in the case study, what do you think was the likely process of conceptualizing the event?

3 As identified by Skybridge, the event provides two challenges for future years, how to develop the event, while keeping it aspirational and tightly budgeted. Imagine that you are planning the above event again for next year.

   (a) If the numbers increase above the current level, the existing venue may not accommodate the large audience and the creative interpretation of the brief. Identify the strengths and weaknesses of the current venue. Suggest an alternative venue that could accommodate this event and list the benefits that your choice of venue would bring.

   (b) In order to keep the event aspirational in future, what vision or idea would you develop for this event? How would you conceptualize it? What are the unique elements in your event concept and how would this be expressed in the event?

4 Can you think of any other companies or organizations where a similar event model could be applied? List the potential stakeholders, and describe the steps that you would take in conceptualizing the event.

CHAPTER 4

The planning function

After studying this chapter, you should be able to:

- understand the importance of planning to ensure the success of an event

- construct an appropriate vision and mission for an event

- construct objectives for an event, which are specific, measurable, achievable, realistic and time specific

- use various techniques for selecting the most suitable strategies to achieve the objectives of a festival, exhibition or event

- construct an appropriate organizational structure for an event which will facilitate the achievement of its objectives

- prepare position descriptions for personnel involved in an event.

What is planning?

In its simplest form, the planning process consists of establishing the current position of an organization, then determining a future desired position for that organization, and the methods needed to achieve it. In other words, the planning process is concerned with the ends and the means to achieve those ends.

Good strategic planning is crucial to the success and survival of an organization. The link between an organization's formal planning processes and its subsequent performance is well documented. For example, Thompson (1997) and Tribe (1997) believed that planning is essential for organizations, particularly those experiencing turbulent environments. Moreover, planning 'should concentrate on identifying and evaluating alternative courses of action, so that opportunities are created. Planning therefore increases awareness' (Thompson, 1997, p. 37). Hannagan (1998, p. 121) highlighted that planning may be seen as 'integrated decision making' that brings together various decisions so that they connect to each other and provide a sound basis for action to be taken.

Successful planning ensures that an organization remains competitive. It has been demonstrated (Johnson and Scholes, 1999) that formalized planning can provide a structured approach to analysis and thinking. It creates ownership of strategies and communicates this to the organization, and provides a useful means of co-ordination. Further, Hannagan (1998) believes that a number of benefits can be gained from planning: it enables managers to detect and solve problems; alternative strategies are highlighted for consideration; staff responsibilities are clarified and uncertainty about the future is reduced, thus minimizing resistance to change.

However, as a cautionary note, both Hannagan (1998) and Thompson (1997) advise that although planning can make managers think and examine, it is essential to adapt to the changing environment rather than rigidly sticking to the plan. Further, Johnson and Scholes (1999) identify that unless monitored effectively, formalized planning can be ineffective. They encourage managers to consider plans in the context of the culture and politics of the organization, ensure that it is an active plan rather than merely a paper exercise, place this in the context of the whole organization, ensure that it does not become overdetailed so as to miss the major issues, and not become obsessed with the plan as conclusive, rather using the plan for overall direction.

In event management, proper planning is also essential. Catherwood and Van Kirk (1992, p. 5), from the accounting firm Ernst and Young, are consultants to major events such as the Olympic games. They state, 'planning is a process that must continuously occur . . . until the end of the event. It is crucial to have as a foundation for this ongoing planning a vision, a statement, or concept that can be easily articulated and understood'.

Without planning, it is possible that the finished product will disappoint not only the intended audience, but also the organizing bodies themselves.

Planning for events

An event plan needs to be both comprehensive and flexible. For an event manager the event plan is an important guide, which must be able to accommodate the wide variety of conditions – meteorological, cultural, economic, political, competitive and demographic – which may change and impact on an event.

Hospitality, Leisure & Tourism Series

Critics of the planning process claim that planning is a time-consuming bureaucratic exercise whose benefits are doubtful, and that planning reduces flexibility, which can be the key to success of a festival or event. But without a plan, members of an event team have little idea of their objectives, and no means to measure their success in achieving them. An effective plan does not reduce flexibility; on the contrary, it provides a clear picture of the current operating environment, allowing a speedy response if that environment changes.

Good event planning is a complex process, involving many important steps, as shown in Figure 4.1. Each of these steps is examined in detail during the course of this chapter.

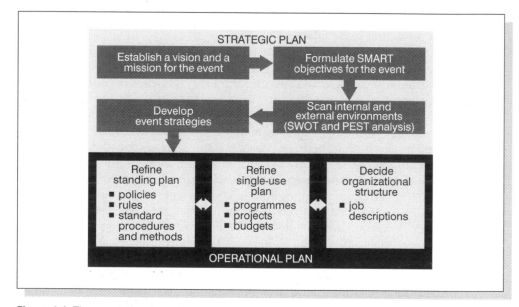

Figure 4.1 The event planning process
Source: adapted from Robbins and Coulter, 1999.

The planning process is usually broken down into two key processes: strategic and operational planning, as listed in Table 4.1. In essence, strategic plans focus on setting the mission, objectives, policies, structure and funding, and deciding on the strategies – the means and schemes – which will achieve them. Operational plans describe specific steps needed to implement these strategies, and establish quantifiable revenue and expenditure budgets. Strategic plans deal with effectiveness (doing the right things), operational plans deal with efficiency (doing things right). Strategic plans are usually single-use plans while operational plans are usually standing plans, which can be activated each time a recurring event is staged (Cole, 1997). In the planning of a festival, exhibition or event, both types of planning are used. Within smaller event organizations, strategic and operational planning are usually conducted by the same person.

Level	Accountability	Goals	Outcomes	Concerns
Strategic	Board/senior management	Guiding, growth in assets, turnover, profit	Long-term implications – success, present survival or failure	Effectiveness, e.g. market position, competitive strategy, values (policies), financial controls
Overlapping concerns				Marketing strategy, resourcing, financial/ sales targets, management information, managing change
Operational	Senior/middle management	Specific, optimum use of resources, achieve agreed targets	Short-term implications – budgeted targets achieved or missed, reliable flow of goods and services to customers	Efficiency, e.g. procedures, production control, selling, quality, employee motivation, cost-benefit ratio.

Source: adapted from Cole, 1997.

Table 4.1 Relationship between strategic and operational planning

Strategic plans

A model of the strategic planning process is illustrated in Figure 4.2. Such a model provides a coherent framework for event managers to follow, and assists in clarifying such key questions as what is to be done, by whom, how, by when. It also helps in identifying the expected outcomes of the event.

Vision and mission

Every event should have a vision and a mission. The vision can be separate from the mission or the two expressed as one, but usually the vision usually describes the long-term goals of the event. The mission describes in the broadest terms the task that the event organization has set for itself, stating the reason for staging the event, its stakeholders and its key objectives. Each event will have a unique mission, which differentiates it from all other events.

How does this mission evolve? All festivals, exhibitions and events occur because one person or a group of people believes that holding an event will fulfil some need in a community, region, organization or company. These needs vary, but are central to vision and mission development.

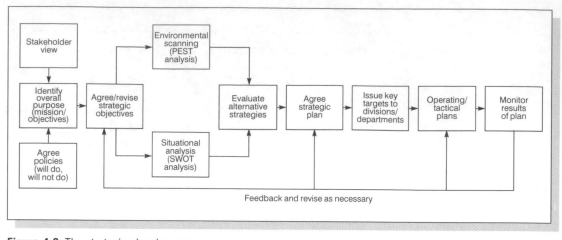

Figure 4.2 The strategic planning process
Source: adapted from Cole, 1997.

For ease of reference, the mission is generally expressed in a concise mission statement of only a few lines. An effective mission statement should answer the following questions:

- Who are our participants (customers)?
- What participant needs are we satisfying?
- What are the organizers trying to achieve?

Once the mission is defined, it can be used to focus the event's organizers upon the task in hand, leading to the formulation of clear event objectives and strategies. It is also an important means to provide all who are involved in the event (either in a paid or volunteer capacity) with a clear understanding of the event and their role in it.

A coherent mission statement can be an invaluable tool for establishing a common direction in a team, and promoting unity among its members.

Notting Hill Carnival Trust has the following mission: 'Develop and sustain the continued success and popularity of Notting Hill Carnival as the largest and safest Street Festival of Arts in Europe, and the best Carnival of its kind in the World.'

This can usefully be compared with the Manchester 2002 Mission for the Commonwealth Games (Figure 4.3). The Manchester statement effectively sets out the mission, answering the questions discussed previously, whereas the Notting Hill statement provides an overall vision for the event. The Manchester 2002 Mission illustrates the need to meet different, sometimes conflicting, needs from a wide variety of stakeholders and agendas, whereas the Notting Hill Carnival mission focuses on development and sustainability. This difference in specificity may be due to the unique opportunity faced by Manchester as a one-off event, compared to Notting Hill Carnival that may learn and develop each year.

Objectives

Once the mission has been decided, the event planner must establish the event's objectives. Well conceived objectives are a core element in the planning

- To deliver an outstanding sporting spectacle of world significance, celebrating athletic excellence, cultural diversity and the unique atmosphere of 'The Friendly Games'.
- To deliver a successful Games on behalf of all competitors, spectators and stakeholders.
- To leave a lasting legacy of new sporting facilities and social, physical and economic regeneration.
- To set a new benchmark for hosting international sporting events in the UK and the lasting benefit they can generate for all those involved.

Figure 4.3 The Manchester 2002 Commonwealth Games Mission
Source: Manchester 2002.

process, and are distinguished by several key features. These can be summed up in the acronym SMART:

Specific: carefully focused on the mission of the event.
Measurable: expressed in a concise and quantifiable form so that they can be assessed after the event.
Achievable: the objectives can be realised given the human, financial and physical resources available to the event organization.
Relevant: applicable to the current environment in which the event organization operates.
Time specific: to be achieved by a designated time.

Depending on the mission of the event, objectives can vary greatly. For example, an event might aim to:

- reach a purely financial target (e.g. raise £50 000 for charity X)
- engage community participation (e.g. attract 50 000 people to the event's activities)
- raise awareness (e.g. after the event, 65 per cent of the population of Belfast will know that whooping cough is a preventable disease in children)
- enhance product quality (e.g. the event will attract ten practitioners with international reputations to display their expertise)
- recover costs or make a profit (e.g. to produce a surplus of income over expenditure of £X)
- ensure participant satisfaction (e.g. 95 per cent of participants sampled will express a satisfied or better rating of the event)
- achieve growth in event dimensions, including public participation (e.g. the event will consist of twenty-five activities, 20 per cent more than the previous year and attract 20 per cent more participants)
- increase efficiency (e.g. with no increase in financial resources, the event will consist of ten more activities than the previous year's event)
- increase market share (e.g. this event will attract more people than any other event of its type in the UK this year).

As with all objectives, the crucial element is that the objectives adhere to the SMART principles. Otherwise they are merely immeasurable vague hopes and desires, without benchmarks for success. Without such benchmarks, event managers cannot determine whether they have been successful in achieving their desired future ends and, just as importantly, identify those objectives that were not achieved. This is always an important part of the process of planning and delivering an event, since it allows event managers to analyse areas where planning was unsuccessful, and decide ways to improve performance for future events.

Service Objectives (External Affairs) for Bath Festivals Trust 2000 (B&NES, 1999) included:

- publication of the long-term vision and further consultation on its elements
- computerization of the Bath Festivals Trust box office
- setting up of the computerized box office to benchmark the number of foreign visitors to the 2000 Music Festival
- address communication issues raised in the South West Arts Appraisal Report on Bath Festivals Trust – with the council and the local arts community
- introduction of a new policy for dressing the city at relevant periods, agreed with the council's Planning Department and the Festivals Forum
- 13 per cent increase (minimum) to over £220 000 in box office income for the Bath International Music Festival
- 30 per cent increase (minimum) to over £400 000 in fundraising income for the Bath International Music Festival
- 100 per cent increase (minimum) to over £60 000 in fundraising income for the Bath Literature Festival.

It is interesting to note that the first four of these 'objectives' are actually strategies. Event managers can often confuse the two, which confuses their thinking and consequent planning. However, both objectives and strategies are time specific to the festival or event's activities for that particular year.

Analysing the external and internal environment

After the event's objectives are decided, the next step in the strategic planning process is to analyse external and internal environments (or surroundings). This can be achieved by using two techniques. First, a political, environmental, sociological and technological (PEST) analysis can be undertaken, sometimes referred to as environmental scanning. Second, the organization can be placed in the context of the environment by performing a strengths, weaknesses, opportunities and threats (SWOT) analysis or, as it is sometimes called, situational analysis.

Environmental scanning – political, economic, social technological (PEST) analysis

The external environment consists of all the outside factors which surround the event and might impact on its success. The internal environment consists of the resources available to the event organization, including physical, financial and human resources.

The external environment is usually assessed first, and consists of many factors. The main factors include:

- *Political/legal*: the deliberations of all levels of government become laws or regulations which affect the way in which people live in a society. For example, the laws regulating the consumption of food and alcoholic beverages have changed radically in the UK since the 1950s, making outdoor food and wine festivals possible.
- *Economic*: the economic climate affects the volume and value of goods and services produced in a region. Economic features such as unemployment, inflation, interest rates, and levels of wages and salaries can impact on the demand for a particular event. For example, in an area of high unemployment, an event featuring conspicuous consumption of material goods would be inappropriate. Alternatively, events that celebrate different stages of the economic cycle can be very successful. For example, harvest festivals, which originated in medieval Europe to celebrate successful farming seasons, are still popular events in rural areas.
- *Social/cultural*: the social life of a particular community results from interaction between the people who live there. Various institutions play a role in a society, such as churches, charities, sporting groups, social groups, occupational groups, business organizations and artistic bodies. The people of an area may come together under the aegis of a community group such as Rotary or Lions to celebrate unique features of that area. Culture can be defined as a historically derived design for living, shared by a discrete group of people. It encompasses such things as food, dress, architecture, language, shared beliefs, myths and values. It also includes artistic endeavours, recreation and leisure activities, and popular culture such as cinema, pop music and dance. Any planned event must address its target audience carefully: for example, planners of youth events must be aware that the youth culture of each generation is quite often very different from its predecessor, and create activities accordingly
- *Technological*: Changes in equipment and machines have revolutionised the way people undertake tasks. A contemporary example of this is the use of the Internet to promote festivals, exhibitions and events. Entering the word 'festival' into an Internet search engine will produce links to a multitude of events in all parts of the globe. Similarly, many sites have been developed to support event professionals, students and educators, by providing information, directories, and resources – WorldofEvents.net (http://www.worldofevents.net) and EPMS.net (http://www.epms.net) developed by the authors of this text are two examples.

There are three further areas that can form part of an effective environmental analysis: covering demographics, meteorological and competitive. These are expanded upon below:

- *Demographic*: the composition of society in terms of age, gender, education and occupation changes over time. A striking example is the entry of the baby boom generation (people born between 1945 and 1960) into middle age. The generation that gave the world rock 'n' roll, blue jeans and relaxed sexual mores is, and will continue to be, a large market for event managers, and will always have very different needs to the preceding and succeeding generations.
- *Meteorological*: the expected weather patterns of a particular area are a basic environmental consideration. This environment must be closely monitored when planning outdoor events!
- *Competitive*: the activities of organizations that operate in the same market are always a reference point for event managers.

Situational analysis – strengths, weaknesses, opportunities, threats (SWOT) analysis ● ● ●

A thorough scanning of the full range of factors that make up the external environment will reveal the event's target market(s), its range of activities, and opportunities for promotion, sponsorship and fundraising. Similarly, threats to the successful operation of the event can also be identified. Over a period of time, environmental factors can change, sometimes dramatically, necessitating adjustments to an event's objectives or design. For example, the ethnic composition of many areas within the UK has undergone marked change, and the resultant shifts in the social and cultural environments of those areas, have affected the demand for festivals celebrating particular cultures. In another example, a predicted reduction in government funding of cultural events is patently a threat to an event organization dependent on such funding for much of its revenue.

When the analysis of the external environment is complete, the next step in the strategic planning process is to undertake an internal analysis of the event organization's physical, financial, informational and human resources to establish its strengths and weaknesses.

Strengths can be such things as management or creative expertise; ownership or access to appropriate physical plant such as stages, sound systems and transportation; access to appropriate technology such as ticketing systems and information processing; access to financial resources; reputation; brand names; large volunteer base; cordial relationships with government; and contacts with potential sponsors. Weaknesses could be the opposite of these or the event organization's competitive position. For example, if two events catering for similar markets are held around the same time, one would probably be in a weaker competitive position than the other. In another example, meteorological conditions can be a strength for an event occurring in July or August, or a weakness if the event is planned for shower-prone April. The British Grand Prix 2000 was a perfect illustration of this – the event was a washout when it was moved to April from its traditional home in the July sporting calendar, leading to a significant loss in revenue. As a result, the event was subsequently returned to July in the 2001 season.

Strategy selection

The scanning process gathers crucial information that will be used by the event manager in selecting strategies to achieve the event's mission and objectives. Strategies must utilize strengths, minimize weaknesses, avoid threats and take advantage of any opportunities that have been identified. A SWOT analysis is a wasted effort if the material, which is gathered by the analytic process, is not used in strategy formulation.

Several generic strategies, which can be adopted by festival and event managers, are summarized below.

Growth strategy

Late twentieth-century human endeavour appears to be characterized by an obsession with size. In events, this is expressed in a desire to be bigger than last year, bigger than other events or bigger than other communities' events. Bigger is often thought to be better, particularly by ambitious event managers. Growth can be expressed as more revenue, more event components, more participants or consumers, or a bigger share of the event market. It is worth pointing out that bigger is not necessarily better, as some event managers have discovered. An example of this is Streets Ahead (a Catalan festival which takes place in Manchester). It adopted a growth strategy from 1995 towards a street festival for the millennium, involving ten local authorities in and around Greater Manchester. In the first year, one authority was involved, the following year two, then four until, by 1999, all ten local authorities were taking part (Allen and Shaw 2000).

It is important to recognize that an event does not necessarily have to grow in size for its participants to feel that it is better than its predecessors – this can be achieved by dedicating attention to quality activities, careful positioning and improved planning. However, a growth strategy may be appropriate if historical data suggest there is a growing demand for the type of event planned or a financial imperative necessitates increasing revenues. The annual Reading Festival substantially increased attendance by incorporating contemporary pop acts into the event's line-up, thereby appealing to a market segment with a strong propensity to attend musical events.

Consolidation or stability strategy

In certain circumstances it may be appropriate to adopt a consolidation strategy – that is, maintaining attendance at a given level by limiting ticket sales. This strategy is effective because supply is fixed while demand grows: eventually ticket prices will be increased, allowing the quality of inputs into the event to be improved. Tickets to performances at the Glastonbury Festival are generally sold well in advance, which allows its managers to ensure high-quality outcomes at no risk of financial deficits.

Retrenchment strategy

An environmental scan may suggest that an appropriate strategy is to reduce the scale of the event but add value to the existing components. This strategy can be applicable when the operating environment of an event changes. Retrenchment can seem a defeatist or negative to adopt such a strategy, particularly to longstanding members of an event committee, but it can be a necessary response to an unfavourable economic environment or in cases where the sociocultural environment has substantially changed. For example, the management of a community festival may decide to delete those festival elements that were poorly patronized and focus on only those that have proven to be popular with its target market. Likewise, exhibitions may delete an accompanying seminar programme and focus on the core purpose of the exhibition.

Combination strategy

As the name suggests, a combination strategy includes elements from more than one of these generic strategies. An event manager could decide to cut back or even delete some aspects of an event that no longer appeals to the targeted market for the event, while concurrently growing other aspects.

Strategy evaluation and selection

Most management writers such as Thompson (1997) and Johnson and Scholes (1999) believe that strategic alternatives can be evaluated by using the three main criteria:

1 *Appropriateness/suitability*: strategies and their component parts should be consistent. That is, strategies selected should complement each other and be consistent with the environment, resources and values of the event company.
2 *Acceptability/desirability*: strategies should be capable of achieving the event's objectives. They should focus on what the environmental scan has identified as important and disregard the unimportant. Event companies should, however, be careful not to overlook potential risks involved in the strategy, for example, financial or environmental risk or the risk of the required skills not being available in the organization.
3 *Feasibility*: the proposed strategy should be feasible. It should work in practice, considering the resources available (e.g. finance, human resource, time). The strategy should also meet key success factors (e.g. quality, price, level of service).

Once again it is important to stress that the strategies chosen must be congruent with the findings of the SWOT analysis, or the environmental scan becomes a waste of time and intellectual energy, and results in inappropriate strategy selection.

Operational plans

Once the strategic thrust of the event has been agreed the implementation of the plan can commence. This process can be carried out by means of a series of operational plans. The connections between each aspect of the planning process are shown in Figure 4.4.

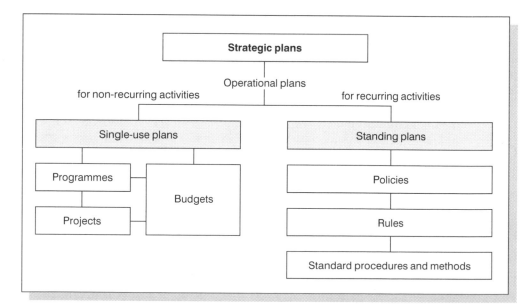

Figure 4.4 The hierarchy of plans
Source: Stoner, Freeman and Gilbert, 1995.

Strategic plans describe the general thrust of how the festival, exhibition or event is to achieve its agreed objectives (which of course are expressed in a way that is SMART). From these strategies are formed the operational plans needed to implement them. These consist of single-use plans and standing plans.

Single-use plans

Single-use plans are designed to achieve a particular objective. Most one-off festivals, exhibitions, and events fall into this category. For example, Leeds Love Parade would have been based on a single-use plan for its 2000 event, as it was the first of its type in the UK. In subsequent years, the parade would differ to a large or small degree, and each event would need its own single-use plan. The plans for many festivals are summarized in their programmes, which can be made up of several projects. Therefore a programme can – depending on the size of the festival – cover a wide range of activities or projects.

Now the planning process formulates the specific actions needed to deliver the programme, in accordance with the stated strategic thrust. This involves deciding various aspects of the event, such as the person or event department responsible for carrying out the plan, the allocation of financial, physical, human and communication resources, and a time frame for each action. The person responsible for the programme may then delegate responsibility for projects, which make up the programme, to their subordinates.

Delegation can be a powerful method to engage the commitment of members of the event team, and highlights the important concept of staff responsibility or empowerment in event management. Many authors, including Heskett, Sasser and Schelesinger (1997) and Hannagan (1998) have shown that people who are given an opportunity to contribute their ideas, suggestions and creativity into the planning process are much more likely to take 'ownership' of their programme or project than if they were merely asked to carry out a process which has been decided by others. Staff who feel ownership of a programme or project are more committed to achieving its desired outcomes, as they have been empowered by participating in the decision-making and planning process.

Events such as Bradford Festival are usually made up of several programmes, each with a set of objectives. Each programme, consisting of several projects, is 'owned' by a member of the management team. Possible programmes for this type of event include a cultural programme to deliver music, drama and art projects, a programme presenting speakers, dance, comedy cabaret and theatre writing, and a community and education programme, involving schoolchildren, students and community groups in production, performance, workshops and display (Bradford Festival, 2000).

Each of these programmes would use a budget as a technique for planning and control (discussed in Chapter 8). The budget is simply a statement of the resources approved to carry out the programme in a temporal and quantified format, and also specifies the anticipated revenues from the programme.

A budget is made up of two components – expenditure and revenue. The expenditure budget lists the amount to be spent on the different resources needed to achieve the programme's objectives and in which accounting period the expenditure is to take place. It includes such cost factors as human (labour and entertainers' fees), physical (logistics and staging, i.e. costs of equipment, supplies and consumables), communications, energy, marketing and financial (insurance, interest, etc.). The revenue budget lists the amount anticipated to be earned from each element or project of the programme from applicable revenue sources. These include box office, sponsorship, government grants, merchandising, sale of goods and services, or for commercial events, the amount allocated from the marketing budget of the company for whom the event is produced.

This budgeting process is an integral aspect of planning and is often used as the process in which alternative courses of action are considered and quantified, and the most appropriate chosen. The key to this process is that it be guided at all times by the event's objectives and the agreed strategies for achieving them. An inexperienced event manager sometimes can disregard this principle during the budget planning process, thereby negating the purpose of strategic planning.

The budget planning process – which implements cost control – is also the link between planning and controlling an event's activities as illustrated by Figure 4.5. Building on the traditional event management model developed by Goldblatt (1997), the model demonstrates the link between planning, evaluation and control, while focusing on ensuring customer satisfaction (quality).

The information contained in the budget acts as the control mechanism for event managers because it allows them to compare actual expenditure and revenue with planned expenditure and revenue. If there is a discrepancy between the two, they can either change activities in an appropriate way so that planned and actual results are congruent or change the plan because circumstances have changed.

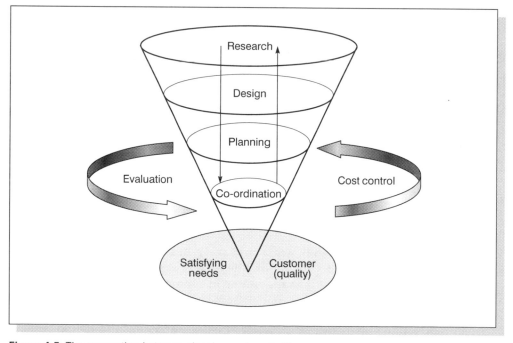

Figure 4.5 The connection between planning and controlling
Source: Bowdin and Church, 2000.

Standing plans

Many festivals, exhibitions and events are not one-off events, but occur at regular intervals – yearly; biennially or, in the case of some major sporting events, every four years. In this case a single set of decisions can outline policies, standard procedures and rules. This is where standing plans are helpful.

Standing plans, as outlined in Figure 4.4, are made up of policies, rules and standard procedures and methods. Thompson (1997) defines policies as guidelines for decision-making. By contrast, rules are explicit statements that tell managers what they can or cannot do. Standard procedures are defined as a series of interrelated sequential steps that can be used to respond to common or anticipated occurrences.

Each event will develop these three elements to produce its own particular standing plan. An event such as the Bradford Festival, for example, might develop a policy that all board members and executive staff must contain representatives from each community in the local area, or that the board must approve all capital expenditure in excess of £5000. Possible rules might include that no volunteer can be asked to work more than eight hours per day, and any programme manager who chooses to ignore this rule would need to be able to justify this decision. A standard procedure might be that any unused tickets be refunded at once, no questions asked, with a smile. The advantage of this trio of standing plans is that managers at all levels of the event organization need not spend time considering issues which arise on a regular basis, as the plan ensures that they will be dealt with in a consistent and coherent manner.

Organizational structure

During the planning process, the organizational structure of the organization must also be decided. In the same way that a house takes its shape from its structural framework, an event organization's strategies and objectives are the product of its structure.

Organizational structure is extensively discussed by leading management authors, including Cole (1996), Thompson (1997), Hannagan (1998), Johnson and Scholes (1999) and Mullins (1999). The majority of event organizations – with the exception of major sporting events such as the Olympic Games – have a small number of staff. Therefore, their organizational structures usually display a low level of complexity. They are characterized by a low degree of differentiation of work between different positions within the organization, minimal geographical dispersion of the organization and minimal vertical levels of decision-making within the organization. For such small organizations, three types of organizational structure are common:

- simple structures
- functional structures
- network structures.

Large organizations make use of further organizational modes such as:

- task forces/matrix structure
- committees.

Hospitality, Leisure & Tourism Series

Simple structures

As the name suggests, a simple structure has a low level of complexity. As Figure 4.6 illustrates, all decision-making is centralized with the manager, who has total control over all the activities of the staff. This is the most common structure in small business (and event organizations) as it is flexible, adaptable to changing circumstances, easy to understand, and has clear accountability – the manager is accountable for all the activities of the event. Thompson (1997) refers to this as an entrepreneurial structure. Because of this flexibility, staff are expected to be multiskilled and perform various functions. This can mean individual jobs are more satisfying, and produce high staff morale. However, because of a lack of specialization, staff may not achieve a high level of expertise in any one area.

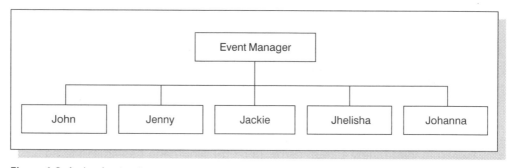

Figure 4.6 A simple structure

This structure has its disadvantages. For example, once the organization grows beyond a certain size decision-making can become very slow – or even non-existent – as a single executive has to make all decisions and carry out all the management functions. Also, if the manager has an autocratic style, staff can become demoralized when their expertise is not fully utilized. There is an inherent risk in concentrating all expertise and information about the management of an event in one person – obviously, sickness at an inappropriate time could prove disastrous for the event.

Functional structures

As the name suggests, a functional structure departmentalizes employees by their function, that is, by their intended output. Figure 4.7 shows a functional organization for an outdoor musical festival. Employees can achieve efficiencies (i.e. produce more output with the same inputs) by specializing is particular tasks, rather than attempting all tasks involved in producing an event.

The advantages of a functional structure can be summarized as:

- staff become expert in their particular specialization
- duplication of equipment and expertise is avoided
- staff feel comfortable working with fellow specialists in their department
- the organization can become more effective (able to achieve its objectives) and more efficient (producing more with less).

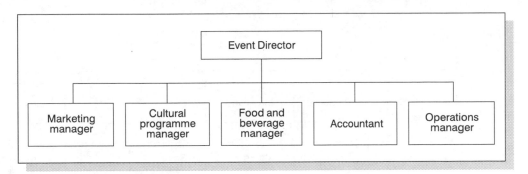

Figure 4.7 A functional structure

Like most constructs, a functional structure can have some disadvantages. These can be summarized as follows:

- Functional managers can lose sight of the organization's objectives in pursuit of their functional tasks.
- There is a potential conflict between functions, which can inhibit the overall success of the event.
- Staff have little understanding of the role and outputs of other functions, and this can cause animosity and a lack of co-operation.
- There is a heavy reliance on the event director to co-ordinate all of the functional activities to ensure event objectives are met.
- Functional managers may find it difficult to move up to an event director's position as they lack 'the big picture', i.e. a broad perspective of an event's activities and outcomes.

Of course, many techniques can be used to overcome some of these disadvantages. Multiskilling strategies can be used to rotate staff through different functional departments and regular meetings between all functional departmental heads will ensure clear communication is maintained. Staff can be kept fully informed of the event's objectives, strategies, tactics and budget by means of regular staff meetings or newsletters, and these methods can also be used to make staff aware of the revenue and expenditure budget position. All these activities are essential elements of the leadership function of the event manager, and will be discussed in Chapter 5.

Matrix structures

Large organizations, such as corporate event and incentive travel organizations, sometimes use a structure that is based on a series of projects working within the overall organization structure. Johnson and Scholes (1999, p. 409) define the matrix structure as 'a combination of structures which often takes the form of product and geographical divisions or functional and divisional structures operating in tandem'. Figure 4.8 illustrates a matrix structure for a corporate event company, where a team is assigned to a particular client account.

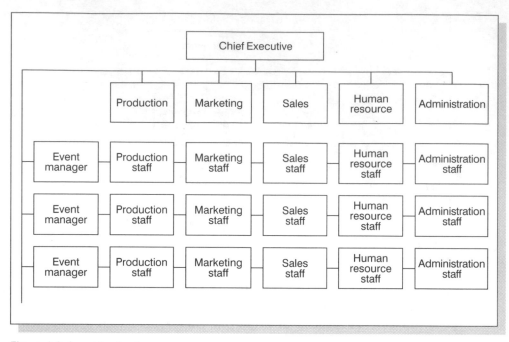

Figure 4.8 A matrix structure
Source: adapted from Hannagan, 1998.

The matrix structure focuses on a project or event manager leading a team of people and skills from across the organization to form a team. The member of staff therefore has two managers – the functional manager responsible for their department, and a project manager for the particular event that they are involved in organizing. In some organizations, a department may have a matrix structure within an organization based on the functional structure. This structure works in organizations where a high degree of co-operation and flexibility can be achieved, as it requires a free flow of communication both vertically and horizontally. The matrix structure can be appropriate for an event organization because of several key advantages:

- It focuses on the end product.
- It stimulates creativity.
- It provides challenges.
- It enables flexibility in an organization.
- It improves communication in and understanding.

The disadvantages of the matrix structure include:

- Excellent communication is required.
- Power struggles can be encourage within the organization.
- There is a risk of duplication of effort.
- The lines of authority can be confused.
- It requires high levels of interpersonal skills across the team.
- If not managed effectively, it may lead to more discussion than action (Hannagan, 1998, p. 207).

An example of organizations that may use such a structure would be corporate event companies. These may have one event manager that acts as the key account (project) manager, drawing together a team from across the organization to make the event happen. As a result, the project manager on one account may act in an operational management capacity in another, thus enabling an effective use of management resources.

Network structures and virtual organizations

Johnson and Scholes (1999, p. 413) define the network structure as 'made up of discrete but interrelated parts consisting of a number of co-operating organizations', as Figure 4.9 shows. It is a fairly new way of thinking about organizational, which made its appearance in management theory during the late 1990s (see Johnson and Scholes, 1999; Keung, 1998).

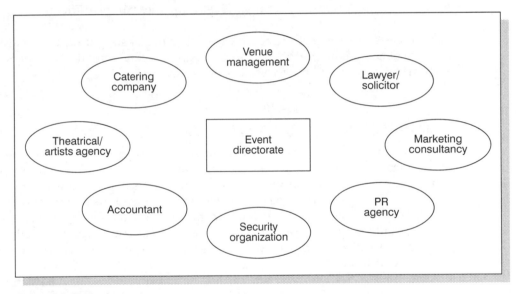

Figure 4.9 Network structure

Most festival or event organizations (with the exception of mega-sporting events, and ongoing commercial events) are by definition of a limited duration, and are inactive for much of the time between events. This makes it impractical to maintain a large organization structure of the functional type, unless it is chiefly composed of unpaid volunteers. The network structure can be quite appropriate for an event organization because of several key advantages:

- It can be more efficient than other structures, which means lower costs and greater output.
- It enables specialist firms with current expertise and experience to be contracted on a needs basis, with no 'downtime'.
- Budgeting can be much more exact as most costs are contracted and therefore known beforehand.

- It is flexible and dynamic as the core management group is made up of only a few people or one individual, and can quickly make decisions and change strategies and tactics if the environment changes
- When the event directorate and the contractors are linked by an effective computer network, communications can be rapid, resulting in swift reaction to any problems which arise.

The disadvantages of this structure include:

- Quality control may be difficult to achieve as the work is performed by contractors.
- Reliability of supply of goods and services can be problematic as contractors may have other clients who are given priority.
- Deficiencies in contractor performance can result in expensive and lengthy legal proceedings.
- Co-ordinating employees from various companies can be difficult.

Nevertheless, the concept of the network structure is supported by contemporary management thinking on downsizing, sticking to core activities and outsourcing, and can be very effective for certain kinds of events.

Task forces and committees

Large organizations, such as local government authorities (LGAs), sometimes decide to produce a one-off event by assembling a task force. This temporary structure is composed of staff with appropriate skills from various departments from within the organization, and disbands once the event has been held, its members returning to full-time duty in their functional department. Once assembled, a task force forms the management group for the event. It performs the planning function described in this chapter and utilizes both internal and external resources to achieve the event's objectives, as it sees fit.

A committee has a similar structure to a task force, and can be defined as a permanent task force. If a local government authority, for example, decided to produce an annual event, an appropriate structure would be a standing committee made up of representatives from the departments of the LGA with a function to fulfil to meet the event's objectives. In this way experience and expertise would be built up over time, allowing the formation of a corporate memory.

Each structure has its advantages when used appropriately. Table 4.2 shows the advantages of each structural design, and its likely application in event management organization. In all cases, the selection of a structure must be based on the available resources, the size, the strategies that have been developed to achieve the event objectives, and the operating environment. The trend over the past ten years has been to 'flatten' the organization structure by reducing the level of middle management and keeping communication and lines of responsibility tightly controlled. Should this trend continue, with the increase in people working from home – due to the increasing availability of the Internet and information technology – and with the use of self-employed freelance managers, the use of structures such as the network or virtual organization is a likely outcome.

Structural design	Advantages	When and where will this design be applied?
Simple/ entrepreneurial	Flexibility, central control, clear responsibility and communication	In small event organizations, in simple and dynamic environments
Functional	Efficient use of specializations, clear responsibility, authority and control, clear promotion path, good vertical communication	In large event organizations which produce a single service
Matrix	Focuses on end product, stimulates creativity, flexibility, improves communication	In large event organizations which produce many events drawing in resources from various departments
Network and virtual organizations	Flexibility, use of specialisms, cost-efficient, partnerships and collaborations	When many reliable suppliers are available
Task force	Flexibility	In large organizations which need to produce a one-off event
Committee	Flexibility, ability to take on larger volumes of work, group assessment of facts, specialist knowledge, co-ordination between work groups, focus for information and action	In large organizations responsible for annual events which need expertise that crosses functional lines

Source: adapted from Cole, 1996; Hannagan 1998; Johnson and Scholes, 1999; Mullins, 1999; Thomson, 1997.

Table 4.2 Organization structure options

The position description

The next step in the planning and organizing process is to decide the structure of each job. In other words, what is each position (or, to use a more common word, job) in the organization is accountable for. In large organizations, this is usually documented in a format known as a position (or job) description.

The usefulness of this part of the planning exercise is well documented in the management literature. Beardwell and Holden (2001) contend that position descriptions are helpful to managers in recruiting, selecting, inducting and training of new employees, and development, job evaluation and performance appraisal of existing employees. Mullins (1999, p. 740) states that job analysis, leading to the job description and person specification is 'Central to a well planned and systematic approach' of human resource planning'. He goes on to stress that although valuable, it is important not to write job descriptions in a bureaucratic manner, which would imply 'a lack of flexibility, imagination or initiative on the part of the job holder'. Mullins highlighted criticism of job descriptions by Townsend, who described them as straitjackets, and Belbin, who suggested that they were an obstacle to progress in organizations as they lead to a lack of co-operation, claims for additional payment based on additional responsibilities or inflexibility with taking on team roles. Beardwell and Holden (2001) report that problems can arise if job descriptions are not regularly updated, which may be the cause of poor employee selection.

It may not be necessary for job descriptions to be formal written documents in small event organizations where a verbal briefing can be sufficient. However, the benefits of written job descriptions for an organization are many and can include:

- Preparing job descriptions can clarify for the event director what role an organization's human resources will play in achieving its objectives.
- A written job description is a record which can be used to avoid misunderstandings between staff and management about the roles and responsibilities of various positions.
- The process of matching each job to a specific set of outcomes can avoid duplication across positions, and reduce ambiguity, overlap and inefficiencies.
- These documents assist in appraisal of personnel involved in the event.

The content of the job description is not fixed but depends on the context. However, the following elements are usually found in part or total in a job description (Mullins, 1999):

- *Job title*: outlines whether this is a new position or replacement.
- *Function*: states in a broad way what an employee has to accomplish.
- *Duties and responsibilities*: lists the tasks the job incumbent needs to accomplish.
- *Specific limitations on authority*: lists the authority the incumbent has to spend money, hire and fire, use resources.
- *Relationships*: specifies the position to which the incumbent reports, which positions report to the incumbent, and people in other organizations with which the incumbent has contact.

The job description may also be extended to include a list of the personal qualities required for a person to perform in that position, sometimes referred to as the job (or person) specification. This can be a useful tool in the selection process, however, Beardwell and Holden (2001) stress that it is important to ensure that the specification is carefully written to avoid discrimination and encourage equal opportunities. It is usual for a job description and job specification to be supported by an organizational chart, which shows the structure and reporting relationships within the organization as a whole.

There are many different ways of accomplishing the task choosing an organizational structure and developing job responsibilities. The process can be formally pursued, resulting in written organizational charts and job descriptions. However, organizations that are small, under the total control of one person and not reliant on government grants, may choose to conduct this process informally, relying on oral communication to disseminate the plan. Whatever method is chosen, it must be done with the particular needs of the organization in mind.

Summary

Planning is the basis for all successful events. To be successful, an event manager must gain a clear understanding of why the event exists (its mission), what it is trying to do for whom (its objectives), and decide the strategies needed to achieve these objectives. These must be set out and quantified in a detailed operational plan and its associated budget. It is also necessary to prescribe policies, procedures and rules for the event to ensure consistency of action among the various participants in its production.

The most common barrier to effective planning is managers' inability to establish measurable objectives (i.e. SMART objectives). If the outcomes of an event are not measurable, then there is no way that management or team success can be judged. A comprehensive plan not only provides a blueprint for the execution of an event, but provides a basis for analysing the actual event outcomes against planned outcomes, enabling an event management organization to deliver better events in the future.

Questions

1 Prepare a mission statement for each of the following events:
   (a) Bradford Mela
   (b) Notting Hill Carnival
   (c) an international music festival
   (d) a lifestyle consumer exhibition (e.g. fashion, gardening, home furnishings)
   (e) an event of your choice.

2 Select one of the above events and complete the following event planning process:
   (a) Prepare a set of objectives and a SWOT analysis for the event.
   (b) Demonstrate how each of your objectives satisfies the SMART principle.
   (c) List the strategies suggested by your SWOT analysis.
   (d) Formulate an operational plan for the event on the basis of the strategies you outlined in (c).
   (e) What type of organizational structure will best suit the planned event?
   (f) Draw a plan of the organizational structure that you selected in (e).
   (g) Write a brief position description for each of the positions on your plan.

3 Image that you are the director of London Jazz Festival.
   (a) What environmental factors would you need to consider when organizing the festival? Classify these as external or internal.
   (b) List the main aspects that you consider necessary to a standing plan for this event. How are these different to the aspects you would include in a single-use plan?
   (c) Construct an organization chart for the festival.
   (d) Write a position description for your job as festival director.

Case Study

The Open Championship

Background

The Open Championship, organized by the Royal and Ancient Golf Club (R&A) at St Andrews, is golf's oldest major championship. It takes place on an annual basis, rotating between nine selected links courses in Scotland and England. The first Open Championship was played over three rounds of Prestwick's twelve-hole course on 17 October 1860 – just eight men played in that first challenge and Willie Park of Musselburgh beat Tom Morris by two strokes with a score of 174. No prizes were awarded until 1873 when Park again triumphed and received £10 – compare this to the 129th Open Championship at St Andrews in July 2000, when 156 players competed for the Claret Cup and a first prize of £500 000 (from a record prize fund of £2.75 million). As one of the world's best known events, with the best golfers, extensive media coverage, and thousands of spectators, it is easy to see the necessity for effective planning.

Attendance at the Open 2000 reached new record levels, with a total of 230 000 passing through the pay-gates over the eight days of the championship. This exceeded the previous record by more than 21 000, also set at St Andrews in 1990, with more than 208 000 spectators. Daily figures for the period of the championship were: Thursday, 20 July, 39 000; Friday, 21 July, 47 000; Saturday, 22 July, 49 000; and Sunday, 23 July, 47 000. The Saturday figure was the highest ever reached on a single day at the Open – beating the previous record established on the Saturday of the 1990 Open at St Andrews when 45 500 watched the third round.

Coverage on the Open Championship website (www.opengolf.org) attracted more than 128 million page views, making it the most visited golf site in the world. Features included: live scoring, up-to-the-minute news coverage, player interviews and extensive webcam coverage. The site also included helicopter-mounted cameras overflying each hole, hole-by-hole graphics and defending champion Paul Lawrie's thoughts on how to tackle the Old Course, plus action colour photography, video clips and sound bites, and a wealth of information on the history of the championship. There was a massive increase in traffic since the 1999 Open – Carnoustie produced just over 25 million page views. Cutting-edge infrastructure put in place for the championship included more than sixty servers throughout the world, configured to handle 1000 requests per second.

Planning for 2001

Memories of the Millennium Open were still fresh in the mind, and half-dismantled grandstands still dominated the skyline over the ancient links of St Andrews in August 2000. However, for the small team in the Championship office of the R&A all thoughts turned to the future, to the Royal Lytham and St Annes 2001 championship, to be played from Thursday, 19 July to Sunday, 22 July. Planning for the 2001 Open began more than two years before the event, with the pace increasing immediately after the 2000 championships, with regular on-site meetings held with club officials, police and contractors.

A delegation from Royal Lytham and St Annes visited St Andrews during the 2000 championship to see at first hand the latest developments in the staging of a modern Open. Although it is only four years since Tom Lehman won the title in the last championship held at Lytham, detailed arrangements are under constant review and refinement.

The Assistant Chief Constable of Lancashire also made the trip to St Andrews to examine the latest traffic measures in action. Despite record crowd levels there were no major delays and the park-and-ride and train-bus links worked well – many people used the Golflink system, travelling to the course by direct train and bus service. Others took advantage of the park-and-ride operation, using the large reduced-rate car park at Guardbridge and completing the journey to St Andrews on free buses under police escort.

Since housing closely confines the course at Lytham, there is a greater need than at many Open venues for park-and-ride facilities. Spectators travelling by car to Royal Lytham and St Annes for Open Championship week must stick to the clearly signposted routes – these have been carefully planned by Lancashire police in consultation with the R&A. Drivers with reserved car park labels follow the appropriate colour-coded Open Golf signs. These designated routes will lead directly to park and ride facilities operating from all main public car parks, which will reduce delays and allow motorists to park at nominal rates and travel free to and from the course on special buses, assisted by police. In a policy that will be strictly enforced, any vehicles parked in the vicinity of the course that are causing any unnecessary obstruction will be towed away.

Following the enormous success and record-breaking attendance at the Millennium Open at St Andrews, detailed planning is under way to increase to number of stand seats available for the 2001 championship at Royal Lytham and St Annes. Because the course at Lytham is bounded on all sides by the railway line, roads and housing, there is a finite amount of space available for all the spectator facilities, which are so much a part of the modern championship. Detailed scrutiny of the site has identified areas, which will allow almost 5000 more seats to be available free of charge than when Tom Lehman won the title at Lytham in 1996.

Spectators will experience a huge range of on-course facilities during the 2001 championships, designed for the maximum enjoyment of watching the world's finest golfers in action. In addition to more than 21 000 grandstand seats around the course and at the practice ground, there will be a comprehensive network of scoreboards throughout the course and the tented village area. A wide variety of food and drink will be available, including the Famous Grouse 19th Hole and the Bollinger champagne tent, and giant television screens within the tented village will keep track of play. The Golf Show will include displays of the latest equipment from major golf manufacturers and an information centre will provide advice on tickets, travel and accommodation. The Royal Bank of Scotland will have comprehensive banking services for spectators, players, officials and exhibitors available in the tented village and there will also be payphones, first aid and left-luggage facilities. In the Junior Golf Tent there will be free tuition from qualified PGA professionals for under-16s.

National and international companies have a wide range of options available to entertain clients and guests at the Open Championship, ranging from a table for six in the Executive Restaurant to a private chalet catering for 100. Tables and chalets can be booked by the day or for the four-day duration of the championship. Each chalet has its own individual company signboard, television, telephone, floral decorations, patio furnishings and flagpole to fly the company flag.

Summary

It can be seen from the above that the Open Championship runs successfully based on many years of experience. The nature of the Open – using extensive temporary facilities built at venues not specifically designed for such large-scale events – requires over two years of detailed planning to ensure that the infrastructure is in place for it to run safely and smoothly. Planning is already underway for the 2002 Open Championship at Muirfield and the 2003 Open Championship at Royal St George's Golf Club (Sandwich, Kent). This involves working effectively with many stakeholders, including organizers, police, club officials, the local authorities and contractors. As a result, the increasing number of spectators and competitors at the event, and millions of viewers worldwide, gain the best possible experience from the Open – the world's oldest major championship.

For further details about the Open Championship, please visit www.opengolf.com.

By David Hill, Championship Secretary, The Open Championship, Royal and Ancient Golf Club, St Andrews, Fife, Scotland, KY16 9JD.

Questions

1 Write a mission statement for the Open Championships.

2 Construct a policy document for the event that lists appropriate policies and procedures for the event.

3 What type of organizational structure appears to be used for this event? Suggest reasons why this structure would suit the requirements of this event.

4 Would you classify the process used in planning the event as a single-use plan or a standing plan? Explain your answer.

5 Identify five other events that rotate between different venues each time they are run. What lessons can organizations planning these events learn from the Open Championship to ensure a successful event?

Leadership and human resources

After studying this chapter you should be able to:

- outline procedures for recruiting and selecting staff and volunteers for an event

- implement effective induction and training programmes for staff and volunteers

- understand what motivates people to perform effectively and efficiently

- understand how effective team-building of volunteers is carried out

- implement procedures to ensure compliance with statutory provisions such as payment of wages, health and safety legislation, and employee and volunteer records.

Introduction – what is leadership?

One definition of management, by the pioneering management writer Mary Parker Follett is 'the art of getting things done through the efforts of others'. This means that the 'others' (staff and volunteers) must first be carefully chosen according to specific criteria; must receive appropriate training; be given direction on what they are to achieve, and how their efforts contribute to the festival, exhibition or event as a whole; be given appropriate rewards; be appropriately motivated to achieve goals set for them; and be treated in accordance with appropriate legislation regulating employees and volunteers.

All these actions contribute to the leadership role of festival, exhibition and event managers. In particular, this chapter deals extensively with the leadership in relation to volunteers, because for many festivals, they constitute the great bulk of the workforce. However, volunteers are not just unpaid labour but people with needs, who probably present a greater leadership challenge than paid employees, since the rewards they seek are intangible, and intrinsic to the job itself; they do not seek the extrinsic reward of a salary.

Human resource issues and leadership are often overlooked in the management of small businesses such as festival, exhibition and event organizations. Effective management of human resources is vital to the success of an organization whose purpose is to produce a customer-focused event. It can be overlooked or assumed to be simply common sense, to the detriment of the event's outcomes. People who are selected without thought, who are poorly trained and have little idea of their function and how it contributes to the event's outcomes are not able to satisfy the expectations of the event's customers by delivering customer service of consistent quality. This chapter outlines procedures and policies that enable event managers to undertake this function effectively.

Human resource requirements

The number and type of human resources required for a particular event is determined through the strategic planning process. That is, the number and type of human resources required depends on the strategies adopted to achieve an event's objectives. For example, if an event's strategy is to focus on quality customer service, the number of people required will be greater than if other strategies, requiring less intensive human resources, are adopted. An example of this is the Manchester 2002 Commonwealth Games, which will utilize a very large number of volunteers in customer contact roles.

Once the strategic and operational plans are agreed on, it is then possible to determine the number and types of human resources required to produce the event successfully. Getz (1997, p. 186) suggests that this procedure can be done using a three-step method:

1 Break down the programme or operational plan into separate tasks. For example, the things that people must do to produce the event can be broken down into preparing the site, setting up fencing, erecting tents, toilets, stages and signs, cleaning up and disposing of waste and returning equipment to owners.
2 Determine how many people are needed to complete the different tasks. For example, do all the tasks have to be done in order, by the same crew or all at once, and do they have to be done by a larger crew?

3 Make a list of the numbers of people, the supervisors and the skills needed to form the best possible crew.

The most difficult task in this process is step 2, particularly if the festival, exhibition or event is new, or the event manager has no experience in a particular type of event. Human resources management writers such as Armstrong (1999) propose the use of work study models to make human resource forecasts, a technique that can be effectively applied to events. They are generally very simple as this example of a musical festival shows.

Number of participants expected: 25 000.
Number of arrivals in peak hour period: 10 000.
Number through one gate per hour: 2000.
Number of gates required: 5.
Number of turnstile operators required: 5.

However, care should be taken to ensure that sufficient staff are available at the event, particularly when considering stewards and security staff. The Health and Safety Executive (HSE, 1999) advise that the number of stewards should be based on the risk assessment, rather than precise mathematical formulas, in order to take into account the unique circumstances of the event.

Armstrong (1999) claims that by far the most common method of human resources planning used in business (and, it can be assumed, also used by festival, exhibition and event managers), is managerial judgement. That is, each of the events' departmental managers calculates how many and what type of human resources he or she requires in order to meet their objectives. In order to forecast human resource needs, they take into account demand forecasts, the site of event, skill requirements, previous instances of similar events and strategies adopted by the event. As Armstrong (1999, p. 322) points out, there are four main methods for forecasting demand for staff: managerial judgement, ration-trend analysis, work-study techniques and modelling, although generally a combination of managerial judgement and another technique would be used, probably because it is intuitive and easy to comprehend.

Once the number of people and the level of skills required are established, the next step is to recruit and select appropriate personnel.

Recruitment and selection

Chapter 4 pointed out that a job or position description is helpful to managers in recruiting and selecting new employees. The process of completing a position description can clarify what personal qualities such as education, training, experience, stamina, social interaction skills, strength and vitality are required for each job type. The job specification lists the education, training and experience an incumbent needs to do the job successfully. The recruitment of paid employees and volunteers is a process that can be illustrated by Figure 5.1.

Some of the important factors to be considered when recruiting and selecting staff are discussed below.

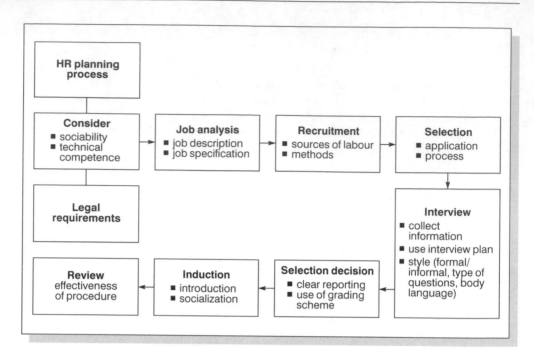

Figure 5.1 The recruitment and selection of paid and voluntary employees
Source: adapted from Mullins, 1999.

Budget

Depending on the size of the event, a budget (i.e. an agreed amount of the event's funds) can be allocated for recruitment costs. These budgeted funds can be used for payment of recruitment agencies or, alternatively, advertising and other recruitment costs such as travel expenses of non-local applicants and search fees for executive placement firms. The act of setting a budget acts as a control mechanism that ensures recruitment costs are realistic and that they are maintained.

Recruitment

It may be appropriate, depending on the types of positions that need filling, to use recruitment agencies, for example, Anne Ellington Associates, Career Contacts, Chess Partnership or ESP Recruitment for full-time staff, or the local job centre or employment agencies to meet temporary staffing needs. However, because of the perceived attractiveness of working on events, it may be cheaper to recruit using advertisements in appropriate newspapers or trade journals, for example, *Manchester Evening News* or *Marketing Event*. In addition, there are an increasing number of Internet-based recruitment services, for example, Stepstone (www.stepstone.co.uk) and Monster.co.uk (www.monster.co.uk). Nevertheless, it must be recognized that the time spent by managers on this quite time-consuming process is also a cost, and therefore it may be more efficient to outsource to an agency.

Voluntary staff • • •

Volunteers are gathered from a wide variety of sources. One source of volunteers, which is sometimes forgotten, is the major sponsor. As part of the sponsorship agreement, the sponsor may provide the event with temporary workers with a wide range of skills, including managerial, financial planning and marketing skills. Universities and further education colleges can also be a source of volunteers, particularly those universities and colleges offering courses in festival, exhibition and event management. Other sources worth investigating are: service clubs, such as Lions Club and Rotary, who can provide food and beverage facilities (from which they raise funds for their activities); community and special interest groups who have some affinity with the mission of the event; and people who have worked on previous events. McCurley and Lynch (1998, pp. 60–76) identify three approaches to volunteer recruitment, warm body, targeting and concentric circle recruitment.

- *Warm body recruitment*: warm body recruitment is generally used for positions that can be done my most people and can be particularly useful when seeking large numbers of volunteers. This method involves distributing advertising posters, use of public television or paid advertising, or contacting local community organizations. Sources from which volunteers can be recruited are:

  - job centres
  - libraries
  - tourist information centres
  - chambers of commerce
  - community centres
  - volunteer organizations
  - shop windows
  - religious groups
  - community service programmes
  - alumni groups
  - senior citizen centres and retirement homes
  - professional organizations (accountants, lawyers)
  - hospital waiting rooms and doctors' surgeries.

- *Targeting recruitment*: with targeting recruitment, the event manager would determine the type of person most likely to do the job and track them down. A starting point may be to look at existing volunteers and find out what motivated them to participate. Are there patterns of behaviour or background (e.g. education, occupation) that can be the focus for recruitment?

- *Concentric circle recruitment*: this method of recruiting volunteers involves starting with the groups of people who are already connected to the event or company and working outwards. It is based on the premise that volunteers are recruited by someone they know, e.g. friends or family, clients or colleagues, staff, employers, neighbours, or acquaintances such as members from the same clubs and societies.

Obviously, the type of event affects the type of volunteer. It would be unrealistic to request senior citizen centres to supply volunteers for a rock festival.

Selection ● ● ●

Application forms can be used to ensure all applicants have supplied equivalent biographical and historical data. However, this is not generally necessary for small organizations if the advertisement is written in such a way that all the qualities sought are clearly spelt out and applicants advised to address these in their letter of application. From this unsuitable applicants can be culled and those thought suitable can be short-listed and invited to attend an interview.

There is a range of methods available for selection. Robertson and Makin (1986, cited in Beardwell and Holden 2001) classified these into three distinct groups:

1 *Past behaviour*: the use of past behaviour can be used to predict future behaviour. That is, the manner in which a person completed a task in the past is the best predictor of the way that person will complete a task in the future. Biographical data (obtained from the curriculum vitae or application form), references and supervisor/peer group ratings can assist this stage.
2 *Present behaviour*: a range of techniques can be used to assess current behaviour, including personality questionnaires/psychometric testing, one or more interviews, self-assessment, portfolios/examples of work and handwriting (graphology). Effective interviewing techniques should be used, by asking appropriate questions that can elicit responses that identify applicant's ability in respect of the critical job requirements. This may include using several interviewers who, in post-interview discussions, can present behavioural evidence to support their ratings of applicant's suitability for the position.
3 *Future behaviour*: if appropriate, interview information can be supplemented with observations from simulations. For example, if the position is for a sponsorship manager, applicants can be asked to present a sponsorship proposal to a potential sponsor.

No matter what methods of selection are employed, it is imperative that these incorporate procedures to ensure all Equal Opportunity legislation is adhered to and no applicant can claim they have suffered discrimination.

Since management can be defined as the art of achieving corporate objectives through the efforts of others, some of the most important decisions event managers make are those on staff selection. As the best predictor of future behaviour is past behaviour, the use of previous employers as referees can clarify whether an applicant is able to perform a task effectively. However, to avoid embarrassment for the applicant, he or she must consent to contacting the referee.

Not all volunteers or employees may be suitable for the various tasks involved in producing an event. It is therefore reasonable to screen volunteers for suitability, usually by interview. Mullins (1999) suggests the use of a plan or form to help structure the interview in a way that aids effective recruitment. An example of such a form is shown in Figure 5.2.

Selection decision – hiring ● ● ●

Because most events are, by definition of a short-term nature, most paid employees will be employed on a contractual basis for a specific period of time. The contract (which can be a legal document, a letter of appointment or merely a

---

Interviewer's checklist

Name of volunteer: Date:

Position sought:
Background relevant to position:

Reasons for applicant to become involved in event

Does applicant understand requirements for position, e.g. training; time involved; criminal record check; etc.?

Applicant's time available to work on event:

Perceived strengths for position:

Perceived weaknesses for position:

Special needs:

Accept   _____ yes   _____ no

Applicant notified _____Date/time

Figure 5.2 Example of an interviewer's checklist
Source: Bradner, 1995.

non-documented verbal agreement) says that the employee agrees to perform certain activities in return for an agreed salary and other emoluments, and lays out the rights and obligations of the employer and employee. Unsuccessful applicants should be informed as soon as possible that they have not been successful.

Induction

To engender and maintain paid staff and volunteers' enthusiasm for their role in the event and for its successful outcome, it is important that staff – particularly volunteers – are given an induction or orientation period. A first step is to discuss the job description with the new member of the event organization. To avoid misunderstandings and later recriminations, it is important that both paid employees and volunteers understand clearly what is expected of them. A simple way to accomplish this is for volunteers to sign a position description. Bradner (1995, p. 75) suggests that the information shown in Figure 5.3 can fulfil this function.

This process ensures the volunteer is aware of what is required of him or her and what benefits he or she is to receive. The event manager knows what tasks the volunteer is capable of and willing to perform. This then becomes the basis of a mutually rewarding experience.

Volunteer job description and contract

Job Title: . . . .

Supervisor: . . . .   Location: . . . .

Objective (Why is this job necessary? What will it accomplish?): . . . .

. . . .

. . . .

Responsibilities (What specifically will the volunteer do?): . . . .

. . . .

. . . .

Qualifications (What special skills, education, or age group is necessary to do this job?): . . . .

. . . .

. . . .

Training provided: . . . .

. . . .

. . . .

Benefits (parking, transportation, uniforms, food and beverage, expenses): . . . .

. . . .

. . . .

Trial period (probation, if required): . . . .

References required (yes or no): . . . .

Any other information: . . . .

. . . .

Date: . . . .

Signature of volunteer (signatures to be added at time of mutual agreement): . . . .

Signature of supervisor: . . . .

Figure 5.3 Example of a job description and contract for a volunteer
Source: Bradner, 1995.

If not handled well, it can be a disturbing experience to become part of a new and unfamiliar organization. An induction period can replace this feeling with a commitment to making an event successful. Getz (1997, p. 189) suggests the following activities be part of an effective induction programme:

- Provide basic information about the event (mission, objectives, stakeholders, budget, locations, product details).
- Conduct tours of venues, suppliers, offices and any other contacts the staff may need.
- Make introductions to other staff and volunteers.
- Give an introduction about organizational culture, history and working arrangements.
- Give an introduction to the training programme.

A well-planned and organized induction period welcomes staff and volunteers to the event organization and engenders a sense of belonging to and enthusiasm for the event and its mission. Bradner (1995) suggests that an induction kit be given to each new employee or volunteer containing such things as:

- an annual report
- a message from the chairperson welcoming staff and volunteers
- a clear name badge
- a staff list
- a uniform, whether it be a T-shirt or something more formal, made of quality fabric
- a list of sponsors
- a list of stakeholders
- any other appropriate items.

It is important that the induction reflect the tone of the event. For example, the atmosphere at an induction for volunteers for a contemporary music festival may be loud and lively whereas a flower carnival's would be dignified, elegant and sedate. Refreshments are served and enthusiastic and knowledgeable staff should make presentations during the induction ceremony.

The outcome of the induction process should be a group of volunteers and staff who are committed to the event, enthusiastic and knowledgeable about their role in it and aware of what part their job plays in the totality of the event.

Training

All staff and volunteers need training of some type if they are to make an effective contribution to the event. This can range from informal, on-the-job training carried out by a co-worker, to a formal programme using an extensive range of training techniques. For staff (particularly volunteers), this training process reinforces the idea that their services are important and they are making a significant contribution to the event. It also enables them to grow personally, to gain new skills and to increase in confidence.

The type and extent of training required can be identified from the gaps that exist between current performance and desired performance. Identification of these gaps comes from:

- performance appraisals of existing staff (what staff identify as training they require to be effective)
- analysis of job requirements (what skills are identified in the job description)
- survey of personnel (what skills staff state they need).

Because of the infrequent nature and short duration of events, training of event volunteers usually takes place on the job under the direction of the event manager or a supervisor. For this to be effective it should be structured to include:

- *Defined learning objectives*: these outline what the trainee should be able to do at the end of the training.
- *Appropriate curriculum*: the content of the training is appropriate to the learning outcomes.
- *Appropriate instructional strategies*: these can take the form of discussion groups, lectures, lectures/discussions, case studies, role-playing, demonstrations or on-the-job training.
- *Well-conducting training*: the trainer is not an expert handing down instructions from on high but a facilitator who can identify, explain and model the skills, observe trainees' attempts and correct their errors
- *Evaluation*: this is to assess whether the trainees have acquired the appropriate skills.

Buckler (1998, pp. 18–19) developed a simple model of learning from his research into learning organizations. The model is based on the premise that the involvement of leaders in the learning process is crucial for success, as learning cannot be effective if the manager does not understand the process. Buckler goes on to argue that effective learning requires interaction between managers (the teacher) and staff (pupils) in order to develop a shared vision of what is to be achieved, remove barriers to learning and encourage innovation/try new ideas in a safe environment. This process of learning can be modelled as shown in Figure 5.4.

Appropriate methods for training event personnel are:

- guided discussions, i.e. asking the group questions which draw on their existing knowledge and then building on that base
- case studies of previous or similar events
- discussion groups to talk about the task involved in order to decide upon a course of action
- role-plays of situations in which personnel may find themselves
- exercises that apply the information received (adapted from Lulewicz, 1995).

As can be seen from the typical comments made by learners in Figure 5.4, essential elements of the training process are reflection and feedback. That is, trainees think deeply about the connections between what they already know about the topic and the new data they receive by relating new knowledge to experience, and using theory to extend experience. Feedback, from trainer, supervisor or peers, or their own reflection, enables trainees to adjust their actions to enable the task to be correctly completed. It is unlikely that anyone has learnt any new skill without this process of reflection and feedback.

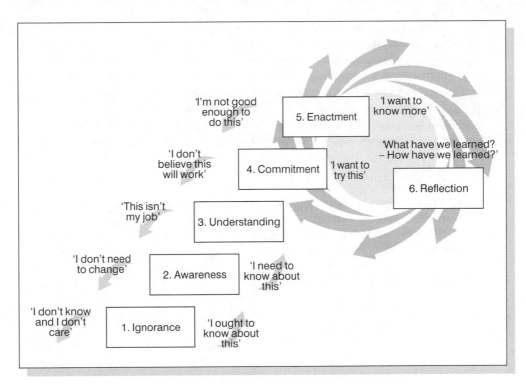

Figure 5.4 A simple model of the learning process
Source: Buckler, 1998.

Motivating staff and volunteers

Motivation is what commits people to a course of action, enthuses and energizes them and enables them to achieve goals, whether the goals are their own or their organization's. The ability to motivate other staff members is a fundamental component of the event manager's repertoire of skills. Without appropriate motivation, paid employees and volunteers can lack enthusiasm for achieving the event's corporate goals, for delivering quality customer service, or can show a lack concern for the welfare of their co-workers or event participants.

At first glance, it may be thought that pure altruism (an unselfish regard for or devotion to the welfare of others) is an important motive for volunteering to assist in events. Although this proposition is supported by Flashman and Quick (1985), the great bulk of work done on motivation stresses that, although people may assert they are acting for altruistic reasons, they are actually motivated by a combination of external and internal factors, most of which have little to do with altruism. As McCurley and Lynch (1998, pp. 11–12, 13) point out: 'Motivation for the long-term volunteer is a matter of both achievement and affiliation, and often recognition is best expressed as an opportunity for greater involvement or advancement in the cause or the organization.' Further, short-term volunteers are motivated by recognition of their personal achievement, which can be achieved by simply thanking them for their contribution. The parameters of reward are discussed in this section.

Much work has been done over many years, by researchers from a variety of disciplines, on what motivates people, particularly in the workplace. The theories proposed by these researchers provide a solid basis for understanding motivation. Theories relevant to the motivation of volunteers are used in this section as a framework to help understand why people are motivated to do something and how this process can be facilitated. The theories of motivation most relevant to festival, exhibition and event workers (both paid and unpaid) are content theories and process theories. Each is discussed along with their relevance to event workers.

Content theories

Content theories concentrate on what things initially motivate people to act in a certain way or, as Mullins (1999, p. 415) points out, 'these theories are concerned with identifying people's needs and their relative strengths, and the goals they pursue in order to satisfy these needs'. This is illustrated in Figure 5.5.

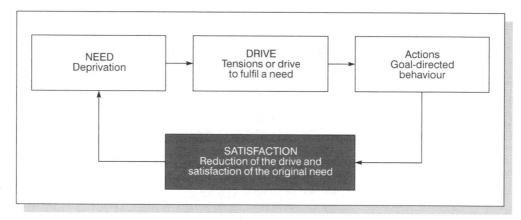

Figure 5.5 Basis of content theories of motivation
Source: Peach and Murrell, 1995.

Content theories say that a person has a need – a feeling of deprivation, which then drives the person towards an action, which can satisfy that need. Abraham Maslow's (1954) hierarchy of needs, illustrated in Figure 5.6, popularized the idea that need is the basis of motivation. In essence, Maslow's theory proposes that lower order needs must be satisfied before people are motivated to satisfy the next higher need. That is, people who are trying to satisfy physiological needs of hunger and thirst have no interest in satisfying the need for safety until their physiological needs are satisfied. The first three needs are perceived as deficiencies; they must be satisfied in order to fulfil a lack of something. In contrast, satisfaction of the two higher needs is necessary for an individual to grow emotionally and psychologically.

Although little empirical evidence exists to support Maslow's theory, it can give insights into the reasons why people volunteer. People who feel a need for social interaction, making new friends or belonging to an organization with perceived prestige are satisfying social needs. Those who have satisfied the first three needs may be motivated by the need for gaining the esteem of friends and family by performing a particular task, which is prestigious in some way. Finally, people may

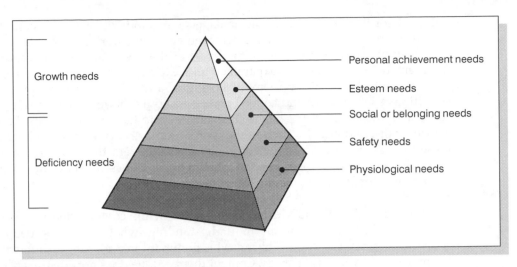

Figure 5.6 Maslow's hierarchy of needs
Source: adapted from Maslow, 1954.

volunteer in order to undertake a task that they believe will help them achieve their potential as a person and thereby be self-fulfilled.

Another researcher who influenced thinking on motivation is Herzberg (1987), who proposed the concept of motivators and hygiene factors. He suggests that what he refers to as hygiene factors do not in themselves motivate people but demotivate if they are perceived to be inadequate in any way. Motivating factors are things such as achievement and recognition. The Herzberg theory is illustrated in Figure 5.7.

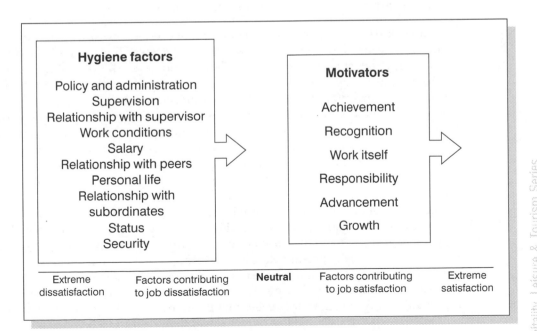

Figure 5.7 Herzberg's two-factor theory
Source: adapted from Herzberg, 1987.

This theory suggests that event managers can motivate staff and volunteers by instituting processes of recognizing achievement, empowering staff so they can take responsibility for the outcomes of their part of the event, and giving opportunities for them to grow in skills, experience and expertise. At the same time, certain hygiene factors can act as demotivators: the attitudes of supervisors; working conditions such as meal and coffee breaks and hours of work; the status of one job compared with another (e.g. stage crews are seen to have higher status than crowd control staff); and policies such as the type of uniforms given to volunteers. Fixing these things will not motivate people but it will prevent them being demotivated. Although Herzberg's work has its contemporary critics, it does supply a useful framework for thinking about how to structure the workplace to maximize motivation.

However, as Peach and Murrell (1995) put it, while content theories focusing on need fulfilment are important in understanding what motivates people, it is sometimes difficult to know which need is dominant in a person, as different people are motivated by different needs. Content theory alone does not adequately describe what motivates work performance.

Process theories

Process theories concentrate on how motivation actually works – what its effects are. Adam's (1965) equity theory and Vroom's (1964) expectancy theory best represent this concept.

Equity theory can be represented by the equation:

$$\frac{\text{My rewards (outcomes)}}{\text{My contributions (inputs)}} = \frac{\text{Your rewards (outcomes)}}{\text{Your Contributions (outcomes)}}$$

Two important characteristics of equity theory, which must be carefully thought about by event managers, are first, that overrewarding some has the same demotivating effect as underrewarding others and, second, that feelings of inequity are based on perceptions that may or may not equate with the event manager's perception of reality and can vary between individuals.

Equity can be defined in this context as the ratio between a person's effort and skills and their rewards (such as recognition, prestige, tasks allocated) compared to the rewards others receive for similar inputs. If inequity is perceived, the aggrieved person may try to make colleagues change their behaviour, either by increasing or decreasing input, depending on the perceived inequity. This process is illustrated in Figure 5.8.

The question of perceived inequity is somewhat problematic for event managers, as it is difficult to know staff's perceptions of how they are being treated. The best way, of course, is to maintain constant and open communication lines between managers and their personnel. By this process event managers can pick up perceptions of inequity and take action to change these perceptions.

Expectancy theory (a kind of process theory) proposes that the motivation to act in a particular way comes from a belief that by doing something a particular outcome will result (expectancy); that this outcome will then result in a reward (instrumentality); and, finally, that the rewards for accomplishing this outcome are sufficient to justify the effort put into doing it (valence).

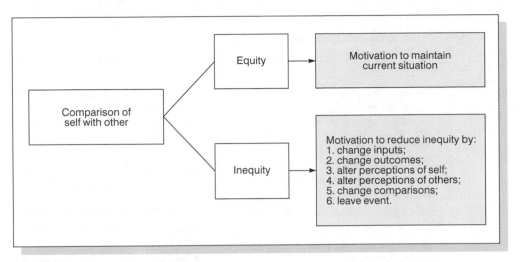

Figure 5.8 Responses to perceived equity or inequity

The application of expectancy theory to the situation of a volunteer working in a community cultural festival might be as follows:

- A volunteer has an *expectancy* that by working on the event opportunities for involvement in cultural activities by the community in which he or she lives will be enhanced.
- The volunteer's role in the festival will contribute (or be *instrumental* in) the goal of enhancing community cultural life.
- *Valence* is the sum of the internal rewards (self-actualization or self-esteem) and external rewards (social interaction, prestige, recognition, increased status within the community).

A salient point is whether volunteers actually believe or expect that by working on the community arts festival, cultural opportunities will be enhanced. If they do, their efforts will be greater than if they did not expect that to happen. Next, if volunteers believe that their efforts will be instrumental in that goal being achieved, they will be motivated to produce their best efforts in helping to achieve that goal. Finally, the reward for achieving this goal must be greater than competing rewards from other activities such as spending time with family, sport and involvement in other organizations. It is from this theoretical framework that Peach and Murrell (1995, pp. 238–9) derive their reward and recognition techniques, which are shown as Table 5.1.

An appropriate system of recognition of effort and extrinsic rewards for performance should be part of any event's human resources management plan. By conscientiously endeavouring to:

- get to know staff and volunteers
- maintaining dialogue between management and staff
- developing an understanding of what motivates each individual
- monitoring changes in the external and internal environments of the event.

Reward systems that work	Recognition techniques that work
Rewards that integrate the needs of the individual and the organization in a win-win understanding	Carefully constructed systems that are built on the motives and needs of volunteers – individualized need recognition for each person
Rewards based on deep appreciation of the individual as a unique person	Recognition integrated into task performance, where clear performance objectives are established
Rewards based on job content, not conditions – rewards intrinsic to the job work best	Corporate growth and development objectives also become opportunities for recognition
Assignment of tasks that can be performed effectively, leading to intrinsic need satisfaction	Longevity and special contributions recognized frequently, not just every ten years
Consistent reward policies that build a sense of trust that effort will receive the proper reward	Recognition grounded deeply on the core values of the organization; what is recognized helps as a role model.
Rewards that can be shared by teams so that winning is a collective and collaborative experience	

Source: Peach and Murrell, 1995.

Table 5.1 Reward and recognition techniques

An event manager can ensure that reward and recognition procedures are appropriate and act as motivators for staff and volunteers.

Techniques for effective volunteer team-building

Volunteers are individuals with different motivations to satisfy different needs, different demographics, and different skills and education. To be effective, they have to be melded into a team committed to achieving an objective. In order for this to happen, effective team-building techniques should be used.

Battle (1988, p. 98) believes that to be successful a leader must be able to mould their people into a team. Battle advocates that the seven steps for effective team-building are to:

- Establish a common objective
- Train the team
- Provide the team with constant communication
- Be enthusiastic at all times
- Execute the agreed plan
- Recognize, reward and motivate the team
- Evaluate progress of the plan regularly.

These steps have been expanded by Nancy McDuff (1995, pp. 208–10), an internationally recognized authority on volunteer programmes, into a fourteen-element formula for effective volunteer teams. These are listed below, with adaptations to suit an event environment.

1   *Teams are a manageable size.* Most effective teams are between two and twenty-five people, with the majority less than ten. If the event uses a large number of volunteers, break them up into smaller teams of around ten.
2   *People are appropriately selected to serve on a team.* Care and attention should be paid to selecting people with the right combination of skills, personality, communication styles, and ability to perform, thereby improving the chances of the team being successful. For example, the crowd control team at an event would have similar personal characteristics and personalities.
3   *Team leaders are trained.* Leaders who find it difficult to delegate and want to do everything themselves make poor leaders. Try to ensure team leaders have training in supervision skills.
4   *Teams are trained to execute their tasks.* It is unrealistic to expect teams to perform effectively without appropriate training. The training should include the team's role in the event and how that role contributes to the overall success of the event.
5   *Volunteers and staff are supported by the event organization.* Teams must feel that the administration is there to support their endeavours, not to hinder them.
6   *Teams have objectives.* The purpose of the team is spelt out in a measurable objective. Having a plan to achieve those objectives helps build trust.
7   *Volunteers and staff trust and support one another.* People trust each other when they share positive experiences. As each team is aware of the event's objectives and how their role helps to achieve those objectives, they trust their co-workers and support their efforts.
8   *Communication between volunteers and the event organization is both vertical and horizontal.* Communication, which means sending 'meanings' and understandings between people, is a process involving an active and continuous use of active listening, the use of feedback to clarify meaning, reading body language, and the use of symbols that communicate meaning. Communication travels in all directions – up and down the reporting line and between teams and work groups. Working together is facilitated by good communication.
9   *The organizational structure promotes communication between volunteers and staff.* The organization's structure, policies and operating programmes permit and encourage all members of the organization to communicate with their co-workers, their managers and members of other departments. This help builds an atmosphere of co-operation and harmony in the pursuit of common objectives.
10   *Volunteers and staff have real responsibility.* A currently fashionable concept of management is 'empowerment'. This means giving staff authority to make decisions about their work and its outcomes. For example, a group of volunteers has the somewhat mundane task of making sandwiches. If they are empowered with the authority to decide what sandwiches to make, how to make them and where to sell them, their enthusiasm for the task will probably be enhanced and there will be a corresponding improvement in outcomes.
11   *Volunteers and staff have fun while accomplishing tasks.* Events are fun things! People working in them expect to have fun as well. Event managers should strive to

engender an atmosphere of humour, fun and affection between co-workers within the culture of the organization. Such things as ceremonies to acknowledge exemplary contributions to the event, wrap-up parties and load-in celebrations can facilitate this.

12 *There is recognition for the contributions of volunteers and staff.* Paid staff should express formal and informal appreciation of the work of volunteers, and the work of the paid staff is publicly recognized and appreciated by volunteers. This mutual appreciation should be consistent, public and visible.

13 *Volunteers and staff celebrate their success.* Spontaneous celebrations with food, drink, friendship and frivolity should be encouraged by management of the event to celebrate achievement of objectives. The event manager should allocate a budgeted amount for these occasions.

14 *The entire organization promotes and encourages the well being of volunteer teams.* Everyone in the organization sees him or herself as part of a partnership and actively promotes such relationships.

Once teams are in place and operating effectively, the event manager should monitor the performance and productivity of the teams by observing their activities and maintaining appropriate communication with team leaders and members. If deficiencies are noticed during the monitoring procedure, appropriate action can be taken in terms of training, team structure or refinement of operating procedures in a climate of mutual trust.

Statutory requirements for staff and volunteers

The Health and Safety at Work Act 1974 is designed to reduce the likelihood and severity of illness and injury at work. Volunteers, being unpaid, are not specifically covered by this legislation. However, the common law rules on negligence, together with statutory requirements placed on employers and the self-employed to ensure the health and safety of those not in their employment, may give volunteers a similar right to recover damages from an event organizer if they are injured or fall sick because of their activities at the event.

According to Health and Safety at Work Act, employers (i.e. event organizers), site/venue owners and self-employed contractors have a statutory duty of care to protect the health and safety of those that may be affected by their work activity. This Act also obligates event staff to take reasonable care for the health and safety of persons participating in an event, and for those whom their acts or omissions at work may affect. Event staff must also co-operate with any requirement imposed in the interests of health, safety and welfare by the employer (the event manager, in this case) or any other person authorized under the Act. Health and safety, risk assessment and legal requirements are discussed further in Chapter 9.

Employment law

Employment law regulates how employers deal with their employees in terms of pay and conditions, and prevents discrimination in relation to race, sex or disability. This legislation generally sets out minimum rates of pay, and conditions such as annual leave and working hours. Of course, there is nothing to stop an event manager from paying more than the minimum wage, as the labour market is not controlled, except by minimum conditions that must be met. Traditionally, the market has been based on the concept of free collective bargaining, however, in recent years, there have been increasing levels of legislation, including the impact of European Union legislation. To ensure compliance with appropriate legislation, event managers who employ paid labour should consult the Department of Education and Employment, which undoubtedly can supply a handbook with details of current labour legislation.

Many paid employees of events are employed as casual workers. To compensate for the irregular nature of their work, these employees may be paid rates above the normal full-time hourly rate. It is the responsibility, and in the best interests, of the event manager to ensure these employees are paid appropriately, particularly during the summer event season when there is increased competition for their services.

A relatively recent change is the introduction of the right to a contract of employment. Under the Employment Rights Act 1996, employees are entitled to receive a contract of employment within eight weeks of commencing employment. The legislation ensures that minimum conditions of employment are established in the contract. Armstrong (1999, pp. 796–7) identifies the following areas typically to be included, with details either discussed or referred to in separate documents (e.g. grievance procedure):

- a statement of job title and duties
- the date employment commenced
- rate of pay, allowances, overtime, method and timing of payment
- hours of work including breaks
- holiday arrangements/entitlement
- sickness procedure (including sick pay, notification of illness)
- length of notice due to and from the employee
- grievance procedure
- disciplinary procedure
- work rules
- arrangements for terminating employment
- arrangements for union membership (if applicable)
- special terms relating to confidentiality, rights to patents and designs, exclusivity of service and restrictions on trade after termination of employment (e.g. cannot work for a direct competitor within six months)
- employer's right to vary terms and conditions subject to proper notification.

If large numbers of employees are used in an event, an enterprise agreement negotiated with employees can engender an atmosphere of trust and of working together to achieve a commonly sought objective.

Records of paid employees must also be kept. These should include:

- Name, address and telephone number
- Employment classification/employee number and national insurance number
- Whether full-time or part-time
- Whether permanent, temporary or casual
- Whether an apprentice or trainee
- Date when first employed
- Date when terminated

- Remuneration and hours worked
- Leave records
- Superannuating contributions.

McCurley and Lynch (1998) advise that it is also sound practice to keep records of volunteers. These may based on employee records, but will include as a minimum:

- contract
- job description
- application/interview forms
- name and address
- role in the event and training received
- skills and expertise
- performance appraisal
- access to special equipment
- willingness to volunteer again.

This type of information facilitates human resource planning for future events.

Summary

The management of human resources is an essential aspect of the event manager's job. Without a motivated, trained, enthusiastic and willing workforce, no event can achieve its desired outcomes. Adherence to the principles and practices of human resource management will assist in achieving the longevity of an event and desired outcomes.

Questions

1 You are the general manager of a community festival. You have calculated that 100 volunteers will be needed for serving food and beverages, ticket sales, gate control and security. Identify sources from which you could recruit these volunteers. Write a volunteer job description and contract for these four tasks and construct an interviewer's checklist for these positions.

2 Prepare an induction programme and a training programme for the volunteers that you have recruited.

3 How would you motivate the volunteers to provide a high standard of quality customer service to the patrons of the festival?

4 In what ways would you empower the volunteers?

Case Study

Eurostar Managers Forum by World Event Management

This case study provides a powerful example of how World Event Management – a global player in corporate events and motivational, incentive and team-building programmes – provides effective communications, production, team-building and on-site event management. The case study is concerned with the use of an event to motivate management teams and to communicate brand messages, based on the Eurostar Manager's Forum, an annual meeting arranged for Eurostar Group, on 7–8 December 2000.

The Eurostar Group, responsible for determining the communication direction and service direction of the overall Eurostar business, comprises three train operating companies from the UK (Eurostar UK), France (SNCF) and Belgium (SNCB). As a result of the geographical and cultural diversity, it is essential that management have a clear understanding of the organization. In order to facilitate this, Eurostar hold an annual two-day meeting of managers from all divisions of the three companies. For 2000, the venue chosen for the event was the New York Convention Centre at Disneyland Paris, with the client managing their own travel, via the Eurostar, and their own logistics at the Sequioa Lodge Hotel, Disneyland Paris.

Diversity of the audience can present a significant challenge. The event was aimed at train operators, not marketeers, plus key distributors and contractors, and therefore the event had to be designed to ensure that the communication message was clear. As you can imagine, taking into account the requirements of 195 managers from three railway companies based in London, Paris and Brussels, speaking three different languages, and each having distinctly different cultures, required clear objectives to be formulated to ensure success. These were identified as follows:

- To understand the power of branding and the Eurostar brand.
- To inform about performance and future developments and plans.
- To encourage a very mixed group to get to know each other better.
- To move the meeting format forward from the last meeting.

Based on these objectives, World Event Management developed a conference that involved and surprised the audience throughout the two days, based around a clear theme, and using a host/facilitator, video inserts, table challenges, breakout workshops and two very different team-building activities.

The theme was developed around a key message – 'Making Our Marque' – to communicate the power of branding, the power of the Eurostar brand and its relevant meaning to an audience of French and English speakers.

Event format

Day 1 ($\frac{1}{2}$ day, p.m.)

For the first day, the audience was seated at round tables for the workshop and reporting back. The delegates were divided into teams by badges with different famous brand names.

In order to keep the day informal, no lectern was used – instead all messages were presented in discussion format. A facilitator was used to introduce the theme, key messages, interact with audience and host discussions with all five speakers.

For the brand exercises, the audience was challenged to map out and present their current and future perceptions of the Eurostar brand. Real customer views were presented as video inserts – in three languages – to add the customers' perceptions into the discussion. During plenary sessions, simultaneous translation was provided in two languages.

The day ended in the early evening with a final team activity – 'Trading Brands' – which focused on using the power of brands to increase company value.

Day 2 ($\frac{1}{2}$ day, a.m.)

On the second day, workshops were used where the audience, in mixed groups, were challenged to develop action plans to improve customer service and company performance. The findings from this were collated but not formally presented back to the group.

In the late morning, the audience took part in a final team activity – 'T-shirt Masterpiece'. The teams summarized the Eurostar brand and message on T-shirts, then each team in turn presented their message on stage.

Evaluating the results

As a result of the event, the following outcomes were achieved:

- A better understanding of company service culture and future strategies.
- Improved working relationships between delegates.
- Enthusiastic participation in both team activities.

World Event Management designed, produced and managed the theme, title and conference logo, the event format, running order, speaker support on screen, two team activities, customer interview films, simtran (simultaneous translation), set and staging, technical support and all stage management.

For further details about World Event Management, please visit www.world-events.com.

Questions

1 Why is this an 'event'? How is it different from and similar to other events that you know of?

2 Who were the event stakeholders?

3 What stakeholders' needs were satisfied by this event?

4 The case illustrates the use of events for motivational purposes. How can events such as this be used to motivate employees and managers? What other needs do they satisfy? On what basis can participants be selected to take part?

CHAPTER 6

The marketing of events

After studying this chapter, you should be able to:

- describe how the marketing concept can be applied to festivals and special events

- understand needs and motivations of festival and event customers

- conduct a market segmentation analysis to establish appropriate target markets for an event

- forecast probable demand for an event

- construct a marketing plan for an event which contains appropriate pricing, promotion, place and product strategies.

Introduction – what is marketing?

Marketing is a term often used, yet there is no standard universal definition. The Chartered Institute of Marketing (CIM, 2001) defines marketing as, 'the management process responsible for identifying, anticipating and satisfying customer requirements profitably'. The entire focus of an organization should be on satisfying the wants and needs of an identified group of people with some homogeneous characteristic – the target market. This is in contrast to a popular view of marketing that assumes it is only concerned with selling or advertising. Marketing does not encompass only these activities, but much more. In 1980, Theodore Levitt, the Harvard University marketing authority, wrote, 'Marketing ... views the entire business process as consisting of a tightly integrated effort to discover, create, arouse, and satisfy customer needs' (Levitt, 1980, p.16). This chapter describes the marketing process.

The following is a definition of marketing in the context of events: 'Marketing is that function of event management that can keep in touch with the event's participants and visitors (consumers), read their needs and motivations, develop products that meet these needs, and build a communication program which expresses the event's purpose and objectives' (Hall, 1997, p. 136).

To illustrate these concepts, the following list shows the marketing activities that an event manager does to produce a successful festival or event:

* analyses the needs of the target market to establish appropriate event components, or 'products'
* establishes what other competitive events could satisfy similar needs to ensure their event has a unique selling point
* predicts how many people will attend the event
* predicts at what times people will come to event
* estimates what price they will be willing to pay to attend
* decides on the type and quantity of promotional activities telling the target market about the event
* decides on how tickets to the event can reach the target market
* establishes the degree of success of the marketing activities.

All these activities, essential for a successful event, are part of the marketing function. This chapter explores how the event manager carries out these functions to achieve the objectives set out in the event strategic plan discussed in Chapter 4.

The need for marketing

Some critics of the marketing concept argue that some cultural festivals and events should not be concerned with a target market's needs, but with innovation, creativity and the dissemination of new art forms. The argument is that consumers' needs are based on what they know or have experienced and therefore innovative or avant-garde cultural experiences will not be accepted by consumers. Thus, if the marketing concept of focusing on customer needs is used, nothing new will ever be produced. As Dickman (1997, p. 685) states, 'administrators were reluctant to even use the word [marketing], believing that it suggested "selling out" artistic principles in favour of finding the lowest common denominator'.

Hospitality, Leisure & Tourism Series

This attitude, while perhaps understandable, is based on a misunderstanding of marketing principles and techniques and can be self defeating for the following reasons:

1 The use of marketing principles gives event managers a framework for decision-making that should result in successful events that still allow for innovation and creativity, but cater for a target market segment that has a need for novelty and the excitement of the new.
2 Sponsoring bodies require some certainty that their sponsorship will be received by the target market they are seeking. Sound marketing practices will help convince them that a festival or event is an appropriate medium for them to communicate to their target market.
3 Local and national government financially assist many festivals and events. They usually only fund those events whose management can demonstrate some expertise in marketing planning and management.
4 Consumers, particularly those resident in major cities, have an enormous range of leisure activities from which to choose to spend their disposable income. This means that a festival or event, which, by definition, can be categorized as a leisure activity, will attract only those who expect to satisfy one of their perceived needs. Therefore, any festival or event needs to be designed to satisfy identified needs of its target market. Failure to do this usually results in an event that is irrelevant to the needs of its target market and does not meet its objectives.

Consumer expectations

The marketing concept is just as applicable to a leisure service such as event as it is to any other product. In fact, it could be even more so, as a leisure service, like other services, is intangible, variable, perishable and inseparable.

For example, consider a customer attending an outdoor jazz and blues festival. Unlike the purchase of goods, there is nothing tangible the customer can pick up, touch, feel or try before purchase. They merely decide to attend the festival based on expectations that a particular need (for entertainment, social interaction, a novel experience, self-education or any number of needs) will be met.

Consumer expectations come from a combination of marketing communications from the festival or event organizer, word-of-mouth recommendations from friends and family, previous experience with this or similar events and the brand image of the event. The service the customer receives – being entertained – is inseparable from the consumption of the service. In other words, instead of purchasing goods in a shop and then consuming them somewhere else, production of and consumption of the service are simultaneous or inseparable. Customers do not purchase by chance, but have to make a conscious decision to travel to the event site.

Even when markets are tightly segmented into a group of people with a common characteristic, members of the group may have differing perceptions of the benefits they have received from the event experience. This comes about because people are slightly different in their perceptions and attitudes, and therefore their perception of the service they receive and the people they receive it from may be variable. For example, two close friends may attend the jazz and blues festival. One may perceive all the services provided as terrific, yet the other may be not as enthusiastic, despite having experienced the same service.

If the weather is poor on the day of the festival and attendance affected, unsold tickets for that day cannot be stored and sold when the weather improves. In other words, leisure services are extremely perishable.

It is these characteristics of leisure experiences such as festivals and events that makes careful, structured thinking and planning of the marketing function integral to the success of any event.

Marketing mix

Getz proposes this definition of marketing for events: 'Marketing events is the process of employing the marketing mix to attain organisational goals through creating value for clients and customers. The organisation must adopt a marketing orientation that stresses the building of mutually beneficial relationships and the maintenance of competitive advantages' (Getz, 1997, p. 250).

This definition introduces the concept of the marketing mix, which Kotler et al. (1999, p. 111) define as 'the set of controllable tactical marketing tools that the firm blends to produce the response it wants in the target market'. Kotler et al. identify these variables as product, price, promotion and place, and each of these variables is discussed in depth in this chapter. 'Controllable' means that the event manager can manipulate or alter these variables in order to achieve an event's marketing objectives.

Product encompasses all the elements, which make up the festival or event. This includes such things as the entertainment offered, standard of service, food and beverage facilities, opportunities for social interaction, consumer participation in the event, merchandising, staff interaction with customers and the 'brand' image the festival or event enjoys among the target market.

Price means the value consumers place on the event experience and are prepared to pay. This value is determined by the strength of the need the leisure experience satisfies and alternative leisure experiences offered by other events and other leisure service providers. The price of an event experience can be varied according to the type of customer (e.g. pensioner concessions) or time of consumption (e.g. discounted price for previews).

Place has two meanings in event marketing. As well as signifying the geographical location of the event, it also means the purchase point(s) for tickets to the event. For example, *place* for an exhibition not only means the venue (e.g. Earls Court), but also the method of distribution of tickets to the event. Are they sold only at the gate, or can they be pre-purchased, and if so, where?

Promotion is, as Middleton (1995) points out, the most visible of the four Ps of the marketing mix. It includes all the marketing communication techniques of advertising, personal selling, sales promotion, some merchandising (e.g. T-shirt sales featuring the event), publicity and public relations, and direct mail. Potential consumers are motivated to purchase the leisure experience offered by the event by the design of these messages.

Some marketing writers have developed variations on the original four Ps. For example, Cowell (1984) proposes a seven-P marketing mix of:

- product
- price
- promotion

- place
- people
- physical evidence (layout, furnishing of venue, sound quality)
- process (customer involvement in the leisure service).

However, the last three Ps are just part of the product element of the marketing mix.

Getz (1997, p. 251) goes one P further and proposes an eight-P mix of:

- product (the service offered)
- place (the location)
- programming (elements and quality of style)
- people (cast, audience, hosts and guests)
- partnerships (stakeholders in producing the event)
- promotion (marketing communications)
- packaging and distribution of tickets
- price.

It is Middleton's view that, 'it helps the understanding of a central marketing concept to focus on an unambiguous, easy to understand four Ps' (Middleton, 1995, p. 66). The product consists of elements, which vary according to the target market, the venue, and other stakeholders. Splitting product into various permutations can cause muddled marketing thinking and action.

Table 6.1 summarizes the four Ps of the marketing mix and considers the variable elements of each.

The term 'promotional mix' refers to the many components that can constitute marketing communications between an event and its potential audience (or consumers). It is these variables that the event manager can manipulate to achieve an event's objectives. However, it must be noted that the product, promotion, and the place (if a ticketing agency or direct mail is to be used) require a commitment to upfront expenditure that is committed before any revenue is obtained from ticket sales. It is therefore important that the marketing planning processes are thorough, thoughtful and realistic in their forecast of both revenue and expenditure. Any muddle in the marketing process can have disastrous consequences for the viability and longevity of any event.

Figure 6.1 shows how the marketing mix fits in the context of the event organization and its environments. Chapter 4 discussed how the strategic planning process went about choosing appropriate strategies that can achieve the event's objectives. Some, if not many, of those strategies are concerned with marketing and will result from a marketing planning process that is embedded in the strategic planning process.

The core of the planning process, as the marketing concept suggests, is the consumer. The event's features should satisfy the needs of a carefully chosen consumer segment. All marketing efforts focus on these needs and how they can be satisfied, either profitably or in a way that achieves the objectives of the event.

The inner ring of Figure 6.1 contains the marketing variables of the four Ps that the event director (or its marketing manager in a large event) can manipulate. However, a realistic estimate of the revenue and sponsorship that an event or festival generates, determines the funds that can be spent on product enhancement, promotion and ticket distribution.

Four Ps	Elements
Product:	
Design characteristics/packaging	Location, staging, entertainment mix, food and beverage provision, seating, queuing, decoration, theme, lighting
Service component	Number of service staff, degree of training, uniforms, standard of service quality
Branding	Prominence given to name of event and what that name means to consumers
Reputation/positioning	Where event is to be positioned in terms of consumer demand – up-market to mass market
Price:	
Time of consumption	Discounted prices at times of low demand
Promotional price	Concessional prices for certain target markets
Promotion:	
Advertising – television, radio, newspaper, magazine, outdoor, Internet	The promotional mix
Sales promotion – merchandising, public relations	
Flyers and brochures	
Personal selling via a sales force	
Place:	
Channels of distribution	Tickets available through an agency such as Ticketmaster, Internet sites (e.g. firstcalltickets.com, LatestEvents.com) or sold by mail from a mailing list

Table 6.1 Event marketing mix

The marketing environment

The marketing efforts of the event do not occur in isolation. They are obviously constrained by the resources of the event organization. For example, if an event has very few volunteers to assist with all aspects of customer interaction, it would be unrealistic to embark on a process of increasing the quality of customer service. In other words, the marketing effort is constrained by the use of available resources.

The environments in which they operate affect all marketing activities. Figure 6.1 shows these to be:

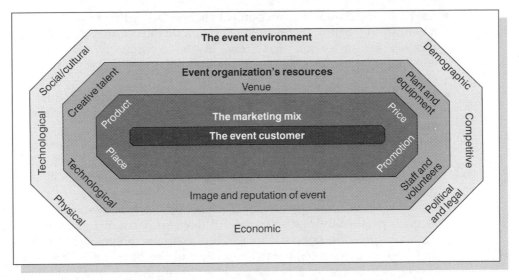

Figure 6.1 How the marketing mix fits in the context of the event organization
Source: adapted from Middleton, 1995.

- *Social/cultural*: events are a part of a society's culture. Changes in a society will lead to changes in the demand for certain events. For example, during the late 1980s/early 1990s the increase in popularity of dance music and its related culture lead to an increased demand for illegal dance events, commonly known as 'raves'. Interest in these illegal gatherings diminished after the mainstream nightclubs organized events to cater for this new market, including high-profile venues such as the late Hacienda in Manchester, that went on to enter the folklore and legend of dance music. These early developments led to the branded dance events and clubs, such as Ministry of Sound in London, Cream in Liverpool, Gatecrasher in Sheffield and the late Back to Basics concept in Leeds. Another example of social change is the greater emphasis many people now place on harm to the physical environment. All events must be seen to be sympathetic to the physical environment or risk a backlash from environmental groups.
- *Technological*: the enormous changes wrought by advances in computer and communication technology have caused many advances in the production of events. A computer program now controls fireworks, a mainstay of many public events. A computer can programme lighting for stage events. Presentations use multimedia; that is, more than one medium to communicate a message, usually audio, video and a slide or PowerPoint presentation. A snapshot of the state of technology and event management would show a spectrum of digital technology use. On end of the spectrum is the event company that is just getting used to e-mail and thinking of developing a website, while at the other end are companies that create, manage and promote only on-line events. In between are events that are managed by a mixture of digital and analogue – paper and screen. The spread of Internet literacy has produced a pressure on events to be shown on the Web in order to meet the expectations of the client, sponsor and other stakeholders.
- *Physical*: outdoor events are constrained by weather conditions. Outdoor venues must be left in a perfect condition or risk the wrath of environmental groups.

- *Economic*: the economic environment changes according to the economic cycle of a country or region. In times of relative hardship, it may not be appropriate to produce lavish events that some in the community view as conspicuous consumption, whereas during 'boom' times demand for such an event could be considerable.
- *Political and legal*: most events are constrained by regulations that control such things as noise levels, parking, security, the sale of alcohol, occupational health and safety, and the hygienic serving of food.
- *Competitive*: events do not take place in a leisure activity void. Consumers have an enormous range of leisure activities from which to choose. Event managers use the four Ps to ensure they can capture a reasonable market share of the leisure pound.
- *Demographic*: means characteristics of people such as age, gender, occupation, income, personality and interests. All developed countries are experiencing an ageing population bought about by the post-war boom in births between 1946 and 1960 and a contemporary reduction in the birth rate. This large group of people is now ageing (the first are over fifty-five years of age) and form a large, usually affluent group of consumers. According to research carried out by the Henley Centre for Forecasting, by 2010 the number of twenty-five to thirty-four year olds will have fallen by 21 per cent, while there will have been an increase of 28 per cent in the number of fifty-five to sixty-four year olds. In addition, the same research identified that the average income will have risen by 30 per cent and disposable income by 16 per cent (Robinson, 2000). These factors will present both an opportunity and a challenge for event organizers in order to develop events that not only tap into the higher income, but also to develop suitable events for the older market. Another demographic change of consequence for event directors is the increase in double-income families, which increases their disposable income and consequently the funds that could be spent on leisure activities. A further demographic phenomenon is the increase in the number of educated and employed women, and women who choose careers over families, at least in the early stages of their working life, which increases the market for cultural activities that appeal to educated women (Brooks and Weatherston, 2000).

The event consumer

The following acronym helps to explain the customer decision-making process (Morgan, 1996, p. 80):

Problem recognition
Information search
Evaluation of alternatives
Choice of purchase
Evaluation of post-purchase experience.

This process (PIECE) can be applied to the decision to attend a festival or event. The consumer identifies a need that may be satisfied by attending an event or other leisure experience, searches for information about such an experience in different

Stage in the consumer decision-making process	Implications for marketing strategies	Marketing decisions
Recognition of the need	Selection of appropriate target market(s)	Which market – mass or focused?
Search for information	Promotional mix variables	Direct mail, publicity, paid advertising or other types of advertising?
Evaluation of the alternatives	Event elements design Promotional message	Change the product? Change the promotional mix?
Choice at point of sale	Ease of purchase	What are the incentives for sellers?
Evaluation of leisure experience	Service quality	What type of post-event research will be undertaken? How will consumer satisfaction be monitored?

Table 6.2 The event consumer decision process and the implications for marketing

media (entertainment section of newspapers, radio shows, magazines) then evaluates the alternatives available. The customer then compares the needs the leisure experience can satisfy against a list of attributes. For example, a customer seeks an opportunity to enhance family ties, and chooses to attend a community festival that contains elements that all members of the family can enjoy. After experiencing (or 'consuming') the event, the customer evaluates the experience in its capacity to satisfy that need. Table 6.2 shows the implications for event marketers of this process.

The starting point for this marketing process is the needs of the customer that may be satisfied by attending a festival or event. Little empirical research on needs and motivations for event customers has been published in the UK. However, academic research carried out in North America in recent years give insights into this issue (Getz 1991; Mohr et al., 1993; Roslow, Nicholls and Laskey, 1992; Saleh and Ryan 1993; Uysal, Gahan and Martin, 1993).

Based on their research of customers of a jazz festival and a handcraft festival in Saskatchewan, Canada, Saleh and Ryan (1993) tentatively suggest a sequential decision making process for festival attendance which supports Morgan's PIECE model. Figure 6.2 illustrates this process. The missing element of evaluation (E) occurs after the leisure experience has occurred.

A study of customers at a community festival in South Carolina by Uysal, Gahan and Martin (1993) and a study of attendees of a North American hot air balloon

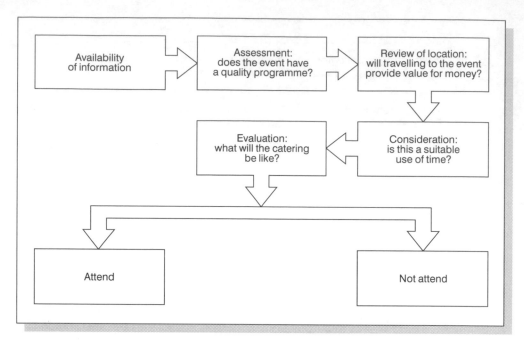

Figure 6.2 A sequential decision-making model for attending a festival or event
Source: adapted from Salah and Ryan, 1993.

festival by Mohr et al. (1993) reported that the five principal motivations (or need satisfiers) for attending festivals are:

- *Socialization*: being with friends, people who are enjoying themselves and people who enjoy the same things.
- *Family togetherness*: seeking the opportunity so the family could do something together and to bring the family together.
- *Excitement/thrills*: doing something because it is stimulating and exciting.
- *Escape*: getting away from the usual demands of life and having a change from daily routine.
- *Event novelty*: experiencing new and different things and/or attending festival that is unique.

Although the motivations for visiting both festivals were the same, the order was slightly different. Visitors to the community festival placed 'escape' at the top of their motivations, whereas visitors to the hot air balloon festival considered 'socialization' to be the most important motivator. This suggests that visitors to specialized festivals are highly motivated by a desire to socialize with people who share their interests, while visitors to community festivals are more motivated by 'escape' from the ordinariness of day-to-day life.

Getz (1991) adapts Maslow's theory of people having a needs hierarchy. Maslow proposed that needs are satisfied in the following order: physiological, safety, social, self-esteem and self-development (see pp. 102–3). Getz adapted this to propose a three generic needs model. Table 6.3, is an adaptation of Getz's theory.

Need and motives	Corresponding benefits and opportunities offered by events
Physical Physical need motivate the need to:	
Eat and drink	Eat and drink new, different food and drink
Exercise	Participate in sporting activities
Relax	Relaxing entertainment
Search for security	Recreation in a secure environment
Find sexual gratification	Meet people
Social/interpersonal The need for belonging, friendship and love motivate:	
Socializing with family and friends	Share a new and different environment
Romance	Meet new people
Links to cultural and ethnic roots	Renew ties to ethnic and cultural groups
Expressions of community and nationalism	Share in the use of appropriate symbols and rituals
Pursuit of recognition for accomplishments	Prestige from attending an event
Personal The need for understanding, aesthetic appreciation, growth and self-development motivates:	
A quest for knowledge	Formal/informal learning
Seeking new experiences	Unique programmes
Creativity	Participation in artistic endeavours
Fulfilment of ambitions	Participate in something unique and special

Source: adapted from Getz 1991

Table 6.3 Needs, motives and benefits offered by events

Morgan (1996) identified five other social factors that can influence consumers' leisure behaviour. These can be described in the context of event participation as follows:

- *Family influences*: the desires of children will often influence the leisure behaviour of their parents. The need for family cohesion and the enhancement of familial ties is a strong motivator for many people. This explains the enormous numbers of children accompanied by exhausted parents to be found at community shows and galas. Many festivals include entertainments for children for this reason.

- *Reference groups*: groups who influence the behaviour of those with whom they come into close contact (such as peers, family, colleagues and neighbours) are called a *primary reference group*. Those who have less frequent contact a *secondary reference group*. Most people tend to seek the approval of members of their reference groups. If it is generally accepted in a particular reference group that attendance at a particular festival is appropriate behaviour, then members of that group are likely to attend. If not, then attendance is very unlikely. Showing examples of a typical reference group (e.g. a nuclear family group) enjoying themselves at a festival can send a message to a target market that may well respond favourably.
- *Opinion formers*: within any group, some people will be opinion leaders. That is, their opinions on new leisure experiences are sought by the group and generally accepted. These opinion leaders are often media or sporting personalities, which is the reason many of them make a very substantial living endorsing new products and leisure services. The adoption of new leisure services follows a normal distribution curve. Innovators (generally opinion leaders within a group) are the first to try the experience. Early adopters who are a little more careful about adoption of the innovation follow them. However, they still act as opinion leaders for the great majority. Laggards are the last to try something new. Therefore, the promotional messages for any new festival or event should be directed at those who have been identified as opinion formers or innovators.
- *Personality*: Brassington and Pettitt (2000, p. 108) define personality as, 'the features, traits, behaviours and experiences that make each of us distinctive and unique'. People can be introverted/extroverted, shy/self-confident, aggressive/retiring, dynamic/sluggish. It is well known that personality affects consumer behaviour. Unfortunately, as personality is difficult to measure in terms of consumer behaviour, it is a marketing tool that is difficult to use. However, festivals that celebrate adventure or sporting prowess would be unlikely to appeal to shy, retiring personalities.
- *Culture*: the UK is an example of a culturally diverse country. Within the UK live diverse groups who have different designs for living. Each of these cultural groups has different buying habits, leisure wants and needs, and attitudes and values. If a particular cultural group is a desired market segment, the four Ps of the marketing mix can be manipulated in order to appeal to that group.

Target market segmentation

Most events do not appeal to everybody. As Hall (1997) observes, the marketing planning activities of event managers must include an understanding of the behaviour of visitors to an event. This includes identifying those market segments that are likely to have their needs satisfied by the event activities or, alternatively to ensure the event contains those elements which can satisfy an identified target market's needs. The process of identifying appropriate target markets is known as market segmentation. Segmentation can occur by geography, demography or lifestyle (psychography).

Geographic segmentation is concerned with the place of residence of event visitors. A community festival, for example, would probably decide to focus on local residents as the first step in their segmentation exercise. However, if the festival is thought to be of interest to other than locals because of its potential product content, the marketing net could be spread wider. The potential geographic spread could be:

- local residents of the area
- day visitors from outside the immediate area
- domestic tourists
- international inbound tourists
- school trips.

The chosen geographic segmentation depends on the leisure experience provided by the festival or event. For example, an event such as an agricultural show (e.g. the Great Yorkshire Show in Harrogate) would have a regional geographic segmentation and probably a national market segment for its more specialized event experiences.

Demographic segmentation concerns the measurable characteristics of people, such as age, gender, occupation, income, education and cultural group. A demographic segmentation tool often used by marketers is a socioeconomic scale based on occupation (usually the head of the household, in family units). Table 6.4 illustrates the traditional JICNARS classification used by British marketers in an event context. Retired people are coded according to their pre-retirement occupation. It is worth noting that in 1998 the government introduced a new National Statistics Social Economic Classification (NS-SEC) for the purposes of official statistics that breaks the population down into seventeen groups based on occupation, size of employing organization, type of contract, benefits and job security. These may enable more clearly defined groups, particularly considering the trend towards the 'middle classes' within the UK population (Brassington and Pettitt, 2000; Rose and O'Reilley, 1998).

Although developed for the UK, these classifications are relevant to all developed countries. Media buyers in advertising agencies first used this method of classification, as the system is a very good predictor of reading and viewing habits. For example, ABC1 adults make up the majority of the readership for broadsheet newspapers, such as *The Times* (77 per cent), *Daily Telegraph* (82 per cent), *Financial Times* (87 per cent) and *Independent* (87 per cent), whereas they account for only a minority of the tabloids readership (e.g. *Daily Star* 17 per cent, *Sun* 22 per cent and *Mirror* 24 per cent) (Chisnall, 1995).

However, these classifications are not always an accurate guide to income. For example, many Cs earn considerable incomes. The essential difference between As, Bs, C1s and the other categories is in the level of education. The higher the level of education, the higher the propensity of a person to participate in cultural activities, including arts and community festivals (Torkildsen, 1999). Morgan observes that the age at which individuals terminate their formal education (16,18 or after higher education at 21 years) can indicate their ambition, intelligence and, importantly for event managers, their curiosity about the world in which they live (Morgan, 1996, p. 103). For directors of festivals and events that include cultural elements, their target market is an educated one.

Other demographic variables are gender and age. Women and men occasionally have different needs and some events cater for these different needs. The years in

Group	Social status	Social grade	Head of household's occupation	Types of events group is likely to attend	% of population
A	Upper middle class	Professional (non-manual)	Professional people, very senior managers in business or commerce or top-level civil servants, retired people (previously grade A), and their widows	Cultural events such as fundraisers for the opera, classical music festivals	3
B	Middle class	Middle managers (non-manual)	Middle management executives in large organizations, (with appropriate qualifications), principal officers in local government and civil service, top management or owners of small businesses, educational and service establishments, retired people (previously grade B) and their widows	Cultural events (but purchasing cheaper seats), food and beverage festivals, historical festivals, arts and crafts festivals, community festivals	14
C1	Lower middle class	All other non-manual workers	Junior management, owners of small establishments, all others in non-manual positions. Jobs in this group have very varied responsibilities and educational requirements. It also includes retired people (previously grade C1) and their widows	Most popular cultural events, some sporting events, community festivals	26
C2	Skilled working class	All skilled manual workers	Skilled manual workers, and those manual workers with responsibility for other people, retired people (previously grade C2) with pensions from their job and widows (if receiving pensions from their late husband's job).	Motor vehicle festivals/shows, sporting events, community festivals	25
D	Working class	All semi-skilled and unskilled manual workers	Semi-skilled and unskilled manual workers, and apprentices and trainees to skilled workers, retired people (previously grade D) with pensions from their job, and their widows (if receiving a pension from their late husband's job)	Some sporting events, ethnic festivals	19
E	Those at lowest level of subsistence	On benefit/ unemployed	Those entirely dependent on the state long term, through sickness, unemployment, old age or other reasons, those unemployed for a period exceeding six months (otherwise classify on previous occupation), casual workers, those without a regular income. Only households without a chief wage earner will be coded in this group	Very little, except occasionally free events	13

Source: adapted from Brassington and Pettitt 2000; Office for National Statistics, 2000.

Table 6.4 A classification of socioeconomic market segments for events

Generation	Born	Age in 2001	Formative years
First World War	Pre-1924	78+	Pre-1936
Depression	1924–34	66–77	1936–46
Second World War	1935–45	55–66	1947–57
Early boomers	1946–54	46–55	1958–66
Late boomers	1955–64	36–46	1967–88
Generation X	1965–76	24–36	1977–88
Echo boom	1977–94	7–24	1989–2001

Source: Getz, 1997.

Table 6.5 The generations born in the twentieth century

which people are born can affect their outlook on life, their attitudes and values, and their interests. Depending on the event, one or several of these generations can be targeted. Table 6.5 shows the different generations born in the twentieth century.

Another method of age segmentation is by life cycle. This relies on the proposition that peoples' leisure habits vary according to their position in the life cycle. Wells and Gubar (1966) developed the original life-cycle model that reflected the life stages of the time (i.e. bachelor, newly married, full nester, empty nester and solitary survivors), however, due to changes in society this has now become outdated (Brassington and Pettit, 2000). The family life cycle, illustrated in Figure 6.3, is reflective of the modern family. For example, single or married/cohabiting people with children are equally the target market for community events that feature elements for both children and adults, whereas AB empty nesters are the perfect market for a cultural festival featuring quality food and drink and arias from well-loved operas.

However, care should be taken not to resort to age stereotypes. Many early baby boomers, in or approaching their fifties, are fit, active and interested in all types of culture, popular and contemporary, as well as high-culture festivals such as classical music or theatre. It could be argued that the most successful community festivals are those which are inclusive of all age groups, rather than focusing on just one age cohort.

Geodemographics – segmenting residential areas according to variables from population census data – was originally developed by the CACI Market Analysis Group as ACORN (A Classification of Residential Neighbourhoods). ACORN classifies residential areas into six main categories (see Table 6.6) with seventeen subgroups and fifty-four types, thus allowing postcode areas to be linked to demographics and buying behaviour for accurate target marketing (Kotler et al., 1999, pp. 391–2).

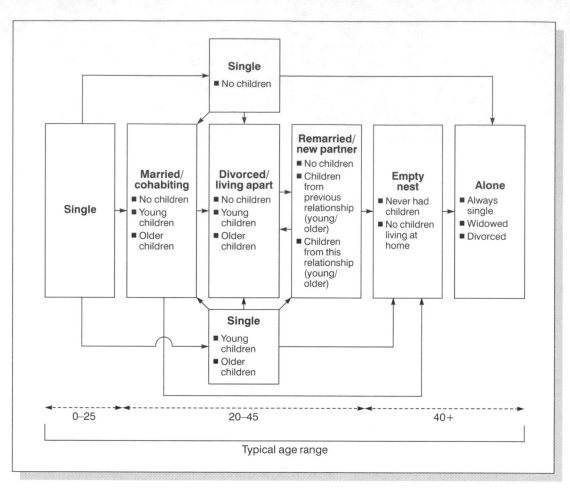

Figure 6.3 The family life cycle
Source: Brassington and Pettitt, 2000.

The Office for National Statistics (ONS) publishes a great deal of data taken from each census that categorizes residential areas according to the demographics of the residents of that area. This information was traditionally published as paper-based documents by the Great Britain Office of Population Censuses and Surveys as, for example, *1991 Census London Postal Districts: Postcode Sector Monitor.* A separate edition is published for every region throughout the UK and is a valuable store of demographic information categorized by geographic area. Data shown include the demographic variables of sex, age, marital status, household membership and relationships, cultural characteristics, qualifications, employment, workplace and household accommodation. The launch of the ONS in June 2000 illustrated a shift toward more accessible official statistics, which includes census, other data and publications being freely available on line for not-for-profit end users (see www.statistics.gov.uk for further information). Directors of community festivals should find this data very useful for product planning.

Psychographics – segmenting a market according to its lifestyle and values – is another segmentation technique that could be a useful planning tool for event

Group	Description	Approximate % of population
A – Thriving	Wealthy achievers, suburban areas Affluent greys, rural communities Prosperous pensioners, retirement areas	20
B – Expanding	Affluent executives, family areas Well-off workers, family areas	11
C – Rising	Affluent urbanites, town and city areas Prosperous professionals, metropolitan areas Better-off executives, inner city areas	8
D – Settling	Comfortable middle-agers, mature homeowning areas Skilled workers, homeowning areas	25
E – Aspiring	New homeowners, mature communities White-collar workers, better-off multiethnic areas	13
F – Striving	Older people, less prosperous areas Council estate residents, better-off homes Council estate residents, high unemployment Council estate residents, greatest hardships People in multiethnic, low-income areas.	21

Source: adapted from Mintel, 2000.

Table 6.6 ACORN classification

directors. This method involves measuring AIO (activities, interests, opinions) dimensions and demographics (Brassington and Pettitt 2000). Table 6.7 illustrates the primary lifestyle dimensions. Based on consumer research, classifications have been developed by various organizations. For example, McCann-Erickson found the following British lifestyles:

- avant guardians: interested in change
- pontificators: traditionalists, very British
- chameleons: follow the crowd
- sleepwalkers: contented underachievers (Kotler et al., 1999, p. 242).

However, like personality segmentation, psychographic segmentation of a market has some serious limitations for an event marketer:

> The main problem . . . is that psychographic segments are very difficult and expensive to define and measure. Relevant information is much less likely to exist already in the public domain. It is also very easy to get the implementation wrong. For example, the organisation that tries to portray

Hospitality, Leisure & Tourism Series

Activities	Interests
Work	Family
Shopping	Home
Holidays	Work
Social life	Community
Hobbies	Leisure and recreation
Entertainment	Fashion
Sports interests	Food
Club memberships	Media
Community	
Opinions	*Demographics*
Themselves	Age
Social and cultural issues	Education
Politics	Income
Education	Occupation
Economics	Family size
Business	Life-cycle stage
Products	Geographic location
Future	

Source: adapted from Brassington and Pettitt, 2000.

Table 6.7 Lifestyle dimensions

lifestyle elements within advertisements is dependent on the audiences ability to interpret the symbols used in the desired way and to reach the desired conclusions from them. (Brassington and Pettitt, 2000, p. 190)

What this type of segmentation can do for an event marketeer is to give another technique for deep thinking about the characteristics of the target market sought.
To be effective, market segments must be:

- measurable; that is, the characteristics of the segment (socioeconomic status, gender age, etc.) must be accessible to the event marketeer
- substantial enough to be worth the effort of targeting
- accessible by normal promotional channels
- actionable by the event organization in terms of the marketing budget and other resources (Morgan, 1996).

Product planning

The product of an event is a leisure experience that has been carefully produced to satisfy a target market's identified needs. The word 'product' is used, as marketing theory applies to both the production of tangible goods and intangible services

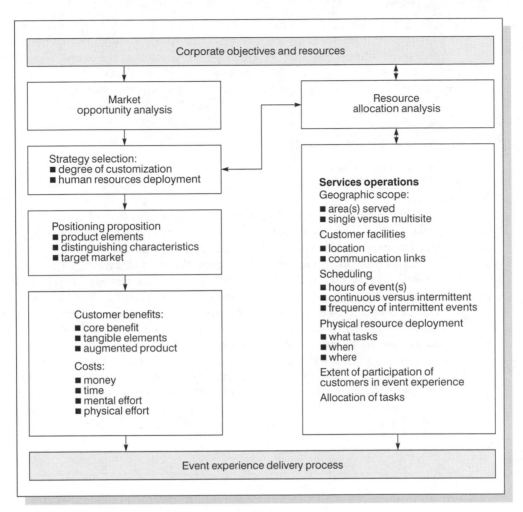

Figure 6.4 The process of creating an event product

(Chapter 3, 'Conceptualizing the event', explores this process). Figure 6.4 illustrates this process diagrammatically.

The new concepts introduced in Figure 6.4 are customer benefits and costs. The section on pricing further explores the concept of costs. Morgan (1996, p. 136) states that a leisure service (or product) contains three elements:

- the core benefit that the customer experience – an enjoyable leisure experience that satisfies some need(s)
- the tangible benefit that helps deliver the core benefit – the venue, the seating, decoration, etc.
- the augmented product; that is the additional features that differentiate this event from its competitors – artists, service quality, and type of people attracted to the event, parking or transportation facilities, ease of access and exit, etc.

The event planner needs to be aware of all three elements.

This introduces an important characteristic of the marketing of services – people are part of the product. In other words, much of the event consumer satisfaction comes from interactions with the other people attending the event. This then means that the event manager needs to ensure that the audience is compatible, and has some homogenous characteristic to facilitate social interaction.

Product development

This section discusses some product development issues that will help in understanding what constitutes a leisure product, how it evolves and how it can be analysed.

Branding gives an event an easily recognizable identity. One of the best known brands in the world is the five interlocking rings of the Olympic Games – a mega-event. Because leisure experiences are intangible, branding is particularly important as it reassures potential consumers that the service will deliver the benefits promised. Clever use of the 'brand' helps the event manager make an intangible phenomenon more tangible for the event consumer.

The *product life cycle* (shown as Figure 6.5) illustrates that all events follow a similar pattern of participation as they go through the stages of introduction, growth, maturity and eventual decline. The history of events within the UK is littered with examples of once hugely popular festivals or events that were once very popular and now no longer exist, or have been rejuvenated. For example, 1998 saw the end of the once popular Phoenix due to lack of ticket sales, and Reading Festival (established as an alternative to mainstream music events) has over the years broadened its musical appeal to incorporate mainstream music (Mintel, 2000).

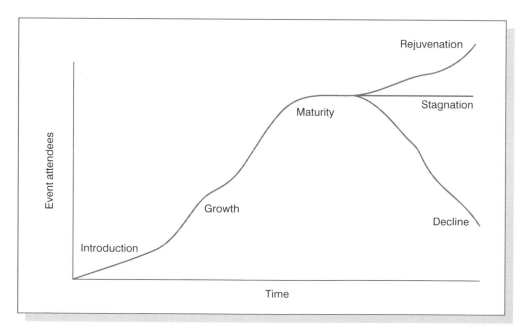

Figure 6.5 The product life cycle

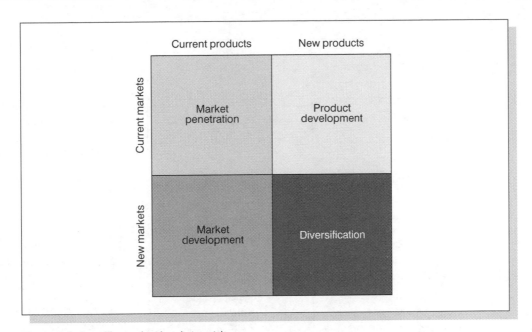

Figure 6.6 Ansoff's product/market matrix
Source: Ansoff, 1957.

To avoid failure or decline, event managers need to monitor closely public acceptance of the content of the content of their event product to ensure that it is still congruent with the leisure needs of contemporary society.

A simple, yet highly useful tool for clear and effective thinking about product strategies is Ansoff's matrix (1957), shown in Figure 6.6. An event that considers its product is appropriate yet is not drawing large numbers may consider a market penetration strategy, i.e. by the use of advertising or other forms of promotion attract more of the same target market. If it is thought that the event leisure experience can reach a different target market(s) without changing the product, a market development strategy can be used. It may be that monitoring of consumer satisfaction shows that the current product offering is not satisfying consumer needs. It would then be necessary to develop new and different products that can. If the event adopted a corporate strategy of growth, it may be appropriate to develop new products for a new market. For example, consumer monitoring might show that the AB section of the population is not attending an event. A product strategy of diversification would result in an event product that would satisfy this target group's needs.

Because leisure services are intangible, inseparable and variable defining service quality is a difficult construct. A definition that examines quality service from the viewpoint of the consumer is: quality service occurs when the consumers' expectations of the leisure service match their perceptions of the service received. Because this is based on perceptions rather than something tangible, not every customer will be satisfied all the time. However, one of the corporate objectives set out in an event's strategic plan should be a measurement of consumer satisfaction such as 95 per cent of event participants will give a satisfied or higher rating of the event. Figure 6.7 shows how consumer dissatisfaction can occur.

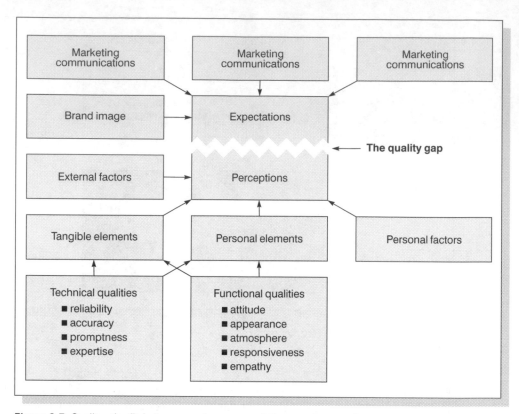

Figure 6.7 Quality: the fit between customer expectations and perceptions
Source: Morgan, 1996, p. 159.

The consumer's perceptions of the leisure experience are formed from the technical and human qualities of the experience as well as any external factors such as wet weather, and personal factors such as an argument with a partner occurring at the event. The consumer's expectations of the event are determined by:

- marketing communications – advertising, publicity, brochures, signs, and price which are used to promote the event
- word-of-mouth recommendations from friends and relatives who describe their experiences of this or similar events
- personal experience of this or similar events.

When the consumer's perceptions of the event match or exceed their expectations, a quality leisure experience has been delivered and the outcome is a satisfied consumer.

Zeithaml, Parasuraman and Berry (1990) are the world's leading researchers on service quality. They have reduced their original ten determinants of service quality to this top five:

- assurance – because staff give the appearance of being knowledgeable, helpful and courteous, event consumers are assured of their well-being

- empathy – the event staff seem to understand the consumers' needs and deliver caring attention
- responsiveness – the staff are responsive to the needs of the consumer
- reliability – everything happens at the event in the way marketing communications promised
- tangibles – the physical appearance of the event equipment, artists and staff met expectations.
- Concentrating on these aspects of service will result in outcomes that meet corporate service objectives.

Pricing

Festivals and events are leisure activities. Most UK residents live in areas that offer many leisure options. This means that price can have a major effect on demand for an event and is an important aspect of an event's marketing mix. However, some events are free of charge to consumers, but there still are costs to the consumer of attending, as well as costs for the producer. This section discusses the non-cash costs of price, how price is used in event marketing, the concept of value for consumers, different types of costs, appropriate pricing strategies and issues involved in pricing.

Price has many uses. In a market economy like Britain's, the more highly sought after a particular good or service is, the higher the price, so fewer people can purchase it. For an event, price can determine the number of consumers who attend the event. For example, a mass-market event such as a lifestyle consumer show must keep its price at a level of affordability to its customers – middle-income, middle Britain. On the other hand, a fundraising event such as the National Society for the Prevention of Cruelty to Children (NSPCC) Firecracker Ball can ask a much higher price as its target market is much smaller (socioeconomic group AB who are supporters of the NSPCC) but wealthier, and therefore willing to pay for a perceived quality experience. However, the high price can represent quality (or 'value for money') to the potential consumer and influence the decision to purchase.

The three foundations of pricing strategies are:

- costs
- competition – the market
- value to the customer.

Value is the sum of all the perceived benefits (gross value) minus the sum of the perceived costs. Therefore, the greater the positive difference between perceived benefits and costs, the greater the net value to the potential consumer. In the NSPCC fundraiser example, potential consumers compare the perceived benefits – dinner, drinks, entertainment, opportunities to socialize with the rich and famous, prestige, novelty of an unusual night out – with the perceived costs – money and non-cash costs. If the NSPCC have adequately communicated these benefits, consumers will perceive that the event offers value and purchase tickets.

Not all costs to the event consumer are cash. Other costs incurred are:

- time – the opportunity cost of the time spent consuming the event experience compared with using that time to enjoy another leisure experience

Hospitality, Leisure & Tourism Series

- the physical efforts required to consume the leisure experience – travel, energy expended
- psychic costs – mental effort to engage in the social interaction required, feelings of perceived inadequacy in certain social settings
- sensory costs – unpleasant climate, uncomfortable seating, unattractive physical environment, and unlikeable companions.

Event managers must consider these elements of consumer costs and attempt either to alleviate any difficulties, or to promote them in such a way that they become part of the event. In most events, the people who attend the event become part of the event product. For example, part of the product of the NSPCC fundraiser is the 'high society' who attends. Alternatively, a middle-aged non-drinker will probably not feel comfortable at an event that is largely attended by young men in their twenties who are enjoying a great deal of alcohol.

Types of event costs are:

- fixed – costs that do not vary according to the number of event consumers; for example, venue hire, interest, light heat and power, volunteer uniforms, artist fees
- variable – costs that vary according to the number of event consumers; for example, number of paper plates used at a food festival, catering at a product launch, extra staff required to service additional customers.

Analysis of costs is the first step in calculating an appropriate price for the event. The next element to consider is the price of competitive leisure experiences. If a similar leisure experience has a price of £x, the choices are to (1) match and charge price £x, (2) adopt a cost leadership strategy and charge £x minus 25 per cent, or (3) adopt a differentiation strategy and use a price of £x plus 50 per cent and use marketing communications to promote the value of the event.

Three generic pricing strategies can be utilized by event managers. A revenue-oriented strategy seeks to set a price that will maximize revenue from the target market. The NSPCC's Firecracker Ball is an example of a revenue-oriented pricing strategy. An operations-oriented pricing strategy seeks to balance supply and demand by introducing cheaper prices for times of low demand and higher prices at time of higher demand. Agricultural shows are examples of events that use an operations-oriented pricing strategy. Finally, a target market strategy uses different prices for different target markets. For example, a three-day music festival could have one price for those who want to participate for all three days (the fanatic market), a day price for the not so keen, and another price to see a headline act.

Figure 6.8 shows the thought processes necessary to construct a coherent pricing strategy. It also necessary to understand if the event is price elastic or inelastic. If lowering the price can increase demand, the event is price elastic. Alternatively, the demand for some events will not change, regardless of price reductions. These events, which are largely of a specialized nature, are said to be price inelastic. Obviously, it would be very foolish to attempt to increase revenue by lowering the price of an inelastic event. Figure 6.9 summarizes all event pricing issues.

Customer satisfaction of pricing is more than just the money paid. Customer pricing satisfaction also involves convenience, security, credit card acceptance, speed, simplicity and effective use of technology. It is essential that the event manager has a good understanding of the event's fixed and variable costs, competitors' pricing, value of the leisure experience to the customer and pricing elasticities.

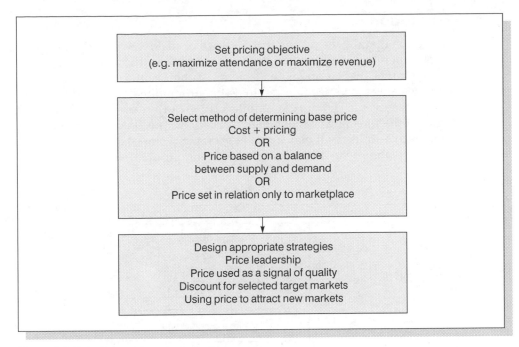

Figure 6.8 Selecting pricing strategies for events

How much should be charged?

- What costs must be covered?
- How sensitive are customers to different prices?
- What are leisure competitors' prices?
- What levels of discounts to selected target markets are appropriate?
- Should psychological pricing (£10.95 instead of £11) be used?

What should be the basis of pricing?

- Should each element be billed separately?
- Should one admission fee be charged?
- Should consumers be charged for resources consumed?
- Should a single price for a bundled package be charged?

Who shall collect payment:

- The event organization, or
- A ticketing intermediary?

Where should payment be made:

- At the event,
- At a ticketing organization, or
- At the customer's home using Internet or telephone?

When should payment be made:

- Then tickets are given out, or
- On the day of the event?

How should payment be made:

- Cash – exact change,
- Credit card,
- EPOS, or
- Token?

Figure 6.9 Pricing issues
Source: adapted from Lovelock, Vandermerwe and Lewis, 1999

Promotion

Promotion literally means to move forward or to advance. In the marketing context, promotion refers to all the communication activities that an event director can use to tell the target market about the benefits of the event and so advance sales. These activities are sometimes referred to as the promotional mix or the communications mix of the event. This mix is an integral part of an event's marketing strategy as Figure 6.10 illustrates. The target market, the positioning of the event and its competitive strategy all play a role in deciding the marketing objectives of an event. Decisions about the make-up of the event product, the pricing strategy to be

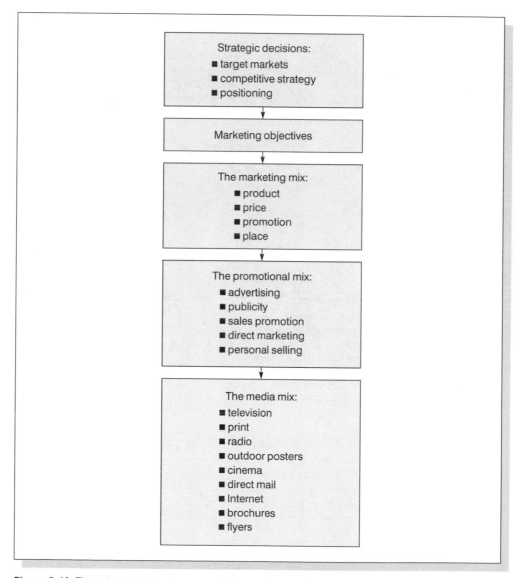

Figure 6.10 The relationship between marketing and promotion strategy
Source: adapted from Morgan, 1996

adopted, how tickets to the event are to reach the target market and by what means are prospective customers to be informed of the event benefits are then made.

Advertising is any form of non-personal promotion paid for by the event organization. Radio, television, newspapers, magazines, the Internet, billboards or mobile platforms such as buses or taxis can be used for advertising. The mainstream media such as television, newspapers and radio can be very expensive to use. The creative process of producing the messages can also be expensive, especially if it is done by an advertising agency.

Publicity includes all those activities not directly paid for that the event uses to communicate with the event's target market. An advantage that event directors have is that people generally enjoy reading about leisure experiences of sport, the arts and entertainment that an event produces. It is therefore somewhat easier to get publicity for an event than for a more mundane activity. However, the event director must be aware that for a story to be used by the media it must be have some news value (i.e. it must be new and of interest to the reader, viewer or listener), be well written and come from a reliable source. It is therefore important that all such publicity has the imprimatur of the event director.

Sales promotion, sometimes called below-the-line promotion by advertising agencies because they do not receive commission on these activities, are those activities that use incentives or discounts to increase sales. Examples of sales promotion are family days at an event where families receive a group discount or a free bottle of fizzy drink when they buy a ticket. Sales promotions have the ability to generate extra sales in particular target market subsegments.

Direct selling is communicating directly with potential customers in the target market group by the use of a mailing list, the telephone or the Internet. An existing event should have collected a list of people who have previously attended the event. These data can be gathered quite simply by, for example, conducting a free raffle that requires attendees to supply their name and address. Other events may also sell their mailing lists. Direct selling may well be the most cost-effective form of promotion for an ongoing event that appeals to a tightly defined target market, which has access to a mailing list.

As Getz (1997, p. 305) points out, the role of the promotional mix is to:

- create or increase awareness of the event
- create or enhance a positive image
- position the event relative to its competition
- inform target markets of pertinent details of the event
- generate demand for the event
- remind target markets of the event's details.

Decisions on promotional strategy must focus on the target market. For example, an event with a large, mass market such as a consumer exhibition (the British International Motor Show, Birmingham, for example) can use television advertising as a promotional device whereas a small community festival's promotional mix is limited to publicity and advertising in the local newspaper. Each of the promotional techniques and their advantages and disadvantages are shown in Table 6.8.

When the appropriate type of promotion and its medium has been chosen, the next step is to decide on the message(s). George and Berry (1981) have some cogent advice on service promotion that has been adapted for event directors:

Promotional type	Medium	Advantages	Disadvantages	Use for
Advertising	Television	Wide reach, conveys excitement and colour, can lend credibility	Expensive to produce and transmit	Large, mass-market events
	Radio	Can be targeted by music tastes, quick to produce, cheaper	Difficult to cut through the clutter of other radio advertisements and programmes	Musical events
	Newspapers	Wide reach, short lead time; local/ regional newspapers tightly target a community	Can be expensive; widely distributed papers may not tightly target the audience	Community festivals
	Magazines or newsletters	Tightly targeted	Long lead times for events	Special interest groups
	Posters/outdoor	Cheap; can be displayed where target market congregates	Can deface buildings, can be ripped down	Youth, community, special interest events
	Flyers	Cheap, effective if well designed, tightly targeted	Need volunteers to distribute	Youth, special interest events
Sales promotion	Price discounts for particular types of customers	Generates revenue	Can dilute revenue if groups not carefully chosen	Large, mass market events
	Cross-promotion with a sponsor	Generates sales for the sponsor, can result in additional sales	Sponsor's image may overtake the event's	Most events
Publicity	Television	Adds credibility; large audience	Must have a televisual angle	All events
	Press	Gives credibility; can be a large or targeted audience	Must be of interest to the general reader	All events
	Speciality magazine or paper	Audience is tightly targeted	Has a long lead time	Special interest events
Direct to target market	Mail, phone or e-mail	Little waste, can be very cost-effective	Results depend on quality of mailing list	Special interest events
	Internet	Cheap to produce as can usually be done by a volunteer; easy to change messages; can be used to sell tickets direct; penetration is increasing	Many people wary of giving credit card information through the Internet	A target market that is technologically advanced

Table 6.8 The advantages and disadvantages of different types of promotion

- advertisements should feature the event's artists and staff, rather than models
- provide tangible clues to counteract the intangible nature of the event by showing physical facilities at the event site
- seek continuity over time by use of recognizable symbols, spokespersons, trademarks or music
- promise what is possible, so as to foster realistic expectations.

Other guidelines worthy of consideration are:

- make the service more tangible and recognizable by using representatives of the target market enjoying the event product to illustrate the benefits of the event
- ensure all promotion is integrated with all other aspects of the marketing mix. Use one consistent image or message so that the target market is not confused.

A question that many event directors find difficult to resolve is the amount to be spent on promotion – the budget. Kotler et al. (1999, pp. 770–2) suggest four methods of deciding the budget that can provide a useful framework for thinking through this question.

1 *Affordable method*: many companies set the budget at the level they think the company can afford. This method tends to ignore the effect of promotion on sales, places advertising low in the list of spending priorities, and leads to uncertainty in annual budgeting which makes long-term planning difficult.

2 *Percentage-of-sales method*: the amount can be decided as a percentage of sales, either based on last year's figures or anticipated sales. Kotler et al. (1999) note that there is little to justify this method, as it wrongly views sales as the cause of promotion rather than the result. What this method can do is to give the event director a comfort zone in which to work. That is, they cannot be criticized because that was the amount spent last year.

3 *Competitive-parity method*: consists of budgeting at least the same if not more that what the competition is spending. Remembering that the competition for an event is all other leisure activities, this may prove very difficult to establish. It is important to have sufficient voice not to get lost in the 'clutter', but matching is certainly not recommended as:
   (a) the leisure market is complex and it is probably impossible to establish what all possible competitors are spending
   (b) it is doubtful if many events have the revenue potential to support such a costly exercise.

4 *Objective-and-task method*: comes from the marketing process of setting marketing objectives, then communication objectives, deciding what tasks are needed to achieve these objectives then estimating the costs of these tasks. For example, a marketing objective of selling 10 000 tickets flows to a communication goal of telling a potential market of 100 000 people of the benefits of the event. The tasks to be decided are creative, the make-up of the promotional mix and the medium (or media) to be used. From this process comes a cost that must be realistic. It would be very foolish to spend £5000 on promotion for an event that has forecast revenue of £7000.

Hospitality, Leisure & Tourism Series

Place

Place refers to both the site where the event takes place (the venue, which has been dealt with earlier) and the place at which consumers can purchase their tickets. For most events, this means deciding on whether to use a ticketing agency. Ticketing agencies widen the distribution network, make it easier for customers to purchase tickets, speed up the entry of customers at the venue, and provide a credit card acceptance service and a telephone booking service. However, they charge both the event organization and the customer. Their use depends on the type of event, any other purchase facility that can be used, the willingness of the target market to pay for a ticketing service and its relative affordability.

However, selling tickets via a ticketing agency, or some other distribution network such as the Internet, does have distinct advantages for the event producer. Ticket sales can be monitored and decisions made regarding the amount of promotion necessary to achieve marketing objectives based on hard information. The security problems inherent in accepting cash at the door are alleviated. As customers pay in advance, the cash flow to the event producer occurs weeks or even months before production, with obvious advantages for the financial health of the event organization.

The use of the Internet (or World Wide Web – WWW) as a distribution medium for events is rapidly gaining in popularity as event directors realize its advantages, which can be summarized as:

- *Speed*: consumers can purchase tickets without leaving their desk of home, without queuing or waiting for a phone operator to become available.
- *Consumer ease*: consumers can view at their leisure the different products of a festival, and select the shows that best suit their pocket and programme, without slowing queues or felling pressured from a box office sales person.
- *Revenue*: ticket revenue comes from the buyer's credit card, which facilitates security and ease of collection.
- *Modernity*: more and more consumers expect services such as events to be available for purchase on the WWW. Without this facility, the event may have an image of being dated.

An interesting example of the use of the WWW for distribution of tickets is the Leeds/Reading Festival (http://www.meanfiddler.com), a multi-show festival. The festival uses on-line ticketing software – Ticketweb.co.uk – to provide an on-line booking system to support their physical box offices, ticket agencies and telephone box office. Consumers have a choice of booking on line, by telephone, or from a box office or retail outlet. However, the booking fee remains even if the consumer chooses the on-line medium, with a fee waiver only if purchased in cash through Gateway Yorkshire in Leeds.

What is of interest is that neither this festival nor any other events found in an extensive search of UK event websites are yet to have their own on-line booking system, which can accept bookings and credit card details electronically without booking fees charged to the consumer. However, due to the rapid escalation of e-commerce and its acceptance by UK consumers, and the ease that a website can be constructed and modified, it seems likely that before too long most major events will have their own on-line booking facility, and perhaps rely on that and venue door sales as their only distribution medium. Research by Firstcalltickets.com (2000) suggests that the on-line ticket market, worth £22.2 million in 1999, will rapidly expand to £400 million by 2005. They claim that this rapid expansion will be due to four key areas:

1 Tickets are a particularly e-friendly compared to other products available on line, which customers wish to touch/view before purchase.
2 The explosion in consumer Internet usage, together with increasing confidence in on-line purchasing.
3 Websites and interactive television box offices transform the ticket-buying process from what can be a mundane and often frustrating task into an entertaining, quick and simple activity.
4 The recent explosion in generic music and sport portals on the Web leading to a rise in demand to buy related tickets on line.

This suggests that on-line ticketing is set to become the preferred ticket distribution channel for events, which could result in reduced overheads and booking fees, and support increasingly focused distribution to the target market.

Marketing research

The need for marketing research in event organizations is based on one simple premise: the lower the quality (or indeed, the complete absence) of data used for marketing decisions, the higher the risk of marketing failure. The data collection is usually organized into a marketing information system that Kotler et al. (1999, p.317) define as 'people, equipment and procedures to gather, sort, analyse, evaluate and

Research category	Uses	Typical marketing use
Market analysis	Marketing planning	Measurement and projections of market volume and target market size
Consumer research	Segmentation and positioning	Quantitative measurement of customer attitudes, profiles and awareness; qualitative assessment of consumer needs and perceptions
Promotion studies	Effectiveness of marketing communication	Measurement of consumer reaction to all types of promotion
Performance evaluation	Control device	Measurement of customer satisfaction with event

Table 6.9 Categories of event marketing research

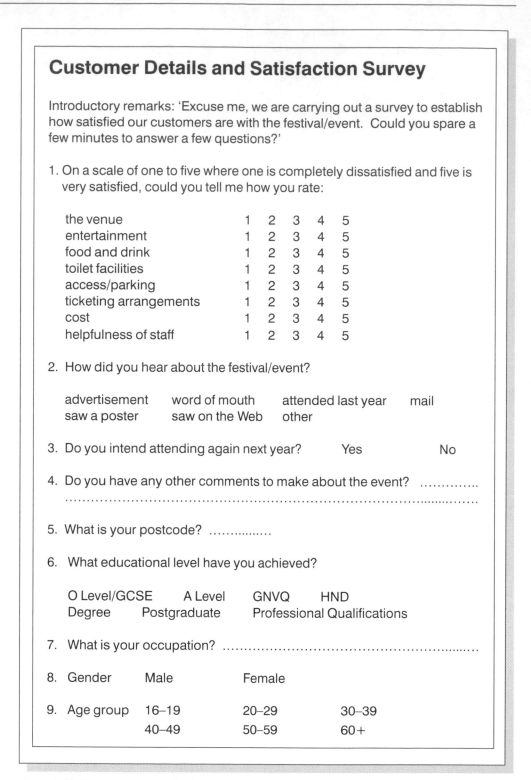

Customer Details and Satisfaction Survey

Introductory remarks: 'Excuse me, we are carrying out a survey to establish how satisfied our customers are with the festival/event. Could you spare a few minutes to answer a few questions?'

1. On a scale of one to five where one is completely dissatisfied and five is very satisfied, could you tell me how you rate:

the venue	1	2	3	4	5
entertainment	1	2	3	4	5
food and drink	1	2	3	4	5
toilet facilities	1	2	3	4	5
access/parking	1	2	3	4	5
ticketing arrangements	1	2	3	4	5
cost	1	2	3	4	5
helpfulness of staff	1	2	3	4	5

2. How did you hear about the festival/event?

advertisement   word of mouth   attended last year   mail
saw a poster   saw on the Web   other

3. Do you intend attending again next year?   Yes   No

4. Do you have any other comments to make about the event? ....
....

5. What is your postcode? ....

6. What educational level have you achieved?

O Level/GCSE   A Level   GNVQ   HND
Degree   Postgraduate   Professional Qualifications

7. What is your occupation? ....

8. Gender   Male   Female

9. Age group   16–19   20–29   30–39
40–49   50–59   60+

Figure 6.11 Sample customer details and satisfaction survey (this survey would be completed by the interviewer)

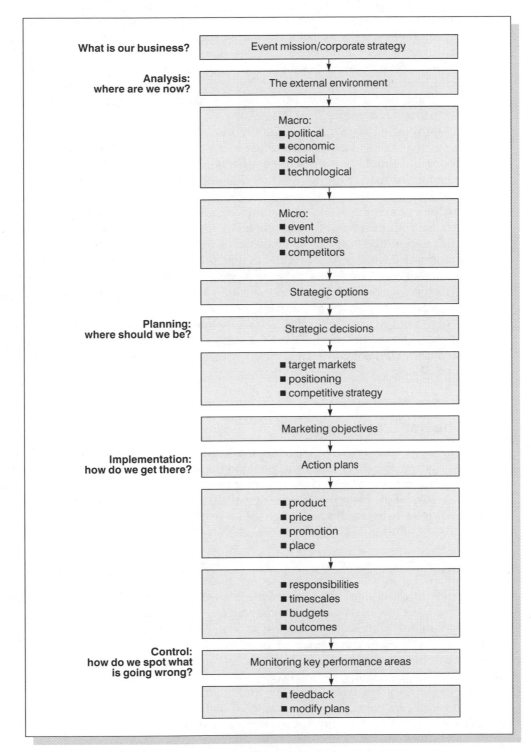

Figure 6.12 Incorporating marketing into the strategic plan
Source: adapted from Morgan, 1996.

distribute needed, timely and accurate information to marketing decision makers'. The type of information required by event managers varies according to the type of event. Table 6.9 shows some useful categories of marketing research. The table, however, looks a little more complex than it really is, as most, if not all, of the information requirements shown can be collected from a simple survey of a random sample of event customers as they leave the event. For those interested in learning more about this topic, an excellent book on research methods is Veal's *Research Methods for Leisure and Tourism* (1997).

Figure 6.11 shows a simple survey instrument that can be used or modified by event managers to collect marketing research data. A randomly selected sample of about 100 should be sufficient to generate useable data that can be processed into meaningful marketing information. Random, in this context, means that all event customers have an equal chance of being selected for the survey. For example, as customers exit the event, every tenth customer is asked to participate, rather than selecting those thought most likely to respond favourably to the request. The information obtained can be analysed using a computer software package such as Statistical Package for the Social Sciences (SPSS), a spreadsheet package such as Microsoft Excel, or simply by using a pocket calculator and a piece of paper. Further guidance on conducting audience/visitor surveys is provided by the Arts Council of England (Arts Council of England, 1999; Verwey, 1999).

One final caveat. Creativity, good judgement and courage to make decisions are important qualities for the event manager. Do not succumb to paralysis through analysis. Marketing research aids competent event management, but does not replace it.

The marketing plan

The next and final step in the marketing planning process is to incorporate marketing objectives and strategies into the strategic plan for the event. Figure 6.12 illustrates this process. The marketing plan is not separate from the strategic plan but part of it. Figure 6.12 also shows that a sound understanding of marketing principles is essential knowledge for an event manager.

Summary

A common misconception held by many in the festival and event area is that marketing means nothing more than advertising. As this chapter has shown, marketing is a structured and coherent way of thinking about managing an event or festival to achieve the objectives of customer satisfaction and either profit or increased awareness of a cause or movement.

The core of the marketing concept is a focus on the customer, in this case the event attendee. This implies that good marketing flows from a complete understanding of the customers – who they are, where they live and what their needs are. This comes from good research and event managers communicating with and observing their customers. From this knowledge come appropriate marketing strategies that can achieve an event's objectives. Given this understanding of the customer and the external environments in which the event operates, appropriate product, price, promotion and distribution strategies can be implemented.

Questions

1 Why should event managers focus on the needs of their customers, rather than the needs of the event organizers?

2 What are the advantages of market segmentation to an event manager?

3 Name five needs that can be satisfied by attending a community festival.

4 What essential ingredients must a publicity campaign contain to be effective?

5 What considerations other than costs must be considered when deciding on price for an event?

6 What factors must be considered when deciding place (distribution) strategies for an event?

7 What happens to the strategic plan once it is written? Why?

8 What are the advantages of conducting consumer research?

9 What elements constitute an effective marketing communication?

10 Why is it important to show representatives of the target market in marketing communication messages?

Case Study

International Confex

Background

Now in its twenty-first year, International Confex – the 'international event for any event' organized by United Business Media – is recognized as Europe's leading annual forum for the meetings, events and corporate hospitality industries and support services. For exhibitors, it is a dedicated forum to showcase brands, products and services. For the visitor, it is more than just a trade show – it is the essential industry forum, where they can meet and network with key decision-makers face to face.

The event

International Confex is split into four industry sectors:

- *UK Venues, Destinations and Incentive Travel*: UK and international visitors planning to organize events within the UK recognize International Confex as the event where they can source the widest range of cities, regions, towns, venues and transport.
- *Overseas Venues, Destinations and Incentive Travel*: UK visitors with overseas budgets and international visitors attend International Confex to source the widest range of countries, cities, regions, towns, venues and transport.
- *Corporate Hospitality and Events*: visitors to International Confex are fully aware of the benefits of hospitality and motivation. They visit the show to source a full range of services such as participation, motivation and activity companies, as well as caterers, sporting venues and events, entertainers, theming and historical venues.

Hospitality, Leisure & Tourism Series

- *Exhibition and Conference Support Services*: International Confex is the leading forum for buyers who source contractual services to help create their meeting or event. These include audiovisual services, stand design and build, staging, lighting, security, production and new technologies such as virtual reality and video conferencing.

In total, main stand holders topped 529 in 2001, with around 1300 companies represented across the four different sectors – filling out the ground floor of Earls Court 1.

For International Confex 2001, training and communications consultancy TradeTalk was appointed to create and manage an integrated education seminar programme. Under the collective title of The Knowledge, a programme of seminar sessions were developed to provide practical 'how to' advice on all aspects of conference, incentive travel, corporate hospitality and events industry. Event Director Andy Lane said: 'People come to the exhibition for information. We plan to create added value by offering them the opportunity to fill in their skills gaps and increase their understanding of their own and related industry sectors.'

Visitor marketing programme

Visitors to International Confex can essentially be broken down into two key groups – specialists and generalists.

- *Specialists*: 38 per cent of visitors to International Confex 2001 indicated that their core job function was an event organizer. These specialist visitors represented blue chip companies, major professional conference organizers, exhibition organizers, agencies and incentive motivation houses.
- *Generalists*: These visitors are responsible for meetings and events as part of a wider job remit. This group encompasses visitors including sales and marketing managers, public relations executives, training and personnel managers, executive PAs and association executives.

International Confex is known as the one show in the meetings and events industry that delivers. To ensure the quantity and quality of visitors at the show, United Business Media undertake a comprehensive marketing campaign. This includes advertising, inserts, direct mail, public relations (PR) and joint exhibitor promotions.

- Advertisements and inserts are placed in leading UK industry trade titles such as *Conference and Incentive Travel*, *Marketing Event*, *Conference and Exhibition Factfinder*, and generalist titles such as *Marketing* and *Marketing Week*, as well as key specialist trade titles across Europe.
- The direct mail campaign occurs about four months before the show. Using United Business Media's extensive databases, appropriate messages are sent to carefully targeted individuals. The direct mail campaign reinforces the advertising campaign to ensure the right messages reach the right people, at the right time.
- PR for the event is achieved through editorial in over sixty worldwide publications. Around twenty industry magazines run previews of the event, detailing who is exhibiting and what they will be promoting at the show.
- Promotional opportunities offered to exhibitors include complimentary visitor tickets and a special VIP (very important person) programme, whereby they can nominate key buyers to the show.

- The International Confex website offers exhibitors the opportunity to promote their company on the Web. Each exhibitor may include up to fifty words free of charge, and has the opportunity to add a hyperlink to their own website, or place a banner advertisement to promote their product.

Evaluation

International Confex is evaluated each year from a variety of perspectives, including extensive on-site visitor evaluation. The statistics from this provide useful information not only for the organizers and exhibitors, but also prove the success of the show for potential exhibitors and visitors. The show itself is ABC audited to ensure that the data produced is authentic, reliable, and verified by an external organization. This confirmed that International Confex 2001 was a highly successful year with a 2 per cent increase in visitor attendance figures on 2000 to 9362.

Visitor surveys are used to evaluate the event overall, and the relative benefits of the four areas covered. In 2001, on-site visitor research showed that:

- 77 per cent of visitors said they would definitely or probably return next year.
- 65 per cent of visitors used the website to pre-register.
- 83 per cent of those visiting the website said they had found it good/excellent for planning their show visit.
- 24 per cent used the show website for information on exhibitions and to look at the floor plan.
- 70 per cent of visitors came to see UK Venues and Destinations.
- 51 per cent of visitors came to see Corporate Hospitality and Events.
- 44 per cent of visitors came to see Overseas Venues and Destinations.
- 53 per cent of visitors were interested in seeing the Exhibition and Conference Support Services sector the show.

In exhibitions, the quantity of visitors is important. However, it is the quality of these visitors that will continue to attract the leading companies to exhibit and as such the evaluation gathers this data. The ABC audit showed that:

- 26 per cent of visitors to International Confex 2001 held budgets of over £500 000 for organizing events.
- 71 per cent of visitors to International Confex 2001 approve or influence approval in the purchasing chain – attracting real buyers to the event.
- 59 per cent of visitors to International Confex 2001 were of managerial level or above.

Finally, from the organizers perspective, one of the ultimate measures of an events success is whether exhibitors book for the following year's event – International Confex 2001 exhibitors valued the show so highly that 65 per cent of them rebooked a stand for International Confex 2002 by the end of the show.

As the 'international event for any event', International Confex is in the spotlight of fellow industry professionals and the industry media. United Business Media use the results of visitor, exhibitor and other sources of evaluation to develop the exhibition on an annual basis to increase the quality and quantity of exhibitors and visitors. It is only through developing and refining the exhibition in the light of evaluation and the external

Hospitality, Leisure & Tourism Series

environment that the International Confex will continue to the leading annual forum for the events industry.

For further details about International Confex, please visit www.international-confex.com.

By Caroline Chan, Event Marketing Manager, United Business Media.

Questions

1 What are the advantages and disadvantages of the marketing campaign used by International Confex?

2 What visitor needs and wants does International Confex fulfil?

3 What alternative distribution strategies could International Confex utilize?

4 The International Confex product includes the opportunity to access an educational seminar programme. What other elements could be included in International Confex to develop the exhibition for the future?

5 Why do you think International Confex is successful in attracting the quality and quantity of visitors? What other strategies could be implemented to ensure that this quality is maintained and developed in the future?

CHAPTER 7

Sponsorship
of events

After studying this chapter, you should be able to:

- define sponsorship in the context of festival and events
- understand why organizations use sponsorship as a promotional medium
- identify appropriate sponsors for an event
- construct an appropriate sponsorship proposal
- plan activities that satisfy a sponsor's needs.

Introduction – what is sponsorship?

To anybody who has not tried to obtain sponsorship, it may seem that it is a simple process of asking a rich, usually transnational, company for money because the company has a philanthropic bent. In return, the company's name is included (usually among many others) in the festival, exhibition or event's marketing communications. However, the process of securing sponsorship is not such a simple undertaking. This chapter outlines a number of strategies that can be used in attempting to secure a sponsor for an event.

Sponsorship is a promotional technique used by businesses, both large and small, for purely commercial reasons. It has nothing to do with philanthropy and is never a donation. It is a commercial transaction that the sponsoring organization uses because it believes that the festival, exhibition or event offers a communication link to its target market that is more effective than, or complementary to, other promotional opportunities such as advertising.

International Events Group (1995, cited in Getz, 1997, p. 216) define sponsorship as 'a cash and/or in-kind fee paid to a property (such as an event) in return for the exploitable commercial potential associated with that property'. Geldard and Sinclair (1996, p. 6), in their comprehensive work on sponsorship, define it as 'the purchase of the, usually intangible, exploitable potential rights and benefits associated with an entrant, event or organisation which results in tangible benefits for the sponsoring company (image/profit enhancement)'.

This definition includes the involvement of government agencies that can sometimes be major sponsors of festivals and events. They are not philanthropists, but are seeking an intangible benefit in return for their sponsorship. These benefits may include:

- enhancing the economic development of a region (e.g. Rugby World Cup 1999)
- enhancement of community's identity (e.g. Millennium Festival)
- increasing social interaction and community development (e.g. Bradford Festival)
- sharing ideas and developing a sense of togetherness (e.g. Science Week)
- developing a community's infrastructure (e.g. the Manchester Commonwealth Games 2002);
- winning popular support for the ruling government.

Companies, on the other hand, usually use the sponsorship of public activities such as festivals and events to:

- generate consumer goodwill towards the company
- generate or increase sales of their products
- increase brand awareness and acceptance
- align a particular brand to a lifestyle
- access niche markets
- provide opportunities for entertainment of clients
- demonstrate product capabilities
- create merchandising opportunities.

Crompton (1994, p. 65) stresses the reciprocal aspect of the sponsorship process. He defines it as 'a reciprocal relationship that involves an organisation and a business

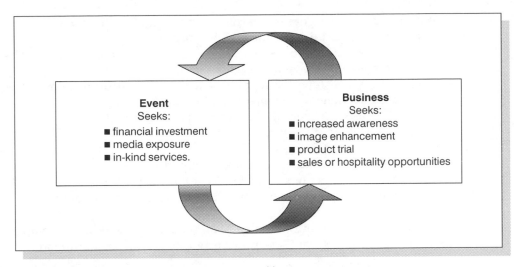

Figure 7.1 Exchange relationship in event sponsorship
Source: Crompton ,1994.

engaging in an exchange which offers commensurate benefits to each entity'. The reciprocity element of sponsorship process is illustrated in Figure 7.1. For the reciprocity element to be effective, sponsorship must benefit both the event committee and the sponsoring company.

Interestingly, the Medici family who ruled Florence from 1434 to 1637 undertook the first recorded instance of sponsorship. Cosimo the Elder (1389–1464) and his grandson, Lorenzo the Magnificent (1448–92), sponsored painters, artists, sculptors and scholars. It is reasonable to assume that they sponsored these artists, many of whom featured in events produced by the family, for much the same reasons that Ernst & Young sponsored the Tate Gallery. That is, the aim of the sponsorship was to generate goodwill towards them from a target audience, to generate awareness and acceptance of their family enterprises, and to entertain their clients with hospitality centred on these artistic endeavours.

Corporate sponsorship of festivals, exhibitions and events

As discussed in Chapter 6, organizations need to communicate to potential customers how their products can satisfy a particular need. Commonly, this is accomplished by advertising in the print or electronic media, by sales promotion, by generating publicity or by personal selling. The sponsoring of festivals, exhibitions and events gives businesses another medium which, if carefully constructed by the festival, exhibition or event organization, can allow businesses to reach a target market in an effective manner that also complements their existing promotional mix. In other words, the sponsorship of the event becomes an integral part of the marketing plan of the business.

In their review of the literature on this topic, Sunshine, Backman and Backman (1995) discovered:

- of the top 200 UK corporate sponsors, the principal benefit they sought was access to specific target audiences followed by corporate image enhancement
- a chain of book stores sponsors college events to engender brand loyalty among new customers who have the potential to be lifelong customers
- another study that reported that the benefits expected from sponsorship were:
  - increased awareness of company and product
  - increased product identification with a particular lifestyle
  - a means of product and market differentiation
  - a means of entertaining key clientele
  - a means of providing merchandising opportunities
  - a means of product or corporate image building
  - an opportunity to represent commitment to a particular community.

According to Geldard and Sinclair (1996), the benefits sought by companies from sponsorship include all of those previously listed, with the addition of:

- exclusivity – the ability to lock a competitor out of an activity
- the opportunity to demonstrate product attributes
- the opportunity to generate sales.

There is no doubt that sponsorship of festivals and events as a promotional medium has increased over recent years. Research into the marketplace by Ipsos RSL illustrates that in the period 1991 to 1998 sponsorship doubled, from £315 to an estimated £640 million (Ipsos RSL, 2000). Crompton (1995) suggests that that the following changes in the operating environment have contributed to that growth:

1 The increase in media outlets (including cable television channels, the Internet, new radio stations and specialist magazines) has made it difficult for product messages to 'cut through the clutter'. One way to be seen by consumers every day is to use sponsorship as a promotional medium.
2 The cost of television advertising increased, while the proliferation of channels has fragmented the viewing audience. The introduction of the remote control, which allows viewers to change channels whenever an advertisement appears, the videotape recorder, which allows viewers to fast-forward commercials in pre-recorded programmes, and the recent introduction of TiVo, which enables the screening out of advertisements from live television, has further reduced the effectiveness of using television as a promotional medium. Some companies therefore see sponsorship as a more cost-effective. However, the consequence of more and more sponsorship of events may be that they too become cluttered to be effective for communication with a target audience.
3 Colour television and the increase in the number of channels caused by the introduction of satellite and cable television has provided many more opportunities for events, especially sports events, to be televised, which consequently has provided more opportunities for the exposure of event sponsors.
4 The banning of direct television advertising can increase sponsorship opportunities. Tobacco companies have provided valuable sponsorship of events because the advertising of tobacco on television was banned. The use of sponsorship enabled their brand image to be reinforced with their target market. This sponsorship by tobacco companies, of course, is now being phased out in the UK.

In 1997 the Labour government made an election pledge to ban all tobacco advertising and promotion, and implemented the ban from December 1999. However, following a legal challenge in the European Court of Justice, this was overturned in October 2000. The government has at the time of writing proposed the Tobacco Advertising and Promotion Bill, which will ban tobacco sponsorship for most events from 30 July 2003. A number of international events, including snooker and Formula One, will have an extension until 1 October 2006, due to the strong reliance that these events have had on sponsorship from tobacco companies (Conway, 2000). Alcohol products can still be advertised on UK television, though for how long is a matter for conjecture if the example of the USA is followed in the UK. Liquor companies seek to access the youth market as the next generation of consumers, therefore they are frequent sponsors of music and sports events.

5 Sport has become increasingly commercialized, which has become accepted as vital to a sport's well-being. It common to see a sporting team run onto a sporting arena with their uniforms, the fence and the ground itself emblazoned with sponsors' names. The acceptance of this seems to have reached all levels of sport, with even the most amateur of events being sponsored. The enormous success of sponsorship activity associated with the 1984 Los Angeles Olympic Games showed companies how effective corporate sponsorship could be. This exercise gave the companies concerned an enormous amount of media coverage and the Games were a financial success. This sort of sponsorship has been a feature of all Olympic Games since then. However, unlike other major sporting events, the playing fields of the Olympic Games are a sponsor's banner-free zone.

6 Sponsorship has also become an effective medium to use to communicate with discrete market segments. Until the 1970s, market segmentation was not widespread and companies moved their products by mass-marketing techniques. With the advent of the concept of market segmentation, companies needed media through which they could communicate with these target markets. As sports, music, or arts fans are spread across the full range of demographics, festivals, exhibitions or events offer an effective medium for this communication. As Sleight (1989, p. 42) notes 'sponsorship works because it fulfils the most important criterion of a communications medium – it allows a particular audience to be targeted with a particular set of messages'.

7 The increase in the number of products and services on the market has been accompanied by a drop in the number of companies by merger and takeover. This has increased the need for producers to enhance their relationships with the retailers of their products. Sponsorship offers innovative and interesting ways to offer entertainment and hospitality to these retailers.

8 Many councils and government services have adopted a user-pays policy. This means the cost of staging festivals has increased as the event organizers have to pay for services such as police security, waste disposal, ambulance protection and rental of the council-owned venue. These extra costs have forced festival and event producers to seek sponsorship to cover these increased costs.

It is difficult not to agree with this diagnosis of Crompton (1995). Since sponsorship has become more attractive to potential sponsors, provided the festival or event manager is careful in selecting an appropriate sponsor(s) and is methodical and creative in constructing the sponsorship package of benefits, mutually satisfying rewards for all parties can result.

Deciding on the appropriate sponsorship for an event

Geldard and Sinclair (1996) warn that sponsorship is not for all events. First, obtaining sponsorship is both time-consuming and can be damaging to the ego when the inevitable refusals occur. Sponsorship is a commercial contract in which the event promises to deliver certain benefits and rights to the sponsor in return for cash or goods and services in kind, which is known as in-kind sponsorship or contra. To ensure these benefits are given to the sponsor requires event management time, planning and effort. It is not a process to be entered into lightly.

If an event cannot offer a sponsor appropriate benefits, then a donation to the event may be appropriate. A donation is a gift with no obligation for benefits to be given in return. In other words, it is philanthropy, which is not sponsorship.

Geldard and Sinclair (1996) propose a checklist to establish if an event is suitable for sponsorship, illustrated in Figure 7.2.

Is the event suitable for sponsorship?

- Does the event have some benefits that can be offered to a potential sponsor?
- Does the target audience approve of commercial sponsorship?
- Are any companies not suitable for sponsoring the event (e.g. tobacco or alcohol companies should not be asked to sponsor events for teenagers)?
- Does the event organization have people with the expertise and time to construct and produce sponsorship packages?
- Does the event have a policy on sponsorship?

Figure 7.2 Checklist to establish if an event is suitable for sponsorship
Source: Geldard and Sinclair, 1996.

A sponsorship policy sets out what the event organization can and cannot do in terms of attracting and delivering sponsorship benefits. The policy would give details of:

- the event's objectives for seeking sponsorship
- the rules for entering into sponsorship
- the level at which accountability and responsibility for sponsorship lay
- what types of sponsors are unsuitable for the event
- how the sponsorship plan is constructed
- how the value of contra/in-kind goods and services is established (usually at the retail price the event would have to pay if they are not sponsored)
- how the benefits gained from a sponsorship are to be valued
- who is the approving authority for sponsorship (e.g. the marketing manager or the event director or the board of directors).

Identifying appropriate sponsorship

As the decision to sponsor an event is usually made because it is part of a corporate marketing strategy, Sunshine, Backman and Backman (1995) suggest that

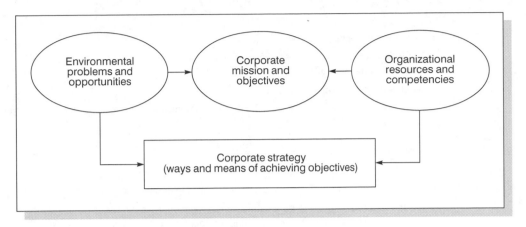

Figure 7.3 Corporate strategy flow chart
Source: Sunshine, Backman and Backman, 1995.

the first step in successfully obtaining an appropriate sponsor is to understand the factors that influence the decision-making process. These factors are illustrated in Figure 7.3.

To fully understand how a company develops marketing strategies, the event manager can undertake research into the company and the environments in which it operates. A reading of the annual report reveals its mission and, generally, the objectives that flow from this statement. The annual report also may reveal the perceived competencies of the company and the resources available to it to achieve its objectives. Event managers must always monitor the business, social, cultural, political and economic environments in which they and businesses operate. This monitoring enables the astute event manager to identify changes in the operating environments of companies that can make a sponsorship effective for them. For example, a manager of a community festival in Leeds may notice the chairperson of a financial services company announcing to the financial press a decision to build a new call centre in the area and how the company is looking forward to building links with the community. A carefully constructed sponsorship proposal stressing the effectiveness of the community festival as a communication medium to the residents of Leeds would have a good chance of success.

Another way to identify potential sponsors is to examine the sponsorship proposal from the sponsor's perspective. Crompton (1993) proposes a memorable acronym of CEDAR EEE that summarizes the screening process that businesses use when evaluating sponsorship proposals. The acronym is derived from:

Customer audience
Exposure potential
Distribution channel audience
Advantage over competitors
Resource investment involvement required
Event's characteristics
Event organization's reputation
Entertainment and hospitality opportunities.

Hospitality, Leisure & Tourism Series

1 Customer audience

Is the demographic, attitude and lifestyle profile of the target audience congruent with the product's target market?

What is the on-site audience?

Is sponsorship of this event the best way to communicate about the product to this target audience?

2 Exposure potential

What is the inherent news value of the event?

What extended print and broadcast coverage of the sponsorship is likely?

Will the extended coverage be local, regional or national? Is the geographical scope of this media audience consistent with the product's sales area?

Can the event be tied to into other media advertising?

Can the company's products be sold at the event?

What is the life of the event?

Are banners and signage included in the sponsorship? How many and what size? Will they be visible during television broadcasts?

Will the product's name and logo be identified on promotional material for the activity?

- Event posters – how many?
- Press releases – how many?
- Point-of-sale displays – how many?
- Television advertisements – how many and on what station(s)?
- Radio advertisements – how many and on what stations(s)?
- Print advertisements – how many and on what stations(s)?
- Internet advertisements (on the event website, banner advertisements) – how many and on what site(s)?

Where will the product name appear in the event programme? Front or back cover? Number and site of programme advertisements? How many programmes?

Will the product's name be mentioned on the public address system? How many times?

Can the sponsor have display booths? Where will they be located? Will they be visible during television broadcasts?

3 Distribution channel audience

Are the sponsorship's advantages apparent to wholesalers, retailers or franchises? Will they participate in promotions associated with the sponsorship?

4 Advantages over competitors

Is the event unique or otherwise distinctive?

Has the event previously had sponsors? If so, how successful has it been in delivering the desired benefits to them? Is it strongly associated with other sponsors? Will clutter be a problem?

Does the event need co-sponsors? Are other sponsors of the event compatible with the company's product? Does the company want to be associated with them? Will the product stand out and be recognized among them?

Figure 7.4 Screening criteria used by businesses to determine sponsorship opportunities
Source: adapted from Crompton, 1993.

If there is co-sponsorship, will the product have category and advertising exclusivity?
Will competitors have access to signage, hospitality or event advertising? Will competition be allowed to sell product on site?

If the company does not sponsor it, will the competitor? Is that a concern?

5 Resource investment involvement required

How much is the total sponsorship cost, including such items as related promotional investment, staff time and administrative and implementation effort?

Will the sponsorship investment be unwieldy and difficult to manage?

What are the levels of barter, in-kind and cash investment?

Does the event guarantee a minimum level of benefits to the company?

6 Event's characteristics

What is the perceived stature of the event? Is it the best of its kind? Will involvement with it enhance the product's image?

Does it have a 'clean' image? Is there any chance that it will be controversial?

Does it have continuity or is it a one-off?

7 Event organization's reputation

Does the organization have a proven track record in staging this or other events? Does it have the expertise to help the product achieve its sponsorship goals?

Does the organization have a reputation and an image with which the company desires to be associated?

Does it have a history of honouring its obligations?
Has the company worked with this organization before? Was it a positive experience?

Does it have undisputed control and authority over the activities it sanctions?

How close to its forecasts has the organization been in delivering benefits to its sponsors?

How responsive is the organization's staff to sponsors' requests? Are they readily accessible?

Is there insurance and what are the company's potential liabilities?

8 Entertainment and hospitality opportunities

Are there opportunities for direct sales of product and related merchandise, or for inducing product trial?

Will celebrities be available to serve as spokespeople for the product? Will they make personal appearances on its behalf at the event, in other markets, or in the media? At what cost?

Are tickets to the event included in the sponsorship? How many? Which sessions? Where are the seats located?

Will there be access to VIP hospitality areas for the company's guests? How many will be authorized? Will celebrities appear?

Will there be clinics, parties, or playing opportunities at which the company's guests will be able to interact with the celebrities?

Figure 7.4 *continued*

These criteria are expanded in Figure 7.4. The task for event managers is to analyse their event using these criteria and then find companies whose marketing needs could be satisfied by the benefits offered by their event.

Obviously, not all criteria outlined are used by all companies all the time when assessing sponsorship proposals. A company may seek a different range of outcomes or benefits from a sponsorship arrangement. Crompton (1993) stresses that companies usually establish measurable objectives for their sponsorship investments. This suggests that it is in the event's best interests to work with the sponsoring company to establish some sort of measurable objective for their sponsorship of the event.

When sponsorship of festivals, exhibitions and events was in its infancy, many decisions regarding sponsorship reflected the personal interests of senior management. This decision base is now almost obsolete. Event managers must find companies that have promotional needs that sponsorship can satisfy, understand the sponsorship decision-making process, construct sponsorship proposals that answer questions raised in that process, and act to ensure what is promised is delivered to the sponsors.

Constructing an effective sponsorship proposal

Once organizations that have marketing links to the target market are identified, the next step is to construct a sponsorship package that can satisfy both the organizations' communication needs and the objectives of the event. These benefits are usually a combination of the following elements and are dependent on the type of event:

- *A promotional medium*: sponsorship is a more efficient means of effectively communicating with a targeted audience (i.e. more target market receivers of the messages at lower cost per impact) than other media. Techniques used include naming rights, where the event is given the name of the sponsor's product (e.g. the Martell Grand National or the Weetabix Women's British Open), advertisements on banners or posters at the venue, advertisements in a programme or on the event website, or a logo shown on all material produced for the event, such as tickets, entry forms, eating and drinking utensils, signs, displays, floats, merchandise or the venue itself.
- *Publicity*: sponsorship provides an opportunity to be associated with an event that is viewed favourably by the target audience. The sponsor's involvement in the event needs then to be mentioned in various media read, listened to or watched by the target audience.
- *Networking*: sponsorship provides opportunities for the sponsor's management and staff to meet people important to their business. These people can either be potential clients, suppliers of product to their business, regulatory authorities or opinion formers.
- *Product sales or demonstration*: sponsorship provides opportunities for product sales or product demonstrations to a target market.
- *Entertainment facilities*: sponsorship provides opportunities for the sponsor to entertain their clients. The sponsorship package needs to be constructed so that it allows the sponsor to offer preferential seating, quality food and beverages, preferential parking and access to unusual or sought after entertainment to its

clients or potential clients. The package can also include introduction to celebrities involved in the event.

- *Access to event by sponsor's staff*: sponsorship can improve staff morale and provide wider awareness of the sponsorship when staff can access to the event at a reduced price. Such a benefit is likely to help maintain good relationships between the event and the sponsor, thereby increasing chances of the sponsorship being continued.
- *Price*: The cost of the sponsorship should be no more than the cost of using another promotional medium. For example, if the cost to reach a similar target market using television is £155,000, a company may view a sponsorship price of £100,000 as an attractive proposition.

Establishing the range of benefits to offer the sponsor can only come from research into each sponsor's needs, and then customizing a package of benefits at a competitive price that will satisfy the needs of that potential sponsor by using all the communication and entertainment benefits the event offers.

Contacting potential sponsors

Fairly casual research (an observant eye and informal questioning) will provide a list of providers of goods and services designed to satisfy the needs of the target market for the festival, event, exhibition or conference. The next step in the sponsorship process is to select appropriate sponsors from this list for the event and conduct in-depth research on their marketing strategies. For example, if the organization uses television advertising to promote its products, can the event complement this advertising programme in some way? Is the organization currently sponsoring an event? If so, is that event complementary or competitive to this event? Does the organization have published guidelines for organizations approaching them for sponsorship? For example, many larger organizations may commit only to certain types of event, or may be tied to particular causes (e.g. charities). They may also allocate their sponsorship budget on an annual basis through the planning cycle, requiring at least six months' notice, therefore proposals arriving after this time would not be considered.

The next step is to contact potential sponsor organization to establish:

- the name and address of the person to whom the proposal should be addressed
- how the event can complement the organization's current marketing communication strategies
- any special needs the organization may have.

Once this is done, a customized formal written proposal can be sent to the decision-maker incorporating all the potential sponsor's special requirements. After a decent interval (about five days), this can be followed up by a telephone call requesting a meeting to present the proposal in person. If, after the meeting, the potential sponsor declines the opportunity to sponsor the event, select another potential sponsor from the list and carry out the steps again.

Once a sponsor has been found for the event, a sponsorship business plan outlining both parties' responsibilities should be drawn up.

Constructing a sponsorship business plan

The first steps to ensuring sponsor's expectations are met is to construct a sponsorship business plan. Geldard and Sinclair (1996) state that once an agreement has been reached with the sponsor(s), a sponsorship business plan should be constructed that includes:

- a quantifiable outcome for the sponsorship package
- corporate or brand image objectives, if applicable
- a time line (or Gantt chart) that details all the activities that need to take place and the time of their implementation
- a forecast the sponsorship programme's costs
- details of the human resource costs needed to carry out the programme.

A sponsorship business plan will generally consist of these components:

- *Introduction*: this puts the plan into context by describing the history, mission and objectives of the event and the role of the sponsor(s) in the event. It names the sponsor(s), their needs and expected outcomes.
- *Background*: this section details the social, cultural economic and political environment in which the event is to operate, the business and competitive environment of the sponsors, their involvement in the event and the length of the sponsorship contract. It also includes details of the target market for the event.
- *Objectives*: this section details the desired outcomes of the sponsorship expressed in specific, measurable, achievable, relevant and time-specific terms. It is helpful to include the reasons why these objectives have been chosen.
- *Target audiences*: this section lists all those organizationally affected by the plan (both in the event's and the sponsor's organization), the event's target market, the event's stakeholders, television audience (if applicable), etc.
- *Action list/time line/accountability*: shown here are all activities that need to be completed to achieve the sponsorship objectives, the deadline for completion of these activities, and who is responsible for completion.
- *Budget*: all sponsorship activities incur costs, including human resource costs, to the event organization. In this section all anticipated costs by cost centre (e.g. prize money, communication costs, promotional costs to support the sponsorship, staff hours spent on sponsorship matters, signage manufacture, professional fees, promotional material, sponsor entertainment) and the revenue from the sponsorship (either cash or in-kind) should be listed. This then shows the income from the sponsorship and the costs incurred in supporting it. Figure 7.5 provides a checklist of items to be included in a sponsorship budget. (See Chapter 8 for more information on budgets). All the details, except perhaps the profit element of the budget, should be given to the sponsor to show the event's managerial competencies.
- *Evaluation*: shown in this section are the key performance areas (KPAs) by which the success or otherwise of the sponsorship is to be measured. Obviously, this has to be written in a form that is measurable.

The construction of the sponsorship business plan is a creative and rewarding task that is essential if sponsor's objectives are to be met. It shows the sponsor that the

---

Items that will incur cash outlays or person hours to support the sponsorship

Cost £

Event programmes

Additional printing

Signage production

Signage erection

Support advertising

Hospitality – food and beverage

Telephone, Internet and fax

Public relations support

Tickets for sponsors

VIP parking passes

Cost of selling sponsorship (staff time at £ _____ per hour)

Cost of servicing sponsorship (staff time at £ _____ per hour)

Legal costs

Travel costs

Taxis and other transport

Evaluation research

Media monitoring

Total costs

Profit margin (must be at least 100%)

Minimum sponsorship sale price

Figure 7.5 A checklist of items to be included in a sponsorship budget

organization is managerially competent and engenders confidence in the event's ability to achieve mutually rewarding outcomes. It requires a good understanding of marketing concepts and principles, the corporate and marketing needs of the sponsor, and creativity to produce innovative and exciting ways for the sponsor to get its message to your target market.

Servicing of the sponsor's needs

Before proceeding to discuss how to appropriately service sponsors, it is appropriate to reinforce the mutual obligations of the event and its sponsor. Geldard and Sinclair (1996) list these as follows:

- The event's obligations to the sponsor
  - to deliver all the benefits promised and outlined in the contract without constant prodding from the sponsor
  - to be genuinely committed to positive sponsorship outcomes for all stakeholders
  - to protect the rights of the sponsor

- to acknowledge the sponsor at every appropriate opportunity
- to provide innovative programmes to assist the sponsor meet their objectives
- to ensure all members of the event organization are aware of the event's obligations to the sponsor and enthusiastic about them being met
- to keep the sponsor fully informed on all relevant matters occurring in the event organization
- to warn the sponsor in advance of potential unpleasant publicity.
- The sponsor's obligations to the event
  - to provide the cash payment or in-kind goods and services agreed to in a timely manner
  - to be genuinely committed to the sponsorship
  - to promote the interests of the sponsorship whenever possible
  - to commit sufficient promotional funds to ensure the sponsorship is a success.

In order to ensure that the event does satisfy the sponsor's marketing needs listed in the sponsorship agreement, it is essential that the event organization services (i.e. looks after) the sponsor. This can include everything from maintaining harmonious relationships between the sponsor's staff and the staff of the event organization, to ensuring sponsor's signage is kept in pristine condition. The following is a list of activities, adapted from Geldard and Sinclair (1996), which will help to exceed the sponsor's expectations, thereby improving future sponsorship relationships.

- *One contact*: one person from the event organization needs to be appointed as the contact point for the sponsor. That person must be readily available (a mobile phone helps), have the authority to make decisions regarding the event and be able to forge harmonious relationships with the sponsor's staff.
- *Understand the sponsor*: a method of maintaining harmonious relationships is to get to know the sponsor's organization, staff, products and marketing strategies. By doing this, it becomes easier to understand all the needs of the sponsor and thus easier to satisfy these needs.
- *Motivate event organization's members about the sponsorship*: keeping members informed of the sponsorship contract, the objectives of the sponsorship and how the sponsor's needs are to be satisfied, will help ensure that the sponsorship will work smoothly to the benefit of both parties. However, if members are not wholly supportive of the sponsorship and the actions necessary to fulfil the needs of the sponsor, the sponsorship can founder very quickly. For example, if members fail to wear the uniform, which bears the logo of the sponsor while being televised, the sponsor has every right to be annoyed.
- *Use of celebrities associated with the event*: if the event includes the use of artistic, sporting, or theatrical celebrities, ensuring the sponsors have an opportunity to meet them in a social setting. Most people enjoy immensely the opportunity to tell anecdotes about their brush with the famous!
- *Acknowledge the sponsor at every opportunity*: the use of all the available media to acknowledge the sponsor's assistance is not only courteous, but probably part of the sponsorship contract. Media that can be used include the public address system, newsletters, media releases, the annual report and staff briefings.
- *Sponsorship launch*: have a sponsorship launch to tell the target market that brand X is to sponsor the event. The style of the launch depends on the type of sponsorship and the creativity of the event director.

- *Media monitoring*: monitor the media for all stories about the event and provide copies to the sponsor. This shows the sponsor that the event takes an interest in the sponsorship and is alert to the benefits the sponsor is receiving.
- *Principal sponsor*: if the event is such that it has many sponsors, ensure that the logo of the principal sponsor (i.e. the sponsor who has paid the most) is seen on everything that the event does. This includes stationery, uniforms, flags, newsletters, stages, etc.
- *Naming rights*: if the event has given naming rights to a sponsor, it has an obligation to ensure that these rights are used in all communications emanating from the event organization. This includes making every endeavour to ensure that the media are aware of and adhere to the name of the event. This sometimes is difficult, but must be attempted.

Stage	Characteristic
Research	Market research and environmental monitoring to identify suitable companies for event sponsoring.
Preparation	Preparation of sponsorship proposal that includes:
	Details of event, including its target markets
	Identification of benefits for the sponsor and their value
	Cash or in-kind products/services requested for the sponsorship
	Responsibilities of each partner in the sponsorship.
Consideration	Stages of consideration by potential sponsors are: Initial contact with event organization by telephone
	Informal discussions between event organization and marketing personnel of potential sponsor
	Formal presentation to potential sponsors's decision maker(s).
Decision	If no, try the next company on the list. If yes, proceed to the next stage.
Agreement	Contract between sponsor and event organization detailing responsibilities of both parties.
Implementation	Carry out activities prescribed in the contract.
Evaluation and feedback	Feedback to sponsor detailing performance of agreed key result areas.

Source: adapted from Hall, 1997.

Table 7.1 Stages in the corporate sponsorship process

Hospitality, Leisure & Tourism Series

- *Professionalism*: even though volunteers manage many events, this does not mean that staff can act like amateurs. Sponsors expect to be treated efficiently and effectively, with their reasonable demands met in a speedy manner. Sponsorship is a partnership. Loyalty to that partnership will be repaid.
- *Undersell and overdeliver*: do not promise what cannot be delivered. Be cautious in the proposal and then ensure that the expectations raised by the cautious proposal are at a minimum met, but probably exceeded.

Summary

The importance of securing sponsorship for an event presents a range of benefits both for the event management and the sponsoring company. In order to attract the most appropriate sponsors to an event, an event committee must research thoroughly those companies and their products that it feels would be most likely to benefit from sponsoring the event. The committee must also prepare a proposal outlining to the sponsor(s) the objectives of the event and the perceived sponsor benefits, and ensure that the working relationship is productive and honours the contract between the two parties. The components of the sponsorship process have been summarized in Table 7.1.

Questions

1 Define sponsorship from the perspective of an event organizer and the marketing manager of a fast-moving consumer goods firm.

2 Define philanthropy and explain why it is not sponsorship.

3 Why do governments sponsor events?

4 Name an event for which sponsorship may be inappropriate and list the reasons for this.

5 What does monitoring the social/cultural/political/technological environments in the context of event sponsorship mean? Name an example of this process

6 Construct a CEDAR EEE analysis for an event with which you are familiar.

7 Construct a sponsorship proposal for an event known to you.

8 Construct a sponsorship budget for the sponsorship of an event known to you.

9 List the key result areas for the sponsorship of the event you used for the previous question.

10 Give details of how you would brief the event's contact person for the event you used in question 8.

Cheltenham Arts Festivals

Background

Cheltenham Arts Festivals Limited (CAF) is responsible for the organization and promotion of three annual arts festivals: the Cheltenham International Jazz Festival (May), the Cheltenham International Festival of Music (July) and the Cheltenham Festival of Literature (October).

The Cheltenham International Jazz Festival is the newcomer among the festivals – since starting in 1996 the festival now attracts an audience of over 10 000. A five-day event, the festival hosts an array of popular international jazz stars alongside the best new and more adventurous artists.

The Cheltenham International Festival of Music is the longest running of the festivals and was also the first of the post-war festivals in the UK. Beginning in 1945 as a showcase for British contemporary music, in recent times Michael Berkeley (Artistic Director) has expanded the festival's repertoire to include contemporary music from across Europe. In addition to presenting orchestral, chamber, choral and solo music alongside contemporary music-theatre and opera, the seventeen-day festival boasts an afternoon series, which features the very best in young and local musical talent, as well as a late-night strand of programming, commencing at ten in the evening.

The Cheltenham Festival of Literature began in 1949 when Gloucestershire writer John Moore organized a gathering of writers to celebrate the written word in Cheltenham. Over the last decade the festival has grown rapidly, with annual ticket sales now exceeding 45 000. At the heart of the festival is the love of literature and the art of the book, with additional strands including *Book It!*, the Children's Festival, *CyberFest*, the virtual on-line Festival, and *Voices Off*, which takes poets, performers, singers and storytellers out to venues all over Cheltenham. The established ten-day Autumn Festival is complemented by a three-day Spring Events Weekend in April.

All three festivals run Education and Outreach Programmes, and there is a related Music Festival Fringe programme.

The CAF is a registered charity, with an annual turnover of £1 million. It aims:

- to promote arts festivals both for residents of Gloucestershire and for the attraction of visitors
- to commission artistic events of the highest quality for the sake of developing the art itself
- to encourage a lively artistic environment within the area of Gloucestershire, acting as both a regional and national model
- to develop audiences for arts events in general, ensuring that our events are accessible to ever wider audiences
- to programme and promote events in such a way as to offer existing audiences a greater understanding and appreciation of the arts
- to fulfil a positive role as a resource for the education sector and for lifelong learning throughout the county.

The CAF has a board of directors and a finance committee, with each festival having its own organization team, whom the Sponsorship and Development Department and the Education Department support. There are around fifteen full-time members of staff working for the festivals. The Press and Publicity Department, Box Office team and other support from Cheltenham Borough Council staff, seasonal help and volunteers supplement their efforts. Each festival also has its own committee, which includes experts from different areas of the relevant art form (for example, education, broadcasting, and publishing).

Sponsorship

The festivals seek funding for events, concerts and projects within the Education and Outreach Programmes from a wide range of sources including public funding bodies, commercial organizations, foundations and trusts. Income from sponsorship accounts for approximately 25 per cent of the turnover of the Jazz Festival, 37 per cent for the Music Festival and 32 per cent of the turnover of the Literature Festival.

The Sponsorship Department comprises a Sponsorship and Development Manager, a Sponsorship Co-ordinator and a Sponsorship Assistant.

A sponsorship launch is held in advance of each festival with the purpose of releasing programme information to potential sponsors and supporters. A sponsorship pack is collated for the launch, containing an overview of the festival themes, an outline of the benefits to be gained through sponsorship and full details of all events, print sponsorship opportunities and Education and Outreach projects available. Packs are also distributed to those unable to attend the launch.

The CAF also produces a corporate sponsorship brochure, intended for distribution to potential new, and predominantly national, commercial sponsors, and a quarterly newsletter which contains news and information about the festivals with particular emphasis on sponsorship and the benefits it brings. This newsletter is targeted mainly at a local and regional audience in the business sector.

The main print vehicle for sponsor accreditation for each festival is the festival brochure, 100 000 of which are distributed locally, regionally and nationally. Accreditation is by way of name/logo associated with the particular event being supported. Sponsors are also accredited in the Music Festival Souvenir Programme, in which they are able to advertise and include their corporate statements.

Other sponsorship benefits offered to commercial sponsors include:

- complimentary and discounted tickets
- opportunities for displays and distribution of promotional material to event audiences
- inclusion in a press release listing all sponsors and supporters of the festival
- accreditation on a permanent board displayed at festival venues
- the co-ordination of corporate hospitality arrangements
- exclusive invitations to meet event participants
- an Internet link from www.cheltenhamfestivals.co.uk to the sponsor's website.

The CAF also runs a patrons' scheme, through which individuals donate an annual sum towards all the festivals. The benefits of patronage include:

- a dedicated ticket booking line
- support of festival events and education projects
- invitations to festival launches
- talks and other special events
- an annual patrons' lunch
- accreditation in festival publicity, if desired.

Many of the Cheltenham Arts Festivals Ltd's patrons also become individual sponsors of festival events.

For more details about the Cheltenham Arts Festivals, please visit www.cheltenhamfestivals.co.uk

By Caroline McKinnes, Sponsorship and Development Manager, Cheltenham Arts Festivals, Town Hall, Imperial Square, Cheltenham, GL50 2JT.

Questions

1 Focusing on one of the festivals, describe the target market in demographic and socioeconomic terms.

2 What factors would a potential sponsor look for when considering whether to sponsor the festivals?

3 How would you break down the festival in order to maximize income from sponsorship for the festival, and the benefits gained by the sponsor?

4 Based on what you have read within the case study, and your identified target markets, what companies would find sponsorship of the festivals a worthwhile investment of their marketing resources? Briefly explain the appropriateness of each sponsor to the festival.

5 Construct a sponsorship pack for the sponsorship launch.

6 Design a corporate sponsorship brochure.

7 In addition to sponsorship, CAF also runs a patrons' scheme. Besides the financial income, what other benefits can be gained for the festivals from running such a scheme?

Control and budgeting

After studying this chapter, you should be able to:

- understand the use of control by management

- identify the control systems used in events and festivals

- analyse the factors that create successful control mechanisms

- identify the key elements of budgetary control and explain the relationship between them

- understand the advantages and shortcomings of using a budget.

Introduction – what is control?

Control consists of making sure that what happens in an organization is what is supposed to happen. The control of an event can range from the event manager simply walking the site and discussing daily progress with staff, to implementing and monitoring a detailed plan of responsibilities, reports and budgets. The word 'control' comes from the Latin *contrarotulare*, meaning 'against the roll': in ancient Rome it meant comparing something to the official records, which were kept on paper cylinders or rolls. In modern times, the word has retained some of this meaning, and the control of any business involves comparing the progress of all key functions against a management plan to ensure that projected outcomes are met.

Event planning can be effective only if the execution of the plan is carefully controlled. To do this, it is necessary to develop proper control mechanisms. These are methods which are designed to keep a project on course and return the project to the plan if it wanders. Control affects every element of the management of events including logistics, human resources and administration, and its basic nature remains the same in every area.

Slack, Chambers and Johnston (2001, p. 306) define control as 'the driving through of the plan, monitoring what actually happens and making changes as necessary'. It is the process of coping with changes that affect plans. Control may mean a plan is revised or it may require intervention in the project to bring it back on track. These activities depend on an effective communication system.

This chapter explores control in the contest of events. It will demonstrate that the choice of workable control mechanisms is central to the success of an event, and discuss budgets, which are the main control system used in events.

Elements and categories of control

The process of control involves establishing standards of performance and ensuring that they are realized. This can be a complex process, but consists of three main steps:

- *Establishing standards of performance*: this can come from several sources, including standard practices within the event management industry, guidelines supplied by the board of management of the event, specific requirements of the client and sponsors, and audience or guest expectations. Standards must be measurable.
- *Identifying deviations from standards of performance*: this is done by measuring current performance and comparing it with the established standards. Since the event budget is expressed in measurable terms, it provides an important method of highlighting areas that are straying from the plan and which require attention.
- *Correcting deviations*: any performance that does not meet the established standards must be corrected. This can entail the use of many types of problem-solving strategies, including renegotiating contracts and delegating.

These three steps are also called the control cycle (Burke, 1999) and are central to the successful delivery of an event. Such a cycle would be applied with varying frequency, depending on the size and complexity of the event itself.

Generally, events are characterized by two types of controls – operational and organizational. Operational controls are used for the day-to-day running of the event. Organizational controls relate to the overall objectives of the event organization, for example whether the event is profitable and satisfies the client's brief. Hicks and Gullet (1976) suggest a further category of controls according to when the controls are applied:

- *Predictive control* tries to anticipate and identify problems before they occur. Predicting cash flows for an event is an important area because expenses are not concurrent with income. For example, venue hire is usually paid for in advance of the event. Similarly, for an event with a small budget, briefing a lawyer is another example of predictive control. Some companies, for instance, may be less likely to pay promised fees to a small company than they would to a larger, more powerful company. Also, the organizers of a small one-off event are not in a position to threaten a defaulting company with withdrawal of further work opportunities. In these, and similar situations, a swift letter from a solicitor who has been briefed beforehand can often hasten payment. Another term for predictive controls is 'feedforward'.
- *Concurrent control* measures deviation from the standards as they occur. The event manager's informal question of 'How's it going?' falls into this category. For example, the monitoring of food stalls during an event is essential to ensure that food safety regulations are being followed. It may be difficult to predict just how a caterer will deviate from the guidelines
- *Historic controls* are mostly organizational controls and can include analysis of major deviations from an event plan so that the next event runs more closely to plan. Such controls review the concluded event and are concerned with the question: 'How were objectives met?'

In order to compare actual and planned progress in managing an event, points of comparison are necessary. These include the following:

- *Benchmarks* are identifiable points in the organization of the event where a high standard is achieved. Benchmarks emphasize quality and best practice. For example, catering of a given high standard could be a benchmark for a corporate party. Attaining a benchmark is often a cause for celebration by the event company.
- *Milestones*, or key dates, are intermediate achievement dates that stand as guideposts for monitoring an event's progress. They mark particularly critical completion times. For example, the arrival of the headline performers at the venue is a critical time, and the submission date of a client proposal is a key date.

Figure 8.1 illustrates the control process and how each element fits into the planning process.

Event control can be expensive in time and money. Its cost and effectiveness depend on the choice of the control mechanisms that make up the control system. Control mechanisms must be:

- *Meaningful and efficient*: they should be directed only at those areas that contribute to the success of the event. These significant areas have to be identified in advance,

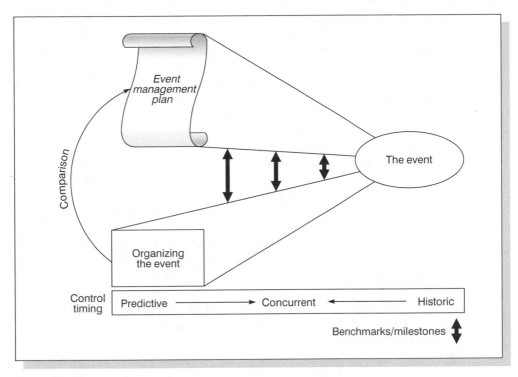

Figure 8.1 The control process

and addressed in the event plan. A limited amount of time is available for measuring and comparing – this process must be streamlined so that it does not become an end in itself.

- *Simple*: controls should not be any more complicated than is necessary. Their aim is practical and they have to be able to be communicated to many levels within an event. For example, an excessively complicated system of controls can alienate a broadly based festival committee.
- *Relevant*: controls must be prepared to match each area of event management and they should be distributed to those who have the responsibility of carrying them out. For example, there is no point in the publicity section having data that concern the budget of the performers.
- *Timely and flexible*: deviations from the plan should be identified early and addressed before they develop further. Concurrent controls should allow sufficient time to correct any gaps with the plan. Flexibility is essential, as the controls may need to respond to revision of the event plan up until the last moment. Sometimes, milestones must be moved to accommodate changes in the event. For example, a benchmark may be an attendance of 1000 people, but if only 800 chairs were delivered, it is no longer a best practice benchmark and must be dropped in case it create a logistical problem.
- *Able to suggest action*: the most useful control mechanisms provide corrective actions to be taken when members of the event team find a gap between the plan and reality. Without these suggestions for action, inexperienced staff or volunteers can become confused and the event manager can be swamped by problems that could readily have been solved by others if guidance had been provided.

When deviations or gaps are identified, the event manager can make a reasoned choice – either to close the gap, or leave it alone and revise the plan. Historic organizational controls, for example, may show a gap between the event objectives and what actually happened. The event manager can choose to change the objectives himself or herself or change aspects of the event. Examples of gaps that can be measured include:

- Ticket sales targets versus actual sales: For the entrepreneur, the sale of ticket is the 'make or break' of the event. Any deviations from the schedule may cause a cash flow problem.
- Supplier compliance versus contract: In the fluid situation of setting up an event there can be many deviations from the plan. In particular, supplier may not send the exact goods as described in the contract. This needs to be anticipated and pre-empted.
- The 'buzz' or event awareness versus the marketing/promotional plan: If the promotion of the event is not creating at least an interest then the plan may have to change.
- Actual logistics versus the operation plan: A small deviation from the plan can create major problems throughout the event. If the delivery trucks to an exhibition arrive in the wrong docks, the delay and confusion can be magnified in a short space of time.
- Entertainment versus crowd response: If the crowd is not responding as expected, it may be time for quick management action.

Control methods

Some of the control methods used in events are very straightforward, whilst others can be complex and require a high level of financial reporting skills. However, they all have the same aim – to highlight areas that have strayed from the plan so that management can take appropriate action.

Reports and meetings

Reports that evaluate the progress of an event are perhaps the most common control method. The reports are presented at the management or committee meetings. The frequency of these meetings will depend on the proximity of the event date. Many event management companies hold weekly meetings with reports from the teams (or subcommittees) and individuals responsible for particular areas. The meetings are run using standard meeting rules, such as those described in Comfort (1996), with a time for team/subcommittee reports. The aim of these reports is to assist the meeting in making decisions.

Typically, an annual community festival would have monthly meetings throughout the year leading up to the event, and increase these to weekly meetings two months before the festival. The weekly meetings may alternate between the festival committee and the general community (which discuss major decisions by the festival committee). In this way, the public can be given some control over the planning of the festival. At the committee meetings, the subcommittees dealing with publicity, sponsorship, entertainment, youth and community relations can report their actions. The reports expose any gaps so that the event co-ordinator can take

Hospitality Leisure & Tourism Series

action to close them. This is also called management by exception, because it assumes everything is flowing well, that the subcommittee handles routine matters and the event co-ordinator need only step in when significant deviations from the plan demand it.

Delegation and self-control

The use of subcommittees at a festival is an example of delegating activities to specialist groups. Part of the responsibility of each subcommittee is to solve problems before they report. Since it is impossible for the event manager to monitor all the areas of an event, this method is valuable because it allows delegated groups to control their own areas of specialization. However, the subcommittee must confine its actions to its own area and the event manager must be aware of possible problems arising across different subcommittees. For example, solving a problem in the entertainment part of an event could give rise to problems in the sponsorship areas.

Quality

There are various systems to control the quality of an event and the event company itself. In particular, quality control is dependent on customer feedback, and on the role played by event personnel in delivering quality service. Integrating the practical aspects of controlling quality with the overall strategy of an event is called total quality management (TQM). It seeks to create an event company that continually improves the quality of its services. In other words, feedback, change and improvement are integral to the company's structure and operations. Event companies use various TQM techniques. One technique is finding and rewarding quality champions – volunteer programmes often have awards for quality service at an event. Different professional organizations, such as the Association of Exhibition Organizers (AEO), Incentive Travel and Meetings Association (ITMA), International Festival and Events Association (IFEA), International Special Events Society (ISES), Meetings Industry Association (MIA) and the Event Services Association (TESA), share the same aim: to improve the quality of events within their respective sectors of the industry. They do this by disseminating information and administering a system of event evaluation through awards for quality, for example, the annual ITMA Awards. Further quality initiatives taken up by event companies, include Hospitality Assured Meetings, Investors in People and BS EN ISO 9000 (formerly BS 5750), although to date few companies have achieved accreditation.

The breakeven chart

This simple graphic tool can highlight problems by finding the intersection of costs and revenue. Figure 8.2 shows a simple but effective breakeven chart for an event that is dependent on ticket sales. For example, the Proms in the Park in Birmingham would have fixed costs of stage, pyrotechnics and administration costs. But, the greater the attendance, the larger are the costs of security, seating, cleaning, toilets and so forth. However, at one point the revenue from ticket sales exceeds the costs. At this point, the breakeven point, the event would be making a profit. If a fixed cost such as venue hire is increased, the extra number of people needed 'through the

Hospitality, Leisure & Tourism Series

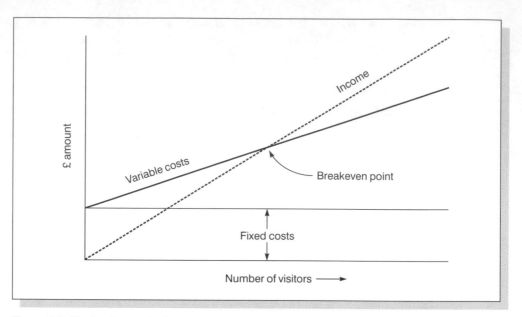

Figure 8.2 The breakeven chart

door' can quickly be calculated. How would the organizers attract the extra people to the event? One means might be increased promotion.

Ratio analysis

There are several ratios that can be used to identify any problems in the management of an event. These can also be used for predictive control as in the earlier example. Their main function is as indicators of the health of the event organization. Dyson (2001) identifies two simple ratios as a useful starting point – known as liquidity ratios, they measure the extent to which assets can be turned into cash. The current assets ratio is calculated as:

$$\frac{\text{Current assets}}{\text{Current liabilities}}$$

It indicates the financial strength of the event company or organization. The second liquidity ratio is known as the acid test ratio. Based on the premise that stock cannot always be turned into cash in the short term, or it may be unwise to do so, this removes stocks out of the equation. The acid test ratio is calculated as:

$$\frac{\text{Current assets} - \text{Stocks}}{\text{Current liabilities}}$$

However, calculation of assets can be difficult, since events by their nature have few current assets except those intangible qualities: goodwill and experience. In a similar way to a film production company, an event company may be formed to create and manage a one-off festival where every asset is hired for the duration of the event.

Return on capital employed (ROCE), sometimes referred to as return on investment (ROI), is a significant ratio for any sponsors or investors in an event, as it assesses the profitability of an event. This is expressed as:

$$\frac{\text{Net profit}}{\text{Capital}} \times 100 = X\%$$

The net profit for a sponsor may be expressed in advertising pounds. For example, media exposure can be measured by column centimetres for newspapers, or time on air for television/radio, and approximated to the equivalent cost in advertising. This ratio is most often used for events that are staged solely for financial gain. An entrepreneur of a major concert performance must demonstrate a favourable ROCE to potential investors to secure financial backing.

Other ratios can provide valuable data. As Brody and Goodman (1988) explain in their text on fundraising events, the ratio between net and gross profit is important is deciding the efficiency of the event for fundraising and in comparing one event to another. This ratio is called the percentage of profit or the profit margin. Another example of an effective ratio is that of free publicity to paid advertising, particularly for concert promoters.

By performing a series of appropriate ratio analyses, an event management company can obtain a clear picture of the viability of the organization and identify areas requiring more stringent control.

The budget

A budget can be described as a quantified statement of plans (in other words, the plan is expressed in numerical terms). The budget process includes costing and estimating income and the allocation of financial resources. The budget of an event is used to compare actual costs and revenues with projected costs and revenues. In particular, maximum expenditure for each area of the event's operation is estimated. To achieve this efficiently, a budget can take many forms. For instance, it may be broken into sub-budgets that apply to specific areas of a complex or large event such as the staging, logistics, merchandising and human resources. Budgets are of particular importance to the management of events because most aspects of the event need payment before the revenue is obtained. Cash flow needs special attention. Most funding or sponsorship bodies need a budget of the event before they will commit their resources. This second part of the chapter expands on these points and provides an example to illustrate them.

Constructing the budget

Two types of budget process can be used in event management. The *master* budget, as the name suggests, focuses on each cost and revenue item of the total event (or event company) and the *functional* budget is constructed for a specific programme element, costs centre or department (Dyson, 2001). An example of the later is a budget devised for a festival that concerns only the activities of one of the performance areas or stages. Such a budget effectively isolates this area of the event from the general festival finance. In this way budgets can be used to compare all the performance areas or stages. The master budget is illustrated in Figure 8.3. It includes box office, marketing, artist fees and staging.

Festival Trust Financial Plan
2000/1 – 2002/3

	Year 1 2000–1	Year 2 2001–2	Year 3 2002–3
INCOME	£	£	£
Ticket Sales	297 330	311 080	322 190
Other Sales	92 290	100 650	103 180
Private Sector Fundraising	345 840	372 020	381 260
Council Grant	347 600	345 290	331 870
Arts Board Grant	150 700	155 430	159 280
Other public sector fundraising	69 630	72 600	73 370
TOTAL	1 303 390	1 357 070	1 371 150
EXPENDITURE			
Artists & Staging	606 980	621 500	622 820
Marketing	125 950	123 200	126 280
Merchandising	24 860	25 520	26 180
Box Office	29 150	29 920	30 690
Salaries	349 030	360 470	369 490
Overheads	134 090	137 280	140 690
Contingency	33 110	37 070	37 950
TOTAL	1 303 170	1 334 960	1 354 100
SURPLUS/(DEFICIT)	220	22 110	17 050

Figure 8.3 Festival Trust Financial Plan 2000–3

The construction of a budget has the advantage of forcing the event management to allocate resources and financially plan the event. It imposes a necessary financial discipline on an event no matter how informally it is organized. In a similar way to the Gantt chart, it can be used for review long after the event is over.

Preparing a budget is illustrated by Figure 8.4. The process begins by establishing the economic environment of the event. The economy of the region and the country (and even European or world economy) may impinge on the event and significantly change the budget. At the time of writing, an example of this is the effect of the rise in value of sterling against other world currencies, in particular those of our European Union partners. This has made it more expensive for companies to place business in the UK, and made it more difficult to sell events within other countries. However, the benefit is that it has made it cheaper for UK residents to holiday and to buy equipment from abroad. To determine the economic environment, it is useful to ask the following questions. What similar events can be used as a guide? Will changes in the local or national economy affect the budget in any way? If it involves international performers or hiring equipment from overseas, will there be a change

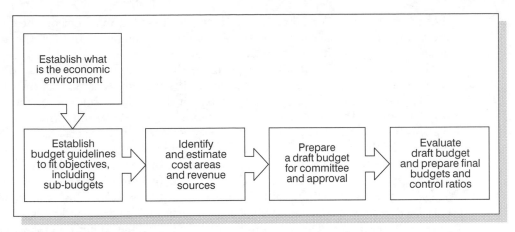

Figure 8.4 The budget process

in the currency exchange rates? These, and many more, questions need to be answered before constructing a budget that will result in reasonable projections of costs and revenue.

The next step is to obtain the guidelines from the client, sponsors or event committee. For example, a client may request that only a certain percentage of their sponsorship be allocated to entertainment, with the rest to be allocated to hospitality. Guidelines must fit with the overall objectives of the event and may require constructing sub-budgets or programme budgets. This is both an *instructive phase*, in

Income	£	Expenditure	£
Grants		Administration	
Donations		Publicity	
Sponsorship		Venue sosts	
Ticket sales		Equipment	
Fees		Salaries	
Special programmes		Insurance	
Concessions		Permits	
Security			
TOTAL		Accounting	
		Cleaning	
		Travel	
		Accommodation	
		Documentation	
		Hospitality	
		Community groups	
		Volunteers	
		Contingencies	
		TOTAL	

Figure 8.5 Generic budget – first level

that the committee, for example, will instruct the event manager on the content of the budget and a *consultative phase*, as the event manager would ask the advice of other event specialist and the subcontractors.

The third step is to identify, categorize and estimate the cost areas and revenue sources. The categories become the items in the budget. A sample of the categories is given in Figure 8.5. This is a summary, or a first-level budget, of the cost and revenue areas. The next level down expands each of these main items, shown in Figures 8.7 and 8.8. The use of computer-generated spreadsheets enables a number of levels in the budget to be created on separate sheets and linked to the first level budget. Cost items take up the most room on a budget and are described below.

Once the costs and possible revenue sources and amounts are estimated, a *draft budget* is prepared and submitted for approval to the controlling committee. This may be the finance subcommittee of a large festival. The draft budget is also used in grant submissions and sponsorships. The funding bodies, including the Millennium Commission, UK Sport, Arts Council and Regional Arts Boards, have budget guidelines and printed forms that need to be filled out and included in the grant application.

The final step is the preparation of the budget and financial ratios that can indicate deviations from the plan. An operating business has a variety of budgets including capital expenditure, sales, overheads and production. Most special events will only require an operation budgets or cash budget. With regard to estimating amounts within the budget, Watt (1998, p. 45) suggests that although it must be, 'as accurate as possible . . . it is always advisable to *overestimate expenditure* and *underestimate income*. To do the opposite is a recipe for disaster'. Figure 8.4 illustrates the budget process.

Cash flow

The special nature of events, exhibitions, conferences, and festivals requires close attention to the flow of cash. Catherwood and Van Kirk (1992), Getz (1997) and Goldblatt (1997) all emphasize the importance of the control of cash to an event. Goldblatt (1997) stresses that it is imperative for the goodwill of suppliers. Without prompt payment the event company faces immediate difficulties. Payment terms and conditions have to be fully and equitably negotiated. These payment terms can ruin an event if they are not given careful consideration beforehand. To obtain the best terms from a supplier, Goldblatt (1997) suggests the following:

- Learn as much as possible about the suppliers and subcontractors and the nature of their business. Do they own the equipment? What are the normal payment terms in their business? Artists, for instance, expect to be paid immediately, whereas some information technology suppliers will wait for thirty days.
- Be flexible with what can be offered in exchange – including sponsorship.
- Try to negotiate a contract that stipulates a small deposit before the event and full payment after it is over.
- Suggest a line of credit, with payment at a set time in the future.
- Closely control the purchasing.
- Ensure that all purchases are made through a purchase order that is authorized by the event manager or the appropriate finance personnel. A purchase order is a written record of the agreement to supply a product at a prearranged price. All suppliers, contractors and event staff should be informed that no purchase can be

made without an authorized form. This ensures that spending is confined to what is permitted by the budget.

- Obtain a full description of the product or service and the quantities required.
- Itemize the price to a per unit cost.
- Calculate any taxes or extra charges.
- Determine payment terms.
- Clarify delivery details.
- Consider imposing penalties if the product or service delivered is not as described.

As Figure 8.6 shows, the ability of an event co-ordinator to affect any change diminishes rapidly as the event draws closer. The supply of goods and services may, of necessity, take place close to or on the actual date of the event. This does not allow organizers the luxury of reminding a supplier of the terms set out in the purchase order. Without a full written description of the goods, the event manager is open to all kinds of exploitation by suppliers and, as the event may be on that day, there may be no choice but to accept delivery.

When considering cash flow, the advantage of the ticketing strategies of events such as Glastonbury Festival is obvious. As tickets are sold months before the event, the management is able to concentrate on other areas of planning. Event companies that specialize in the corporate area obtain a similar advantage. Generally they are paid upfront. This allows the event manager or producer the freedom to negotiate terms and conditions with the suppliers without having to worry about the cash flow. A cash flow timing chart similar to the Gantt chart is often helpful in planning events. This shows the names of the suppliers and their payment requirements. It includes deposit dates, payment stages, payment on purchase, monthly fixed cost payments and thirty-, sixty- or ninety-day credit payments.

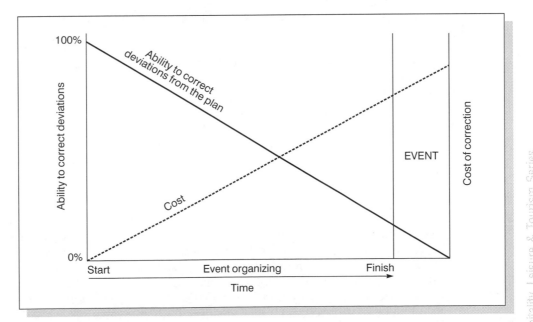

Figure 8.6 Control, cost and time
Source: adapted from Burke, 1999.

Costing

The cash flow at an event is heavily dependent on the cost of goods and services. These are estimated for the construction of the budget. The prediction, categorization and allocation of costs is called the costing. In relation to the breakeven chart (see Figure 8.2), two types of costs have been identified. These are described in the following text.

Fixed costs or overheads are costs associated with the event that occur no matter how many people come to the event. They include the unchanging expenses concerned with the operation of the event management company, for example, rent, staff salaries, telephone and other office expenses. At a large festival these may include rates and interest on loans. When deciding on a budget these costs need to be apportioned reasonably to the various event areas. This process is called absorption of the overheads by the cost centres. Cost centres, for example, include entertainment, catering, staging or travel. If the fixed costs are incorrectly absorbed the cost centre will be wrongly described. For a correct financial picture of the future event, the overheads have to be reasonably spread to all areas. The aim of an event company is to reduce the fixed costs without effecting the quality of the event.

Variable costs are expenses that purely concern the event and are directly related to the number of people who attend the event. Food and beverage costs are related directly to the number of people at an event. The more people at an event the more tickets need to be printed, possibly more staff, and certainly more food.

This division is not as clear-cut in the event industry as in other industries. It is sometimes clearer, instead, to talk in terms of *direct costs* (the costs directly associated with the event, whether variable of fixed) and *overheads* (costs associated with the running of the event company). In this case the direct costs are the major costs and the aim of the event company is to control these costs. Figure 8.7 lists the detailed budgeted costs of a one-off event.

Catherwood and Van Kirk (1992) divide the costs of an event into four main categories:

- operational or production costs including event staff, construction, insurance and administration
- venue/site rental
- promotion – advertising, public relations, sales promotion
- talent – costs associated with the entertainment.

To obtain the correct cost of each of the elements contained in the budget categories (sometimes called cost centres) there is a common costing process involved. The steps are listed below:

1 *Conceptual estimate* or 'ball park figure': this would be used in the conceptual development stage of the event to give management an idea of what costs are involved. Generally this would have an accuracy of plus or minus 25 per cent.
2 *Feasibility study*: this includes comparing costs in similar events, e.g. the cost of a headline speaker varies according to their career and popularity. Asking other event managers what was paid for the speaker gives the event producer a basis for negotiating a fair price and a more realistic budget estimation.
3 *Quote or definitive estimate*: this is the cost quote in reply to the tender. The larger festivals will put out to tender many of the elements of the event including sound,

lights and security. A near correct estimate can be made on this basis. For small events, the quote may be obtained by ringing a selection of suppliers and comparing the costs. However, it is rarely the case that the costs are comparable, as there are so many unusual features or special conditions. Once an event company has built up a relationship with a supplier, it tends to stay with that supplier.

Tips on reducing costs

With careful and imaginative planning, costs can be reduced in a number of areas:

1 *Publicity*: an innovative event may need a large publicity budget that is based on revenue from ticket sales. The event manager's aim should be to reduce this wherever possible. Established festivals may need very little publicity as 'word of mouth' will do all the necessary work. For example, Bradford Festival 2000, with a budget of £684 511, spends relatively little on publicity (8 per cent of total expenditure) because it has built up such a reputation with its target audience and has developed an extensive collection of media partners for the event (Bradford Festival, 2000). The more innovative the event the greater the possibility for free publicity. The Rugby World Cup, for example, gained an enormous amount of free publicity due to the efforts of one of the main sponsors, Guinness.

2 *Equipment and suppliers*: suppliers of products to events have down times during the year when their products may be hired cheaply. In particular theatrical productions at the end of their run are a ready source of decoration and scenery. Annual events like the summer festivals may have equipment in storage that can be hired.

3 *In-kind gifts*: many organizations will assist events to achieve cross-promotional advantages. Entertainment can be inexpensive if there is a chance that they can promote a performance or product at the event. For example, a supplier may agree to supply their beer freely to the party for the media and guests prior to the event in exchange for the rights to sell it at the concert.

4 *Hiring charges*: hire charges of large infrastructure components such as tents and generators and headline acts can be reduced by offering work at other festivals and events. The large cultural festivals around the UK, including the Edinburgh International Festival and the Harrogate International Festival, can offer a festival circuit to any overseas performer. Costs can therefore be amortized over all the festivals.

5 *Priorities cost centres*: at some time it will be necessary to cut costs. This must be planned by knowing beforehand the effect on the overall event if one area or part of it is significantly changed or eliminated. In project management this is called sensitivity analysis (Burke, 1999). Estimates are made of the effect of cost changes on the event and the cost centres are placed in a priority list according to the significance of the effect. For example, a sensitivity analysis could be applied to the effect of imposing a charge on a programme that was previously available free. While this could significantly increase revenue, it may produce a negative effect in sponsorship and audience satisfaction, which may well be translated into the reduction of revenue.

6 *Volunteers*: costs can be reduced using volunteers instead of paid staff. It is important that all the skills of the volunteers are fully utilized. These skills should

	£			£
Administration	Office rental		Insurance	Public liability
	Fax/photocopy			Workers comp.
	Computers			Rain
	Printers			Other
	Telephone		SUB-TOTAL	
	Stationery		Permits	Liquor
	Postage			Food
	Office staff			Council
	SUB-TOTAL			Parking
				Children
Publicity	Art work			SUB-TOTAL
	Printing		Security	Security check
	Poster leaflet distribution			Equipment
	Press kit			Staff
	Press ads			SUB-TOTAL
	Radio ads		Accounting	Cash and cheque
	Programmes			Audit
	SUB-TOTAL			SUB-TOTAL
Venue	Hire		Cleaning	Before
	Preparation			During
	SUB-TOTAL			After
Equipment	Stage			SUB-TOTAL
	Sound		Travel	Artists
	Lights			Freight
	Transport			SUB-TOTAL
	Personnel		Accom.	
	Toilets			SUB-TOTAL
	Extra equipment		Documentation	Photo/video
	Communication			SUB-TOTAL
	First aid		Hospitality	Tent
	Tents			Food
	Tables and chairs			Beverage
	Wind breaks			Staff
	Generators			Invitations
	Technicians			SUB-TOTAL
	Parking needs		Community	Donations
	Uniforms			SUB-TOTAL
	SUB-TOTAL			
Salaries	Co-ordinator		Volunteers	Food and drink
	Artists			Party
	Labourers			Awards and prizes
	Consultants			SUB-TOTAL
	Other		Contingencies	
	SUB-TOTAL			SUB-TOTAL

Figure 8.7 Projected costs – second level

be continually under review as new skills may be required as the event planning progresses. For charitable functions, volunteers will often absorb many of the costs as tax deductible donations.

Revenue

Anticipating potential sources of revenue should be given as much attention as projecting expenses. The source of the revenue will often define the type of event, the event objectives and the planning. A company product launch has only one source of revenue – the client. Company staff parties, for example, are paid by the client with no other source of revenue. The budget then has only one entry on the left-hand side. A major festival, on the other hand, has to find and service a variety of revenue sources such as sponsors and participants. This constitutes a major part of festival planning.

Revenue can come from the following sources:

- ticket sales – most common in entrepreneurial events
- sponsorship – common in cultural and sports events
- merchandising
- advertising
- in-kind
- broadcast rights – an increasingly important source of revenue in sport events
- grants – local government, national government, Millennium Commission, Arts Council, UK Sport, Regional Arts Board
- fundraising – common in community events
- the client – the major source for corporate events.

Figure 8.8 features an expanded list of revenue sources. For many events, admission fees and ticket prices need careful consideration. It will impact on the cash flow and the breakeven point. One or more of three methods can decide the ticket price:

1 *Covering costs*: all the costs are estimated and added to the projected profit. To give the ticket price, this figure is then divided by the expected number of people that will attend the event. The method is quick, simple and based on knowing the breakeven point. It gives a 'rule of thumb' figure that can be used as starting point for further investigations in setting the price.
2 *Market demand*: the ticket price is decided by the prevailing ticket prices for similar or competing events. In other words, it is the 'going rate' for an event. Concert tickets are decided in this way. In deciding on the ticket price, consider elasticity of demand. For instance, if the ticket price is increased slightly will this affect the number of tickets sold?
3 *Perceived value*: the event may have special features that do not allow a price comparison to other events. For instance, for an innovative event the ticket price must be carefully considered. By its nature this kind of event has no comparison. There can be variations in the ticket price for different entertainment packages at the event (at many multi-venue events the ticket will include admission only to certain events), for extra hospitality or for special seating. Knowing how to grade the tickets is an important skill in maximizing revenue. There are market segments that will not tolerate differences in pricing, whereas others expect it. It can be a culturally based decision and may be part of the design of the event.

Income		£			£
Grants	Local government		Ticket sales	Box office	
	Central government			Retail outlets	
	Millennium Fund			Admissions	
	Arts Council			SUB-TOTAL	
	Other		Merchandise	T-shirts	
	SUB-TOTAL			Programmes	
Donations	Foundations			Posters	
	Other			Badges	
	SUB-TOTAL			Videos	
Sponsorship	In kind			SUB-TOTAL	
	Cash		Fees	Stalls	
	SUB-TOTAL			Licences	
Individual contributions				Broadcast	
	SUB-TOTAL			SUB-TOTAL	
Special programmes	Raffle		Advert sales	Programme	
	Auction			Event site	
	Games			SUB-TOTAL	
	SUB-TOTAL		Concessions		
				SUB-TOTAL	

Figure 8.8 Revenue sources – second level

Tips for increasing projected income

Income can be increased using a number of methods.

Ticket scaling

There are many ticketing strategies that strive to obtain the best value from ticket sales. The most common strategy is to vary the pricing with seat position, number of tickets sold and time of sale. Early-bird discounts and subscriptions series are two examples of the latter. Another strategy involves creating a special category of attendees. This could include patron, special clubs, ' friends of the event', people for whom the theme of the event has a special meaning or those who have attended many similar events in the past. For example, for a higher ticket price, patrons are offered extra hospitality, such as separate viewing area, valet parking and a cocktail party.

In-kind support and bartering

One way to increase income is to scrutinize the event cost centres for areas that could be covered by an exchange with the supplier or bartering. For example, the advertising can be expanded for an event with a programme of 'give-aways'. These are free tickets to the event given away through the press. Due to the amount goodwill surrounding a fundraising event, bartering should be explored as a method of obtaining supplies.

Merchandising

The staging of an event offers many opportunities for merchandising. The first consideration is, 'Does the sale of goods enhance the theme of the event?' The problems of cash flow at an event, as stated earlier in this chapter, can give the sale of goods an unrealistic high priority in event management. It is easy to cheapen a 'boutique' special event with the sale of 'trinkets'. However, the attendees may want to buy a souvenir. For example, a large choir performing at a one-off spectacular event may welcome a video of the choir at the event. This could be arranged with the choir beforehand and result in a guaranteed income. As a spin-off the video could be incorporated into promotional material for use by the event management in bidding for future events.

Broadcast rights

An increasingly important source of revenue, particularly in sport events, is the payment for the right to broadcast. Live television broadcast is a lucrative area for potential – but it comes at a price. The broadcast, rather than the needs and expectations of the live audience, becomes master of the event. Often the live audience becomes merely one element in the television entertainment. As a result, the audience may include 'fillers' – people who fill any empty seats so that the camera will always show a capacity audience.

If the entire event is recorded by high-quality video equipment, future broadcast rights should also be investigated. For example, in many countries there is a constant demand for worthwhile content for pay television (cable or satellite). At the time of writing, Internet broadcast is in its infancy. There have been a number of music and image broadcasts but they have been limited by the size of the bandwidth. There can be no doubt that this will become an important medium for the event industry.

Sponsorship leverage

Leverage is the current term for using the event sponsorship to gain further support from other sponsors. Very few companies or organizations want to be the first to sponsor a one-off event. However, once the event has one sponsor's support, sufficient credibility is gained to enable an approach to other sponsors. For example, gaining the support of a major newspaper or radio station allows the event manager to approach other sponsors. The sponsors realize that they can obtain free publicity.

Special features

When an event is linked to a large population base, there are many opportunities for generating income. Raffles, for example, are frequently used to raise income. At a concert-dance in Bath, all patrons brought along a prize for a raffle drawn on the night. Each received a ticket in the raffle, as part of the entry fee to the event. The prizes ranged from old ties to overseas air tickets. The raffle took two hours to get through, but every person received a prize and it became part of the entertainment of the evening.

Holding an auction at an event is also an entertaining way to increase event income. For example, the Childline Next St Clements Ball (held in October 2000) included auction items such as a trip on a Sunseeker powerboat, a football signed by the England team and a pair of British Airways Club Class return tickets. The sale of the football shirts after a major match, complete with the mud stains, has been a way of raising revenue.

Reporting

The importance of general reporting on the progress of the event planning has been described in this chapter. The budget report is the means to highlight problems and suggest solutions. It is an efficient way to communicate this to the event committee and staff and should be readily understood. It is important that appropriate action is taken in response to the report's suggestion. Figure 8.9 is a list of guidelines for a straightforward report.

- The report should relate directly to the area of the event management area to which it is addressed.
- It should not contain extraneous information that can only obscure its function. Brevity and clarity are the key objectives.
- The figures in the report must be of the same magnitude and they should be comparable.
- It should describe how to take remedial action if there is a significant problem.

Figure 8.9 Reporting guidelines

The most common problem in an event is the cost 'blow out'. Event managers often encounter unforeseen circumstances that can cost dearly. For example, the subcontractor that supplies the sound system can go bankrupt; the replacement subcontractor may prove more expensive. One of the unwritten laws of project management is that the closer the project is to completion the more expensive are any changes. Appropriate remedial action may be to go for the cheaper catering or to find extra funding. This could be a raffle to pay for the extra sound. Figure 8.7 shows graphically how the cost of any changes to the organization of an event escalates as the event date nears.

The main problem of a budget, particularly for events, is blindly sticking to it without regard for changes in the plan. It is a tool of control and not an end in itself. The elegance of a well laid out budget and its mathematical certainty can obscure that it is a slave to the event objectives, not its master. A budget is based on reasonable projections made within an economic framework. Small changes in the framework can cause large changes in the event's finances. For example, extra sponsorship may be found if the right products are added to the event portfolio. A complicated, highly detailed budget may consume far more time than is necessary to make the event a success.

Time is a crucial factor in event management. Keeping rigidly within budgetary standards can take up too much time and energy of the event management, limiting time for other areas.

Finally, a budget that is constructed by the event management may be imposed on staff without adequate consultation. This can lead to losing valuable specialist staff if they find themselves having to work to unreasonable budgetary standards. In particular, an innovative event requires the creative input of all the staff and subcontractors. At these events, informal financial control using a draft budget is often far more conducive to quality work than strict budgetary control.

Summary

There is little point in expending effort in creating a plan for an event if there is no way to keep control of it. The event plan is a prerequisite for success. The control mechanisms to keep the project aligned to the plan need to be well thought out and easy to understand by the management team. When the event strays from the plan there needs to be ways to bring it back into line or to change the plan.

An estimate of the costs and revenues of an event is called the budget and it acts as the master control of an event. With a well-reasoned budget in place, all sections of an event know their spending limits and can work together. The cash flow of an event needs special considerations. When is the cash coming in? Moreover, when does it need to go out? An event that does not have control mechanisms, including a well-thought-out budget, is not going to satisfy its stakeholders. Not only will it fail, but also organizations will never know the reason for its failure. A sound budget gives management a solid bedrock on which to build a successful event.

Questions

1 What controls do you use to get from home to work or schools?

2 List the milestones for a swimming event involving at least 1000 competitors.

3 Identify the best practices for a corporate conference dinner.

4 Identify the cost centres and revenue sources for:
   (a) a corporate staff party
   (b) a concert (include a breakeven chart)
   (c) a wine and food festival
   (d) the Commonwealth Games 2002 in Manchester

5 If it were necessary to cut costs at the above events, what areas would be the first to feel the effects?

6 What 'economies of scale' can be expected from multi-venued festivals?

7 Anticipate the possible cash flow problems at a large cultural festival in a city.

CHAPTER 9

Legal and risk management

After studying this chapter, you should be able to:

- explain the central role of event ownership in event administration

- identify the necessary contracts for events and their components

- construct a risk management plan

- understand the variety of rules and regulations governing events

- describe the process of gaining insurance.

Introduction – what are the legal issues?

A key question in event administration is 'who owns the event?' The legal owner of an event could be the event co-ordinator, the committee, a separate legal entity or the sponsors, but it is important to recognize that the ownership of the event entails legal responsibility and therefore liability. The members of an organizing committee can be personally held responsible for the event. This is often expressed as 'jointly and severally liable'. The structure of the event administration must reflect this, and the status of various personnel, such as the event co-ordinator, the subcontractors and other stakeholders, must be clearly established at the outset. Likewise, sponsorship agreements will often have a clause as to the sponsor's liability, and therefore the extent of their ownership of the event. All such issues need to be carefully addressed by the initial agreements and contracts.

The organizing committee for a non-profit event can become a legal entity by forming an incorporated association. Such an association can enter into contracts and own property. The act of incorporating means that the members have limited liability when the association incurs debts. It does not grant them complete exemption from all liability such as negligence. By law, an association must have a constitution or a list of rules, which state the procedures and powers. These include auditing and accounting matters, the power of the governing body and winding up procedures. Community and local festival events often do not form a separate incorporated association as they can come under the legal umbrella of a body such as a local council. This gives the event organizing committee a good deal of legal protection as well as access to administrative support. For a one-off event, this administrative support can save time and resources because the administrative

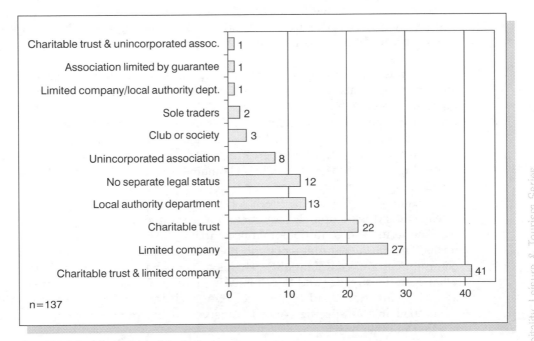

Figure 9.1 Legal structure of festivals
Source: Allen and Shaw, 2001, reprinted with permission, British Arts Festival Association.

Hospitality, Leisure & Tourism Series

infrastructure, such as fax machine, telephone lines, secretarial help, and legal and accounting advice, is already established.

Establishing an appropriate legal structure for an event management company is an exercise in liability minimization. Several structures are possible for an event company, which could operate as a sole trader, partnership, charitable trust, or a company limited by liability. Figure 9.1 illustrates the legal structure of a sample of festivals, with just over half being limited companies and just under half registered as charities (Allen and Shaw, 2001). Each of these legal structures has different liability implications. Legal advice may be required to determine the most appropriate structure for a particular circumstance.

Contracts

A contract is an agreement between two or more parties that sets out their obligations and is enforceable by law. It describes the exchange to be made between the parties. A contract can be a written or an oral agreement. In the world of event management, an oral contract is of little use if problems occur in the future. Therefore, it is appropriate to put all contractual agreements in writing. This may frequently take the form of a simple letter of agreement, no more than a page in length. However, when large amounts of money and important responsibilities are involved, a formal contract is necessary. As Goldblatt (1997) explains, a typical event industry contract will contain:

- the names of the contracting parties, their details and their trading names
- details of the service or product that is offered (e.g. equipment, entertainment, use of land, expert advice)
- the terms of exchange for such service or product
- the signature of both parties indicating understanding of the terms of exchange and agreement to the conditions of the contract.

To make this mutual obligation perfectly clear to all parties, the contract would set out all the key elements. This would consist of the following: financial terms, including payment schedule; a cancellation clause; delivery time; the rights and obligations of each party; and an exact description of the goods and services being exchanged.

Contracts and contract terms have subjected to scrutiny over recent years, due to event management, suppliers, performers and venues being caught out with hidden terms. In order to address this, Chris Hannam (of Stagesafe) has developed a sample contract, terms and conditions and notes for use for the Production Services Association (PSA) for use between service companies, artist management agencies, freelances and self-employed contractors. The sample contract is presented as Figure 9.2. The terms and conditions that accompany this include areas such as payment terms, insurance requirements for both client and supplier, health and safety commitment and confidentiality. This is accompanied by a schedule that outlines what both the supplier and the client will provide. The complete sample contract is available for download from the PSA website (www.psa.org.uk). Although developed in this specific context, it serves to illustrate a format that could be applied in other areas.

Event management companies may need a wide range of contracts to facilitate their operation. Some of these are shown in Figure 9.3.

THIS AGREEMENT is made the < *Date* > day of < *Month*.. >

BETWEEN < *Insert your name or Co name* >of:

< *Insert your address* .... > (The Supplier)

AND < *Insert your customers name* > of:

< *Insert your customers address* .... > (The Client).

CONTRACT DETAILS CONTRACT NO: < *Insert your job No* >

EVENT, PRODUCTION OR TOUR:. < *Insert name of job/tour* >

DURATION OF THE AGREEMENT: From: < *Insert Start Date* > **To:** < *Insert Finish Date* >

1. The Supplier agrees to supply goods/services in accordance with the Schedule attached hereto or as subsequently agreed in writing by the parties hereto.

2. It is hereby agreed that prior to the signing hereof The Client has had ample opportunity to examine The Supplier's Terms of Business attached hereto and shall be deemed to have unequivocally accepted them.

3. The total contract price shall be < *Insert price and currency* > plus VAT (if applicable)

4. The terms of payment are: < *Insert Payment Terms* >

5. In the event of cancellation of this Agreement by The Client and without prejudice to any rights hereunder or under the Terms of Business attached hereto, The Client will indemnify The Supplier as a result of such cancellation for < .... >% of the contract price. Interest at a rate of < >% per month is liable to be charged on any outstanding balances.

6. It is a fundamental term of this agreement that the stipulations as to payment contained be fully adhered to by The Client (including an absolute requirement of payment to be made within the times stipulated but subject to the proviso contained in Condition 4) and if for any reason The Client shall be in breach of such stipulations The Supplier shall have the right at its absolute and sole discretion and without prejudice to its other rights hereunder forthwith and without notice to dismantle remove or otherwise bring to an end any works service goods or other things supplied by the supplier hereunder and to terminate forthwith this agreement and be under no further liability hereunder to provide any of the services or goods herein agreed.

Signed for and on behalf of   )
The Supplier   )

Date.

Signed for. and on behalf of   )
The Client   )

Date.

IN ADDITION TO SIGNING THE AGREEMENT, THE CLIENT IS REQUESTED TO INITIAL ALL PAGES OF THIS AGREEMENT, THE TERMS OF BUSINESS AND SCHEDULES, IN THE TOP RIGHT HAND CORNER

Figure 9.2 A sample contract. *Source*: Hannam, 2000.

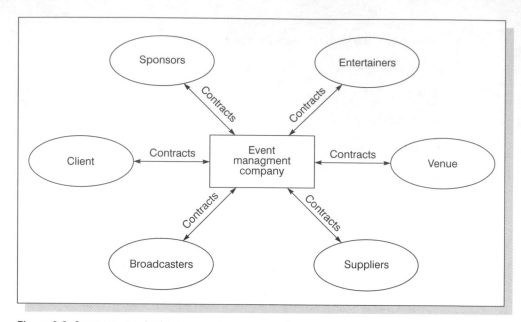

Figure 9.3 Contracts required by an event management company

An event of medium size would require a set of formal contracts covering:

- the event company or coordinator and the client
- the entertainers
- the venue
- the supplier (e.g. security, audiovisual, caterers)
- the sponsor(s).

For smaller events these may be arranged by letters of agreement, without going into too much detail.

Different contracts have different 'styles' and the event manager must to be familiar with them. Some of these contracts are discussed in the following text.

Entertainment

A common feature of entertainment contracts is the 'rider'. This is an attachment to the contract, usually on a separate piece of paper. Hiring a headline performer may necessitate signing a twenty- to thirty-page contract. The contract often contains a clause requiring the event company to provide the goods and services contained in the rider, as well as the performance fee. The rider can include such things as a technical specification (e.g. size of PA system required, microphone, technician requirements, lighting), hospitality specification (e.g. food, drink, relaxing accommodation), and venue specification (e.g. payment terms, insurance requirements) (Kemp, 1995; Vasey, 1998). The event company ignores this to their peril. The rider can be used by the entertainer's agent as a way of increasing the fee in real terms, which can have serious consequences for the budget of an event. For example, a university student union that employs a well-known rock group at a minimal fee for a charity function would find its objectives greatly damaged by a rider stipulating reimbursement of food, accommodation and transport costs for thirty people.

Another important clause in the entertainment contract is exclusivity. For example, a headline act may be the major attraction for an event. If the act is also performing at a similar event in the same period, for example the summer festival season, this could easily detract from the uniqueness of the event. A clause to prevent this is therefore inserted into the contract. It indicates that the performer cannot perform within a specified geographic area during the event or for a certain number of days prior to and after the event. The intricacies of an entertainment contract, together with the expense, led Stayte and Watt (1998) to suggest that event managers obtain legal advice from a solicitor experienced in dealing with entertainment/music contracts.

The contract must contain a clause that stipulates the signatories have the right to sign on behalf of the contracting parties. An entertainment group may be represented by a number of agents. The agents must have written proof that they exclusively represent the group for the event.

Venue

The venue contract will have specialist clauses, including indemnifying the venue against damages, personnel requirements and provision of security staff. The contract can also contain the following elements:

- *Security deposit*: an amount, generally a percentage of the hiring fee, to be used for any additional work such as cleaning and repairs that result from the event.
- *Cancellation*: outlining the penalty for cancellation of the event and whether the hirer will receive a refund if the venue is rehired at that time.
- *Access*: including the timing of the opening and closing of the doors, and actual use of the entrances.
- *Late conclusion*: the penalty for the event going overtime.
- *House seats*: this is the reserved free tickets for the venue management.
- *Additions or alterations*: the event may require some changes to the internal structures of the venue.
- *Signage*: this covers the signs of any sponsors and other advertising. Venue management approval may be required for all promotional material.

When hiring a venue, it is important to ascertain exactly what is included in the fee. For example, just because there were chairs and tables in the photo of the venue does not mean that they are included in the hiring cost.

Sponsor

The contract with the sponsor would cover issues related to quality representation of the sponsor such as trademarks and signage, exclusivity and the right of refusal for further sponsorship. It may specify that the sponsor's logo be included on all promotional material, or that the sponsor has the right to monitor the quality of the promotional material. Korman (2000) highlights that sponsors will generally ask for exclusivity within their own brand sector or may demand sole rights to gain full benefit from the event. He further identifies that minor sponsors should be managed to ensure that they do not establish a portfolio of rights that may damage public perception of the major sponsorship, and that sponsors are kept to a minimum to ensure that the message is clearly projected. As a result of these issues, the level of sponsorship – sole sponsor, headline sponsor, minor or major sponsor, or supplier – needs clearly stating in the contract. The contract would also describe the hospitality rights such as the number of complimentary tickets supplied to the sponsor.

Broadcast

Broadcast contracts can be very complex, due to the large amount of money involved in broadcasting and the production of resultant merchandise such as videos and sound recordings. The important clauses in a broadcast contract address the following components:

- *Territory or region*: the broadcast area – local, national or international – must be defined. If the attached schedule shows the region as 'World', the event company must be fully aware of the rights it is bestowing on the broadcaster and their value.
- *Guarantees*: the most important of these is the one stating that the event company has the rights to sign for the whole event. For example, some local councils require an extra fee be paid for broadcasting from their area. Also, performers' copyright can preclude any broadcast without written permission from their record and publishing companies. Comedy acts and motivational speakers are particularly sensitive about any broadcasts and recordings.
- *Sponsorship*: this area can present difficulties when different levels of sponsorship are involved. Sometimes the rights of the event sponsor and the broadcaster's sponsors can clash.
- *Repeats, extracts and sub-licences*: these determine the allowable number of repeats of the broadcast, and whether the broadcaster is authorized to edit or take extracts from the broadcast and how such material can be used. The event company may sign with one broadcaster, only to find that the rights to cover the event have been sold on for a much larger figure to another broadcaster. In addition, a sub-licence clause may annul many of the other clauses in the contract. The sub-licenser may be able to use its own sponsors, which is problematic if they are in direct competition with the event sponsors.
- *Merchandising*: the contract may contain a clause that mentions the rights to own products originating from the broadcast. The ownership and sale of any of the recordings can be a major revenue source for an event. A clause recently introduced found in these sorts of contracts concerns future delivery systems. Multimedia uses, such as CD-ROMs, cable television and the Internet are all relatively recent, and new communications technologies continue to be developed, for example, the launch of WAP mobile phones. It is easy to sign away the future rights of an event when the contract contains terms that are unknown to the event company. It is wise to seek out specialist legal advice.
- *Access*: the physical access requirements of broadcasting must be part of the staging and logistical plan of the event. A broadcaster can easily disrupt an event by demanding to interview performers and celebrities. It is important to specify how much access the broadcaster can have to the stars.
- *Credits*: this establishes, at the outset, the people and elements that will be listed in the titles and credits.

The broadcaster can offer all kinds of assistance to the event company. They have an interest in making the area presentable for television and will often help decorate the site. The level of assistance will depend on its stake in the event. For example, Channel Four's involvement in Party in the Park (Hyde Park, London), through their T4 youth brand, has led to many kinds of synergies between the event, the sponsors and the broadcaster.

Constructing a contract

The process of constructing a contract is illustrated in Figure 9.4 and comprises five main steps: the intention, negotiation, initial acceptance, agreement on terms and signing. This process can be facilitated if the event management has standard contracts, where the name of the supplier and any special conditions can be inserted. This saves the event company going through unfamiliar contracts from sponsors, suppliers and entertainers, which can be very time-consuming.

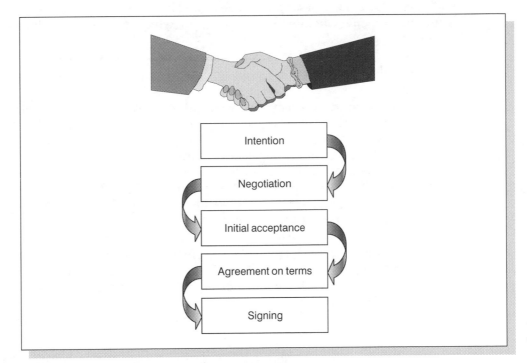

Figure 9.4 The process of constructing a contract

For large events and more complex contracts a 'heads of agreement' is sent after the negotiations are completed. This is a summary of any important specific points, listing the precise service or product that is being provided. The contract can be renegotiated or terminated with the agreement of all parties. The final version should contain a clause that allows both parties to go to arbitration in the advent of a disagreement.

Trademarks and logos

Another kind of ownership issue for event management is its ownership of trademarks and logos. Protection of trademark ownership is generally covered within legislation, including the Trade Marks Act 1994 and the Copyright, Designs and Patents Act 1988. However, specific legislation has been drawn up to protect the Olympics through the Olympic Symbol Etc. (Protection) Act 1995, which specifically prevents the use of their logo, motto and related word by any other party without the permission of the British Olympic Association. This illustrates the importance of the ownership of event symbols.

The event company has to be aware of the risks of misrepresenting their event. There is a danger, when promoting an event, to exaggerate the benefits. Descriptions of the product must always be accurate, as disgruntled consumers may take legal action to gain punitive damages when they feel that advertising for an event has made false claims. The Trade Descriptions Act 1968 can be used to argue such cases. This makes it an offence if a trader:

- applies a false trade description to any goods
- supplies or offers to supply any goods to which a false trade description is applied
- makes certain kinds of false statement about the provision of any services, accommodation or facilities.

In the events context, this may involve a music festival advertising that a certain performer will be taking part or implying the support of associations or organizations when this is known not to be true. It may also include a company implying sponsorship approval or affiliation with an event when it is not, for example, through ambush marketing. Nic Couchman and Dan Harrington of Townleys solicitors (Couchman and Harrington, 2000, p. 2) identify that ambush marketing, sometimes referred to as 'parasitic marketing', can take many forms, but will usually fall into two distinct groups:

(A) Activities traditionally considered piracies – these will usually have a clear-cut remedy in law. They are activities which clearly constitute infringements of the proprietary rights in an event, for example unauthorised use of a registered event logo on merchandise, false claims to be official suppliers to a particular team or use of copyright broadcast material on a website; and

(B) Other activities – more subtle practices for which the remedy is less clear-cut or may not even exist.

They go on to identify that typical examples of type (B) activities include: unauthorized or unofficial merchandise; unauthorized or unofficial publications; unauthorized sales promotion activity or publicity stunts; unauthorized broadcasts/virtual advertising/Web advertising of sports content/live screenings/films/video/photography/telephone commentary/'sponsored'; on-line text and audio commentary information lines/pager services; and unofficial corporate hospitality.

Duty of care

A fundamental legal principal applied to events is that of taking all reasonable care to avoid acts or omissions that could injure employees, contractors, users, participants and visitors. This is called duty of care and is covered by the area of law known as torts. A tort is a breach of duty owed to other people and imposed by law, and in this it differs from the duties arising from contracts, which are agreed between contracting parties. Unlike criminal law, which is concerned with punishment and deterrence, the law of torts is concerned with compensation. Within the UK, duty of care is enshrined within legislation, including the Occupiers Liability Act 1957 and 1984, Supply of Goods and Services Act 1982 and the Health and Safety at Work etc Act 1974 (HSE, 1999; Stayte and Watt, 1998).

For event management, duty of care means taking actions that will prevent any foreseeable risks of injury to the people who are directly affected by, or involved in, the event. This would include the event staff, volunteers, the performers, the audience or spectators and the public in the surrounding areas.

Risk assessment and management

Events are particularly susceptible to risks. Risk is not necessarily harmful. One reason that an event company wins the job of organizing an event is that other companies perceive it to be too risky. Risk is the basis of the entrepreneur's business, without which there would be no competitive advantage. Without risk, there would be no tightrope-walking or extreme sports. Part of what makes an event special is the risk – it has not been done before. The unique venue, large crowds, new staff and volunteers, movement of equipment and the general excitement are a recipe for potential hazards. The event manager that does not heed advice on risk prevention is courting disaster and foreshortening their career in the event industry. The sensible assessment of potential hazards and preventative action is the basis of risk management, and is a legal requirement under the Management of Health and Safety at Work Regulations 1992. According to the Health and Safety Executive (HSE, 1999, p. 7) risk may be defined as 'the likelihood that harm from a hazard is realised and the extent of it'.

Every part of event management has potential risks. Various publications exist to assist the event manager in managing risk, including general publications offered by the Health and Safety Executive (HSE, 1998) and guidelines developed for exhibitions (AEO, BECA and EVA, 2000), music events (HSE, 1999), outdoor events other than pop concerts and raves (NOEA, 1993; 1997), sporting grounds (Department of National Heritage and the Scottish Office, 1997) and crowd safety (HSE, 2000). Possibly the best known out of these, affectionately referred to as the Purple Guide, is *The Event Safety Guide* (HSE, 1999). Designed to provide advice for the safe management of music events, concerts and festivals, the guide separates events into five phases where risk can be assessed:

- *Build-up*: this involves planning the venue design, selection of competent workers, selection of contractors and subcontractors, and construction, for example, of the stage, marquees, and fencing.
- *Load in*: this involves planning for the safe delivery and installation of equipment and services which will be used at the event, for example, stage equipment used by performers, lighting and sound systems.

Step 1   Identification: look for the hazards

Step 2   Decision: decide who might be harmed and how

Step 3   Evaluation/control: evaluate the risks and decide whether the existing precautions are
         adequate or whether more should be done

Step 4   Recording: record your findings

Step 5   Review: review your assessment and revise it if necessary

Figure 9.5 Five steps to risk assessment
Source: HSE, 1998, p. 3.

- *Show*: this involves planning effective crowd management strategies, transport management strategies and welfare arrangements and planning strategies for dealing with fire, first aid, contingencies and major incidents.
- *Load out*: this requires planning for the safe removal of equipment and services.
- *Breakdown*: this includes planning to control risks once the event is over and the infrastructure is being dismantled, including disposal of waste-water and rubbish.

A good risk management strategy will also cover any other area whose operations are crucial to the event and which may need special security and safety precautions, such as ticket sales and other cash points and communications. In every area, risks must be identified and pre-empted, and their management integrated into the event plan. As with many aspects of event management, risk management can be represented as a cycle. Figure 9.5 identifies the five steps that need to be taken to assess the risks associated with staging event.

Identification

Pre-empting problems requires skill through experience and knowledge. Something that appears safe to some of the event staff may well contain hidden dangers. A sponsor's sign at an event may look securely mounted when examined by the marketing manager, but it would require specialist knowledge by the stage hands to be assured that it is secure. Since the event manager cannot be an expert in every field, it is best to pool the experience of all the event staff and volunteers, and convene a risk assessment meeting. Such a meeting should aim to gather risk management expertise. For large events, a consultant may be hired. The meeting is also an opportunity to train and motivate event staff in the awareness, minimization and control of risk.

Identification techniques

A range of techniques is available for event managers to assess and manage the risks involved in an event, including work breakdown structure, test events, internal/external risk, fault diagrams, incident reports and contingency plans.

- *Work breakdown structure*: decomposing the work necessary to create an event into manageable parts can greatly assist in the identification of risks. It provides a visual schema as well as the categorization of the event into units with specific skills and resources. Isolating the event areas in this way gives a clear picture of the possible problems. This analysis may not reveal the problems that result in a combination of risks. For example, a problem with the ticketing of an event may not be severe on its own. However, if it is combined with the withdrawal of a major sponsor the result may require the event to be cancelled.

- *Test events*: large sporting events often run smaller events to test the facilities, equipment and other resources. The pre-conference cocktail party is used to test some of the aspects of the conference. Many music festivals will run an opening concert on the night before the first day as a means of testing the equipment.
- *Internal/external risk*: to assist the analysis it is useful to have a classification according to the origin of the risk. Internal risks arise in the event planning and implementation. They may also be a result of the inexperience of the event company. These risks are generally within the abilities of the event company to manage. External risks arise from outside the event organization and may need a different control strategy. It would focus on mitigating the impact of the risk.
- *Fault diagram*: risk can also be discovered by looking at their impact and working backwards to the possible cause. This is a result to cause method. For example, a lack of ticket sales would be a terrible result for an event. The fault diagram method would go back from this scenario through the various aspects of the event to identify its cause. The list of causes is then used to manage the risk.
- *Incident report*: almost all large public events have an incident report document. These may be included in the event manual and are meant to be filled out by the event staff when there is an incident. This is not to be confused with an accident report book, which is a legal requirement for all events under the Reporting of Injuries, Diseases and Dangerous Occurrences Regulations 1995 (RIDDOR).
- *Contingency plan*: an outcome of the risk assessment may be a detailed plan of viable alternative integrated actions. The contingency plan contains the response to the impact of a risk and involves decision procedure, chain of command and a set of related actions. An example of contingency planning was the response to the extreme weather conditions on New Year's Eve 2000. As a result of heavy snow and wind, followed by a quick thaw and heavy rain, many events were cancelled. However, the event at Belfast City was transferred from the outdoor venue to Belfast Waterfront (indoors) and the event was a success.

Decision

Decide on who may be harmed. This may include, for example:

- people particularly at risk, e.g. young workers, trainees
- people not familiar with the site, e.g. contractors, visitors
- members of the public.

Evaluation/control

Once the risks are identified they can be listed in order of importance. They are given priority according to their probability of occurrence and the severity of the results. Risk assessment meetings can often bring out the 'prophets of doom' who give an unrealistic pessimistic pall over the event planning. This is itself, a risk that has to be pre-empted. It is important that the meeting be well chaired and focused, since the time needed for risk assessment must always be weighed against the limited time available for the overall event planning. An effective risk assessment meeting will produce a comprehensive and realistic analysis of potential risks.

After the potential risks have been evaluated, event managers need to create mechanisms to control any potential problem. In *Five Steps to Risk Management*, the Health and Safety Executive (HSE, 1998) suggest that managers ask the following questions: can I get rid of the hazard altogether? If not, how can I control the risks so that harm is unlikely? They go on to propose that the following principles should be followed in controlling risk, in order:

- try a less risky option
- prevent access to the hazard e.g. through security, barriers.
- organize work to reduce exposure to the hazard
- issue personal protective equipment
- provide welfare facilities, e.g. wash facilities to remove contamination – and first aid (HSE, 1998, p. 5).

Specific event risks ◦ ◦ ◦

The assembly of large numbers of people will inevitably lead to hazards, however, the risks associated with these will vary according to the nature of the event (HSE, 1999). These risks include crowd management, alcohol, communication, environment and emergencies.

- *Crowd management*: there are many factors that impinge on the smooth management of crowds at an event. The first risk is correctly estimating the number of people who will attend the event. No matter how the site is designed, too many attendees can put enormous strain on the event resources. For example, gatecrashers at Glastonbury Festival 2000 doubled the licensed capacity to an estimated 200 000 people on site. This led to the cancellation of Glastonbury 2001, due to increased safety fears in the wake of the Roskilde tragedy and prosecution of the organizer for alleged breach of the licence. Even at free events, too few attendees can significantly affect the event objectives. For example, the launch of Millennium Square in Leeds on New Year's Eve 2000 saw only hundreds, rather than the anticipated thousands, of visitors attend due to the extreme weather conditions on the evening. Crowd risk management is also a function of the type of audience and their standards of behaviour. A family event will have different priorities in risk management to a rock festival. The expectations of the crowd can be managed with the right kind of information being sent out prior to the event. The HSE guide, *Managing Crowds Safely* (HSE, 2000), provides general guidance for managing crowd safety in a systematic way, covering the areas of planning, risk assessment, putting precautions in place, emergency planning and procedures, communication, monitoring crowds and review.
- *Alcohol*: events can range from a family picnic with the audience sipping wine while watching a show, to New Year's Eve mass gatherings of youth and heavy

consumption of alcohol. Under the law, both events are treated the same. The results of the latter can cause an event to be cancelled. The alcohol risk management procedures can permeate every aspect of some events including limiting ticket sales, closing hotels early, increased security, and roping off areas. The European Football Championships 2000, hosted jointly by the Netherlands and Belgium, illustrate the negative impact that alcohol can have, with violence, civil disruption, arrests, restaurants and bars closed, and the threat of England team being expelled from the tournament.

- *Environment*: of increasing concern to the general community is the risk to the environment posed by modern businesses. There are both dangerous risks such as pollution, spills, effluent leakage, and the more indirect risks minimised by waste recycling, water and energy conservation. The impacts, and therefore the priorities for their control, will vary over the event project life cycle.

- *Emergency*: an awareness of the nearest emergency services and their working requirements are mandatory for event management. The reason for calling in the outside emergency service is that the situation is beyond the capabilities of the event staff and requires specialist attention. It is important to understand the chain of command when emergency services arrive. They will be outside the control of the event management who would act purely in an advisory capacity. They may be called in by any attendee at an event. Commenting on the potential consequences of a major incident, the HSE (1999, p. 31) advise that a multi-agency approach will generally be required, including the event management, policy, fire authority, National Health Service (NHS) including ambulance service, local authority, local emergency planning officer, stewards and first-aiders. As a result, procedures, demarcation of duties and responsibilities should be agreed in writing with all relevant parties within the planning stage.

Recording

It is advisable that all hazards and action taken are recorded by all organizations, however, by law only those employing more than five employees are legally required to do so. Records should be suitable and sufficient to demonstrate, should the need arise, that the risk assessment took place, the people affected were identified, significant hazards were dealt with, precautions were taken and the remaining risk was low. Accurate records can assist the event manager in monitoring hazards and provide evidence should this be demanded, for example, in a compensation claim (HSE, 1998).

Review

Evaluating the success and failures of the risk control is central to the success of future events. The event company must be a 'learning organization'. The analysis of and response to feedback is essential to this process.

The *Event Safety Guide* provides advice within thirty-three chapters on specific arrangements for health and safety at music and similar events. The chapter headings, presented in Figure 9.6, can provide organizers with a useful basis for planning their requirements (HSE, 1999, p. 2)

☐ Planning and management	☐ Camping
☐ Venue and site design	☐ Facilities for people with special needs
☐ Fire safety	☐ Medical, ambulance and first-aid
☐ Major incident planning (emergency planning)	management
☐ Communication	☐ Information and welfare
☐ Crowd management	☐ Children
☐ Transport management	☐ Performers
☐ Structures	☐ TV and media
☐ Barriers	☐ Stadium music events
☐ Electrical installations and lighting	☐ Arena events
☐ Food, drink and water	☐ Large events
☐ Merchandising and special licensing	☐ Small events
☐ Amusements, attractions and promotional displays	☐ Classical music events
☐ Sanitary facilities	☐ Unfenced or unticketed events, including radio roadshows
☐ Waste management	☐ All-night music events
☐ Sound: noise and vibration	☐ Unlicensed events
☐ Special effects, fireworks and pyrotechnics	☐ Health and safety responsibilities

Figure 9.6 Checklist for planning risk assessment requirements
Source: HSE, 1999, p. iii.

Insurance

Central to any strategy of liability minimization is obtaining the correct insurance. Event Assured, one of the leading UK providers of insurance to events, provide helpful suggestions regarding insurance. These include the following, focused on legal liabilities:

- The contract with the venue – are you assuming any additional responsibilities beyond Common Law?
- Are you providing adequate security for your exhibitors property left at the venue? You could be held liable for theft if you have not taken reasonable precautions.
- Are you assuming liabilities or entering into contracts that may be outside the scope of your existing liability insurance? Make sure that your insurance contains the correct definitions of your business activities and geographical extent of cover. There is a continuing duty of disclosure under insurance contracts, so it is important to advise your insurers of any new, additional or unusual activities that may be undertaken at the event.
- If the contract states that certain minimum levels of cover are required, do you need to arrange extra cover for this event?
- Unless there is a specific limitation of liability in the contract, assume the worst could happen, and buy as much liability insurance as you can afford. It sounds far-fetched, but your liability could extend to the value of the whole building, and all the people inside it, and even adjoining premises!

- Are you accepting responsibility for the negligence of other parties such as the venue owners, contractors or event exhibitors? Ideally you should resist accepting responsibility for the actions of any other party unless you are in control of what they do. Avoid waiving any rights against other parties.
- If a main contract makes you responsible for the actions of subcontractors, or exhibitors, make sure that your contracts with subcontractors and exhibitors require them to indemnify you in like manner.
- Check the insurances of bone fide subcontractors – limits of liability and wordings. Make sure they contain a clause, which indemnifies you for their negligence.
- If possible, exhibition organizers/owners should control the insurance held by exhibitors by setting up a block policy, and making booking insurance part of the booking form. You can then offer an insurance, which offers the right clauses and limits. Exhibitors will benefit from knowing that there is a standard cover available designed to meet their obligations under their stand agreement.
- For labour only subcontractors, make sure that your insurers are aware of who they are, what they are doing, and what you are paying them. You are likely to be in an 'employer–employee' relationship with such persons, and need to make sure that Employers Liability Insurance operates.
- Are you responsible under equipment hire contracts for liabilities arising out of the use of the plant and for operators? If so, tell your insurers and arrange additional cover if necessary.
- If you are a professional event organizer (i.e. organizing the event for a client), then what are your professional liabilities? Even if the contract makes no mention of this, you will have a liability for negligent acts, errors or omissions, which arises at Common Law under a contract for the provision of professional services. Public liability insurance does not cover this – you may need professional indemnity insurance.
- Think also about the following: libel, slander, breach of copyright, breach of confidence, plagiarism (Event Assured, 2000).

There are many kinds of insurance that can be taken out for events. These include: weather insurance; personal accident insurance for the volunteer works; property insurance, including money; workers compensation insurance; public liability; employers liability. The choice of the particular insurance cover is dictated by the risk management strategy developed by event management, based on legal requirements.

Regulations, licences and permits

There are long lists of regulations that need to be satisfied when staging event. The bigger and more innovative the event, the larger the number of these regulations. The correct procedure in one local authority or county within the UK may be completely different in another. The principal rule is to carry out careful research, including investigating similar events in the same area and seeking advice on what permits and licences are necessary to allow an event to proceed.

It is always the responsibility of an event company to find out and comply with all pertinent rules, regulations and licensing requirements. For example, in reviewing the Public Entertainment Licence for Glastonbury Festival, the report

Insurance

- Public liability insurance – £25 million indemnity
- Insurance for loss or damage to goods, materials, equipment, stands or exhibits
- Employers liability insurance
- Personal accident insurance for participants

Legislation, including:

1 Principal regulations applying to exhibitions include: The Local Government Act 1972; The Health and Safety at Work, etc, Act 1974; The Fire Precaution Act 1971 (as amended); The Building Regulations 1981 (as amended); The Management of the Health & Safety at Work Regulations 1999; The Environmental Protection Act 1990; The Town and Country Planning Act 1990; The Manual Handling Operations Regulation 1992; The Personal Protective Equipment at Work Regulation 1992; The Workplace (Health Safety and Welfare) Regulations 1992; The Provision and Use and Work Equipment Regulations 1998; The Construction (Design & Maintenance) Regulation 1994; The Environment Act 1995; The Institution Structural Engineers Temporary Demountable Structures Recommendations 1999; The Health & Safety (Safety Signs and Signals) Regulations 1996; The Fire Precaution (Workplace) Regulations 1997; Reporting of Injuries, Diseases and Dangerous Occurrences Regulations 1995 (RIDDOR); COSHH (The Control of Substances Hazardous to Health Regulations 1999).

2 Association of Exhibition Organizers Guide – organizers should take note of recommended practice.

3 Children and Young Persons Act 1933 and the Children (Performances) Regulations 1968 – apply where children are involved in the event.

4 Childrens Act 1989 – management of cr'eche facilities.

5 City Veterinary Department – where animals involved, written statement required from City Vet that arrangements are satisfactory.

6 Betting and Gambling – subject to appropriate licences.

7 Video Performance Limited – if music videos are to be played.

8 TV Licence – for temporary television broadcasting.

9 Complex Structures Site Inspection Certificate – generally to be provided by Chartered Engineer with professional indemnity insurance.

10 ExCel Special Permit – if the event is to be filmed or recorded for television or radio.

11 Fairground and Amusement Parks: Code of Safe Practice at Fairs – independent safety certificate for rides and simulators.

12 Trading standards – all exhibitors must comply with trading standards law for consumer rights.

13 Home Office Licence – radio transmissions, on-site communications.

14 Excel Permits – Mooring, on-site parking, hot working (for welding etc.)

15 Food Hygiene/Food Safety/Labelling – Food Safety Act 1990, Food Safety (General Food Hygiene) Regulations 1995, Food Safety (Temperature Control) Regulations 1995, The Food Labelling Regulations 1996, Department of Health Assured Safe Catering System.

16 Liquor licensing – for selling alcohol, licence required from Licensing District of Newham and the police notified.

17 Exhibition Venues Association 'Regulations for Stand Electrical Installations', The Electricity at Work Regulations 1989, British Standard 7671 1992 (IE364) 'Requirements for Electrical Installations' – electric on stands, features, displays or exhibits.

Figure 9.7 Legal requirements for events at ExCeL
Source: adapted from London International Exhibition Centre PLC, 2000.

from the Environmental Health Manager to the licensing authority at Mendip District Council includes input from a wide range of authorities including Environmental Health, Avon and Somerset Police, Somerset Fire Brigade and Festival Medical Services (Anderson, 2000). Many local authorities apply environmental noise control protocols to control the impact of noise on communities, with guidance available from the Noise Council (Noise Council, 1995; HSE, 1999). Not only that, but event managers must make it a practice to pay particular attention to workplace health and safety regulations.

Figure 9.7 describes some of the permits, licences, insurance and regulations with which an event must comply to take place at ExCeL, London. It is evident that an event manager may need to seek legal advice to ensure that all relevant regulations are taken into account – industry associations can prove to be a useful source of information in this respect.

Permits and licences allow special activities during an event, such as the handling of food, pyrotechnics, sale of alcohol, sale of tickets, street trading and road closures. The Performing Right Society (PRS) and Phonographic Performance Ltd (PPL) issue licences for the performance of their members' works. They function as a collection society, monitoring and collecting royalties on behalf of their members (music composers and their publishers). So when an event company decides to set fireworks to music, it is not just a matter of hiring a band or pressing 'play' on the sound system.

Many regulations, permits and licences change with each local authority and country within the UK, and reinterpretations of the old rules are proclaimed regularly. For example, at the time of writing representatives of the Core Cities Group of major cities (e.g. Liverpool, Birmingham, Leeds and Manchester) are currently working with the District Surveyors Association to develop a consistent system of licensing guidelines (Mellor, 2000). The Local Government (Miscellaneous Provisions) Act 1982 (London Government Act 1963 in London), which controls places used for public music and dancing, and similar entertainment, is administered by local authorities and often its interpretation will vary from council to council. Local authorities have similar powers for private events under the Private Places of Entertainment (Licensing) Act 1967 (HSE, 1999).

This complex area needs the close attention of event management. Companies must undertake detailed research into all regulations affecting their event and should allocate time to deal with the results of that research. Government agencies can take a long time to respond to requests. Therefore it is imperative to begin early in seeking any permits or licences, and to factor delays and difficulties with obtaining them into the time frame of the event planning process.

Summary

Event managers have a duty of care to all involved in an event. Any reasonably foreseen risks have to be eliminated or minimised. The process of doing this is central to a risk management strategy. Liability minimisation is part of this strategy. This includes identifying the ownership of the event, careful structuring of the event management, taking out insurance and adhering to all the rules and regulations pertaining to events. Specific legal issues of concern to the event management include contracting, trademarks and trade practices. Legal matters can be complex and interpretation can differ from council to council and between countries within the UK, particularly between England/Wales and Scotland. The information discussed within this chapter provides a brief overview of issues to consider, however, as regulations and guidelines are subject to constant change, it is highly recommended that any event company seek legal advice when unsure of these matters.

Questions

1 List the areas covered by the contract between the event company and supplier of audiovisuals.

2 What are two methods of minimizing liability?

3 Contrast the risks involved in staging an outdoor concert to those involved in producing an indoor food fair. What risk management strategy could be used to reduce or eliminate these risks?

4 What actions can be taken to reduce the cost for overall liability insurance? Should the event company be covered for patrons to be covered after they leave the event?

5 What licences and permits are needed for a street party?

Case Study

Glastonbury Festival 2001 – the big issues

Michael Eavis, organizer of Glastonbury Festival, announced in January 2001 that Glastonbury Festival 2001 would not be taking place. The decision to take a year off was not taken lightly, but was due to a simple cause: gatecrashers – or, more accurately, fence-jumpers. Although the 2000 event passed off without major incident it is widely recognized that the number of people on site was significantly in excess of the number permitted by the Public Entertainment Licence. The site is licensed for 100 000 people – with the addition of gatecrashers the site was completely full.

In assessing trends and risks for the 2001 event, the festival acknowledged that the rate of increase in numbers of gatecrashers suggested that there is a strong likelihood that the site could be dangerously overcrowded in 2001. After considerable work to develop controls, the festival and the authorities were not sufficiently confident that effective controls could be put into place in time for 2001. However, all parties believed that a year off would allow sufficient time for adequate systems to prevent non-ticket holders entering the site to be introduced, and for the key message of the dangers of overcrowding to be publicized.

The issue has come to a head following concerns raised by the Mendip District Council and by the police. Mendip District Council since confirmed their intention to prosecute Michael Eavis over breaches of the terms of the licence. The prosecution also alleged breaches of noise limits as well as attendance numbers.

The numbers game

Various methods – some more credible than others – have been used to estimate the numbers present in 2000, but the festival acknowledges that there were tens of thousands of gatecrashers. Although there have always been some people who gain entry to the festival without a ticket, 2000 saw these numbers reach astonishing proportions. In the early 1970s gaining free admission was part of the culture of the events, and it is widely known that Michael Eavis was inspired by his visit to the Bath Blues Festival in 1970 – where he entered through a hole in the fence! But that was a long time ago, and anyone who saw the film of the Isle of Wight festival from that era, replete with very 1960s-style hippies condemning the 'capitalist' fence, will probably have had an inner smile at how outdated and clichéd that behaviour seems now – particularly when compared with the enormous advances in production values, quality and quantity of entertainment, and audience safety and welfare resources which have come to characterize the modern Glastonbury Festivals.

Organization

If Glastonbury is by far the best known music festival throughout Europe, its closest rival for that title must surely be Roskilde, a weekend event in Denmark usually held on the weekend after Glastonbury (although in some years the events have run simultaneously). The year 2000 saw a tragic event at Roskilde, where nine people were killed in a front-of-stage crush. This event shocked many, not least the Avon and Somerset Police who have frequently referred to the tragedy when voicing their concerns over Glastonbury's control of numbers on site. The police in Britain are exercising great caution for large-scale events – following their experiences at Notting Hill Carnival 2000, on Millennium Eve in London, and in the light of the Roskilde tragedy – and are looking to become more familiar with the complexity and competence of Glastonbury's large management team.

It is worth noting that in the aftermath of Roskilde, organizers, governments and promoters' associations have been looking around for the best models and guidelines for safe event management, and it is little surprise that the best resources have been found here in the UK.

Glastonbury Festivals have long recommended the Health and Safety Executive's publication *The Event Safety Guide* (*ESG*) as the standard reference work for an introduction to safe event planning. The *ESG* is now being voluntarily adopted in many other countries. It is notable that some of the core recommendations of the *ESG*, particularly designs and specifications of front-of-stage barriers, were not followed at Roskilde. In other developments, the Production Services Association (PSA) – the trade body representing live event professionals – has been called in as consultants to promoters' organizations and European governmental departments.

Most of Glastonbury's key personnel are PSA members – many were core contributors to the *ESG*, as were staff of Mendip District Council. A great deal of expertise has been pioneered around Glastonbury Festival, and the local authority, service providers, festival staff and contractors have become recognized experts in their fields.

Glastonbury Festival – 2002 and beyond

Even before the Mendip District Council meeting in October 2000, at which the council and the police's concerns over the issue of potential overcrowding were given formal voice, work had begun to address the issue. Michael Eavis consulted Eve Trackway, the contractors who had provided the perimeter fence in recent years, to look at improved fencing solutions. A prototype of a new fence, commissioned by the festival, was demonstrated in September. At 20 feet high the fence dwarfs the previous structure and has a number of other features which make it vastly more formidable as an obstacle to freeloaders. Michael stated that he was prepared to install a finalized version of the fence for the entire perimeter at a cost of £1.5 million. Feedback was invited from all parties including the festival's own safety and emergency personnel, the emergency services and the local authority.

It was agreed that such an imposing new fence would be a major step forward in preventing overcrowding. It was also recognized that the presence of the structure brought with it some added responsibilities, and several vital ideas for improving fencing yet further came forward. The festival is now considering several final choices of design and is committed to providing a vastly improved perimeter fence for 2002.

It was also agreed that the fence is only a partial solution. Other aspects of event planning can significantly help to dissuade people from attempting to enter without tickets and to avoid crowding on site. Amongst the main ideas under consideration are:

- *Public transport*: ensuring that only ticket holders are permitted to use the special bus, coach and train services to the festival. Practical discussions with the main service providers are well advanced.
- *Vehicle ticket checks*: these would be carried out at some distance from the site, before traffic turns off main routes. Checks would ensure that all vehicle occupants had a festival ticket. Once checked, vehicles would be issued with their car-parking permit. Only vehicles with parking permits will be waved through; other vehicles will be directed straight on.
- *Remote car parks*: instead of using adjacent land the car parks may be established some distance away and shuttle transport for ticket holders provided.
- *Internal controls on access to trouble spots*: this has been strongly proposed by some authorities with regard to the main arena(s). The need to control the density of crowds in certain key areas of the site is being carefully examined. The festival is opposed to fencing the arenas and would naturally want to retain the complete freedom of all ticket holders to move at will through all parts of the site other than the obvious secure work areas, but organizers and authorities are aware of certain specific points and times where crowd densities tend to be very high and are in need of careful management.
- *Other factors*: these include increasing the number, professionalism, resources, legal empowerment and monitoring of perimeter and gate security staff; seeking the co-operation of the local community in not providing private parking nor other facilities to non-ticket holders; developing a legally informed strategy in co-operation with all relevant parties to prevent intrusion and damage to the fence.

Although it is accepted that many fans were disappointed at the decision not to run Glastonbury Festival in 2001, it was believed that taking a year out to effectively consider the above issues will ensure a safe event and improved experience for all festival-goers for many years to come. With the increasing pressures placed on organizers through local authorities, the police and other agencies, and even tighter licence conditions, festivals such as Glastonbury and other large-scale events will increasingly develop their management and control systems to ensure that all risks are minimized.

For further details about Glastonbury Festival of Contemporary Performing Arts, please visit www.glastonburyfestivals.co.uk.

By Glastonbury Festivals Limited, Worthy Farm, Pilton, Shepton Mallett, Somerset, BA4 4BY.

Questions

1 With regard to crowd safety, what lessons can be learned from the experience of Glastonbury Festival? How would you apply these if you were organizing the next festival?

2 Some festival-goers believe that increasing fencing, tightening security and implementing other measures to control them are damaging the festival experience. As the event organizer, what message would you have for these festival-goers?

3 Can you think of any other ways of dissuading people without tickets from attempting to access Glastonbury Festival?

Case Study

Love Parade, Leeds

Background

The Love Parade ran for the first time in the UK in Leeds in July 2000. Following discussions with the Berlin Love Parade organizers, Radio One undertook to organize the dance music based event in the UK. The event concept involved a parade of twenty floats, sponsored by the leading dance music clubs in the UK, leading to a large, free open-air dance music event. Radio One signed an agreement to use the name 'Love Parade' in the UK and financially underwrote the event – they also promoted it and stimulated interest in the event. Logistik were ultimately tasked with putting together the event, managing it, staging it and running it. A third party was contracted to get support from all the big dance clubs in the UK who bought floats. Leeds City Council's role was as host and to help ensure the event went off well.

The concept

The mission was initially to establish and run a Love Parade in the UK, in association with the German event. Historically, there has been a lot of animosity between Germany and England and events such as this are positive in developing cultural links. The Love Parade in Berlin is well documented – it was established to celebrate the fall of the Berlin Wall, which proved to be an excellent stimulant for running an event. The underlying principle for both the German and UK events was that everybody, regardless of class, money, background or status, had an equal opportunity to attend, join in with the event, and they could do so regardless of their financial position in life. Radio One supported this event wholeheartedly as it was an event open to everyone, clearly relating to their ethos of One Love.

The aims were to hold a free, safe and well-attended event. These were clearly achieved. In addition, the objective, from an organizer's point of view, was to develop the event in such a manner that it could be developed and move on to another city – in 2001 the event planned to move to Newcastle.

Hospitality, Leisure & Tourism Series

Audience size

In order to determine the potential audiences for the Love Parade, a number of previous events were researched, including the Road Shows, the Big Sundays and other events organized by Radio One, together with experience at previous dance events. The resulting audience was estimated at being 250 000 (based on aerial photography and working out the number of people per square metre). This unprecedented audience resulted from two areas. First, there was a high level of support from the youth press as it was unique and it caught the youths' imagination. Second, Radio One succeeded in their promotion of it – the event itself caught people's imagination, with a worldwide fellowship of people who love music, love to party, love to have a good time, behave themselves and to link up with Berlin.

The venue, facilities and staff

The venue for the event changed from the City Centre to Roundhay Park in Leeds four weeks before the event, due to concerns expressed by the police over the growth in anticipated audience. Roundhay Park is basically a big open field and, as a result, the event site was built from scratch, including a large volume of toilets, food franchises, drinks franchises, bars and standpipes with free water. West Yorkshire Ambulance Service and the Drugs Advisory Group in Leeds provided first-aid stations and counselling. Transport was provided with a bus service running up to Roundhay from the City Centre. On site, three free stages and twenty free floats were provided for the audience to watch.

The management structure included a parade manager, site manager, production manager, stage manager, float managers, float stewards, event managers and an event director. The team also included approximately 500 stewards from ShowSec International, a health and safety team, plus 600 police officers, West Yorkshire Ambulance Service, Drugs Advisory Services and Leeds City Council Cleansing Services. In addition to this, contracts for services were signed with many suppliers.

The licensing and planning process

Planning commenced a year in advance where tacit agreement for the event was obtained from Leeds City Council, followed by the normal system of multi-agency discussion. Within the licensing framework, there is a fairly well understood set of steps that you go through to obtain a public entertainment licence. The basis is that a meeting is organized with the multi-agency group where the concept and aims are explained, from which will come hundreds of questions. Following this, a number of submeetings follow with environmental health (sound and toilets), the highways department (road closures) and the police (public order). The process involves risk assessments, safety plans, crowd control statements and mission statements.

Documentation is refined to incorporate the above items and this is then built into the event plan. In this respect, simple is best. Whilst you can write reams of documentation, which can be as detailed as you want it to be, it has to be broadly understood by all those that are involved with the event, not just a key group of people who happen to be in a meeting. All the people involved in the event, from the management team to the stewards and the medics, have got to have a good understanding of what's drawn from these meetings, understand what is being aimed for, and what to do in the event of x, y and z. Regardless of the size of the event, you still need a simple plan that everyone understands and can work to. This is the normal process for organizing events – obviously it was a lot more complicated for Love Parade due to the scale of the event. Because of the nature of this event, it was very difficult to stick to any sort of well-understood and pre-agreed formulas for getting permissions for the event through Leeds City Council and other agencies. Very quickly people realized that the event that they had agreed to had changed somewhat, because Radio One were the promoters and it was going to be a lot bigger. There was concern in some quarters that they were hosting the equivalent of the Notting Hill Carnival for dance music, and peoples' attitudes changed. There was debate within Leeds City Council and with the multi-agency group, led by the police, about how the event could best be licensed and whether it should be licensed at all. The debate went on right up until the actual event – ultimately it had a public entertainment licence at Roundhay Park (and a drinks licence), however this was only resolved a few weeks before the event.

As a company, Logistik have insurance for employees, public, professional, and hired in plant insurance. In addition, specific insurance was taken out to cover the Love Parade and increased the amounts on the other insurance to cover this size of event. The insurance indemnified everyone involved.

Consultation

Consultation with the local community was limited and not as it should have been due to the short time that was available following the move to Roundhay Park. As organizers, it can be problematic keeping the balance between canvassing opinion and planning the event, when some communities clearly object to events taking place near them, particularly on this scale. Although there was only a short time available before the event, meetings were arranged with a number of community groups, followed by further meetings and correspondence after the event to listen to people's views. Some of these were irate and unreasonable, but a lot of them were well meaning and contributed constructively. The city council also put together a questionnaire that was distributed to the local community to gain feedback. There was a fair amount of consultation afterwards but this did not make up for the fact that there was not enough time to conduct effective consultation beforehand.

Evaluation

Generally, whether the event was a success depends on who is asked – it has to be looked at on balance and in the context of what was achieved. You could ask three different people 'was the event a success?' and, depending on their age, outlook on life and geographical position (where they lived), they would give you three completely different answers. If you were under thirty and came to the event specifically to enjoy yourself, you would say it was an absolutely phenomenal success with 250 000 people, no major incidents in terms of injury, people had a really good time, it was a friendly atmosphere and there were no public order problems. If you talked to people who own shops in Leeds, the majority would think it was a success because it brought a huge amount of income into the city – an economic impact of around £15 million was reported purely in relation to the Love Parade. However, if you were a resident, living near Roundhay Park, who does not like dance music and does not like their normal everyday life being interrupted, then you would have a completely different view on the success of the event. Those residents probably believe that it was not right for two reasons. First, clearly such a huge event has a massive impact and disrupts people's lives – no matter what you do, that is a consequence of holding this sort of event. Second, culturally a lot of older people have a great distrust and dislike of dance music and even of the type of people and their motivation for coming along. If you look at it from those people's point of view, they would say it was a terrible event and it should not have been allowed. They were supported by some journalists in the very conservative local press who were outspoken about their opposition to the event and the problems that it caused.

In Logistik's view, the event was a success – it went off predominantly well and safely (against a huge amount of opposition) and it showed that if you give young people something to do and put together something that is meaningful to them, they will come along in huge numbers, enjoy themselves and behave themselves. However, Logistik have learned a lot from developing this event and there are a number of areas where we can improve for next time. First, we now fully understand the differences between the cultures of the police and the cultures of people who they perceived would be coming to the event. The Leeds Love Parade illustrated that many of the initial fears were unfounded. Second, the well-documented funding issue should be resolved with the police at the start of the process. With the experience of Leeds Love Parade, the event will be further developed for the planned move to Newcastle. Issues raised during the Leeds experience, including the size of the event, together with the concerns of residents and other stakeholders, will be addressed within the planning stages to ensure that the event meets the increasingly stringent requirements of the multi-agency groups, whilst delivering an event that continues the ethos of the Love Parade.

For further details about Love Parade, please visit www.bbc.co.uk/radio1/loveparade
For further details about Logistik events, please visit www.logistik.co.uk
By Peter Haywood, Joint Managing Director, Logistik Ltd.

Questions

1 What characteristics of Leeds do you think lead to it being chosen as the location for the first Love Parade in the UK?

2 What contracts and licences were considered necessary for the event? From what you know of the event, do these measures seem adequate? If not, what other areas of the event might usefully have been covered by written agreements?

3 The increased size of the event affected the perceived risk involved in staging it, leading to the move to Roundhay Park. What could organizers do to control the size of the event?

4 What lessons can be learned regarding the planning of the event, and how would you apply these lessons if you were organizing the next Love Parade?

CHAPTER 10

Logistics

After studying this chapter, you should be able to:

- define logistics management and its evolution
- understand the concept of logistics management and its place in event management
- construct a logistics plan for the supply of customers, event products and event facilities
- use event logistics techniques and tools.

Introduction – what is logistics?

> One of the hardest tasks, for logisticians and non-logisticians alike is to look at a list and spot what's not there. (Pagonis, 1992, p. 73)

Placing the word 'logistics' into its historical context provides an understanding of its use in present event management. Logistics stems from the Greek word *logistikos*, 'skilled in calculating'. The ancient Romans used the term for the administration of its armies. The term evolved to refer to the practical art of the relocation of armies. Given the complexity of modern warfare, logistics became a science that included speed of operations, communications and maintenance of the armed forces. After the Second World War, modern business applied the experience and theory of logistics as they faced similar problems with transport and supply to those faced by the military.

The efficient movement of products has become a specialized study in the management discipline. Within large companies, especially international companies, a section can be devoted to co-ordinating the logistics requirements of each department. Logistics has become a discipline in its own right. This has lead to consolidation into a separate independent function in companies, often called integrated logistics management. The Institute for Logistics and Transport (TILT) define logistics as, 'The time-related positioning of resources to meet user requirement', where resources may be transports, storage, or information (TILT, 2001). Canadine (2001) notes that logistics is generally being used to operate the supply chains in order to satisfy a customer. He also highlights that an alternative definition of logistics is, 'The detailed organization and implementation of a plan or operation', where the plan or operation is to satisfy customer needs. The benefit of efficient co-ordination of logistics in the event company is that a company's product value can be improved.

For a complete understanding of event logistics, this chapter is divided into sections dealing with the tasks of event logistics and the role of the logistics manager.

The elements of event logistics

The various elements of event logistics can be organized into a system, illustrated in Figure 10.1. This system is used to analyse the logistic elements of an event.

Whereas most logistics theory concerns the supply of products to the customers, event logistics includes the efficient supply of the customer to the product, and the supply of facilities to and from the event site. In this sense, it has more in common with military logistics than modern business logistics. Business logistics is an ongoing activity and is part of the continual management of a company. Military and event logistics often concern a specific project or campaign rather than the continuing management. There is a definite preparation, lead up, execution and shutdown. As well, issues such as inventory control and warehousing that are the basis of business logistics are not as important to a one-off event.

The areas of importance to event logistics can be categorized as:

- *Supply*: this is divided into the three areas of customer, product and facilities. Supply also includes the procurement of the goods and services.
- *Transport*: the transport of these goods and services can be a major cost to an event and requires special consideration.

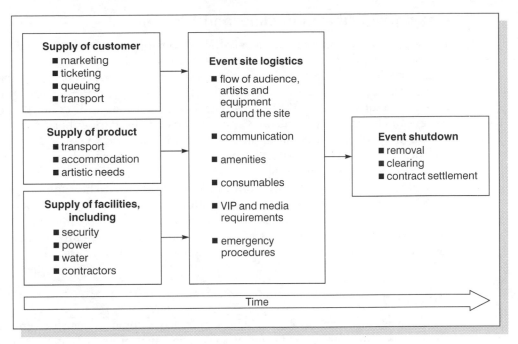

Figure 10.1 Elements of the logistics system

- *Linking*: logistics is part of the overall planning of an event and is linked to all other areas. With large multi-venue events, the logistics becomes so complex that an operations or logistics manager is often appointed. The logistics manager functions as part of the overall network management structure outlined in this chapter.
- *Flow control*: this refers to the flow of products, services and customers during the event.
- *Information networks*: the efficient flow of information during the event is generally a result of efficient planning of the information network. This concept is expanded in the section on on-site logistics.

All these areas need to be considered when creating a logistics plan. Even for small events, such as a wedding or a small product launch, a logistics plan needs to be incorporated in the overall event plan. For these sorts of events, logistics comes under the title 'Staging', which is described in Chapter 11.

Supply of the customer

The customers of the event are those who pay for it. They can be the audience (concerts and festivals), spectators (sport), visitors (exhibitions), delegates (conferences) and the sponsors or the client (corporate events). The customers have expectations that have to be met for a successful outcome. These expectations will include aspects of logistics.

Linking with the marketing and promotion

The supply of customers is ultimately the responsibility of marketing activities. The numbers, geographical spread and expectations of the customers will affect the logistics planning. The targeting of specialist markets or widespread publicity of an event will require a logistics plan with very different priorities. For example, the transport requirements of the customers will vary according to the distance travelled. The majority of the audience of Party in the Park either drives from the surrounding area, or uses the shuttle bus service. Therefore, vehicle access, parking and the availability of an effective bus service are a priority at the event site. The British International Motor Show in Birmingham, with its nationwide publicity campaign, has a large audience from all corners of the UK. This offers opportunities for special negotiations with coach operators, train companies and hotels. If the publicity of an event is spread nationwide the logistics will be different to a product launch that only concerns the staff and customers of a company. In this way the logistics are closely linked to the marketing of an event.

Ticketing

Ticketing is important to events whose primary income is from the entrance fee. Most corporate events, including office parties and product launches, and many public events are free. However, for other events, such as sport events, the extent of ticket sales can determine success or failure (Graham, Neirotti and Goldblatt, 2001). Ticket distribution is regarded as the first major decision in event logistics.

The pricing and printing of the tickets is generally not a logistics area. However, the distribution, collection and security are of concern, and with free events, form an effective means of controlling numbers. In the UK, tickets for events can be sold through various distributors like Ticketmaster for a fee, or they can be sold by mail or through the Internet, for example, through Aloud.com. Glastonbury Festival has traditionally sold out of tickets months in advance, however, in recent years people have waited until closer to the event to purchase tickets in order better to judge the weather. Selling tickets at the gate gives rise to security problems in the collection, accounting and depositing of funds. The ticket collectors need training to deal with the public, as well as efficiently moving the public through the entrance. The honesty of the staff may also be a security concern. Events that have successfully managed this include The Open Championship, which each year have support through sponsorship from the Royal Bank of Scotland to provide cashiers/ticket staff. In larger venues, an admission loss-prevention plan is used to minimize the possibility of theft.

It is not unusual to sell tickets through retail outlets. The Millennium Dome attempted this on a grand scale by using National Lottery outlets as a distribution channel to sell tickets. Inventory control and cash receipts are two areas that require special attention when using retail outlets for ticket distribution. Numbering of the tickets and individual letters of agreement with each outlet are the most efficient methods of control. The letter of agreement would include the range of ticket numbers, level of the tickets (discount or full price) and the method of payment. Depending on the size of the event, the ticketing can be crucial to the event's success and take up a significant amount of the event director's time. Figure 10.2 is a checklist of ticketing an event.

Does the artwork on the ticket contain the following?

- Number of the ticket
- Name of the event
- Date and time of the event
- Price and level of the ticket (discount, complementary, full price, early bird)
- Seating number or designated area (ticket colour coding can be used to show seating area)
- Disclaimer (in particular, this should list the responsibilities of the event promoter)
- Event information, such as a map, warnings and what to bring/not to bring
- Artwork so that the ticket could be used as a souvenir (part of the ticket could be kept by the patron)
- Contact details for information

Printing

- When will the tickets be ready?
- Will the tickets be delivered or do they have to be collected?
- If there is an error or a large demand for the tickets, will there be time for more to be printed?

Distribution

- What outlets will be used – retail, Ticketmaster, Internet, mail or at the gate?
- Has a letter of agreement with all distributors, setting out terms and conditions, been signed?
- What method of payment will be used (by both the ticket buyer to the distributor and in the final reconciliation) – credit card, cash, direct deposit?
- Are schedule of payment and reconciliation forms available?
- Does the schedule of communications refer to ticket sales indicate sales progress and if more tickets are needed?

Collection of tickets

- How will the tickets be collected at the gates and transferred to a pass-out?
- How experienced are the personnel and how many will there be? When will they arrive and leave?
- Is a separate desk for complementary tickets needed site of ticket collection site?
- What security arrangements are in place for cash and personnel?
- How will the tickets be disposed of?

Reconciliation of number of tickets with revenue received

- What method of reconciliation will be used? Is an accountant being used?
- Is the reconciliation ongoing, at the conclusion of the event, or at the end of the month?
- Is the system robust to allow for independent auditing, such as ABC auditing of exhibition visitor numbers?
- Has a separate account been set up just for the one event to assist the accountancy procedure?

Figure 10.2 Ticketing – logistics checklist

An innovative method of ticketing for festivals is to use the hospital-style wristbands, called crowd control bands. These are colour coded to indicate the level of the ticket – a day ticket, a weekend ticket or a special performer's ticket. The use of these wristbands introduces a visual method of control during a large event, as the sale of food and drinks is only allowed if the wristband is shown. In this way, the food vendors become part of the security for the event.

The Internet is increasingly used for the distribution of tickets for large events, concerts and conferences. This use of the Internet illustrates the linking of logistics and marketing, as discussed in Chapter 6. Originally the World Wide Web was used in the marketing of events by means of advertising them through a website. The introduction of encrypted data enabled the increase in the privacy and security of payment methods and the sale of tickets from a site. The site collaborates with the existing ticketing system, and can be connected to travel agencies.

Queuing

Often the first experience a customer has at an event is the queue for tickets or parking. Once inside the event, customers may be confronted with queues for food, toilets and seating. An important aspect of queue theory is the 'perceived waiting time'. This is the subjective time that the customers feel that they have waited. There are many rules of thumb about diminishing the customers perceived waiting time. In the catering industry, the queuing for food can affect the event experience. An informal rule is one food or beverage line for every seventy-five to a hundred people. Figure 10.3 lists some of the factors to consider in the logistics of queuing.

The Atlanta Olympics and the Millennium Dome have successfully used entertainers to reduce the perceived waiting time at the entrance and exhibit queues. Exit queuing can be the last experience for the customer at an event and needs the close attention of the event manager. At London's New Year's Eve celebrations, the authorities planned to use 'staggered entertainment' to spread the exit time of the crowds and avoid overcrowding on the London Underground. Within football stadia it is common practice to keep fans of one team within the ground until the opposing team's fans have dispersed, to avoid confrontation. Nightclubs may employ similar tactics, by raising lights shortly before the end of the evening and circulating security staff to avoid customers all waiting until the final record has been played.

- How many queues and possible bottlenecks will there be?
- Have an adequate number of personnel greeters, crowd controllers, ticket collectors and security been allocated?
- Is signage (including the estimated waiting time) in place?
- When will the queues form? Will they form all at once or over a period of time?
- How can the perceived waiting time be reduced (e.g., queue entertainers)?
- What first-aid, access and emergency procedures are in place?
- Are the lighting and sun and rain protection adequate?
- Are crowd-friendly barricades and partitions in place?

Figure 10.3 Queuing: factors to consider

The oversupply of customers at a commercial event can give rise to a number of security and public safety problems that should be anticipated in the logistics plan. Equally, free events can attract too many customers if not carefully controlled. Only pre-sale tickets, and ticketing free events, will indicate the exact number of the expected audience. When tickets are sold at the entrance to an event, the logistics plan has to include the possibility of too many people. Oversubscription may be pleasing for the event promoter, but can produce a logistical nightmare of what to do with the excess crowd.

Customer transport

Transport to a site is often the first physical commitment by the audience to an event. The method and timing of arrival – public or private transport – is important to the overall logistics plan. The terms used by event managers are *dump*, when the audience arrives almost at once, and *trickle*, when they come and go over a larger period of time. Each of these needs a different logistics strategy. This first impression of the event by the audience can influence all subsequent experiences at the event. For this reason, it is the most visible side of logistics for customers. Graham, Neirotti and Goldblatt (2001) comment on the importance of spectator arrival and departures at sport events. They stress that arrival and departure is a part of the event hospitality experience. The first and last impression of an event will be the parking facility and the traffic control.

The organization of transport for conferences takes on a special importance. Shone (1998) emphasizes the linking of transport and the selection of the venue. The selection of the conference venue or site has to take into account the availability and cost of transport to and from the site. Also, the transport to other facilities has to be considered. A venue that involves a 'long haul' will increase overall costs of a conference or event as well as add to the organizational confusion. It can also make the conference less attractive to delegates and, therefore, impact on delegate numbers.

For large events, festivals and parades, further logistic elements are introduced to the transport of the customer to the event. In particular, permission (council, highways department, police) and road closures need to be part of the logistics plan. Another requirement would be to plan sufficient signage to the event to ensure that customers, and equipment, arrive quickly and with the minimum of disruption to the local community. Events such as The Open Championship have signage commencing on main routes miles from the site as part of a co-ordinated transport plan to ensure that people are directed to the appropriate car parks. A leaflet, *The Provision of Temporary Traffic Signs To Special Events*, is available from the Department of the Environment, Transport and Regions to assist event managers in planning this aspect of the event. Guidance can also be gained from professional signage companies such as Royal Automobile Club (RAC) signs service or Automobile Association (AA) signs. Figure 10.4 lists the elements of customer transport that need to be considered for an event.

Solving logistics problems (e.g. transport and parking) can become a significant issue for event organizers and will form part of the licence requirements for the event. For example, for Glastonbury Festival 2000, wheel-wash and road-sweeping facilities were put in place as a contingency against poor weather, to ensure that mud was not deposited on the roads, which would cause a safety hazard.

- Have the relevant authorities (e.g. local council, police) been contacted for information and permission?
- Has adequate signage to the site been implemented?
- What public transport is available? Are timetables available?
- Has a backup transport system been organized (in case the original transport system fails)?
- Is the taxi service adequate and has it been informed of the event? (Informing the local taxi service is also a way of promoting the event.)
- What quality is the access area? Do weight and access restrictions apply? Are there any special conditions that must be considered (e.g. underground sprinkler systems under the access area)?
- Is there adequate provision for private buses, including an area large enough for their turning circle, driver hospitality and parking?
- Is there a parking area and will it be staffed by trained personnel?
- Is a towing and emergency service available if required?
- Has transport to and from drop off point been organized (e.g. from the car park to the site or venue entrance and back to the car park)?
- At what rate are customers estimated to arrive (dump or trickle)?
- Is there adequate access and are there parking facilities for disabled customers?

Figure 10.4 Customer transport checklist

Supply of product – product portfolio

Any event can be seen as the presentation of a product. Most events have a variety of products and services – a product portfolio – all of which go to create the event experience for the customer. The individual logistic requirements of the various products need to be integrated into a logistics plan.

For a large festival the product portfolio may include over 200 performing groups coming from around the UK and from overseas. For a small conference the product may be a speaker and video material. For an exhibition the product may include not only relevant exhibition stands focused on the theme of the event, but also displays and an educational seminar programme. It should be remembered that the product could also include the venue facilities. This is why the term 'the event experience' is used to cover all the aspects of the customers' experience. It can include, for example, the audience itself and just catching up with friends, in which case, the people become part of the product portfolio.

Transport

If the product portfolio includes products coming from overseas, the logistics problems can include issues such as carnet and customs clearance. A licence allows the movement of goods across an international boarder with an ATA Carnet, issued by Chamber of Commerce for exporting goods temporarily, or TIR Carnet, issued by the Road Hauliers Association or Freight Transport Association for importing goods temporarily. A performing artist group coming into the UK is required to have clearance for all its equipment, and needs to pay any taxes on goods that may be sold at the event, for example videos or compact discs (CD)s.

A large account with an airline company can allow the event manager an area of negotiation. In exchange for being the 'preferred airline' of the event, an airline company can grant savings, discounts, free seats or free excess charges.

The artistic director would forward the transport requirements for the performers to the logistics manager well before the event. This one aspect of logistics illustrates the linking of the various functional areas of a large event.

Importing groups from overseas provides the logistics manager with an opportunity to communicate with these groups. The 'meet and greet' at the airport and the journey to the site can be used to familiarize the talent (i.e. the artists) with the event. Such things as site map, rehearsal times, accommodation, dressing room location, equipment storage and transport out can be included in the artist's event or festival kit.

Accommodation

The accommodation requirements of the artists must be treated separately from the accommodation of the audience. The aim of the event manager is to get the best out of the 'product'. Given that entertainers are there to work, their accommodation has to be treated as a way of increasing the value of the investment in entertainment. Substandard accommodation and long trips to the site are certain ways of reducing this value. Often these requirements are not stated and need to be anticipated by the logistics manager.

Artist needs on site

A range of artist' needs must be catered for, including transport on site, storage and movement of equipment, stage and backstage facilities, food and drink (often contained in the rider), sound and lights. All these have a logistic element but are described in detail in Chapter 11.

As with accommodation, an efficient event manager will anticipate the on-site needs of the artists. Often this can only be learned from experience. In multicultural Britain, the manager needs to be sensitive to requirements that are culturally based, such as food, dressing rooms (separate) and appropriate staff to assist the performer.

Supply of facilities

The supply of the infrastructure to an event site introduces many of the concepts of business logistics. The storage of consumables (food and drink) and equipment, and the maintenance of equipment become particularly significant. For a small event taking place over an evening, or conferences and exhibitions in permanent venues, most of the facilities will be supplied by the venue. The catering, toilets and power, for example, can all be part of the hiring of the venue.

Larger or more innovative events require the sourcing of many of the facilities. Some of these are discussed in detail in Chapter 11. An inaugural outdoor festival will need to source just about all the facilities. To find the best information about the availability and cost of the facilities, the event manager should look for a project in the area that required similar facilities. For example, toilets, generators, fencing and security are also used by construction and mining companies. Some facilities can be sourced through film production companies. Many of the other facilities travel with the various festivals. Large tents and sound systems need to be booked in advance.

Innovative events, like a company-themed Christmas party in an abandoned car park, will require a long lead time to source the facilities. For example, it may take months to source unusual and rare props and venues for an event. These lead times can significantly affect the way the event is scheduled.

On-site logistics

The site of an event may vary from an old warehouse for a dance event to an underground car park for a Christmas party, to a 50-acre site for a festival. Logistic considerations during the event become more complex with the size of the event. The flow of materials and people around the site and communication networks become the most important areas of logistics.

Flow

With larger festivals and events, the movement of audience, volunteers, artists and equipment can take a larger part of the time and effort of the logistics manager than the lead-up to the event. This is especially so when the site is physically complex or multi-venued, and the audience numbers are large. During the lead up time to an event, the subcontractors can take care of many of the elements of logistics. For example, the movement of the electricity generators to the site would be the responsibility of the hire company. However, once the facilities are on site, it becomes the responsibility of the logistics manager for their positioning, movement and operation.

The access roads through a large festival and during the event would have to accommodate:

- artist and equipment transport
- waste removal
- emergency fire and first aid access and checking
- stall set up, continual supply and removal
- security
- food and drink supplies
- staging equipment set up, maintenance and removal
- site communication.

As illustrated by Figure 10.5, even during a straightforward event, many factors of the traffic flow must be considered. The performers for an event will need transport from their accommodation to the stage. Often the performers will go via the equipment storage area to the rehearsal rooms then to the stage. At the conclusion of the performance, the performers will return their equipment to storage then retire for a well-earned rest in the green room. For a community festival with four stages, this toing and froing can be quite complex.

At the same time as the performers are transported around the site, the media, audience and VIPs are on the move. Figure 10.5 does not show the movement of the food vendors' suppliers, water, security, ambulances and many more. When any one

1 Performers' accommodation → equipment storage area → rehearsal area → stage → equipment storage area → social (green room)

2 Media accommodation → media centre → stages → social area

3 VIP accommodation → stages → special requests

4 Audience pick-up points → specific venue

Figure 10.5 Some of the traffic patterns to consider when planning an event

of the major venues empties there is further movement around the site by the audience. This results in peak flow times when it may be impossible, or unsafe, to move anything around the venue except the audience. These peaks and lows all have to be anticipated in the overall event plan. For example, movement of catering from the main production kitchens to the various hospitality units around Lord's Cricket Ground could only take place before spectators arrived and at set times when crowd density would be lighter, for example, avoiding morning coffee, lunch and afternoon tea service. Getting the timing wrong could lead to a thirty-minute journey, from what would normally take ten minutes.

Each event contains surprising factors in traffic flow. For the Brit Awards, taking place at Earls Court, for example, co-ordinating 2000 limousines, mostly containing celebrities, together with taxis and other traffic, could cause significant logistical problems on this main route through London. However, getting the limousines to set down customers at local hotels solves this. The case study of the Vodafone Ball, organized by Skybridge Group, also illustrates the point as it requires meticulous planning, with 9500 guests sitting down to a silver-service meal at the same time and 1200 catering staff to co-ordinate. The previous year's event, involving 7400 guests, earned a place in the *Guinness Book of Records* for the largest silver-served sit-down meal in the world, which recognizes the success of the planning involved.

Communication

On site communication for the staff at a small event can be just the mobile phone or the loud-hailer of the event manager. With the complexity of larger events, however, the logistics plan must contain an on-site communications plan (Figure 10.6). The size of the communications plan will depend on the size of event – at one end of the scale this may simply be a list of names, positions and mobile telephone numbers; at the other, it may also include fax, pagers, radio assignment numbers, on-site locations, extension numbers and lines of responsibility illustrating who is responsible to whom in the organization structure. Contractor contact details may be included on the main plan, however, on larger or more complex events, each contractor or service area (e.g. security, stewarding and catering) may be assigned a separate radio channel. It may be preferable for all communications to be directed through a main communications control centre, rather than via mobile phones, to ensure that operational issues are not confused and lines of communication remain clear. Policies should be implemented on radio usage to guarantee professionalism is maintained at all times.

Name	Position	Location/ base	Contact mobile number	Radio number	Reporting to	Responsible for
Jane Smith	Event Director	Roving	07771 XXX XXX	001	Board	Event Manager
Jackie Brown	Event Manager	Main Office	07771 XXX XXX	002	Event Director	Overall
Alan White	Assistant Event Manager	Area 1	07771 XXX XXX	003	Event Manager	All staff in Area 1
Caroline Black	Assistant Event Manager	Area 2	07771 XXX XXX	004	Event Manager	All staff in Area 2

Figure 10.6 Simple communication plan

On-site signage is an important part of communicating to all the attendees of the event. It may be as simple as messages on a whiteboard in the volunteers' dining area, or involve large on-site maps showing the public the location of facilities. Two important issues in on-site signage are position and clarity. A direction sign that is obscured by such things as sponsors' messages diminishes its value. For large events the signage may need a detailed plan. The issues to consider are:

- Overall site placement of signs – at decision points and danger spots, so that they are integrated into the event.
- Types of signs needed such as directional, statutory (e.g. legal and warning signs), operational, facility and sponsor.
- The sign literacy of attendees – what sort of signs are they used to reading?
- Actual placement of signs – entrance, down the road, height.
- Supply of signs, their physical maintenance and their removal.
- Maintaining the credibility of the signs. If a facility is moved, then the signs will need to be amended.

The most effective way of communicating with the audience at an event is to have the necessary information in the programme. Figure 10.7 shows the type of essential information that can be included in the programme for the audience, spectator or visitor.

Amenities and solid waste management

For large festivals, events and exhibitions, the layout of the amenities is always included in the logistics site map. Figure 10.8 is an example of a large festival logistics site map that shows the layout of amenities.

Accommodation – whether accommodation is provided onsite or available nearby? May include contact details

Banking facilities – where are the nearest banking facilities? Are these on site?

Cameras – are there any restrictions on camera usage? For example, some events may ban all cameras, others only commercial cameras.

Catering/bar facilities – what catering/bar facilities are available onsite? Where are they located?

Clothing – is there a compulsory or suggested dress code?

Directions – where is the event situated? Are there any special routes for getting there?

Disabilities – what extra facilities/services are provided for people with disabilities?

First aid – where are these situated? Assistance from the St John Ambulance or Red Cross may be acknowledged.

Information/meeting point – is there an area onsite where people can arrange to meet or have any queries answered?

Lost and found – where is office located for lost and found children or items of value?

Organizer/security – where are the organizer and security offices located?

Rules – are there any rules that visitors, spectators or the audience must observe?

Telephones – where are the nearest telephones located?

Tickets – remind visitors/audience of the requirement to bring their ticket to the event and of any restrictions (e.g. is access restricted to certain areas?).

Toilets – where are toilets located?

Video/viewing screens – for sporting events and festivals, where are video screens located? For greenfield sports (e.g. golf), where will scores be posted?

Website – what is the address of the event website? What type of information may be found there?

Figure 10.7 Event programme information

The site map is an indispensable tool for the event manager, and is described later in this chapter. The schedules for the maintenance and cleaning of the amenities are part of the plan. For smaller events, these areas may be the sole responsibility of the venue management and part of the hiring contract.

Responsibility for cleaning the site and restoring it to its original condition is of particular importance to an event manager, as it is generally tied to the nature of the event. For example, Leeds Festival in 2000 at Temple Newsam in Leeds attracted a huge audience to a delicate area. Merely the movement of the audience destroyed the grass and resulted in local residents being suspicious of any further events in their area. If an event takes place in the countryside, such as an open-air concert, a motor sport event, a cross-country race or a corporate team challenge, extra care must be taken by the event manager to minimize the impact on the environment, particularly in protected areas such as National Parks. An environmental impact assessment may generally assist the event manager in managing this. However, the National Parks may have their own specific guidelines and rules for such events. Lake District National Park Authority (1999) note that although the impact of large

Hospitality, Leisure & Tourism Series

Key

1 Arena One: Cream	9 Bars	17 Hospital
2 Arena Two: Golden	10 Cloakroom	18 Box Office
3 Arena Three: Cream-House US	11 Water Point	19 Evian Swimming Pool
4 Arena Four: Big Beat Boutique	12 Football Pitch	20 Picnic Area/Food Stalls
5 Arena Five: Bugged Out!	13 Ladies Powder Room	21 Information/Welfare
6 Arena Six: Metalheadz	14 Toilets	22 Internet Cafe
7 Radio One: Outdoor stage	15 Meeting Point	23 The Smirnoff SCAD jump
8 Fun Fair	16 First Aid	24 Chill Out

Figure 10.8 Creamfield's 2000 site map
Source: Slice, 2000.

events can be significant, e.g. the Three Peaks Race, even small events can raise issues and therefore size is not the major issue. They observe that, 'It is more important that the organisers of any event have taken account of the potential problems, and made every effort to avoid them, or reduce them to an acceptable level' (Lake District National Park Authority, 1999, p. 50). In order to be able to manage the events effectively, it is advised that the event manager effectively liaise with local bodies, local communities, and include areas such as transport, parking, toilet provision, marshalling (for sporting events) and safety within the plan. Guidelines provided by sporting bodies and user groups, for example, those developed by the Institute of Charity Fundraisers, can be a useful source of advice to event organizers, based on years of experience. Motor sport events are highlighted as causing particular concerns, and as a result, specific criteria have been developed to minimize the impact of this type of event. These relate to when the events can take place, which routes are allowed, restrictions placed on vehicle numbers and that all houses along the route are notified. Overall, the principles to consider when planning events in greenfield sites may form part of the licence conditions and include the following:

- traffic arrangements (e.g. planning effective routes to minimize traffic on narrow lanes, unsuitable routes, or local villages/towns, protecting verges and keeping routes clear)
- parking management (e.g. solid ground, plan for if vehicles get stuck, road cleaning)
- waste management (e.g. collection and minimisation of litter inside and outside the site)
- drainage considerations for the site (including effective road surfaces for vehicle access)
- safety (e.g. uneven surfaces for audience/spectators)
- noise control.

Well-maintained toilets can be a very important issue with the audience. In particular their number, accessibility and cleanliness. HSE (1999) provides useful guidance in this respect. Requirements for minimum number of toilets for public entertainment buildings are outlined in BS6465: Part 1 1994, however, for licensed entertainment, the location and number of toilets should be agreed with the local authority and may be a term within the licence. The number of units required will depend on the type of event, for example, those with higher fluid intake or where camping will take place. However, a general rule of thumb for a music event opening six hours or more is one toilet for every 100 females, and one toilet per 500 males plus one urinal per 150 males. Hand-washing facilities should be provided with no less than one per ten toilets, together with suitable hand-drying provision. The HSE (1999) also remind organizers of their responsibilities for people with special needs, for example, those requiring wheelchair access, and suggest a minimum of one toilet with hand-washing facilties per seventy-five people, although this should relate to anticipated numbers. One need only look at the press coverage of the summer festivals in the mid to late 1990s in order to recognize the importance to customers of clean toilets, which resulted in significant improvements over the past couple of years. The logistics manager has to be aware of 'peak flows' during an event and the consequences for vehicle transport of the waste and opening times of treatment plants.

The collection of solid waste can range from making sure that the venue manager has enough bins, to calling for a tender and subcontracting the work. The number of bins and workers, shifts, timelines for collection and removal of skips should all be contained in the logistics plan as it interrelates with all the other event functional areas. This is a further example of linking the elements of logistics. A plan for primary recycling – recycling at collection point – would include both the education of the public (signage) and specialist bins for different types of waste (aluminium, glass, paper). Effective management of the event, for example, by banning the audience from bringing in glass bottles, can not only reduce the physical impact on the environment and reduce clear up costs, but can also increase safety.

Consumables: food and beverage

The logistics aspects of food and beverage on a large multi-venue site primarily concern its storage and distribution. Food stalls may be under the management of a stall manager as there are regulations that need to be followed. The needs of the food stalls including transport, gas, electricity and plumbing are then sent on to the logistics manager. In particular the sale of alcoholic beverages can present the logistics manager with specific security issues.

At a wine and food fair, or beer festival, the 'consumables' are the attraction. The collection of cash is often solved by the use of presale tickets that are exchanged for the food, wine or beer 'samples'. The tickets are bought at one place on the site, which reduces possible problems with security, cash collection and accounting. Figure 10.9 lists some of the main factors to consider when including food and beverage outlets at an event.

As well as feeding and watering the public, logistics includes the requirements of the staff, volunteers and performers. This catering area, often called the green room, provides an opportunity to disseminate information to the event staff. A strategically placed large whiteboard in the green room may prove to be an effective means of communicating with volunteers.

Last, but not the least, is the catering for sponsors and VIPs. This generally requires a separate plan to the general catering. At some festivals a 'hospitality tent' is set up for the 'special guests'. This aspect of events is covered in the Chapter 11 on staging.

The VIP and media requirements

The effect on event logistics by media coverage of the event cannot be overestimated. Even direct radio broadcasts can disrupt the live performance of a show – both in the setting up and the actual broadcast. The recording or broadcast of speeches or music

---

- Has a liquor licence been granted?
- What selection criteria for stall applicants (including design of stall and menu requirements) will be used?
- What infrastructure will be needed (including plumbing, electrical, gas)?
- Does the contract include provisions for health and safety regulations, gas supplies, insurance, and workers' payment?
- What position on the site will the stalls occupy?
- Have arrival, set up, breakdown and leaving times been set?
- What cleaning arrangements have been made?
- Do stallholders understand the need for ongoing inspections, such as health, electricity, plumbing, waste (including liquids) disposal and gas inspection?
- Are there any special security needs that must be catered for?
- How and when will payment for the stall be made?
- Will the stallholder provide in-kind support for the event (including catering for VIPs, media and performers)?

Figure 10.9 Food and beverage – factors to consider

often requires separate microphones or a line from the mixing desk. This cannot be left until just before the performance. Television cameras require special lighting, which often shines directly into the eyes of the audience. The movement of production crew and television power requirements can be distracting to a live performance, and need to be assessed before the event.

Media organizations work on very short timelines and may upset the well-planned tempo of the event. However, the rewards in terms of promotion and even finance are so large that the media logistics can take precedence over most other aspects of the event. The event manager in consultation with event promotions and sponsors often makes these decisions. This is an area that illustrates the need for flexible negotiations and assessment by the logistics manager.

The VIP requirements can include special security arrangements. Once again it is a matter of weighing up the benefits of having VIPs with the amount of extra resources that are needed. This, however, is not the logistic manager's area of concern. Once the VIPs have been invited their needs have to take precedence over the public's.

Emergency procedures

Emergency procedures at an event can range from staff qualified in first aid, to using the St John Ambulance or Red Cross service, to the compilation of a comprehensive major incident or disaster plan. The location of first aid should be indicated on the site map and all the event staff should be aware of this. The number of first-aiders, medical and ambulance provision will depend on the nature and size of the event. The HSE (1999) recommends that a ratio of 2:1000 (for the first 3000 attending) may be appropriate for smaller events, with no less than two first-aiders on site. However, exact requirements should be established as part of the risk assessment process and included within the event plan. The HSE (1999) provide a method of estimating these. Large events require an emergency access road that has to be kept clear. These issues are so important that a local council will immediately close down an event that does not comply with their regulations that concern emergencies. The HSE (1999) and Home Office (2000) offer guidance in the preparation of a major incident plan. The HSE (1999, p. 32) define a major incident as one 'that requires the implementation of special arrangements by one or more of the emergency services, the NHS or local authority' for treatment, rescue and transport of a large number of people, and associated issues, such as dealing with enquiries and the media. They suggest that the following areas are considered when planning the major incident plan:

- identify the key decision-making workers
- stopping the event
- identify emergency routes and access for emergency services
- requirements of people with special needs
- identify holding areas for performers, workers and the audience
- the script of coded messages to inform staff and announcements for the audience
- alert/communication procedures, including public warning
- procedure for evacuation and containment
- identify rendezvous points for emergency services and ambulance loading points
- locate nearest hospitals and traffic routes

Hospitality, Leisure & Tourism Series

- identify temporary mortuary facilities
- identify roles, contact list and communications plan
- location of emergency equipment and availability
- documentation and message pads.

The emergency plan must be developed for major incidents, with further plans covering minor incidents. The above provides a useful starting point for areas to consider, but you are strongly advised to obtain a copy of *The Event Safety Guide* (HSE, 1999) or other appropriate guidance notes currently available for exhibitions, outdoor events and sporting grounds (see references).

Shutdown

As Pagonis (1992) points out, military logistics is divided into three phases: deployment, combat and redeployment, and it is often the case that redeployment takes the most effort and time. The amount of time and effort spent on the shutdown of an event are in direct proportion to the size of the event and its uniqueness. Repeated events, like many of the festivals mentioned in this chapter, have their shutdown schedule refined over many years. It can run quickly and smoothly. All the subcontractors know exactly how to get their equipment out and where they are placed in the order of removal. The event manager of a small event may only have to sweep the floor and turn off the lights.

Most difficulties arise in inaugural events, large events and muti-venued events. In these cases, logistics can be as important after the event as at any other time, and the need for planning most apparent. The breakdown and removal of site structures, the collection of equipment, the exits of the various traders, to name a few areas, should all be part of the schedules contained in the logistics plan. The plan for the breakdown of the event is part of the initial meetings and negotiation with contractors. A major parameter in working out the Gantt chart or a critical path is the acquittal of equipment. This includes not just the removal of the equipment but repairing and cleaning.

As emphasized by Catherwood and Van Kirk (1992) the shutdown of an event is the prime security time. The mix of vehicles, movement of equipment and general feeling of relaxation provides a cover for theft. The smooth flow of traffic from an event at its conclusion must also be considered. Towing services and the police may need to be contacted.

Finally it is often left to the person in charge of logistics to organize the final thank you party for the volunteers and staff. Figure 10.10 provides a checklist of points to consider when performing the shutdown.

Techniques of logistics management

We will now consider the role of the logistics manager and their relationship with other functional areas and managers of an event.

The event logistics manager

As mentioned throughout this chapter, the logistics manager has to be a procurer, negotiator, equipment and maintenance manager, human resource manager,

Crowd dispersal

- Exits/transport
- Safety
- Related to programming
- Staggered entertainment

Equipment

- Load-out schedule including correct exists and loading docks
- Shut down equipment using specialist staff (e.g. computers)
- Clean and repair
- Store – number boxes and display contents list
- Sell or auction
- Small equipment and sign off
- Schedule for dismantling barriers

Entertainment

- Send-off appropriately
- Payments – cash
- Thank you letters/awards/recommendations

Human resources

- The big thank you
- Final payments
- Debrief and gain feedback for next year
- Reports
- Celebration party

Liability

- Records
- Descriptions
- Photo/video evidence

Onsite/staging area

- Cleaning
- Back to normal
- Environmental assessment
- Lost and found
- Idiot check
- Site/venue hand-over

Contractors

- Contract release
- Thank you

Finance

- Pay the bills
- Finalise and audit accounts – best done as soon as possible
- Thank donors and sponsors

Marketing and promotion

- Collect press clippings/video news
- Reviews of the event – use a service
- Market research on community reaction

Sponsors and grants

- Release grants: prompt reports
- Meet sponsors and enthuse for next time
- Government and politics
- Thank services involved
- Reports to councils and other government organizations

Client

- Glossy report, video, photos
- Wrap up and suggestions for next time

Figure 10.10 Event shutdown checklist

map-maker, project manager and party organizer. For a small event, logistics can be the direct responsibility of the event manager. Logistics becomes a separate area if the event is large and complex. Multi-venued and multi-day events usually require a separate logistics manager position.

Part of the role of the logistics manager is to efficiently link all areas of the event. Figure 10.11 illustrates the lines of communication between the logistics manager and various other managers for a multi-venued event. It is a network diagram

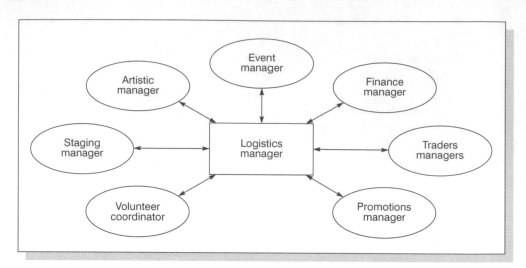

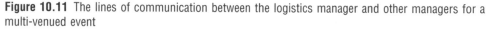

Figure 10.11 The lines of communication between the logistics manager and other managers for a multi-venued event

because, although the event manager or director has ultimate authority, decision-making authority is usually devolved to the various submanagers who work at the same level of authority and responsibility as the event manager.

The information required by the logistics manager from other festival managers is shown in Table 10.1. The clear communication within this network is also partly the responsibility of the logistics manager.

Logistics techniques

The tools used in business and military logistics can be successfully adapted to event logistics. Because an event takes place at a specific time and specific place, the tools of scheduling and mapping are used. The dynamic nature of events and the way that the functional areas are so closely linked means that a small change in one area can result in crucial changes throughout the event. For example, the incorrect placement of an electric generator can lead to a mushrooming of problems. If the initial problem is not foreseen or immediately solved, it can grow so much that the whole event is affected. This gives initial negotiations and ongoing assessment a special significance in event logistics. The logistics manager needs to be skilled in identifying possible problem areas and needs to know what is *not* on the list.

Project management

An event or festival comes under the general term of a project. As it has a life expectancy, the term used for the event, from inception to completion, is the event project life cycle. Almost all of the methodology of project management can be applied to events.

Project management is becoming more common as stakeholders and the business environment are demanding it as a means of creating common standards. In the current era of change, project management methodology is being used in fields as

Position	General role	Information sent to logistics manager
Artistic Director	Selection and negotiation with artists	Travel, accommodation, staging and equipment requirements
Staging Manager	Selecting and negotiation with subcontractors	Sound, lights, and backstage requirements, programming times
Finance Director	Overseeing budgets and contracts	How and when funds will be approves and released and the payment schedule
Volunteers Co-ordinator	Recruitment and management of volunteers	Volunteers selected to assist and requirements of the volunteers (e.g. parking, free tickets)
Promotions Manager	Promotion during the event	Requirements of the media and VIPs
Traders Manager	Selecting suitable traders	Requirements of the traders (e.g. positioning, theming, electricity, water, licence agreements)

Table 10.1 Information required by the logistics manager from the other festival managers

diverse as software development, business change management and now in event management. The language of project management is the language of modern business. Authors such as Burke (1999) and Slack, Chambers and Johnston (2001) have extensively discussed project management, with the latter presenting it as a five-stage process (Figure 10.12).

Stage 1: Understanding the event environment

The first stage in project management is to clearly understand the environment in which the project is taking place, referred to in chapter four as environmental scanning. The aim of this stage is to identify all the elements in the environment that may affect the event – it may be useful at this stage to consider the needs of stakeholders, as illustrated previously in Figure 3.1.

Stage 2: Event project definition

Before moving on to planning the event, the next stage is to clearly identify what it is that is being done, through clear definition of objectives (SMART), outlining the scope of the work, and developing the strategy for implementation – focusing on

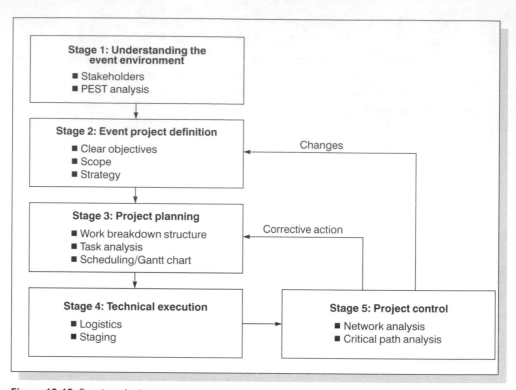

Figure 10.12 Event project management process
Source: adapted from Slack, Chambers and Johnston, 2001.

how the project will be completed. The strategy will include the identification of milestones, which are discussed further later. One of the first steps in this methodology is to clearly identify the scope of work through listing the tasks necessary in the event. Deciding what is not required, as much as what is required may assist this.

Stage 3: Project planning

The project planning stage serves to determine the activities, time and resources required to achieve the objectives, together with the schedule required to bring the project in on time. Monitoring these areas allows the manager to assess the impact of changes to the plan (Slack, Chambers and Johnston, 2001). There are a range of tools and techniques available for the project manager to assist them in their task, including work breakdown structure and scheduling (through Gantt charts).

Work breakdown structure

Fundamental to project management is the ability to break down all the work in a project into manageable units. The graphic representation of this analysis is referred to as work breakdown structure (WBS). The units are assigned necessary resources so that there are outcomes or deliverables. For example, the work involved in promoting an exhibition may be divided first by paid advertising and publicity. This can then be further subdivided according to the media used – television, the Web, print. Each unit in this subdivision is then assigned resources such as money, time, staff, equipment and supplies. The WBS is used as a basis of costing and risk management. The costs of each unit are added together to give the total cost of the work to create the event. An outcome of the WBS process is the responsibility or task sheets that communicate to the event staff their responsibilities and when they need to complete them. Once the work has been allocated in this way, a schedule of work can be created.

Scheduling: Gantt chart

One of the most important tools used in logistics is the bar chat or time line or Gantt chart. Gantt charts are bar charts that are used in project management as a visual representation of the schedule. The steps to creating a Gantt chart are:

1 *Tasks*: breakdown the logistics of the event into manageable tasks or activities. For example, one of the tasks for security of the event is the erection of the perimeter fence. This can be further broken down into the arrival of the fencing material, the arrival of volunteers and equipment, and the preparation of the ground.
2 *Time lines*: set the timescale for each task. Factors to consider are the starting time and completion time. The availability, hiring costs, possible delivery and pick-up times and costs are other considerations in constructing a time scale. For example, a major factor in the arrival of large tents is their hiring costs. These costs can depend on the day of the week on which they arrive rather than the duration of the hire.
3 *Priority*: set the priority of the task. What other tasks need to be completed before this task can start? Completing this priority list will create a hierarchy of tasks or a work breakdown structure.
4 *Grid*: draw a grid with the days leading up to the event across the top and a list of the tasks down the left-hand side of the grid. A horizontal bar that corresponds to each task is drawn across the grid. For example, the task of preparing the ground for the fencing is dependent on the arrival of materials and labour at a certain time and takes one day to complete. The starting time will be when these prior tasks are completed and the length of the time line will be one day. The horizontal bars or timelines are often colour coded so that each task may be easily recognized when the chart is completed for all activities.
5 *Milestones*: as the chart is used for monitoring the progress of the event, tasks that are of particular importance are designated as milestones and marked on the chart. For example, the completion of the security fence is a milestone as it acts as a trigger for many of the other event preparation activities.

Figure 10.13 illustrates an example of a Gantt chart. This chart would be common to many small festivals.

In his work on project management, Burke (1999) stresses that this display provides an effective presentation which conveys the activities and timing accurately and precisely, and can be easily understood by many people. It forestalls unnecessary explanations to the staff and sponsors and gives a visual representation of the event. Time lines are used in events no matter what their size. The arrival of goods and services on time at even a small event can add significant value to the event.

Hospitality, Leisure & Tourism Series

Tasks	F	S	S	M	T	W	T	F	S	S	M	T	W	T	F	S	S
Clear and prepare site											Opening night ◇						
Generators arrive						☐											
Lighting on site																	
Tents arrive																	
Stages arrive and set up																	
Site security																	
Sound system arrives																	

◇ **Milestone:** start of festival

Figure 10.13 Simplified Gantt chart for the set-up of a small festival

The advantages of a Gantt chart are that it:

- visually summarizes the project or event schedule
- is an effective communication and control tool (particularly with volunteers)
- can point out problem areas or clashes of scheduling
- is readily adaptable to all event areas
- provides a summary of the history of the event.

For the Gantt chart to be an effective tool, the tasks must be arranged and estimated in the most practical and logical sequence. Underestimation of the times – or length of the timeline – can give rise to 'cost blow out' and render any scheduling ineffective. As Lock (1988, p.89) points out: 'Extended schedules produced in this way are an ideal breeding ground for budgetary excesses according to Professor Parkinson's best known law, where work is apt to expand to fill the time available.'

Stage 4: Technical execution

The technical execution of the event, referred to in event planning models as implementation or the operational plan, will differ according to the nature of the particular event, although the principles will remain the same. The technical execution of events is discussed elsewhere in this text.

Stage 5: Project control

Although presented as the final stage, project control should take place throughout the project management process. Slack, Chambers and Johnston (2001, p. 530) identify that control will require three major decisions:

- how to monitor the event in order to check progress
- how to assess this performance by comparing observed performance to the plan
- how to intervene in the project in order to bring it back to plan.

A range of tools are available to event managers in order to assist them in monitoring and control, including Gantt charts (discussed earlier) and network analysis.

Network analysis: critical path analysis

One important aspect of any logistic plan is the relationship of tasks to each other. There is a difficulty in graphically showing this on a chart. This is the reason for the development of network analysis. With larger events the Gantt chart can become very complex, and areas where there is a clash of scheduling may be obscured by the detail of bars and colours. A vital part of logistics is giving tasks a priority. For example, the arrival and setup of the main stage in an event is more important than finding an extra extension cord. However, on a Gantt chart all the tasks take on equal importance. The tool of network analysis was developed to overcome these problems.

Network analysis was created and developed by defence force projects in the USA and UK during the 1950s and now has widespread use in many project-based industries. The basis of network analysis is critical path analysis, which uses circles (or in some cases squares) to represent programmed events and arrows to illustrate the flow of activities. Thus, the precedent of programmed events is established and

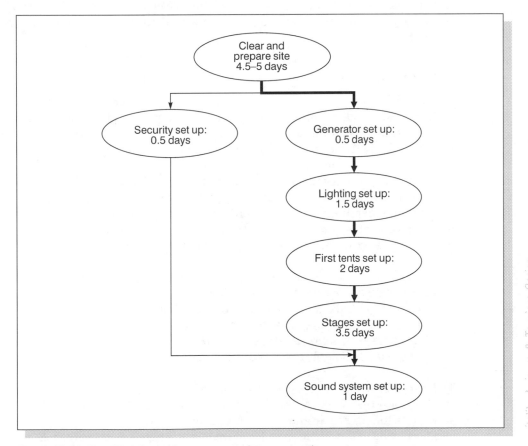

Figure 10.14 Simplified Gantt chart represented as a network

the diagram can be used to analyse a series of subevents. From the diagram, the most efficient scheduling can be found. This is known as the critical path. Figure 10.14 illustrates a network derived from the Gantt chart shown in Figure 10.13. The critical path is shown as an arrow. At the event site this means that, for example, if the generator did not arrive on time everything along the critical path would be directly affected. The lights would not be put up, and without evening light or electricity to run the pneumatic hammers, the tents could not be erected. Without the protective cover of the tents, the stage could not be constructed and so the sound system could not be set up. The critical path is indeed critical.

There are a number of software packages available to help create the Gantt chart and the critical path. These are project management programs, which are used in the construction industry. Unfortunately, most of these packages are based on a variable completion time or completion within a certain time. In the event industry the 'completion time' (i.e. when the event is on) is the most important factor, and every task has to relate to this time. The event manager cannot ask for an extension of the time in which to complete all the tasks.

Time charts and networks are very useful as a control and communication tool, however, like all these logistics techniques they have their limitations. Catherwood and Van Kirk (1992) describe how the Los Angeles Olympic Organizing Committee gave up on the critical path chart, as it became too unwieldy. There were 600 milestones. Rather than assisting communication and planning, it only created confusion. The solution was for the committee to return to a more traditional method of weekly meetings.

Site or venue map

A map of the event site or venue is a necessary communication tool for the logistics manager. For small events, even a simple map can be an effective tool that obviates the need for explanations and can quickly identify possible problem areas. The map for larger festivals can be an aerial photograph with the logistic features drawn on it. For smaller events, it may be a sketch map that just shows the necessary information to the customer. The first questions to ask are 'what is the map for?' and 'who will be reading it?' A logistics site map will contain very different information than the site map used for promotion purposes. Of necessity, the map needs to filter information that is of no interest to the logistics plan. Monmonier (1996, p. 25) in his highly respected work on mapping summarizes this concept thus:

> A good map tells a multitude of little white lies; it suppresses truth to help the user see what needs to be seen. Reality is three dimensional, rich in detail, and far too factual to allow a complete yet uncluttered two-dimensional scale model. Indeed, a map that did not generalize would be useless. However, the value of a map depends on how well its generalized geometry and generalized content reflect a chosen aspect of reality.

The three basic features of maps – scale, projection and the key (showing the symbols used) – have to be adapted to their target audience. Volunteers and subcontractors, for example, need to clearly read and understand it. The communication value of the site map is also a matter of where it is displayed. Some festivals draw the map on the back of the ticket or programme.

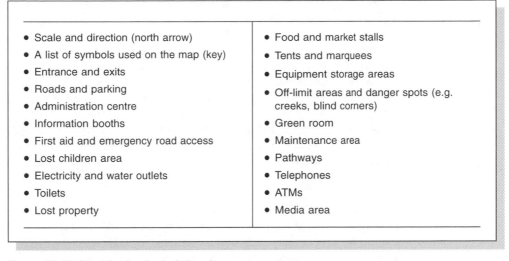

- Scale and direction (north arrow)
- A list of symbols used on the map (key)
- Entrance and exits
- Roads and parking
- Administration centre
- Information booths
- First aid and emergency road access
- Lost children area
- Electricity and water outlets
- Toilets
- Lost property
- Food and market stalls
- Tents and marquees
- Equipment storage areas
- Off-limit areas and danger spots (e.g. creeks, blind corners)
- Green room
- Maintenance area
- Pathways
- Telephones
- ATMs
- Media area

Figure 10.15 Checklist for the logistics site map

The checklist of items to be included in a site map can be very detailed. Figure 10.15 shows a standard checklist of the logistics for a small festival.

With many sporting events, a sketch map on the ticket shows how to find the site, parking, and the location of seats and facilities. The back of tickets generally includes a list detailing the behaviour expected of event participants. The festival site shown in Figure 10.8 is a promotional map for the audience, originally presented in full colour with points of interest to the public displayed. For corporate events a simple map of the venue at the entrance – in particular showing seating, toilets, food areas and bar – can relieve the staff of a lot of questions! Further, the logistics map for volunteers, staff, performers and all other personnel would provide further details, including the placement of site offices, contractors compounds and service routes.

Negotiation and assessment

No matter what the size of the event, the mutual agreement on supply and conditions is vital. In particular, the special but changing nature of one-off events requires the techniques of dynamic negotiation to be mastered by the logistics manager. Marsh (1984, p. 1) in his work on negotiation and contracts, defines negotiation as 'a dynamic process of adjustment by which two parties, each with their own objectives, confer together to reach a mutually satisfying agreement on a matter of common interest'.

Logistical considerations need to covered by the initial negotiations with subcontractors. Agreement on delivery time and removal times is an indispensable part of the timelines as they form the parameters of the critical path.

It needs to be stressed that the management of events in the UK is a dynamic industry. The special nature of many events means that many aspects cannot be included in the initial negotiation. Decisions and agreements need to be continually reassessed. Both parties to the agreement have to realize that the agreement needs to be flexible. However, all possible problems should be unmasked at the beginning, and there are logistics tools to enable this to happen.

Having prepared the schedules and site map, an important tool to use is what Pagonis (1992, p. 194) describes as the 'skull session':

> Before implementing a particular plan, I usually try to bring together all of the involved parties for a collective dry run. The group includes representatives from all appropriate areas of command, and the goal of the skull session is to identify and talk through all the unknown elements in the situation. We explore all problems that could emerge, and then try to come up with concrete solutions to those problems. Skull sessions reduce uncertainty, reinforce the interconnection of different areas of specialisation, encourage collaborative problem solving, and raise the level of awareness as to possible disconnects in the theatre.

Goldblatt (1997) calls this gap analysis. Gap analysis is studying the plan to attempt to identify gaps that could lead to a weakening in the implementation of the logistics plan. Goldblatt (1997) recommends using a critical friend to review the plan look for gaps in your logical thinking.

The identification of risk areas, gaps and 'what ifs' is important in the creation of a contingency plan. For example, as Glastonbury Festival takes place during one of the hottest months of the year, the supply of water was identified as a priority area. For the 1997 festival, a permanent water main was constructed, supplemented by water carts, and drinking water made available to the general public through standpipes. On site, there was also an attempt to encourage water conservation through an association with WaterAid.

Control of events logistics

The monitoring of the logistics plan is a vital part of the overall control of an event. An important part of the plan is the identification of milestones – times when crucial tacks have to be completed. The Gantt chart can be used to compare projected performance with actual performance. It is a simple monitoring device, with the actual performance written on the chart as the tasks occur.

The aim of the logistics manager is to create a plan to enable the logistics to flow without the need for active control. The use of qualified subcontractors with experience in events is the only way to make this happen. This is where the annual festival with its established relationships to the suppliers has the advantage over the one-off, innovative event. The objective of the event director is to enjoy the event without having to intervene in any on-site problems!

Evaluation of logistics

The ultimate evaluation of the logistics plan is the success of the event and the easy flow of event supply and operations. However, the festival committee, event director and/or the sponsors may require a more detailed evaluation. The main question to ask is if the logistics met their objectives. If the objectives as set out in the plan are measurable, then this task is relatively straightforward. If the objectives require a qualitative approach, then the evaluation can become imprecise and open to many interpretations.

An evaluation enables the logistic manager to identify problem areas that enables improvement and therefore adds value to the next event. The term 'logistics audit' is used for a systematic and thorough analysis of the event logistics. Part of the audit concerns the expectations of the audience and whether they were satisfied. For very large events, the evaluation of the logistics may be contained in the overall evaluation undertaken by an external research company. Evaluation is discussed further in Chapter 12.

The logistics plan

Whether the event is a school class reunion or a multi-venued festival, a written logistics or operations plan needs to be part of the communication within the event. It could range from a one-page contact list with approximate arrival times, to a bound folder covering all areas. The folder for a large event would contain:

- general contact list
- site map
- schedules, including time lines and bar charts
- the emergency plan
- subcontractor details, including all time constraints
- on-site contacts, including security and volunteers
- evaluation sheets (sample questionnaires).

All these elements have been described and discussed in this chapter. These can make up the event manual that is used to stage the event. The manual needs to be a concise document, as it may be used in an emergency. An operations manual may only be used once but it has to be able to withstand the rigours of the event itself. Some organizations have a generic manual on their intranet that can be adapted for all their events in any part of the world.

Although this text emphasizes the importance of planning, overplanning can be a significant risk, particularly with a special event, as there is often a need to respond and take opportunities when they arise. Artistry and innovation can easily be hampered by a purely mechanistic approach to event creation. The secret is to ensure that the plan is structured sufficiently well to ensure a safe event, whilst allowing creativity to shine through.

Summary

Military logistics is as old a civilization itself. Business logistics is a recent science. Events logistics has the advantage of building on these areas, using the tools of both and continually improving on them as the events industry grows.

This logistics system can be broken down into the procuring and supply of customers, products and facilities. Once on site the logistics system concerns the flow around the site, communication and the requirements of the event. At the conclusion of the event, logistics concerns the breakdown of structures, cleaning and managing the evacuation of the site or venue.

For small events, logistics may be the responsibility of the event manager. However, for larger events a logistics manager may be appointed. The logistics manager's role within the overall event management and his or her relationship with other managers was described. For both small and large events, the tools of business and military logistics are used. The logistics of an event need to be treated as any other area of management and have in-built evaluation and ongoing control. All these elements are placed in a plan that is a part of the overall event plan.

Logistics is an invisible part of events. It enables the customers to focus completely on the event without being distracted by unnecessary problems. It only becomes visible when it is looked for or when there is a problem. It enables the paying customer, the public, client or sponsor to realize and even exceed their expectations.

Questions

1 What are the logistics areas that need to be contained in initial the agreements with the suppliers to an event?

2 Set out an emergency plan for a small event.

3 List the logistics tasks for (a) a street parade, (b) a product launch and (c) a company party.

4 Create a Gantt chart for the street parade or an event. Identify the critical path.

Case Study

Electrical services at Glastonbury Festival

GE Energy Rentals (absorbing Showpower Inc., who in turn acquired Templine Ltd in 1997) have been the main electrical power contractors for the Glastonbury Festival since 1990. This entails providing all the generators, the cabling, electrical distribution (to the highest standards of safety) and lighting for the main site, all the stages and market.

There are three distinct areas to the operation:

1 *The site*: this involves mainly lighting and the power sources for it. The site lighting performs much the same function as street lighting in a city, highlighting main routes and any obstacles, such as bridges or ditches, and for security. Another major part of this side of the job, is toilet lighting. It is a requirement of the council's licence for the event that all the toilets (there are about 1200 of them!) be adequately lit when it is dark. These toilets are clustered in small groups (of about forty toilets) all over the 550 acres of the site, so getting power to them is one of the most challenging parts of the job. There are also vital services such as the site medical centre, water pumps, etc. to be powered. The main site roadways and the vast circular perimeter fence are lit by seven to ten watchtowers, each with several floodlights, its own generator and an illuminated property lock-up. Approximately 4 miles of festoon lighting, with a bulb every 5 metres support this! The watchtowers, along with many other site functions, now require power for most of the week before the festival and a couple of days after it. The floodlights, stage lighting and countless campfires make the festival site a huge, stunning feature on the Somerset landscape after dark.

2 *The stages*: for all the stages and performance areas GE Energy Rentals Ltd provide generators and the cable and distribution. Large amounts of electrical power are needed for the stage lighting systems, PA systems, video screens, lasers, etc. For the main music stages this now also involves power for live television and radio outside broadcasts. These supplies are generally larger (400A three phase for main stage

lighting) and the distribution much more complex than for site supplies. They are, however, clustered into smaller areas than the site wiring. Stage supplies are backed up with spare generators in case of failure. All the stages have extensive backstage villages of Portacabin dressing rooms, offices, hospitality and catering areas, and loading bays that also need power and lighting.

3 *Market*: the market power for the festival is a major undertaking, organizing and providing the power for most of the 600+ stalls. The timescale generally follows that of the site, except that the power is required for food storage (refrigeration) and security (lighting), twenty-four hours per day from the Monday before the festival to the Monday following. During the operational phase the markets are quite intensive as the large number of users causes issues, with some attempting to use more than they have paid for (causing overloading of sections of the system) and others plugging in faulty equipment leading to tripping of sections. In bad weather conditions (such as the mudbaths of 1998 and 1999) these problems are amplified several times!

Timescale

To install, operate and then remove an installation of this size and complexity in the short time available, while meeting the very high standards of safety required, requires considerable planning and teamwork. The overall timescale is as follows:

1 *Six months prior to event*: power requirements for the markets are established. The process commences in January with forms sent out with the pitch applications for stalls at the festival. There then follows a process of collating the returned forms, chasing payments and attempting to anticipate those stallholders who will eventually require power, but are delaying informing us to delay payment! An outline plan is drawn up and the generators and major elements of the cabling and distribution allocated.

2 *Two months prior to event*: power requests are collated from the other festival area organizers and those who have not yet responded are chased up. Discussions commence with the main subcontractors regarding the supply of men and equipment. Plant is also booked at this stage (e.g. forklift trucks, accommodation and storage cabins).

3 *One month prior to event*: detailed planning begins – each year's plan is based on the previous year, amended as the power requests come in. The site and performance areas are separated and described, power requirements ascertained and generators allocated. This is completed, in conjunction with the all-important site map, on computerized tables and schedules. About this time we usually have a meeting with Michael Eavis to discuss any special or new points and to agree a budget. With the plans taking shape it is possible to identify the number of generators required, usually about 100 units (including markets) with twenty-five self-contained lighting tower units ranging from 600 kW to 6 kW. These are sourced from our fleet, especially the stage generators, and cross-hired from outside suppliers.

4 *Three weeks before event*: the first part of what will eventually grow into a crew of about thirty electricians and assistants arrive on site to start erecting the watchtowers, floodlights and 4 miles of festoon lighting. Transport for plant and equipment to, around, and from site are finalized.

5 *Two weeks before event*: the main crew arrives on site – all need to be accommodated and fed for three weeks in a bare field! Installation begins with site requirements, and the inevitable toilet-chasing as last minute changes to the plan occur. The on-site office

is set up with all the plans and schedules on the walls to act as the nerve centre of the operation. Security commences on the gates, and site crew catering starts, requiring power and lights.

6 *One week before event*: the generators arrive on site and have to be allocated, positioned with trucks and cranes, and wired up and tested for safety. Stage areas need to be made ready for the arrival of the lighting and PA rigs by about the Wednesday of show week.

6 *Doors open!* All site licence requirements must be met and are checked by local council staff.

7 *Showtime!* All systems are up and running. All the generators must be refuelled twice a day – each refuelling circuit takes about twelve hours to complete, so it is like painting the Forth Bridge. The generators will use about 100 000 litres of diesel fuel in the next four days. To reduce the risk of a major spillage, on-site storage is kept to about 1.5 days' supply – in separated bonded tanks – with regular tanker deliveries throughout the event. The on-call crew attends to any breakdowns or last minute additions. The other members of the crew get a chance to enjoy the festival, or just catch up on some sleep!

8 *Post-event – the aftermath*: immediately after the last band come off stage any generators wanted urgently elsewhere must be got away before the traffic builds up. Extra lighting is rigged up for the lighting and PA de-rigs. Another area requiring power is the litter recycling machinery. On Monday morning, the clear-up begins. All the wiring and distribution units have to be collected and loaded onto trucks. People who cannot tell the difference between cables and toilets can make this very unpleasant! The lights are taken down and the generators loaded onto a fleet of articulated trucks and returned to the hire companies. This phase of the operation usually takes about seven days. When the site is clear the crew leave site and on to the next job. Some power is left *in situ* for a week or two more for site crew catering, the fencing crew, etc. Following this, all that remains is to sort out of the paperwork, bills, hire return notes, payments and, of course, collect a cheque from Michael. At this point we look back at the event, take stock and start to plan for next year!

This all adds up to one of the largest jobs of the year for GE Energy Rentals Ltd. For all its size and complexity, the electrical system for the Glastonbury Festival would seem small beer compared to the engineer's responsible for the electrical system of a real city of 100 000. But then, they don't have to build it, use it, and remove it all within five weeks!

For further details about GE Energy Rentals Ltd, please visit:
www.geenergyrentals.com.

By Bill Egan, GE Energy Rentals Ltd, Unit 7, io Centre, Cabot Park, Avonmouth, Bristol BS11 0QL.

Questions

1 Create a Gantt chart that displays the electrical supply to Glastonbury Festival.

2 What aspects of electricity supply are 'sensitive' (i.e. a small change in one area of logistics will have a large effect on the electricity supply to the festival)?

3 Create a risk assessment list for the festival electricity supply that would be used as the basis of a 'skull session'.

Staging events

After studying this chapter, you should be able to:

- analyse the staging of an event into its constituent elements

- demonstrate how these elements relate to each other and to the theme of the event

- understand the safety elements of each aspect of staging

- identify the relative importance of the staging elements for different types of events

- use the tools of staging.

Introduction – what is staging?

The term 'staging' originates from the presentation of plays at the theatre. It refers to bringing together all the elements of a theatrical production for its presentation on a stage. Most events that use this term take place at a single venue and require similar organization to a theatrical production. However, whereas a play can take place over a season, an event may take place in one day or night. Examples of this type of event are product launches, company parties and celebrations, awards ceremonies, conference events, concerts, large weddings, corporate dinners and opening and closing events.

Staging can also refer to the organization of a venue within a much larger event. A large festival may have performance areas positioned around the site. Each of these venues has a range of events with a distinct theme. At Glastonbury Festival of Contemporary Performing Arts (Pilton, Somerset), there are fifteen performance areas, each with its own style. Because it is part of a much larger event, one performance area or event has to fit in with the overall planning of the complete event and has to fit in with programming and logistics. However, each performance area is to some extent its own kingdom, with its micro-logistics, management, staff and individual character. On a larger scale, BBC Music Live 2000 involved concerts the length and breadth of the UK, each with its own event manager, stage manager and light and sound crews, together with the involvement of television production crews to broadcast a live performance of Lou Reed's song 'Perfect Day' synchronized from thirty-eight locations. This perfectly illustrated the interaction of event staging and television broadcast skills (Ball, 2000).

The main concerns of staging are as follows:

- theming and event design
- choice of venue
- audience and guests
- stage
- power, lights and sound
- audiovisuals and special effects
- catering
- performers
- crew
- hospitality
- the production schedule
- recording the event
- contingencies.

This chapter analyses the staging of an event according to these elements. It demonstrates how these elements revolve around a central event theme. The type of event will determine how important each of these elements is to the others. However, common to the staging of different events are the tools: the stage plan, the contact and responsibility list, and the production schedule.

Theming and event design

When staging an event, the major artistic and creative decision to be made is that of determining what the theme is to be. The theme of an event differentiates it from other events. In the corporate area, the client may give the theme of the event. For example, the client holding a corporate party or product launch may want medieval Europe as the theme, or Hollywood, complete with actors and film set. Outside the corporate area, the theme for one of the stages at a festival may be blues music, debating or a children's circus. Whatever the nature of the event, once the theme is established, the elements of the event must be designed to fit in with the theme. This is straightforward when it comes to deciding on the entertainment and catering. With the medieval corporate party, the entertainment may include *jongleurs* and jugglers, and the catering may be spit roasts and wine. However, audiovisuals may need a lot of thought in order to enhance the theme. The sound and lights must complement the entertainment, as they do not fit in with the period theme. Figure 11.1 illustrates the elements of staging and it emphasizes the central role of the theme of the event. However, it should be remembered that, within events, these areas are not so clearly defined. For example, there is generally a close working relationship between audiovisual, special effects, light and sound staff in order to produce the event.

Clare Pasquil, Senior Project Manager at Theme Traders expresses the importance of staging in the following way:

> At Theme Traders our mission is to create unique and unforgettable events. Funnily enough, meticulous planning and staging are crucial when trying to create a spontaneous and vibrant atmosphere. This can be understood in terms of 'staging' because things like lighting, space, noise and furniture are tools of 'mood' to be manipulated. Bad lighting, unwanted noise or bad use of space and access can make or break a party by affecting the response of guests to their environment. Similarly, responses to event features such as lighting and entertainment can help steer guests around a venue without them being aware of it. Stage managing their environment can often ensure

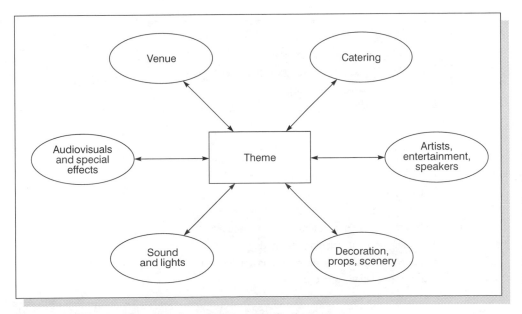

Figure 11.1 The elements of staging revolve around the theme

Hospitality, Leisure & Tourism Series

that the guests do not have to be 'ferried' around and will 'naturally' go home at the right time! It is interesting that the most tightly staged environment will often inspire guests to feel a natural part of a very exciting party.

Choice of venue

The choice of a venue is a crucial decision that will ultimately determine many of the elements of staging. Figure 11.2 lists the major factors in the choice of a venue. The venue may be an obvious part of the theme of the event. A corporate party that takes place in a zoo is using the venue as part of the event experience. However, many events take place within 'four walls and a roof', the venue being chosen for other factors. It can be regarded an empty canvas on which the event is painted. Events can be staged in a range of unusual spaces, from unused factories, parkland, car parks or shopping centres, to floating stages on water or using flat-back trailers from articulated lorries in a supermarket car park. The event manager can exploit the surroundings and characteristics of the venue to enhance the event experience. In these situations, the traditional roles of stage manager and event manager become blurred. When the audience and the performers mix together and where they and the venue become the entertainment package, the delineation between stage and auditorium is no longer appropriate.

An event that uses a purpose-built venue, for example, an arena or exhibition centre, will find that much of the infrastructure will be in place. Two documents that are a good starting point for making an informed choice about the venue are the venue plan and the list of facilities. However, because there are so many factors in an event that are dependent on the venue or site, an inspection is absolutely necessary. For music events, the HSE (1999) suggest that main considerations for the site visit are available space for the audience, temporary structures, backstage facilities, parking, camping and rendezvous points, together with some idea of

- Location
- Matching the venue with the theme of the event
- Matching the size of the venue to the size of the event
- Venue configuration, including sight lines and seating configuration
- History of events at that venue, including the venue's reputation
- Availability
- What the venue can provide
- Transport to, from and around the venue; parking
- Access for audience, equipment, performers, VIPs, staff and the disabled
- Toilets and other facilities
- Catering equipment and preferred caterers
- Power (amount available and outlets) and lights
- Communication, including telephone
- Climate, including microclimate and ventilation
- Emergency plans and exits

Figure 11.2 The factors in venue selection

proposed capacity, concept for the entertainment and rough calculations of space requirements. For conference events, Shone (1998) identifies that location will be the key consideration, with the venue needing to be close to a main motorway and within an hour's travelling time of a major city and airport (if international delegates are expected). Further, Owen and Holliday (1993) recommend that the event manager makes a preliminary unannounced visit to the venue to check the ambience and courtesy of staff before making arrangements. Rogers (1998) suggests that there are a number of points to consider when short-listing conference venues. These include:

- the type of venue (hotel, conference centre, university or, more unusually, football stadia or stately homes)
- the conference rooms and facilities available (including combination of room sizes and style of seating for the requirements of the event)
- accommodation and leisure options (depending on residential requirements and opportunities for social activities)
- an identifiable point of contact.

The final consideration when choosing an event is whether it requires a physical location at all. With the ongoing development of videoconferencing, and the extensive developments in the Internet, events can take place in 'cyberspace'. With some events, e.g. music concerts, the event takes place live in venue in the traditional manner, however, with the introduction of webcasting, a worldwide audience can view or experience the event simultaneously. In this instance, access to technological support and facilities, for example, a large bandwidth telephone line, will be a consideration. In other areas, for example, exhibitions and conferences, technology has been deployed in such a way that it may support the live event experience, through the website hosting supporting materials for visitors to view and in some cases interact with. Relatively recent advances in Internet technology, together with faster telecommunication infrastructure, have enabled conferences to take place solely on line, with delegates interacting, either visually through videoconferencing or through text with instant messaging. Exhibitions can take place virtual exhibition venues, which can either be modelled on the live exhibition venue as a means of supporting the event experience or can take place solely in the virtual world without the boundaries of traditional venues and limited only by imagination and the available technology. The value of such developments is only just beginning to be realized, with some commentators predicting the death of live events, whilst other, more enlightened, observers view these developments as a further medium to support or enhance the live event experience.

Audience/guests

The larger issues of audience (customer) logistics have been discussed in Chapter 10. The event staging considerations concerning the audience are:

- position of entrances and exits
- arrival times – dump or trickle
- seating and sight lines
- facilities.

Goldblatt (1997) emphasizes the importance of the entrance and reception area of an event in establishing the event theme, and suggests that the organizer should look at it from the guest's point of view. It is in this area that appropriate signage and meeting and greeting become important to the flow of 'traffic' and to the well-being of the guests. An example of a carefully planned entrance was the launch of Virgin Atlantic's service to Shanghai, where Terminal 3 of Heathrow Airport was transformed into a mini-Shanghai, with passengers leaving the departure lounge through a giant dragon's mouth (de Smet, 1999).

Once the guests have entered the event area, problems can occur that are specific to the type of event. In the case of conferences, audiences immediately head for the back rows. Interestingly, the HSE (1999) mention the opposite problem at non-ticketed music events, where the area in front of the stage is rushed as soon as the gates are open. Graham, Neirotti and Goldblatt (2001) note a similar occurrence at sport events. The solutions, therefore, is in the type of admission. For example, organizers can adopt reserved seating methods, by using ticket numbers or roping-off sections, and using a designated seating plan. The style of seating can be chosen to suit the event; theatre-, classroom- and banquet-type seating are three examples. Ultimately, the seating plan has to take into consideration:

- type of seating – fixed or movable
- the size of the audience
- the method of audience arrival
- safety factors including emergency exits and fire regulations
- placement and size of the aisles
- sight lines to the performances, speakers or audiovisual displays
- disabled access
- catering needs.

The facilities provided for the guests will depend on the type of event. Referring to Figure 11.3, the corporate event will focus on audience facilities as they relate to hospitality and catering, whereas a festival event will concentrate on audience facilities as they relate to entertainment. For example, there are no chairs for the audience at the BBC Proms in the Park (Hyde Park, London), but because of the theme of the event spectators are happy to bring their own or to sit on the ground. At the other end of the spectrum, the 2001 London and UK DatebooK Ball at the Dorchester Hotel (London) had high-quality furnishings and facilities.

The stage

A stage at an event is rarely the same as the theatrical stage complete with the proscenium arch and auditorium. It can range from the back of a truck to a barge in a harbour. It is important to note that, in event management, the term 'stage' can also be applied to the staging area and not just to a purpose built stage. However, all stages require a stage map called the stage plan. The stage plan is simply a bird's-eye view of the performance area, showing the infrastructure such as lighting fixtures, entrances, exits and power outlets. The stage plan is one of the staging tools (as shown in Figure 11.10) and a communication device that enables the event to run smoothly. For large events, the stage plan is drawn in different ways for different people, and supplied on a 'need-to-know basis'. For example, a stage plan for the

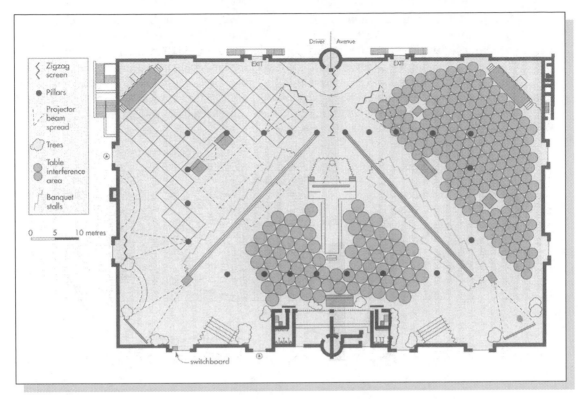

Figure 11.3 An example of a stage plan
Source: Roger Foley, Fogg Productions (www.fogg.com.au)

lighting technician would look different to the plan for the performers. A master stage plan would contain a number of layers of these different plans, each drawn on separate layer of transparent paper. Other plans that are used in event design are the front elevation and side elevation. In contrast to the bird's-eye view that the stage plan gives, these plans show the staging area as a ground-level view from the front and side, respectively. They assist in establishing the sight lines, i.e. the audience's view of the staging area and the performers.

Tim Simpson, Art Director at Theme Traders, described the value of clear stage plans:

> Creating and designing magnificent events is based on two main things: Your ability to be creative and your planning technique. Visiting a venue is vital. Producing clear and accurate plans is also a must. The crew that you have working on the day/night may not have been to the venue before and therefore clearly drawn plans, diagrams and overall illustrations are their lifeline. Plans underline your commitment to accurate planning and therefore success.

An example of when a large stage plan for a special event was used was for the Vodafone Ball 2000 at Earls Court, London (presented as a case study in Chapter 3). The 9500 guests were treated to a choice from thirteen zones of entertainment that reflected the theme, 'Rocking All Over The World', including 'Curtain Call' with performances from West End Theatre, 'Cavern Club' rock and blues, 'Electric Avenue' with pinball machines and simulators, and a full scale fairground.

Where the staging of an event includes a large catering component, the stage plan is referred to as the venue layout, seating plan or floor plan. This occurs in many corporate and conference events where hospitality and catering become a major part of the staging. Figure 11.4 illustrates how the focus on the elements of staging changes according to the style of event.

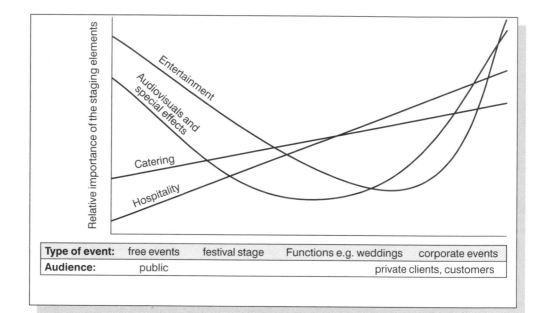

Figure 11.4 Relationship between type of event and the relative importance of the elements of staging

The stage manager is the person in control of the performance and responsible for signalling the cues that co-ordinate the work of the performers. The scheduling of the event on the particular stage is generally the responsibility of the event manager. The stage manager makes sure that this happens according to the plan. The public face of the event may be called the master of ceremonies (MC) or compère. The compère and the stage manager work closely together to ensure that all goes according to the plan. The compère may also make the public announcements such as those about lost children and programme changes.

The combination of electric wiring, hot lights, special effects, the fast movement of performers and staff in a small space that is perhaps 2 metres above ground level makes the risk management of the stage area particularly important. At the event, stage safety is generally the responsibility of the stage manager. Figure 11.5 lists a selection of safety considerations.

The backstage area is a private room or tent near the performance area set aside for the performers and staff. It provides the crew with a place to relax and the performers with a place to prepare for the performance and to wind down

- There must be a well-constructed stage, preferably constructed professionally by a company with adequate insurance.
- There must be clear well-lit access points to the stage.
- All protrusions and steps should be secured and clearly marked.
- Equipment and boxes should be placed out of the way and well marked.
- There should be work lights that provide white lighting before and after the event.
- All electric cabling must be secured.
- A first-aid kit and other emergency equipment should be at hand.
- There must be a clear guideline as to who is in authority during an emergency.
- A list of all relevant contact numbers should be made.

Figure 11.5 Factors to consider in stage safety

afterwards. It can be used for storage of equipment and for communication between the stage manager and performers, and it is where the food and drink are kept.

Power

Staging of any event involves large numbers of people, and to service this crowd electricity is indispensable. It should never be taken for granted. Factors that need to be considered concerning power are:

- type of power – three phase or single phase
- amount of power needed, particularly at peak times
- emergency power
- position and number of power outlets
- types of leads and distance from power source to device
- the correct wiring of the venue as old venues could be improperly earthed
- the incoming equipment's volt/amp rating
- safety factors, including the covering leads and the possibility of electricity earth leakage as a result of rain
- regulations regarding power.

Lights

Lighting at a venue has two functions. Pragmatically, lights allow everyone to see what is happening; artistically, they are central to the design of the event. The general venue or site lighting is important in that it allows all the other aspects of the staging to take place. For this reason, it is usually the first item on the checklist when deciding on a venue. Indoor lights include signage lights (exit, toilets, etc.) as well as lighting specific areas for catering and ticket collection. Outside the venue, lighting is required for venue identification, safety, security and sponsor signs.

Once the general venue or site lighting is confirmed, lighting design needs to be considered. The questions to ask when considering lighting are both practical and aesthetic. They include the following.

- Does it fit in with and enhance the overall event theme?
- Can it be used for ambient lighting as well as performance lighting?
- Is there a backup?
- What are the power requirements (lights can draw far more power that the sound system)?
- Will it interfere with the electrics of other systems? For example, a dimmer board can create an audible buzz in the sound system.
- Does it come with a light operator, i.e. the person responsible for the planning of the lighting with lighting board?
- What light effects are needed (strobe, cross-fading) and can the available lights do this?
- What equipment is needed (e.g. trees and cans), and is there a place on the site or in the venue to erect it?
- Does the building have permanent trusses available for rigging lighting?
- How can the lighting assist in the safety and security of the event?

The lighting plot or lighting plan is a map of the venue and shows the type and position of the lighting. As Reid (1995) points out, the decisions that the event manager has to make when creating a lighting plan are:

- placement of the lights
- the type of lights, including floods and follow spots
- where the light should be pointed
- what colours to use.

Sound

The principal reason for sound equipment at an event is so that all the audience can clearly hear the music, speeches and audio effects. The sound system also is used to:

- communicate between the sound engineer and the stage manager (talkback or intercom)
- monitor the sound
- create a sound recording the event
- broadcast the sound to other venues or through other media, including television, radio and the Internet.

This means that the type of equipment used needs to be designed for the:

- type of sound to be amplified including, spoken work and music
- size and make-up of the audience, e.g. an older audience may like the music at a different volume to a younger audience.
- acoustic properties of the room, e.g. some venues have a bad echo problem, so attaching drapes or material to the walls may alleviate this.
- theme of the event, e.g. a bright silver sound system may look out of place at a black tie dinner.

The choice of size, type and location of the speakers for the sound at an event can make a difference to the guest's experience of the sound. Figure 11.6 shows two

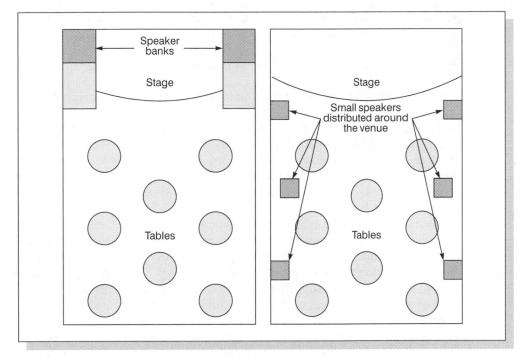

Figure 11.6 Two examples of audio speaker layout

simplified plans for speaker positions at a venue. The speakers may be next to the stage, which is common at music concerts, or distributed around the site. They may also be flown from supports above the audience. At a large site, with speakers widely distributed, the sound engineers need to take into account the natural delay of sound travelling from the various speakers to the members of the audience. A ducting system could also be installed above audience height to avoid tripping hazards caused by trailing cables.

For small events, a simple public address (PA) system may be used. This consists of a microphone and microphone stand and one or two speakers. It is basically the same as a home stereo system with a microphone added, and generally only has enough power to reach a small audience. The quality of sound produced makes them only suitable for speeches.

For larger events that have more complex sound requirements, a larger sound system is needed. This would incorporate:

- microphones, which may include lapel mikes and radio mikes
- microphone stands
- cabling, including from the microphones to the mixing desk
- mixing desk, which adjusts the quality and level of the sound coming from the microphones before it goes out the speakers
- amplifier
- speakers, which can vary in the frequency of sound given out, from bass speakers to treble speakers that enhance the quality of the sound within a certain sound spectrum

- sound engineer, sound technician, or front of house engineer, who looks after all aspects of the sound, in particular the sound quality that is heard by the audience
- backup equipment including spare leads and microphones.

The next step up from this type of system includes all of the above plus:

- monitor speakers (also called wedge monitors) that channel the sound back to the speaker or performer so they can hear themselves over the background sound
- monitor control/mixing desk
- monitor engineer who is responsible for the quality of sound going through the monitors.

If an event needs a sound system managed by a sound engineer, time must be allocated to tune the sound system. This means that acoustic aspect of the venue is taken into account by trying out various sound frequencies within the venue. This is the reason for the often heard 'testing, one, two, one, two' as a sound system is being prepared. The sound engineer is also looking for any sound feedback problems. Feedback is an unwanted, often high-pitched sound that occurs when the sound coming out of the speakers is picked up by the microphones and comes out of the speakers again, thereby building on the original sound. To avoid the problem of feedback, microphones are positioned so that they face away from sound speakers. The tuning of a large sound system is one of the main reasons for having a sound check or a run-through before an event. Figure 11.7 shows a simplified sound run-through prior to an event.

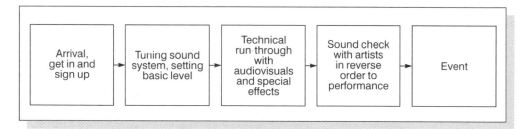

Figure 11.7 A simple flow chart for a sound system

Volume and subsequent leakage during an event can become a major problem. Local councils can close an event if there are too many complaints from residents. At some venues, for example, there are volume switches that automatically turn off the power if the sound level is too high. At multi-venue events, sound leakage between stages can be minimized by:

- thoughtful placement of the stages
- careful positioning of all the speakers (including the monitors)
- constant monitoring of the volume level
- careful programming of the events on each stage in a way that avoids interference.

Audiovisual and special effects

Many event managers hire lighting and sound from separate companies and integrate their services into the overall design of the event. However, there are suppliers that provide both lighting and sound equipment and act as consultants prior to the event. These audiovisual companies can supply a fully integrated system of film, video, slides and often special effects. However, most audiovisual companies are specialists in flat-screen presentations and the special effect area is often best left to specialists in this field. For example, pyrotechnicians require different skills and licences from ice sculptors. Complex events that use a variety of special effects and audiovisuals require a co-ordinator who is familiar with the event theme and knows how to link all the specialist areas to each other. This co-ordinator is called the event producer. Although the terms 'event manager', 'stage manager' and 'event producer' are confusing, they are terms that are used in the industry. The position of event producer is created when there are many different specialists involved in the event. Organizers of corporate events, including product launches and conferences, often subcontract the audiovisual elements, because the specialist knowledge required means an expert is needed to operate these systems effectively. The decision to use an audiovisual company for an event depends on:

- how the audiovisual presentation fits in with the overall event design
- the budget allocated to the event
- the skills of the audiovisual company, including its technical hardware, software and the abilities of the audiovisual producer and writer.

For large-budget events, the audiovisual company will act as a consultant, with the producer and writer researching and creating a detailed audiovisual script.

According to Goldblatt (1997), special effects at an event are used to attract attention, generate excitement and sustain interest. In larger events, for example the Millennium Eve celebrations along the River Thames in London, the pyrotechnics become part of the overall logistics planning. Event managers and planners must fully realize the importance of event decoration, scenery and appropriate props as an enhancing tool for the staging of any event.

Because much of the audiovisual and special effects technology is highly complex, it is often 'preprogrammed'. This means that all lighting, audiovisual and sound 'presets' (technical elements positioned prior to the event), including the changing of light and sound levels and the cueing of video or slide presentations, can be programmed into the controlling computer. The computer control of much of the audiovisuals means that the whole presentation can be fully integrated and set up well in advance. Because these aspects are prearranged, including all the cue times, the advantage is that few technicians are needed to control these operations during the event. The disadvantages are that spontaneity can be taken from the event and, the more complex the technology, the more things can go wrong. Moreover, the technology becomes the master of the cue times and it is nearly impossible to take advantage of any unforeseen opportunities.

Catering

Catering can be the major element in staging, depending on the theme and nature of an event. Most purpose-built venues already have catering. For example, the

Wembley Exhibition and Conference Centre has a contract a catering company. The dinners that take place in the conference centre can only use the in-house caterers. Figure 11.8 illustrates some of the many factors to be considered in catering.

There are general principles that can be followed when planning the catering for events. For example, at a corporate function or formal dinner, a ratio of 1:10 (one member of staff to serve ten customers) is appropriate, whereas at a Christmas party, a ratio of 2:30 (two members of staff to serve three tables of ten customers) may suffice. Staffing numbers will be varied depending on the style of service being adopted, for example, whether silver served or plated, the complexity of the menu, the requirements of the client and the speed of service required. For example, a formal dinner, where the top table dictates the serving of all other guests, may require more staff than if a rolling service can be operated, with tables cleared and the next course served as each table finishes. In this way, teams of staff can work together in order to ensure that all elements of the meal arrive in front of the guest at the same time. Theatre can play a large part in formal meals. For example, using an MC to call guests into the dining area, the top table entering to the synchronized

---

In house or contracted out?

The advantage of in-house catering is the knowledge of the venue. The advantage of contract catering is that the event manager may have a special arrangement with the caterer that has been built up over time; the event manager can choose all aspects of the catering; and the catering can be tendered out and a competitive bid sought.

Quality control factors to consider

- Appropriateness and enhancement of the event theme.
- Menu selection and design, including special diets and food displays.
- Quality of staff and supervision.
- Equipment, including style and quantity, and selection of in-house or hired.
- Cleanliness.
- Culturally appropriateness – a major consideration in a culturally diverse society.
- Staff to guest ratio.

Costs

- Are there any guarantees, including those against loss and breakage?
- What are the payment terms?
- Who is responsible for licences and permits: the caterer, the venue or event management?
- What deposits and up front fees are there?
- What is the per capita expenditure? Is each guest getting value commensurate with client's expenditure?

Waste management:

- Must occur before, during and after the event.
- Must conforming to food hygiene and food safety regulations and environmental concerns.
- Must be appropriate to the event theme.

Figure 11.8 Issues to be considered when arranging catering for an event

clapping of all other guests, and through the tight co-ordination of waiting staff. For example, having all waiting staff entering the room in a formal line before 'breaking off' to take up their positions; upon the signal of the banqueting manager, usually involving the raising of an arm, the top table is served, followed immediately by the all the other tables. In this way, the status of VIP guests on the top table is maintained.

As Graham, Neirotti and Goldblatt (2001) stress, the consumption of alcoholic beverages at an event gives rise to many concerns for the event manager. These include the special training of staff, which party holds the licence (venue, event manager or client); and the legal age for consumption. The possible problems that arise from the sale of alcoholic, for example, increased audience noise at the end of the event and general behavioural problems, can affect almost all aspects of the event. The decision whether to allow the sale or consumption of alcoholic beverages can be crucial to the success of an event and needs careful thought.

There are a variety of ways that the serving of alcoholic can be negotiated with a caterer. The drinks service can be from the bar or may be served at the table by the glass, bottle or jug. A caterer may offer a 'drinks package', which means that the drinks are free for, say, the first hour of the catered event. A subtle result of this type of deal is that the guest can find it hard to find a drinks waiter in the first hour.

Performers

The 'talent' (as performers are often called) at an event can range from music groups to motivational speakers to specially commissioned shows. A performing group can form a major part of an event's design. The major factors to consider when employing artists are:

- *Contact*: the event's entertainment co-ordinator needs to establish contact with the person responsible for the employment of the group. This could be the artist, an agent representing the artist, or the manager of a group. It is important to establish this line of authority at the beginning when working with the artists.
- *Staging* requirements: a rock band, for example, will have a more detailed sound requirement than a folk singer. These requirements are usually listed on document called the spec (specification) sheet. Many groups will also have their own stage plan illustrating the area needed and their preferred configuration of the performance area.
- *Availability for rehearsal, media attention and performance*: the available times given by the artists' management should include the time it takes for the artists to set up on stage as well as the time it takes to vacate the stage or performance area. These are referred to as the time needed for 'set up' (load in) and 'breakdown' (load out).
- *Accompanying personnel*: many artist travel with an entourage that can include technicians, cooks, stylists and bodyguards. It is important to establish their numbers, and what their roles and needs are.
- *Contracts and legal requirements*: the agreement between the event manager and the performers is described in Chapter 9. Of particular importance to the staging are minimum rates and conditions, the legal structure of the group and issues such as workers' compensation and public liability. Copyright is also important as its ownership can affect the use of the performance for broadcast and future promotions.

- *Payment*: most performing groups work on the understanding that they will be paid immediately for their services. Except for 'headline' acts that have a company structure, the thirty-, sixty- or ninety-day invoicing cycle is not appropriate for most performers, who rarely have the financial resources necessary to wait for payment.

Performers come from a variety of performance cultural backgrounds. This means that different performers have different expectations about the facilities available for them and how they are to be treated. Theatre performers and concert musicians, for example, expect direct performance guidelines – conducting, scripting or a musical score. Street and outdoor festival performers, on the other hand, are used to less formal conditions and to improvising.

Supervision of performers in a small theatre is generally left to the assistant stage manager, whereas a festival stage may not have this luxury and it may be the stage manager's responsibility. Regardless of who undertakes it, supervision cannot be overlooked. The person responsible needs to contact the artists on arrival, give them the appropriate run sheets, introduce them to the relevant crew members and show them the green room (the room in which performers and invited guests are entertained). At the end of the performance, the artists' supervisor needs to assist them in leaving the area.

The crew

The chapter on leadership and human resources (Chapter 5) discussed the role of staff and volunteers at an event. While a large festival or sport event will usually rely on the work of volunteers, staging tends to be handled by professionals. Dealing with cueing, working with complex and potentially dangerous equipment and handling professional performers leaves little room for indecision and inexperience. Professionalism is essential when staging an event. For example, the staging of a concert performance will need skilled sound engineers, roadies, security staff, stage crew, ticket sellers and even ushers (the roadies are the skilled labourers that assist with the set up and breakdown of the sound and lights). The crew is selected by matching the tasks involved with their skills and ability to work together.

The briefing is the meeting, before the event, at which the crew members are given their briefs, or roles, that match their skills. The name and jobs of the crew members are then kept on a contact and responsibility sheet. The briefing tends to be more informal than the later production meeting. The event producer should not forget that the crew comes with an enormous amount of experience in the staging of events. They can provide valuable input into the creation and design of the event.

It is also interesting to note that the changes in the events industry, particularly in the audiovisual area, are reflected in the make-up and number of crew members. As Edward Stagg, Senior Lighting Designer at Theme Traders points out:

> Over the last ten years technicians have found it increasingly difficult to keep up with ever expanding technology. The introduction of computerized lighting consoles have reduced programming time dramatically and they only need one person to operate them. Intelligent lighting has also reduced the need for crew as they facilitate movement and changes in beam characteristics on command. There are many fantastic things technology has given to our events but simplicity still has to remain forefront in our minds.

Hospitality

A major part of the package offered to sponsors is hospitality (Catherwood and Kirk, 1992). What will the sponsor expect event management to provide for them and their guests? This can include tickets, food and beverage, souvenirs and gifts. As well as the sponsors, the event may benefit in the long term by offering hospitality to other stakeholders and VIPs. They can include politicians, media units, media personalities, clients of the sponsor, potential sponsors, partners and local opinion formers. They are all referred to as the guests of the event.

The invitation may be the first impression that the potential guest receives, and it therefore needs to convey the theme of the event. It should create a desire to attend as well as imparting information. Figure 11.9 is a checklist for making sure that the various elements of hospitality are covered.

Invitations

- Is the design of high quality and is it innovative?
- Does the method of delivery allow time to reply? Would hand delivery and e-mail be appropriate?
- Does the content of the invitation include time, date, name of event, how to reply (RSVP), directions and parking?
- Should promotional material be included with the invitation?

Arrival

- Has timing been planned so those guests arrive at the best moment?
- What are the parking arrangements?
- Who will do the meeting and greeting? Will there be someone there to welcome them to the event?
- Have waiting times been reduced? For example, will guests receive a welcome cocktail while waiting to be booked into the accommodation?

Facilities

- Is there a separate area for guests? This can be a marquee, corporate box (at a sporting event) or a club room.
- What food and beverage will be provided? Is there a need for a special menu and personal service?
- Is there a separate, high-quality viewing area of the performance with good views and facilities?
- Has special communication, such as signage or an information desk, been provided?

Gifts

- Have tickets to the event, especially for clients, been organized?
- What souvenirs (programmes, pins, T-shirts, CDs) will there be?
- Will there be a chance for guests to meet the 'stars'?

Departure

- Has guest departure been timed so that they do not leave at the same time as the rest of the audience?

Figure 11.9 A hospitality checklist

In their informative work on sports events, Graham, Neirotti and Goldblatt (2001, pp. 85–92) describe ten strategies to achieve success in the provision of hospitality to guests:

1 Know the guests' needs and expectations.
2 Plan what the sporting event is expected to achieve for the guest, e.g. networking, incentive, promotional activity.
3 Understand arrival patterns of guests in order to plan, for example, staffing requirements.
4 Plan according to what has preceded or will follow the guests arrival, for example, meal requirements.
5 Create appealing invitations to capture the prospective guests attention.
6 Understand the protocol for the specific sport event, as most have specific guidelines.
7 Focus on first and last impressions to gain maximum impact.
8 Exceed the guest's expectations, particularly through providing extra amenities, for example, parking, welcome signs, and information desk in hotel lobby.
9 Be responsive to changes in the guests' needs during the event.
10 Evaluate the event so that it can be improved next time.

Corporate sponsors may have a variety of reasons to attend the event and these have to be taken into account in hospitality planning. Sodexho Prestige (2000) suggest that the main drivers for corporate hospitality are building relationships with potential customers, rewarding customers, raising corporate awareness, increasing business/ sales and to develop informal contact in a relaxed setting.

The hospitality experience is of particular importance at the corporate events. In one sense, such an event is centred around hospitality (see Figure 11.4). As it is a private function, there is no public and the members of audience are the guests. Most of the items on the hospitality checklist, from the invitations to the personal service, are applicable to staging these events. For the guests, the hospitality experience is fundamental to the event experience.

The production schedule

The terms used in the staging of events come from both the theatre and film production. A rehearsal of the event is a run through of the event, reproducing as closely as possible the actual event. For the sake of 'getting it right on the night', there may also need to be a technical rehearsal and a dress rehearsal. A production meeting, on the other hand, is a get-together of those responsible for producing the event. It involves the stage manager and the event producer, representatives of the lighting and sound crew or audiovisual specialists, representatives of the performers and the MC. It is held at the performance site or on stage as near to the time of the event as possible. At this crucial meeting:

- final production schedule notes are compared
- possible last minute production problems are brought up
- the flow of the event is summarized
- emergency procedures are reviewed

- the compère is introduced and familiarized with the production staff.
- the communication system for the event is tested (Neighbourhood Arts Unit, 1991, p.50).

The production schedule is the main document for staging. It is the master document from which various other schedules, including the cue or prompt sheet and the run sheets, are created. Goldblatt (1997, p. 143) defines it as the detailed listing of tasks with specific start and stop times occurring from set up of the event's equipment (also known as load in) through to the eventual removal of all the equipment (breakdown or load out). It is often a written form of the Gantt chart (see Chapter 10) with four columns: time, activity, location and responsibility. Production schedules can also contain a description of the relevant elements of the event.

Two particularly limited times on the schedule are the 'load-in' and 'load-out' times. The load in refers to the time when the necessary infrastructure can be brought in, unloaded and set up. The load-out time refers to the time when the equipment can be dismantled and removed. Although the venue or site may be available to receive the equipment at any time, there are many other factors that set the load-in time. The hiring cost and availability of equipment are two important limiting factors. In most cases, the larger items must arrive first. These may include fencing, tents, stage, food vans and extra toilets. Next could come the audiovisual equipment and, finally, the various decorations. Supervision of the arrival and set up of the equipment can be crucial to minimizing problems during the event. The contractor who delivers and assembles the equipment often is not the operator of the equipment. This can mean that once it is set up, it is impossible to change it without recalling the contractor.

Load-out can be the most difficult time of an event, because the excitement is over, the staff are often tired and everyone is in a hurry to leave. Nevertheless, these are just the times when security and safety are important. The correct order of load-out needs to be on a detailed schedule. This is often the reverse of the load-in schedule. The last item on the checklist for the load-out is the 'idiot check'. This refers to the check that is done after everything is cleared from the performance area, and some of the staff do a search for anything that may be left.

The run sheets are lists of the order for specific jobs at an event. The entertainers, for example, would have one run sheet while the caterers would have another. Often the production schedule is a loose-leaf folder that includes all the run sheets. The cue sheets are a list of times that initiate a change of any kind during the event and describe what happens on that change. The stage manager and audiovisual controller use them.

Recording the event

By their very nature, events are ephemeral. A good quality recording of the event is essential for most event companies, as it demonstrates the ability of the organization and it can be used to promote the event company. It can also help in evaluating the event and, if necessary, in settling later disputes, whether of a legal or other nature. The method of recording the event can be on video, sound recording or as photographs. Making a sound recording can be just a matter of putting a cassette in the sound system and pressing the record button. With digital cameras now available at low prices, extensive photographs can be taken at minimal cost, which can then be used on the company Internet site to provide cases of successful events. However, any visual recording of the event will require planning. In particular, the correct lighting is needed for depth of field. Factors that need to be considered for video recording are:

- What is it for – promotion, legal purposes or for sale to the participants?
- What are the costs in time and money?
- How will it effect the event? Will the video cameras be a nuisance? Will they need white lighting?;
- What are the best vantage points?

Recording the event is not a decision that should be left to the last minute; it needs to be factored into the planning of the event. Once an event is played out there is no going back.

Contingencies

As with large festivals and hallmark events, the staging of any event has to make allowances for what might go wrong. 'What if' sessions need to be implemented with the staff. A stage at a festival may face an electricity blackout; performers may not arrive; trouble may arrive instead. Therefore, micro-contingency plans need to be in place. All these must fit in with the overall event risk-management and emergency plans. At corporate events in well-known venues, the venue will have its own emergency plan that needs to be given to everyone involved.

Summary

The staging of an event can range from presenting a show of multicultural dancers and musicians at a stage in a local park, to the launch of the latest software product at the most expensive hotel in town. All events share common staging elements including sound, lights, food and beverage, performers and special effects. All these elements need to create and

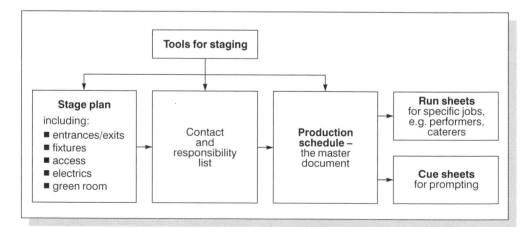

Figure 11.10 A summary of the tools necessary for staging an event

enhance the event theme. The importance of each element depends on the type of event. To stage an event successfully a number of tools are used: the production schedule, the stage plan and the contact and responsibility list, all of which are shown in Figure 11.10.

Questions

1 Analyse an event into its staging elements and discuss the relationship between these elements.

2 Choose a theme for a company's staff party. How would you relate all the elements of staging to the theme?

3 Compile a stage plan, contact responsibility list and production schedule with the relevant run sheets for:

(a) a corporate party for the clients, staff and customers of a company
(b) a fun run with entertainment
(c) a large wedding
(d) one of the stages for a city arts festival.

Case Study

Theming – a marketing tool

Theming, styling, designing, creating, setting the scene and building an atmosphere are all areas covered on a day-to-day basis by Theme Traders – a specialist event management company based in Cricklewood, London.

Theming is similar to marketing. When a company plans the launch of a new product or service, all the Ps have to be considered – presentation, product, positioning and price. These are all the areas that have to be taken into account when planning and theming an event.

Through the 1980s and early 1990s, themes such as 'Wild West Ho Downs', 'Hawaiian Beach Parties', 'Arabian Nights', 'Science Fiction' and 'Bond Parties' were all the rage and these perennial 'themes' will never die. However, what event managers should always ask their clients is what they want to achieve – in a budget-driven world objectives are the name of the game. Heaven forbid that someone should have a party just for fun!

When a city bank asks for a party for 1300 people to be designed, the questions are endless – other than the standard issues (for example, age of guests, sex, venue and type of food), the most important enquiry for the event manager concerns what the client wants to achieve. In order to choose the 'style' and put a creative team to work, the event manager needs to know if this is a 'thank you' party, a celebration, or perhaps an event to 'schmooze' their top ten clients? Is there a need to create a moody mysterious scene, a fun and funky setting or is it to be a full on 'party party' with games and entertainment for the staff?

When one of those lovely 'ladies who lunch' comes to Theme Traders and asks them to arrange a top-notch summer party to celebrate her husband's fiftieth birthday, they might suggest a retro 1960s and 1970s evening, Austin Powers style – this could include bubble columns and lava lamps, animal print draping, a circular bed covered in fluffy pink material, psychedelic colours and glitter boots – or a night of rock 'n' roll where the birthday boy can go back to his teens, air guitar in hand and play to the strains of Pink Floyd and Deep

Purple! But without asking the right questions the event manager could easily get it all horribly wrong – as the chief executive of a major blue chip company, he wants a sophisticated stylish party with a string quartet and a harpist!

Last summer, Theme Traders were asked to design the launch party for a new Internet company, cooldiamonds.com – now a highly successful Internet site where you can buy the best diamonds in the world or, alternatively, a cheeky diamond stud for your belly button! The brief was a mix of sophistication and fun. The directors wanted to invite a young sector of the press, trendy designers from Bond Street, clients from Knightsbridge and city business associates – including their bank manager!

It had to be somewhere central, so Theme Traders chose a beautiful room overlooking the Thames in a top London hotel. In essence, the event had to ooze sophistication but they wanted the youngsters to be able to party, the designers to be able to 'chill' and the Knightsbridge and city set to be able to enjoy deluxe dining in exclusive surroundings. The evening was to be special, unique, inviting and rich. After all, they were launching a luxury item!

One of the Theme Traders creative teams brainstormed the proposal, appointed an art director to the project and one of their senior event managers was assigned to make it all happen. At this stage, an illustration is often produced, which helps the client to focus on the creative team's ideas. Through experience, there is rarely any point in providing more than one illustration as the creative team have usually made a critical decision on how the party will appear through extensive brainstorming, therefore eliminating other second-rate ideas along the way. A crew from the showroom was assigned to the project and all the different departments worked together on the event. All events and parties at Theme Traders are the result of teamwork. Everyone employed is creative, not necessarily through his or her qualifications, but as people. It is essential for Theme Traders to be able to 'paint' a picture for their clients, and to bring that picture to life.

The result? The room was divided into two main areas blending one 'atmosphere' into the other. Using rich midnight blue velvet the entire area was draped with custom-made star cloths through which peeped twinkling silver white lights. At one end, low fluffy cloud-like tables were laid out with enormous soft pastel coloured cushions and beanbags around a starry dance floor. Lit with different shades of blue and white beams and gobos, the cooldiamonds.com logo shimmered everywhere! Over the dance floor hung rotating mirror balls that threw tiny diamond-like specs all around the room. In the 'champagne' area the tables were dressed to the floor with the same rich velvet material. In every centrepiece was a waterfall gently cascading over silver stones around the flicker of tiny tea-lights.

The mood of the whole room was changed as the evening progressed with creative use of lighting. Lighting designers had set the tone of the evening adding shades of blue and indigo which highlighted and brightened the 'diamond' effect around the room as the evening progressed. All in all a cool but rich atmosphere was produced swimming in dreams and desires. The client was delighted!

What the client actually said after the event was that Theme Traders had solved their problem. They thought they would have to have two events, use different venues, incur double the expenses and basically could not see a way through their dilemma. Providing two very distinct arenas for two audiences in the same venue and at the same time could be considered a dilemma, but dilemmas like this are second nature to Theme Traders and they thrive on the challenge. Carefully mixing colours, fabrics and lighting to enhance moods, change atmospheres and make dreams come true – that is Theme Traders' speciality!

For further details about Theme Traders, please visit www.themetraders.com.
By Sally Bentley, Head of Human Resources, Theme Traders, The Stadium, Oaklands Road, London, NW2 6XN.

Questions

1 What process is involved in developing the theme for the event?

2 What benefit does theming bring to an event?

3 How do the elements of staging relate to the theme for the cooldiamonds.com event?

4 Based on the brief given, brainstorm alternative themes for the cooldiamonds.com event.

5 From the results of question 4, choose one theme for further development.

   (a) How will this theme deliver the clients requirements.
   (b) Referring to the elements of staging, describe how you would conceptualize and implement this theme. You may wish to illustrate your answer to focus your idea.

Evaluation and reporting

After studying this chapter, you should be able to:

- understand the role of evaluation in the event management process

- know when to evaluate an event

- understand the evaluation needs of event stakeholders

- create an evaluation plan for an event

- apply a range of techniques including questionnaires and surveys in evaluating events

- describe and record the intangible impacts of events

- understand the role of economic impact studies in the evaluation of events

- prepare a final evaluation report

- use event profiles to promote the outcomes of events and to seek sponsorship

- apply the knowledge gained by evaluation to the future planning of an event.

Introduction – what is event evaluation?

Event evaluation is the process of critically observing, measuring and monitoring the implementation of an event in order to assess its outcomes accurately. It enables the creation of an event profile that outlines the basic features and important statistics of an event. It also enables feedback to be provided to event stakeholders, and plays an important role in the event management process by providing a tool for analysis and improvement.

The event management process is a cycle (see Figure 12.1) in which inputting and analysing data from an event enables more informed decisions to be made and more efficient planning to done, and improves event outcomes. This applies to individual repeat events, where the lessons learnt from one event can be incorporated in the planning of the next. It also applies to the general body of events knowledge, where the lessons learnt from individual events contribute to the overall knowledge and effectiveness of the events industry.

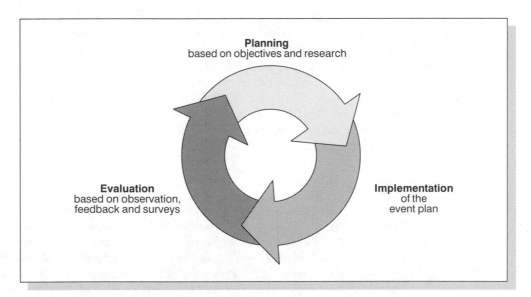

Figure 12.1 Evaluation and the event management process

Edinburgh, for example, has learnt to cope with an influx of visitors that nearly doubles the population of the city for the Hogmanay celebrations, by applying the lessons learnt each year to the logistics planning for the next year's festival. As discussed in an earlier chapter, Glastonbury Festival has been developed and refined over a period by intelligently feeding back information from one year's celebrations into the planning for the next.

Lessons learnt from one event can also be transferred to other events or to the whole events industry. The disaster at the FA Cup semi-final between Liverpool and Nottingham Forest at Hillsborough, Sheffield, in 1989, during which ninety-six fans were killed, led to a major review of the way that football grounds were designed, and improved crowd management techniques. The 1991 World Student Games in Sheffield left a legacy of event knowledge and experience, which has been applied to more recent events such as the European Football Championships in 1996, the Rugby Union World Cup in 1999 and informed development of the UK Major Event Strategy. Innovations in terms of event communications, products and technologies are constantly spread and refined through the process of event evaluation leading to better event planning, implementation and further evaluation. It is an upward spiral leading to the improvement of individual events, and to an ever-growing and more knowledgeable events industry.

When to evaluate events

Evaluation is a process that occurs throughout the event management cycle. However, three key periods have been identified by Getz (1997) and others as to when it is useful to focus on the evaluation process.

Pre-event assessment

Some form of assessment of the factors governing an event usually takes place in the research and planning stage. This is sometimes called a feasibility study, and is used to determine what level of resourcing an event is likely to require, and whether or not to proceed with the event. Such a study may involve market research as to the probable audience reaction to the event, and is likely to involve some degree of research and prediction with regard to attendance figures, costs and benefits. It will often compare the event with profiles and outcomes of previous similar events. The study may result in establishing targets or benchmarks against which the success of the project will be measured.

Monitoring the event

Event monitoring is the process of tracking the progress of an event through the various stages of implementation, and enables factors governing the event to be adjusted. For example, ticket sales may be perceived as slow in the lead-up to an event, and this may result in increased advertising or publicity effort. Monitoring the budget may result in the trimming of expenses, or the freeing up of money for other areas of expenditure. Observation during the event may lead to changes which improve the delivery of the event, such as adjusting sound volume, or altering the dispersal of security or cleaning personnel to match changing crowd patterns. This process of monitoring is vital to quality control, and will also provide valuable information in the final evaluation of an event, and for future planning purposes.

Post-event evaluation

The most common form of evaluation, however, is post-event evaluation. This involves the gathering of statistics and data resulting from an event, and interpreting them in relation to its mission and objectives. An important aspect is usually a feedback meeting of key participants and stakeholders, where the strengths and weaknesses of the event are discussed, and observations are recorded for future reference. Post-event evaluation may also involve some form of questionnaire or survey of the event participants or audience, which seeks to explore their opinions of the experience and to measure their levels of satisfaction with the event. It often involves the collection of data on the financial expenditure of the participants, so that the cost can be compared with the revenue generated by the event. The nature of the evaluation will be determined largely by the purpose of the event and audience for which it is intended.

Reporting to stakeholders

One of the prime reasons that event managers evaluate events is to report to stakeholders.

- The host organization will want to know what the event achieved. Did the event come in on budget and on time? Did it achieve its objectives? How many people attended, and were their expectations met? For future planning purposes it might be useful to know where the attendees came from, how they heard about it and whether they intend to return next year.
- The event sponsor may have other measures. Was the level of awareness of the product or service increased? What penetration did the advertising achieve? What media coverage was generated? What was the profile of the people who attended?
- Funding bodies will have grant acquittal procedures to be observed, and will usually require audited financial statements of income and expenditure along with a report on the social, cultural or sporting outcomes of the event.
- Councils and government departments may want to know what the impact was on their local, regional or national economies.
- Tourism bodies may want to know the number of visitors attracted and what they spent, not only on the event, but also on travel, shopping and accommodation.

Quantified event outcomes can be very helpful to event organizers in promoting the profile and acceptance of the event. The City of Edinburgh Council, together with other stakeholders in the Edinburgh Festivals (including the organizers and the Scottish Tourism Board), use the economic impacts of the Edinburgh Festivals very effectively in promoting support for, and acceptance of, the events. For example, in a press release announcing traffic and safety arrangements for Edinburgh's Hogmanay, the City of Edinburgh Council, noted that, 'Edinburgh's Hogmanay is now in the same league as the Edinburgh International Festival in terms of its position on the world's "must see" list, and the impact it has on the city's economy. For an outlay of around £1.4 million, including the cost of the safety measures, the economic return is in the region of £30 million' (City of Edinburgh Council, 2000c).

Similarly, Bath and North East Somerset Council has used economic impact studies to underline the contribution of arts to the cultural economy of Bath and North East Somerset (B&NES, 2000).

Evaluation procedures

In order to meet the many and varied reporting requirements of event stakeholders, it is necessary for the event manager to plan carefully the evaluation of the event. The evaluation will usually be more effective if it is planned from the outset, and built into the event management process. Planning should include consideration of:

- what data is needed
- how, when and by whom it is to be gathered
- how it is to be analysed
- what format to use in the final reporting.

Data collection

The process of implementing the event may provide opportunities for useful data to be collected. For example, participants may be required to fill in an event entry form, which can be designed to provide useful information on numbers, age, gender, point of origin, spending patterns and so on. Ticketed events allow for a ready means of counting spectators, and the ticketing agency may be able to provide further useful information, such as the postcode of purchasers. For non-ticketed events, figures on the use of public transport and car parks, and police crowd estimates can be used in calculating attendance figures. Event managers should look out for and make use of all opportunities for the collection of relevant data.

Observation

An obvious but critical source of data collection is the direct observation of the event. Staff observation and reports may provide information on a number of aspects of the event, including performance quality, audience reaction, crowd flow, and adequacy of catering and toilet facilities. However, staff will provide more accurate and useful data if they are trained to observe and are given a proper reporting format, rather than being left to rely on casual and anecdotal observation. From the outset, staff should be made aware that observation and reporting on the event are part of their role, and should be given appropriate guidance and benchmarks. They may be given checklists, and asked to evaluate items such as performance quality and audience reaction on a scale of 1 to 5, or by ticking indicators such as below average, average, good, very good or excellent.

At all outdoor events, stage managers should be required to complete a written report on each event, giving their estimates of attendance figures, weather conditions, performance standards and crowd reaction, and commenting on any unusual occurrences or features. Likewise, security staff should be required to report on crowd behaviour, any incidents, disturbances or injuries, and to estimate the size of crowds on the day assisted by photographs taken at regular intervals by security cameras at strategic locations throughout the park. By compiling these reports with statistics from attraction operators, and factors such as competition from other major events in the city, management is able to form profiles of individual events and to track trends over time.

Other key players in an event such as venue owners, councils, sponsors, vendors, police and first-aid officers can often provide valuable feedback from their various perspectives.

- Venue owners may be able to compare the performance of the event with their normal venue patterns and comment usefully on matters such as attendance figures, parking, access, catering and facility usage.

- Councils may be aware of disturbance to the local community, or of difficulties with street closures or compliance with health regulations.
- Sponsors may have observations based on their attendance at the event, or may have done their own surveys on audience reaction, awareness levels and media coverage.
- Vendors may have information on, for example, volume of sales and waiting time in queues that will be valuable in planning future catering arrangements.
- Police may have observed aspects such as crowd behaviour, traffic flow and parking, and may have constructive suggestions for future planning.
- First-aid providers may have statistics on the number and seriousness of treatments for injuries such as cuts, abrasions or heat exhaustion that will assist in future planning of safety and risk assessment.

All of these key stakeholders may have observations on general planning issues such as signage, access, crowd management, communication and the provision of facilities that will have implications for the improvement of the event. It is important that their observations are recorded and incorporated into the evaluation and planning stages of the event management process.

Feedback meetings

All stakeholders should be made aware at the outset that they will be given an opportunity to provide feedback, and that this is a vital part of the event planning process. They should be encouraged to contribute their professional observations and assessment. This may be done at a single 'debriefing' meeting or a series of meetings, depending on the complexity of the event. It is often useful for the date and agenda of this meeting to be made known to all parties early in the process, so that if it is not possible for them to communicate their observations during the heat of the event, then they are aware that a suitable forum will be provided during the finalization of the event. This meeting should ensure that neither congratulations nor recriminations overshadow the important lessons that are to be learnt from the event and incorporated into future planning. It is important that all parties are listened to and that their comments are taken into account in the future planning of the event.

The topics to be addressed at the meeting will be determined by the nature and size of the event. However, the checklist in Figure 12.2 is a useful starting point.

Questionnaires and surveys

Questionnaires can range from simple feedback forms targeting event partners and stakeholders to detailed audience or visitor surveys undertaken by trained personnel. The scale of the questionnaire will depend upon the needs and resources of the event. Simple feedback forms can usually be designed and distributed within the event's own internal resources. They may seek to record and quantify basic data, such as the expenditure of event partners, the observations of stakeholders and their assessment of event management and outcomes.

Surveys are used in order to ascertain reliable statistical information on audience profiles and reaction, and on visitor patterns and expenditure. They may be implemented by direct interviews with participants, or may rely on participants

Hospitality, Leisure & Tourism Series

CHECKLIST FOR EVENT EVALUATION

Aspect	Satisfactory	Requires attention	Comments
• Timing of the event			
• Venue			
• Ticketing and entry			
• Staging			
• Performance standard			
• Staffing levels and performance of duties			
• Crowd control			
• Security			
• Communications			
• Information and signage			
• Transport			
• Parking			
• Catering facilities			
• Toilets			
• First aid			
• Lost children			
• Sponsor's acknowledgement			
• Hosting arrangements			
• Advertising			
• Publicity			
• Media liaison			

Figure 12.2 Event evaluation checklist

filling in written forms. They may be undertaken face-to-face, by telephone or by mail. Face-to-face interviews will usually generate a higher response rate, but techniques such as incentives for participation may improve the response rate of postal surveys. To undertake effective surveys requires expertise and the commitment of considerable organizational resources. For event organizers with limited in-house experience and expertise, professional assistance can be called upon for tasks ranging from the design of survey forms to the full implementation of the survey process.

In the case of repeat events, a single well-designed survey may satisfy the basic research needs of the event. Some event organizers may wish to repeat the survey each year in order to compare successive events and to establish trends, or may want to embark on more ambitious research programmes in order to investigate other aspects of the event. Whatever the scale and approach that is decided on, experts such as Getz (1997), Veal (1997) and the publication by the UK Sport (1999c) suggest certain basic aspects that should be kept in mind:

- *Purpose*: identify clearly the purpose and objective of the survey. A clearly stated and defined purpose is most likely to lead to a well-targeted survey with effective results.
- *Survey design*: keep it simple. If too much is attempted in the survey, there is a danger that focus will be lost and effectiveness reduced. Questions should be clear and unambiguous, and should be tested by a 'trial run' before the actual survey.
- *Size of sample*: the number of participants must be large enough to provide a representative sample of the audience. The sample size will depend on the level of detail in the survey, the level of precision required and the available budget. If in doubt, seek professional advice on the size of the sample.
- *Randomness*: the methodology employed in the selection of participants must avoid bias of age, sex and ethnicity. A procedure such as selecting each tenth person to pass through a turnstile may assist in providing a random selection.
- *Support data*: the calculation of some outcomes will depend on the collection of support data. For example, the calculation of total visitor expenditure will require accurate data on the number of visitors to the event. Then the spending pattern revealed by the survey can be multiplied by the number of visitors to provide an estimate of the total visitor expenditure for the event.

What to evaluate

Events have both tangible and intangible impacts. Surveys most commonly measure tangible impacts such as economic costs and benefits, as these can most easily be measured. However, it is also important to evaluate the intangible impacts of events, even if this evaluation needs to be more narrative based or descriptive. Some of the intangibles that are hard to measure include the impacts on the social life and well-being of a community, the sense of pride engendered by events, and the long-term positioning of a tourist destination or place.

The parade and events staged for the London gay and lesbian communities as London Mardi Gras have been a focus for Gay Rights and Pride. The Bradford Mela aims to celebrate Asian cultures and educate other residents, fostering a culture of racial tolerance. The Eistedfodd Festival, alternating between north and south Wales each year, has provided a strong focus for Welsh national identity. While all of these events have undoubted social worth, it may be difficult and perhaps even counterproductive to quantify this in anything other than descriptive terms.

While the London Mardi Gras has developed out of Gay Pride marches of the 1980s, their website contains a clear statement of the social and cultural values underpinning the event:

It is an opportunity for individuals, not-for-profit organisations and commercial companies to participate in a community event.

Members of our community must be able to play a part in the organisation of the event and also planning its development, themes and content.

It must reflect the diversity and cultures of our community.

It will be free and open to anyone who wants to take part without the need for an invitation, prior arrangement or having to belong to an organised group.

It will be made as accessible as possible for all the members of our community who wish to attend.

It must be attractive to take part in and interesting to watch.

It must contain an element of campaigning for the rights of the members of our community to be accepted as equal members of society.

It should contain banners, costumes, bands and floats representing our community.

Participants will be encouraged to provide interest and activity throughout the event, not just at its head. (London Mardi Gras, 2000)

Commenting on the publication of an evaluation report on A Quality of Light (an international visual arts festival held at various locations in West Cornwall during 1997), Graham Long, South West Arts Chief Executive, noted:

A Quality of Light has defied geography. It has shown that it is possible to mount a major international arts event even in one of the most remote and rural parts of the country. It's been great for those who've seen the work – and for the economy and profile of Cornwall. A Quality of Light has generated £1.4 million for the economy of West Cornwall and people have been reading about it across the country and abroad. Most of that money came from outside Cornwall. That's an amazing return on the total investment of £300,000 in the project. The arts make economic sense.

(Chaloner, 1998)

Economic impact studies

All event managers will be familiar with constructing a simple financial balance statement of the income and expenditure of events. Until recent times, this form of reporting was considered sufficient, as most events were staged for their inherent social, cultural or sporting value to the community. However, the growing involvement of governments, tourism and arts bodies, companies and sponsors has brought with it an increasing need to consider the wider impacts of events.

Economic impact studies set out to measure the costs and benefits of an event by comparing income and visitors' expenditure with the costs of putting on the event. UK Sport (1999c, p. 12) define the economic impact as, 'the total amount of additional expenditure generated within a city, which could be directly attributable to the event'. They have published simple guidelines for measuring the economic impact of sport events, which can be applied to most other events. Their publication outlines a basic methodology (illustrated in Figure 12.3), and includes sample questions for the visitor survey (Figure 12.4). This is discussed further below.

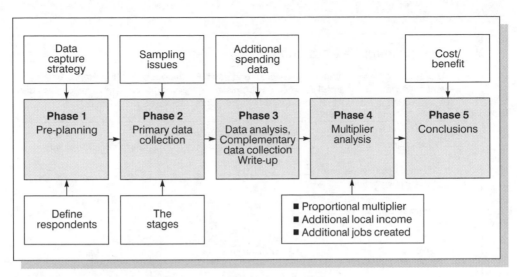

Figure 12.3 Five phase approach to economic impact evaluation
Source: adapted from UK Sport, 1999c.

Phase 1: Pre-planning

This involves planning the data collection strategy, including the likely respondents. Points to consider include:

- How many of each respondent group will attend?
- When will they be arriving?
- Where will they be staying?
- When to conduct the survey?
- Any unique circumstances, for example children involved therefore limited funds?

Phase 2: Primary data collection

This phase involves data gathering using the survey questionnaire. UK Sport highlights the fact that each event is unique, therefore the survey questionnaire will need to be adapted in order to meet the objectives of the event and to achieve meaningful data. The objectives and stages of the research method are:

- To quantify the proportions of respondents who live in the host city and those who are from outside the host city.
- To group respondent types by their role in the event, e.g. media, spectators and competitors.
- To identify basic characteristics of respondents from outside the host city by gender, composition of part by size and broad place of domicile.
- To determine the catchment area of the event by local, regional, national and international responses.

Hospitality, Leisure & Tourism Series

[*Event Name*] Visitors' Survey

We are asking for your help. We are looking to establish the economic importance of this event. We would be grateful if you could complete the following survey. Information provided will be treated in the strictest confidence. No individual responses will be identified.

1. Please state nationality

2. Where do you live? (please specify town or city)

3. Which of the following are you?

Athlete	1 ☐	Coach	2 ☐
Official	3 ☐	Journalist/media	4 ☐
Spectator	5 ☐		

If you are a resident of Cityville thank you very much for your co-operation, however your assistance is no longer required. Please return this form to a research steward

4. Are you attending the event alone?

Yes 1 ☐   No 2 ☐

If YES: please go to QUESTION 5a

If NO: How many other ADULTS (over 16) are there in your party today?

If NO: How many CHILDREN (15 and under) are there in your party today?

5a. In which TOWN/CITY are you staying tonight?

5b. Is this -

At Home?	1 ☐
With Friends/Relatives?	2 ☐
A Guest House?	3 ☐
An Hotel?	4 ☐
A Camp Site?	5 ☐
Other?	6 ☐

If Other: please specify _____

For Official Use Only

Date
- ☐ 27th June
- ☐ 28th June
- ☐ 29th June

Gender
- ☐ 1   Male
- ☐ 2   Female

1. ☐ 1   British
- ☐ 2   Other European
- ☐ 3   North American
- ☐ 4   South American
- ☐ 5   African
- ☐ 6   Asian
- ☐ 7   Other
- ☐ 99   Missing

2. ☐ 0   Sheffield
- ☐ 1   Yorkshire
- ☐ 2   North
- ☐ 3   Midlands
- ☐ 4   South
- ☐ 5   Other UK
- ☐ 6   Western European
- ☐ 7   Central European
- ☐ 8   Eastern European
- ☐ 9   North America
- ☐ 10   South America
- ☐ 11   African
- ☐ 12   Australia
- ☐ 13   Other
- ☐ 99   Missing

5a. ☐ 1   Sheffield
- ☐ 2   Yorkshire
- ☐ 3   North
- ☐ 4   Midlands
- ☐ 5   South
- ☐ 6   Other UK
- ☐ 7   Other
- ☐ 99   Missing

Figure 12.4 Visitors survey. *Source*: adapted from UK Sport, 1999c.

6. How many nights are you staying in CITYVILLE? [_____]

If you are NOT STAYING OVERNIGHT in CITYVILLE, please go to QUESTION 8.

7. If you are STAYING OVERNIGHT in CITYVILLE:
How much are you spending on ACCOMMODATION
PER NIGHT? [_____]

8. How much will you spend in CITYVILLE TODAY on the following -

Food & Drink? £ [_____]
Entertainment? £ [_____]
Travel? £ [_____]
Programmes/Merchandise? £ [_____]
Shopping/Souvenirs? £ [_____]
Other? (Parking, petrol, etc.) £ [_____]

9a. How much have you budgeted to spend in TOTAL during your stay in CITYVILLE?

Total Expenditure £ [_____]

9b. Does this include expenditure on others?

Yes 1 ☐   No 2 ☐

If YES: How many others is this expenditure for? [_____]

10. Is the EVENT the main reason for you being in CITYVILLE today?

Yes 1 ☐   No 2 ☐

11. Are you combining your visit to the EVENT with a holiday?

Yes 1 ☐   No 2 ☐

If YES: Where are you going? [_____]

For how long? [_____]

Can you provide us with a rough idea of your total budget for this part of your trip? £ [_____]

Thank you for taking the time to complete this survey.
Please return this form to a research steward.

Figure 12.4 *continued*

- To quantify the number of people from outside the host city who will be staying overnight in the host city and from this subsample to quantify how many are staying in commercially provided accommodation.
- To quantify how many nights those staying in commercial accommodation will spend in the city and how much per night such accommodation is costing.
- To quantify for both those staying overnight and day visitors, the amount spent per day on six standard categories of expenditure.
- To quantify how much in total people have budgeted to spend in a host city and on how many other people this expenditure will be made.
- To establish the proportion of people whose main reason for being in the host city is the event under investigation.
- To determine if any respondents are combining their visit to the host city with a holiday, so that the spending associated with the holiday, and the location of the spending, can be used to estimate any wider economic impact in other cities or regions due to staging of the event (UK Sport, 1999c, p. 12).

Phase 3: Data analysis, complementary methods and writing up

The data collected by the survey questionnaire should be analysed using a statistical package (e.g. SPSS), or a spreadsheet package (e.g. Microsoft Excel). The data should be analysed by using three filters. First, is the respondent a local or visitor? Second, which group do they belong to? Finally, based on their group type, are they a day visitor or staying overnight?

In addition to questionnaire analysis, it is useful to use complementary methods in order to understand the significance of the findings. This may take the form of observing the event or qualitative interviews with the event organizer and other stakeholders, including local hotels, restaurants and shops. The final area of data to collect, sometimes referred to as 'organizational spend', is additional expenditure in the host area directly attributable to the event but not collected by the questionnaire. Once the data is collected from the sources discussed above, the final writing up of the report can begin.

Phase 4: Multiplier analysis

The data collected may be analysed further, depending on the needs of the host organization or other stakeholders. Multiplier analysis involves calculating the amount of additional income retained in the city after allowing for 'leakage' from the local economy, for example, to suppliers or staff from outside the area. Using multipliers has been discussed by various authors, including Hall (1997) and Getz (1997), who warn that caution is required in calculating multipliers as it can lead to the impacts being exaggerated. UK Sport suggests that one of the most common methods used is the proportional income multiplier, illustrated in Figure 12.5.

Phase 5: Conclusions

The final phase involves an evaluation of the costs of the staging the event, compared with the benefits. However, it should be remembered that events might make a direct loss at the time of the event, with rewards achieved in the longer term. Data from studies such as this will allow stakeholders (such as local authorities) to evaluate their

(a) $$\frac{\text{Direct impact + Indirect impact + Induced impact}}{\text{Initial visitor expenditure}} = \text{Proportional income}$$

(b) Proportional income $\times$ Local multiplier (e.g. 0.20) = Additional local income

(c) $$\frac{\text{Aditional local income}}{\text{Average annual full-time wage}} = \text{Additional jobs created (full-time equivalent job years)}$$

Direct impact   – Total expenditure by visitors (hotels, food, etc.) stays in the local economy from locally produced goods and services. Additional wages, salaries and profits for local business were direct recipients of the visitor expenditure.

Indirect impact – Benefit from visitor expenditure, but not directly received (e.g. suppliers to hotels and restaurants).

Induced impact – Benefit from respending of visitor expenditure in local economy.

Figure 12.5 Economic impact equations
Source: adapted from UK Sport, 1999c.

economic development policies for growth in tourism, leisure and sports. For example, the World Student Games in 1991 left Sheffield with a political argument due to a direct loss of £10.4 million, however, in the longer term, Sheffield benefited from an investment of £147 million in new and refurbished facilities that are still providing income to the city today through major events (Bramwell, 1997).

The methodology takes into account the complexity of estimating the number of visitors from outside the region. It seeks to distinguish visitors attracted by the event or who have extended their visit because of the event, from those who would have visited the region anyway. In the case of an event that extends for more than one day or that has multiple events, it also takes into account the need to identify the number of days or events attended, and to weight this in calculating the results of the survey.

The survey form allows distinction between residents and non-local residents. This is important as it is generally accepted that local residents spending money at events does not usually lead to an increase in local income, as local residents would have spent money whether the event took place or not. This is sometimes referred to as 'deadweight expenditure' (UK Sport, 1999c).

Calculating the economic impact of events is a complex task involving many factors. However, by applying the guidelines and the survey shown in Figure 12.3, a simple and useful snapshot of the economic impact of an event can be readily obtained.

Media monitoring and evaluation

Media coverage is an important aspect of an event. This coverage can be both positive and negative, depending on the event outcomes, the impact on the community and the kind of relationship built up with the media. It is important to monitor and record this coverage as part of the documentation of the event. If the event is local, it may be possible to do this by keeping a file of newspaper articles and by listening and looking for radio and television interviews and news coverage. For larger events, a professional media-monitoring organization may need to be employed to track media coverage from a variety of sources. They will usually provide copies of print media stories and transcripts of radio interviews and news coverage. Audio and videotapes of electronic coverage can be obtained for an additional charge. This coverage provides an excellent record of the event, and can be used effectively in profiling the event to future potential sponsors and partners.

A further issue is content analysis of the media coverage as this is not always positive. Negative media coverage can impact on the reputation of the event, and by implication on stakeholders such as host organization and sponsors. Some media monitors will attempt to place a monetary value on media coverage, usually valuing it at around three times the cost of equivalent advertising space on the grounds that editorial coverage is likely to be better trusted by consumers and is therefore worth more. Such valuations should be regarded as approximate only, but may provide a useful comparative assessment of media coverage. For example, media coverage of the 2000 Love Parade in Leeds was valued by Yorkshire Tourist Board at £2.5 million. This included national radio coverage by Radio One (the organizer) and radio, television and newspaper reports covering the event.

Event evaluation reports and profiles

Once information has been collated from data collection, observation, feedback meetings and surveys, a final event evaluation report should be completed and distributed to all stakeholders. The information should give rise to a profile of the event, which can be included in the executive summary of the report. This profile can form the basis for a media release promoting the outcomes of the event, and for the start of planning for the next event and approaches to sponsors. Figure 12.6 provides an example of a media release based on the profile of the Network Q Rally.

Finalization

Once the event is over and before administration is disbanded or preparation for the next event is begun, it is important to tidy up loose ends and to bring the event management process to a satisfactory conclusion. The following is a useful checklist of tasks to be completed when finalizing the event:

- Hold a debriefing meeting and provide an opportunity for feedback by all stakeholders.
- Settle accounts and prepare an audited financial statement.
- Ensure all contractual and statutory obligations have been fulfilled.
- Prepare and distribute to all key stakeholders a full report on event outcomes.
- Make recommendations for future refinements and improvements to the event.
- Thank all staff, participants and stakeholders for their support of the event.

Press Release: 9914

MSA REPORT REVEALS ECONOMIC IMPACT
OF WORLD RALLY CHAMPIONSHIP

A report commissioned by the Motor Sports Association (MSA) reveals that competitors and spectators at the 1998 Network Q Rally of Great Britain spent 11.1 million UK pounds in the area of the event. The world-wide television coverage of the event stimulated a further 17.25 million pounds of subsequent tourist spending in Wales alone.

An independent team measured the economic impact of the four-day rally on 7,814 businesses, employing 81,271 people in 20 counties. Their report concludes that the Network Q Rally 'is one of the largest spectator sporting events in Great Britain' and that the event 'would not happen at nearly this scale unless it was part of the FIA World Rally Championship'.

The study shows that 134,921 spectators paid to watch the 1998 event; 60% of them were visitors from outside the 10,503 square miles covered by the rally. Of the £11 million spent, 6.7 million pounds represented money flowing into the economies from outside. The main benefactors were hotels, motels and campsites (2.1 million pounds), eating and drinking establishments (3.3 million), retail stores (2.6 million pounds) and local transport services (2.2 million pounds).

The average spectator spent 83 UK pounds per day on tickets, parking, lodging, food, drink, entertainment and tourist purchases. Occupancy at local hotels reached 100%, at a time of year (November) when most establishments would otherwise be quiet.

The rally created over 500 temporary jobs, notably at Rally HQ in Cheltenham and at the offices of the promoters, Silverstone Circuits.

MSA Chief Executive John Quenby commented: 'We already know from independent figures that the UK motor sports industry is a major contributor to our national economy, with at least 50,000 full-time jobs and an annual turnover of 1.3 billion pounds.

'This report is the first systematic evaluation of the economic impact of a major rally. It shows that no fewer than 69 parliamentary constituencies gained direct employment benefits from the Network Q Rally of Great Britain.

'What is particularly gratifying is that so much income flows into the area immediately surrounding the route and then remains in that area, strengthening the social fabric of the community.'

The 40-page independent report – 'The Economic Impact of the Network Q Rally of Great Britain' – was prepared for the MSA by American economic historian William Lilley III (former Staff Director of the US House of Representatives Budget Committee) and Laurence J DeFranco (an expert in geo-economics).

The complete report can be seen on the FIA website (http://www.fia.com).

Figure 12.6 Media release on economic impact of 1998 Network Q Rally
Source: Motor Sports Association, 1999.

Summary

Event evaluation is a process of measuring and assessing events throughout the event management cycle. It provides feedback that contributes to the planning and improvement of individual events and to the pool of knowledge of the events industry.

Feasibility studies identify the likely costs and benefits of an event, and help to decide whether to proceed with it. Monitoring the event establishes whether it is on track, and enables the event manager to respond to changes and adjust plans. Post-event evaluation measures the outcomes of the event in relation to its objectives. The exact nature of this evaluation will depend on the perspectives and needs of the stakeholders.

A range of techniques are used in event evaluation, including data collection, observation, feedback meetings, questionnaires and surveys. Good evaluation is planned and implemented from the outset of the event management process, with all participants made aware of its objectives and methodology. As well as tangible impacts, events have intangible benefits which cannot always be quantified, and may need to be recorded on a narrative or descriptive basis. These include social and cultural impacts on a community, and the long-term profile and positioning of a tourism destination. Calculating the economic impact of an event can be complex and expensive, but a simple methodology is available to carry out a basic study. The media coverage of an event should be monitored in house, or by using professional media monitors. Once information is gathered from all sources, an event evaluation report should be compiled and distributed to all stakeholders. This report can provide the basis for media releases to promote the outcomes of the event, and for future planning and seeking of sponsorship. In finalizing the event, it is important to tidy up loose ends and to feed lessons learnt from the event back into the event management process.

Questions

1 Identify an event that you know well, or one that you have an involvement with in some capacity. Design an evaluation plan intended to provide a profile of the event, and to provide a basis for reporting to key stakeholders.

2 Imagine that you are employing staff to work on a particular event. Design a report sheet for them to record their observations of the event. Decide what aspects you want them to observe and what benchmarks you want them to use.

3 Select an event that you are familiar with and identify the stakeholders that you would invite to a final evaluation meeting. Write an agenda for the meeting designed to encourage feedback on the event in an organized manner.

4 Imagine that you are a tourist officer for your region. Design a questionnaire for a major local event in order to evaluate the impact of the event on local tourism.

5 Obtain copies of three evaluation reports from libraries or direct from event organizations. Compare and contrast the methodology, style and format of the reports.

6 Choose an event that has considerable impacts both positive and negative, on its host community. Use a narrative approach to describe these impacts, and to evaluate the social costs and benefits to the community.

7 Using the same event as in question 6, design a brief for a professional organization to carry out an economic impact study of the event.

8 Identify a high-profile event in your region, and monitor as closely as you can the media generated by the event, including print media, radio and television coverage.

9 Choose an event that you have been associated with and assemble as much data as you can on the event. Using this data, create a written profile of the event.

10 Based on the written profile from question 9, draft a media release outlining the outcomes of the event and the benefits to the local community.

Case Study

The Notting Hill Carnival

The Notting Hill Carnival takes place annually in the streets of Notting Hill, an area in West London. The carnival began in 1964 and provided an opportunity for West Indians to celebrate and commemorate their ancestors' 'freedom from slavery' which is celebrated every year in all parts of the Caribbean.

The first carnival had not been planned as a carnival. In the early 1960s in Notting Hill, there was an event called the Notting Hill Festival, which was a low-key street celebration attended by approximately 200 people, mostly children. In 1964 a Notting Hill social worker, Rhaune Laslett, being aware of the growing number of West Indian children in the area who were not taking part in the festival, decided to add some West Indian culture to the festival as an attraction. She invited a steel band, which was normally present at the Colherne pub in Earls Court, to play at the festival. When the steel band came onto the streets of Notting Hill, nearly every West Indian in the area, adults as well as children, came onto the streets and began to follow the steel band in a processional manner as they did back home, particularly in Trinidad the birthplace of steelpan, playing whatever makeshift instruments (dustbin lids, bottle and spoon, comb and paper) they could lay their hands on.

After that first event, the steel band became a feature of the Notting Hill Festival and the reputation of the festival grew as the only event at which West Indian culture was celebrated. Between 1964 and 1974, no more than 3000 people attended the festival which by then had a change in leadership and became exclusively a forum for West Indian culture, led by West Indians. However, the event was not widely known amongst West Indians from the different communities in London. The revellers tended to be exclusively Trinidadian because of the dominance of the steelpan music and its size was due to word-of-mouth transference of information within that community.

The first attempt to market the carnival on a London-wide scale came in 1975 with the advent of a new radio station in London, Capital Radio. That station had a community slot as part of its programming and announced the fact that there was a West Indian carnival being held in Notting Hill. One hundred and fifty thousand West Indians turned up from many different islands in the West Indies and not just Trinidad. A wider range of West Indian culture was present, most notably the influence of the Jamaican Sound System which brought a more contemporary edge to the carnival as black music was about to invade the English pop charts with Roots, Reggae and the Tamla Motown hits. The Sound Systems played that type of black music and so attracted younger black people to the carnival and they immediately identified with the ethos of the celebration.

In 1976, 250 000 young black people attended the carnival and the authorities, without warning, decided to stop the event and so sent in several thousand police officers. A riot ensued as the young people protested against the suppression of the event, with numerous casualties on both sides. This riot was the first public acknowledgement of ownership of the event by the West Indian community – the riot united the West Indian community in appreciation of their history and in celebration of their ancestors' 'freedom from slavery'. The riot characterized the event in the eyes of the press and British public as a violent affair and brought the Notting Hill Carnival to the attention of the press and, so, the world.

The Notting Hill Carnival is organized by the Notting Hill Carnival Trust, a registered charity that was established some ten years ago to pursue the development of the carnival and the safety of the 2.5 million people that are in attendance. The trust is assisted by the Metropolitan Police Service, the Royal Borough of Kensington and Chelsea, the City of Westminster, London Underground Limited, St John Ambulance Service, London Fire and Civil Defence Authority and London Ambulance Service.

Today, the Notting Hill Carnival boasts an audience of 2.5 million people over August Bank Holiday Sunday and Monday. It is probably the best known carnival in the world with numerous applications from other carnivals to participate in the event. The carnival has a strong multicultural character and is known for its capacity to cater for all age groups, the creativity of the designers, artists and communities that create the hugely attractive costumes, and the range of music available from top DJs and groups free of charge, hence its attractiveness to young people. Each year, audience attendance at the carnival grows by approximately 5 per cent. Each year an increasing number of visitors and participants from Europe are attracted to the carnival.

The Notting Hill Carnival comprises a range of events that take place over a two-week carnival season.

- *Carnival Press Launch*: two hundred members of the press are invited to the Carnival Press Launch to get a taste of carnival culture and be positively cultivated by the carnival community.
- *Carnival Costume Gala*: this takes place the weekend before the carnival and is the event where the artistry of the Kings, Queens, Male Individuals and Females Individuals are judged. Two hundred costumes perform individually, portraying their themes through costume design and performance. The event is usually held at the Olympia Exhibition Centre and boasts an audience of 500 people.
- *The Calypso Monarch Competition*: this takes place on the Friday of the carnival weekend where ten Calypsonians compete for the title of Calypso Monarch. They compose and sing their own calypsos, which must be based on contemporary issues of politics and life generally.
- *The Steelbands Panorama*: this takes place the evening before the carnival procession where ten steel bands compete for the title of Champions of Steel. Each steel band has up to 100 players who perform innovative musical arrangements of calypsos of the season. It boasts an audience of 7000 people.
- *The Two Days of the Carnival*: this comprises a street procession on both days. At which costumes, steel bands, mobile and static sound systems perform in the streets to commemorate the 'freedom to walk the streets' which their ancestors had been denied during the period of slavery. The audience, 'Carnival revellers', are encouraged to join the procession. The emphasis is on the right of each individual to be part of the celebrations, '*Every spectator is a participant*'.

In spite of its phenomenal success and its benefit to the community, the Notting Hill Carnival is not wholly funded from the public purse. The trust operates on an expenditure budget of £600 000, 28 per cent of which comes from three publicly funded sources (London Arts, London Boroughs Grants, Kensington and Chelsea) and the remaining 72 per cent of funds comes from private sponsors. The majority of that money is spent on developing the arts of carnival and ensuring the safety of the public through the provision of stewards and route marshals. The high reliance on sponsorship and the discretionary nature of sponsorship detract from the stability and predictability of the event and make planning extremely difficult.

As a result of funding, the marketing of the event is not based on using wholly traditional methods. The tenor of the marketing drive is to capitalize on as many free opportunities as possible through the press and any high-profile sponsors. The Notting Hill Carnival does not advertise nor does it produce posters, tickets or any other tools of promotion. The carnival is promulgated by word of mouth from a public that has a good time from year to year. High-profile sponsors approach the carnival and are attracted by its high public profile, its multicultural character and its 2.5 million revellers – 65 per cent of whom are between the ages of 16 and 25 years.

It is to be noted that the carnival is very much a public event that happens by custom and not by licence. Its legal status has not yet been adequately defined and so the event is anomalous in every sense of the word – it cannot be defined as a public event because of the high reliance on private/sponsorship funds, nor can it be defined as a private event because of its free nature and openness to the public.

From the organization's point of view, any marketing thrust, whether it be conventional or unorthodox, should lead to an enhancement of the carnival's image, its stability, its credibility, its financial viability, its creativity and its commemoration for posterity of the black community's freedom from slavery. The practical ways employing a number of marketing strategies in which these are achieved and developed on from year to year include:

- Forming strategic alliances with key sections of the media. Thus each year, the 'official Notting Hill Carnival Magazine' is published and distributed by the *Evening Standard*, London's only evening paper, with a circulation of 1 million copies. The magazine thereby reaches people from all walks of life who receive a free copy with their evening paper and get a positive image of carnival culture.
- The BBC are encouraged to make an annual television documentary on the carnival, filming and broadcasting live.
- The BBC are encouraged to host a live radio stage event in the carnival area during the carnival; the Notting Hill Carnival is then able to capitalize on the promotion of their event at the carnival.
- A press office of the Notting Hill Carnival is established two months before the carnival each year to co-ordinate and capitalize on any press enquiries. Press enquiries are international and news of the carnival is broadcast through many different media and languages. The press are fed with up-to-date information.
- The Notting Hill Carnival hosts a roadshow throughout the year, going from town to town in England and abroad, taking the carnival message and encouraging others to develop carnivals along similar lines of freedom of expression.
- The creation and development of a good Internet site where all aspects of the carnival, the planning, the culture and the gloss can be profiled.
- The pre-carnival events are used to promote a more positive profile of the carnival to people who cannot cope with the crowds on the two days, but love the arts of the carnival. They are held in a comfortable environment and afford the individual the opportunity to get close to the arts of the carnival.

Given all this potential for exposure in the press and media generally, sponsors are keen to capitalize on the carnival's high profile and to pursue brand association. The concept of the 'title sponsor' has been an effective marketing tool as the credibility and image of the title sponsor can enhance the credibility of the event. Thus in 1995, the Notting Hill Carnival acquired its first title sponsor from the soft drinks brand 'Lilt' (a product of Coca-Cola). No sooner had Coca-Cola announced its intention to be the title sponsor than other big name competitors wanted to be associated with the event. The Notting Hill Carnival was subsequently sponsored by Virgin Atlantic Airways Limited and is currently sponsored by Western Union (the money transfer company).

The Notting Hill Carnival is now a major well-publicized event that is important to society on many different levels. While its economic impact is not quantifiable – but is estimated to be in the region of £250 million – its societal impact through education and the facilitation of better racial harmony is probably the most valuable outcome of its marketing strategies. It would appear that the public has more than just an understanding of the event and identifies with its ethos, ensuring its assimilation into mainstream culture. The carnival has become more than just an event – it has become a way of life.

For further details about Notting Hill Carnival, please visit www.nottinghillcarnival.org.uk

By Claire Holder, Chief Executive, Notting Hill Carnival Trust, 332 Ladbroke Grove, London, W10 5AH.

Questions

1 The above provides an extensive insight into the development of the Notting Hill Carnival, which has led to the culture, and ethos, of the event as it appears today. What are the main features of the Notting Hill Carnival? How has history influenced these?

2 Who are the stakeholders in the Notting Hill Carnival?

3 In evaluating the carnival, what are the long-term benefits for London and the host community?

4 How has London used the Notting Hill Carnival to create an identity for the area?

5 The current marketing strategy focuses on developing the image of the event and maximizing opportunities raised by sponsors.

   (a) In evaluating the strategy, what other methods are available to the organizers to further develop the image of the carnival?
   (b) Suggest alternative sponsors for the carnival. Identify what benefits the proposed sponsors will gain, and what these sponsors will bring to the carnival.

7 Write a brief requiring a consultant to prepare an economic impact study of the Notting Hill Carnival.

8 At the time of going to press, the Greater London Authority are conducting a major review of Notting Hill Carnival, following concerns over its growth in size and the implication of this on public safety. What are the outcomes of this review? What implications do these have on the future of the carnival?

Edinburgh International Festival

The Edinburgh International Festival was founded in 1947 in the aftermath of a devastating world war. The founders believed that the Festival should enliven and enrich the cultural life of Europe, Britain and Scotland and provide a platform for the flowering of the human spirit. The programmes were intended to be of the highest possible standard, presented by the best artists in the world. The achievement of many of those aims over the years has ensured the Edinburgh International Festival is now one of the most important cultural celebrations in the world.

Both the political world and the world of the arts are now very different from the immediate post-war years and the Festival has developed significantly in the interim. However, the founders' original intentions are closely reflected in the current aims and objectives of the Festival:

- To promote and encourage arts of the highest possible standard.
- To reflect international culture in presentation to Scottish audiences and to reflect Scottish culture in presentation to international audiences.
- To bring together a programme of events in an innovative way that cannot easily be achieved by other organizations.
- To offer equal opportunity for the general public to experience and enjoy the arts, and encourage participation through other organizations throughout the year.
- To maintain the educational, cultural and economic well-being of the city and people of Edinburgh and Scotland.

The Festival brings to Edinburgh some of the best in international theatre, music, dance and opera and presents the arts in Scotland to the world. Around the International Festival, a number of other festivals have grown, the largest of which is the Fringe. There is also the Military Tattoo, a Jazz Festival, Film Festival and Book Festival. All of these are administered separately from the International Festival. A recent survey showed that the festivals generate £125 million for the economy of Edinburgh and sustain nearly 4,000 jobs across Scotland.

Festival finances

All artists and companies in the annual three-week event appear at the invitation of the Festival Director. The Festival's budget covers all of the costs associated with delivering the programme including artists' fees, travel, venue hire and promotion of the event. The Festival has four main revenue sources: public sector grants, ticket sales, sponsorship and donations, and other commercial income.

- **Public sector grants:** In 2000 grants from the City of Edinburgh Council and the Scottish Arts Council totalled £1 975 000 – 34% of total income.
- **Ticket sales:** The Festival sold an average of 75% of its available seats in 2000 (£2.4 million of income, including VAT, representing 34% of total income). The average ticket price was £16 in a range between £5 and £50. Ticket yield has been substantially increased in recent years, by extending the price range at the top end whilst pegging the lower prices. It is not possible to generate significant additional ticket sales revenue without abandoning the current accessible pricing policy.
- **Sponsorship and donations:** The Festival is Scotland's most successful arts organization at generating income from this area. The total of £1 702 980 raised in 2000 represents 28% of the Festival's total income and a 10% increase on 1999 at a time when many organizations are reporting a fall in income from the corporate sector.
- **Commercial income:** In 2000, £179 548 (4% of total income) was raised from this source, which includes broadcasting fees, merchandising and programme sales. The development of The Hub, the new home for the Edinburgh International Festival, means that there is potential for growth in income from this source. However, given that The Hub is not a purely commercial resource, but has an educational and artistic remit, it is not expected to contribute more than £200 000 per annum profit to the Society, and not until 2002.

The total income and expenditure are summarized in Figure A1.1.

Revenue grants from the local authority and from central government have been at the core of the Festival's finances since 1947. This public subsidy helps define the style and tone of the Festival presented, enabling a subsidized ticket pricing policy that ensures access to the widest possible audience.

Public sector support for the Festival has declined in cash terms since 1994, from £2.035 million in 1994 to £1.975 million in 2000. After taking inflation into account, this represents a reduction of 21%, or £436,000. Over the same period, the Festival's earned income has steadily increased. Whilst costs have been kept rigorously under control, it has been necessary to invest in infrastructure to achieve these substantial earnings.

Any further erosion in public sector support will inevitably lead to fundamental changes in the nature of the event itself. Current income sources, detailed earlier, illustrate that the Festival is already heavily reliant on earned income (66%). Even if it were possible to increase these income streams (which is highly debatable, at least in the short-term), it would result in a different style of Festival – one reliant on private donors, corporate money and high priced tickets – and requiring a different style of programming. This would lead to a smaller audience and to the exclusion of a large section of its current audience base. The alternative is to cut back the scope

Income and expenditure account for the 2000 Edinburgh International Festival (all figures net of VAT)

	2000	1999		2000	1999
	£	£		£	£
Earned income					
Ticket sales	2 046 226	1 770 816	Cost of presentations	4 747 898	3 947 766
Sponsorship and donations	1 702 980 528	1 548	Marketing, public affairs & box office	759 369	759 282
Advertising and other	179 548	191 662	Fundraising and sponsorship	246 665	229 227
Interest receivable	50 669	37 638	Administration	695 303	682 281
	3 979 423	3 548 644			
Grant income					
City of Edinburgh Council	1 200 995	1 174 405			
Scottish Arts Council	775 000	775 000			
SAC Lottery Millennium Award	94 779				
	2 070 774	1 949 405			
Total income of the festival	6 050 197	5 498 049	Total cost of the festival	6 449 235	5 618 556
(Deficit)/Surplus for the Festival before the supplementary grant				(399 038)	(120 507)
Supplementary grant from City of Edinburgh Council to finance deficits from previous years				218 995	
(Deficit)/Surplus for the year				(180 043)	(120 507)
(Deficit)/Surplus on General Fund				(398 900)	(218 857)

Figure A1.1 Edinburgh International Festival Income and Expenditure Account

Source: Edinburgh International Festival, 2001

of the Festival with resultant effect on the economic impact, worldwide promotion of the City and amenity for the audience.

In summary, it is no longer possible to undertake the Festival without a major increase in resources. The Council of the Festival Society adopted a four-year business plan in February 2000. A cornerstone of the plan is to re-instate the 1994 funding levels of support from public bodies in 2001. The Society is working with a range of stakeholders, including the City Council and the Scottish Arts Council, to assist these bodies and the Scottish Executive to come to a satisfactory decision about future levels of support. All of the various stakeholders in the Festival now face hard choices about how much money they are prepared to invest in its future, and what kind of Festival they want. It is only through re-instating funding that the Edinburgh International Festival will continue to maintain and develop its role in Scotland's cultural future.

For further information about Edinburgh International Festival, please visit www.eif.co.uk

By Edinburgh International Festival
The Hub, Castlehill, Royal Mile, Edinburgh, EH1 2NE
Tel: 0131 473 2001

Questions

1 Edinburgh International Festival is one of the largest internationally known festivals in Britain. What factors do you think have led to its growth and success?
2 Edinburgh International Festival is reliant on public funding for 34% of its funds, yet this area has been in decline. From what you have been told in the case study, what affect will this reduction in funding have on the event?
3 In the long-term, various options exist for the organizers, including a shift in income streams to other areas, such as corporate sponsorship, or reducing the size of the event.
    (a) Evaluate the stated alternatives in the light of what is known from the case study.
    (b) How would a shift in income stream change the style of the festival and programming?
    (c) What effect would this change have on the image portrayed by the festival?

References

Adams, J. S. (1965). Inequity in social exchange. In *Advances in Experimental Social Psychology* (L. Berkowitz, ed.), New York, Academic Press.

Allen, K. and Shaw, P. (2001). *Festivals Mean Business: The Shape of Arts Festivals in the UK*. London, British Arts Festival Association.

Anderson, S. (2000). Agenda item: Glastonbury Festival 2000, 12 October (Internet) Mendip, Mendip District Council. Available from <http://www.glastonbury-festivals.co.uk/MENDIP DC 2000 REPORT.PDF> (accessed 16 January 2001).

Anon. (1998). Live players go to centre stage. *AV Magazine*, February, 15–16.

Anon. (2000). *Rugby World Cup 1999 Economic Impact Evaluation: Summary Report*. Edinburgh, Segal Quince Wicksteed Limited and System Three.

Ansoff, I. (1957). Strategies for diversification. *Harvard Business Review*, September–October, 113–124.

Armstrong, M. (1999). *A Handbook of Human Resource Management Practice*. 7th edn. London, Kogan Page.

Arnold, A., Fisher, A., Hatch, J. and Paix, B. (1989) The Grand Prix, road accidents and the philosophy of hallmark events. In *The Planning and Evaluation of Hallmark Events* (G. J. Syme, B. J. Shaw, D. M. Fenton and W. S. Mueller, eds) Aldershot, Avebury.

Arts Council of England (1999). *Guidance Notes on Carrying out Audience/Visitor Surveys*. London, Arts Council of England.

Association of Exhibition Organizers, British Exhibition Contractors Association and Exhibition Venues Association (AEO, BECA and EVA) (2000). *The Guide to Managing Health and Safety at Exhibitions and Events*, Berkhamstead. AEO, BECA and EVA.

Bath and North East Somerset District Council (B&NES) (1999). *Bath Festivals Trust: Annual Report and Service Specification 1999–2000* (Internet) Bristol, Bath and North East Somerset District Council. Available from <http://www.bathnes.gov.uk/Committee_Papers/CCL/cl990322/14bathre.htm> (accessed 4 February 2001).

Bath and North East Somerset District Council (B&NES) (2000). *Bath and North East Somerset Arts Impact Assessment.* (Internet) Bristol, Bath and North East Somerset District Council. Available from <http://www.bathnes.gov.uk/copy-ofintranet/Committee_Papers/CCL/cl000124/14app.htm> (accessed 5 December 2000).

Bath and North East Somerset District Council (B&NES) (2001). *Bath and North East Somerset Council's Draft Arts Strategy for 2001–2004*, 29 January (Internet) Bristol, Bath and North East Somerset District Council. Available from <http://www.bathnes.gov.uk/Committee_Papers/CCL/CCL010122/18app1.htm> (accessed 4 February 2001).

British Arts Festivals Association (BAFA) (2001). *New Research Shows that Festivals Mean Business* (Internet) London, British Arts Festivals Association press release, March. Available from <http://www.artsfestivals.co.uk/press.html> (accessed 26 April 2001).

Ball, S. (2000). Thank you for the music. *Access All Areas*, May, 15, 32.

Barnes, P. (1999). Bournemouth makes Labour's part swing. *Access All Areas*, October, 44, 3.

Barrett, J. (2000). About (Internet) London, The Championships. Available from <http://championships.wimbledon.org/about/index.html> (accessed 3 February 2001).

Battle, R. (1988). *The Volunteer Handbook*. Austin, Texas, Volunteer Concepts.

BDS Sponsorship Ltd (2001). *Sponsorship – What is it?* (Internet). Available from: <http://www.sponsorship.co.uk/sponsorship/main.htm> (accessed on 8 February 2001).

Beardwell, I. and Holden, L. (2001) *Human Resource Management: A Contemporary Perspective.* 3rd edn. London, Pearson Education.

Bear Necessities of Golf (1998). (Internet) Electronic Telegraph, Issue 1310, 26 December. Available from: <http://portal.telegraph.co.uk/html Content.jhtml?html=%2Farchive%2F1998%2F12%2F26%2Fsogile26.html> (accessed 8 February 2001).

Belfast City Council (2000a) *Events Unit Performance Improvement Business Plan*, 10 April (Internet) Belfast, Belfast City Council. Available from <http://www.development.belfastcity.gov.uk/events/pdf/perform.pdf> (accessed 7 February 2001).

Belfast City Council (2000b). *Events Unit Strategy*, 2 February (Internet) Belfast, Belfast City Council Development Department. Available from <http://www.-development.belfastcity.gov.uk/events/pdf/finaldraft.pdf> (accessed 7 February 2001).

Bradford Festival (2000). *Bradford Festival 2000 Review.* Bradford, Bradford Festival.

British Federation of Festivals for Music, Dance and Speech (BFF) (2001). *General Information* (Internet) Macclesfield, British Federation of Festivals for Music, Dance and Speech. Available from <http://www.festivals.demon.co.uk> (accessed 21 January 2001).

Blakey, P., Metcalfe, M., Mitchell, J. and Weatherhead, P. (2000). Sports events and tourism: effects of motor car rallying on rural communities in mid Wales. In *Reflections on International Tourism: Developments in Urban and Rural Tourism* (M. Robinson, N. Evans, P. Long, R. Sharpley and J. Swarbrooke, eds) Sunderland, Centre for Travel and Tourism with Business Education Publishers.

Bowdin, G. A. J. and Church, I. J. (2000). Customer satisfaction and quality costs: towards a pragmatic approach for event management. In *Events beyond 2000 – Setting the Agenda. Proceedings of the Conference on Evaluation, Research and Education, 13–14 July* (J. Allen, R. Harris, L. K. Jago and A. J. Veal, eds) Australian Centre for Event Management, University of Technology.

Bradner, J. (1995). Recruitment, orientation, retention. In *The Volunteer Management Handbook* (T. Connors, ed.) New York, John Wiley & Sons.

Bramwell, B. (1997). Strategic planning before and after a mega-event. *Tourism Management*, **18**(3), 167–176.

Brassington, F. and Pettitt, S. (2000). *Principles of Marketing*. 2nd edn. Harlow, *Financial Times*, Prentice-Hall.

Britannica.com (2001) (Internet) *Encyclopedia Britannica*. Available from <http://www.britannica.com> (accessed 10 April 2001).

Brody, R. and Goodman, M. (1988). *Fund-raising Events: Strategies and Programs for Success*. New York, Human Sciences Press.

Brooks, I. and Weatherston, J. (2000). *The Business Environment: Challenges and Changes*. 2nd edn. Harlow, *Financial Times*, Prentice-Hall.

Buckler, B. (1998). Practical steps towards a learning organisation: applying academic knowledge to improvement and innovation in business performance. *The Learning Organisation*, **5**(1), 15–23.

Burke, R. (1999). *Project Management: Planning and Control Techniques*. Chichester, 3rd edn. Chichester, John Wiley & Sons.

Business Tourism Forum and the Business Tourism Advisory Committee (1999). *Business Tourism Leads the Way*. London, British Tourism Authority.

Canadine, I. C. (2001). *Transport, Logistics and All That!* Corby, Institute of Logistics and Transport (Internet). Available from <http://www.iolt.org.uk/whoweare/allthat.htm> (accessed 6 February 2001).

Carling, P. and Seeley, A. (1998). *The Millennium Dome*. House of Commons Library Research Paper 98/32, 12 March. London, House of Commons Library Business & Transport Section.

Cartwright, G. (1995). *Making the Most of Trade Exhibitions*. Oxford, Butterworth-Heinemann.

Catherwood, D. W. and Van Kirk, R. L. (1992) *The Complete Guide to Special Event Management: Business Insights, Financial Advice, and Successful Strategies from Ernst & Young, Advisors to the Olympics, the Emmy Awards and the PGA Tour*. New York, John Wiley & Sons.

Chaloner, H. (1998). *A Quality of Light Boosts Cornwall's Economy* (Internet). Available from <http://www.southwesttourism.co.uk/prodev/light.htm> (accessed 8 January 2001).

Chartered Institute of Marketing (CIM) (2001). *Information and Library Services*. Maidenhead, Chartered Institute of Marketing (Internet). Available from <http://www.cim.co.uk/libinfo/index.htm> (accessed 4 January 2001).

City of Edinburgh Council (2000a). *Minutes: The City of Edinburgh Council: Appendix 1*, 24 August.

Chisnall, M. (1995). *Consumer Behaviour*. 3rd edn. London, McGraw-Hill.

City of Edinburgh Council (2000b). *Edinburgh Launches Hogmanay Programme for 2000/2001*. City of Edinburgh District Council press release, 23 November.

City of Edinburgh Council (2000c). *Edinburgh's Hogmanay Traffic and Safety Arrangements Announced*. City of Edinburgh District Council press release, 15 November.

Cole, G. A. (1996). *Management: Theory and Practice*. 5th edn. London, Letts.

Cole, G. A. (1997). *Strategic Management*. London, Letts.

Comfort, J. (1996). *Effective Meetings*. Oxford, Oxford Business English Skills.

Conway, L. (2000). *The Tobacco Advertising and Promotion Bill*. House of Commons Research Paper 00/97, 20 December. London, House of Commons Library (Internet). Available from <http://www.parliament.uk> (accessed 31 January 2001).

Cook, A. (2000). Survey shows wasted spend. *Marketing Event*, March, 11.

Couchman, N. and Harrington, D. (2000). Preventing ambush/parasitic marketing in sport. *Sports and Character Licensing*, (4), March 2000 (Internet). Available from <http://www.townleys.co.uk/ambush%20marketing.htm> (accessed 31 January 2001).

Coulson, C. and Coe, T. (1991). *The Flatter Organisation: Philosophy and Practice*. Corby, Institute of Management.

Cowell, D. (1984). *The Marketing of Services*. London, Heinemann.

Crofts, A. (1992). *Corporate Entertaining as a Marketing Tool*. London, Mercury Books.

Crompton, J. (1993). Understanding a business organisation's approach to entering a sponsorship partnership. *Festival Management and Event Tourism*, **1**(3), 98–109

Crompton, J. (1994). Benefits and risks associated with sponsorship of major events. *Festival Management and Event Tourism*, **2**(2), 65–74.

Crompton, J. (1995). Factors that have stimulated the growth of sponsorship of major events. *Festival Management and Event Tourism*, **3**(2), 97–101.

Dale, M. (1995). Events as image. In *Tourism and Leisure – Perspectives on Provision* (D. Leslie, ed.), vol. 2. Brighton, LSA.

Smet, L. de (1999). Enter the dragon. *Access All Areas*, September, 20–21.

Deeley, P. (1998). Old Trafford in crackdown on rowdy element (Internet) *Daily Telegraph*, 1 July. Available from <http://www.telegraph.co.uk:80/et?ac=004296952912049&rtmo=VkZP5Vkx&atmo=rrrrrrrq&pg=/et/98/7/1/scdeel01.html> (accessed 5 February 5 2001).

Department for Culture, Media and Sport (DCMS) (1999). *Tomorrow's Tourism: A Growth Industry for the New Millennium*. London, Department for Culture, Media and Sport.

Department of National Heritage and the Scottish Office (1997). *Guide to Safety at Sports Grounds*. 4th edn. London, HMSO.

Destination Sheffield (1995) *An Event-led City and Tourism Marketing Strategy for Sheffield*. Sheffield, Destination Sheffield.

Dickman, S. (1997). Issues in arts marketing. In *Making It Happen: The Cultural and Entertainment Industries Handbook* (R. Rentschler, ed.) Kew, Victoria, Centre for Professional Development.

Dyson, J .R. (2001). *Accounting for Non-accounting Students*. 5th edn. Harlow, *Financial Times*, Prentice-Hall.

Edinburgh International Festival (EIF) (2000). *Edinburgh International Festival Annual Review 1999*. Edinburgh, EIF.

Edinburgh International Festival (EIF) (2001) *Edinburgh International Festival Annual Review 2000*. Edinburgh, EIF.

English Sports Council (1999). Memorandum submitted by the English Sports Council. In *Fourth Report: Staging International Sporting Events. Volume II Minutes of Evidence* (Select Committee on Culture, Media and Sport). London, The Stationery Office.

English Tourism (1999). Tourism and sport in England (Internet) London, English Tourism. Media brief, July 1999. Available from <http://www.englishtourism.org.uk> (accessed 19 January 2001).

Evans, G. (1996). Planning for the British Millennium Festival: establishing the visitor baseline and a framework for forecasting. *Festival Management and Event Tourism*, **3**(3), 183–196.

Event Assured (2000). *Risk Check List for Event Organisers – Risk and your Event* (Internet) Event Assured Advice Centre, 28 April. Available from <http://www.event-assured.com/advice.htm> (accessed 28 December 2001).

Exhibition Liaison Committee (1995). *The Exhibition Industry Explained*. Exhibition Liaison Committee.

Firstcalltickets.com (2000). *Ticket Sales Book Net Success* (Internet) Firstcalltickets.com press release, 9 May. Available from <http://www.firstcalltickets.com/aboutus/pressreleases/pr0425.html> (accessed 20 April 2001).

Flashman R. and Quick, S. (1985). Altruism is not dead: a specific analysis of volunteer motivation. In *Motivating Volunteers* (L. Moore, ed.) Vancouver, Vancouver Volunteer Centre.

Fletcher, M. (2000). Calling time on the gender gap. *Marketing Event*, October, 23–24.

Fuller, M. (1998). *Basingstoke Arts Festival Feasibility Study: Report of the Director of Arts, Countryside and Community*, 15 January (Internet) Hampshire, Hampshire County Council Recreation and Heritage Committee. Available from <http://www.hants.gov.uk/> (accessed 15 November 2000).

Gartside, M. (1999). Cornwall 'bungles' total eclipse. *Access All Areas*, September, 1–2.

Geldard, E. and Sinclair, L. (1996). *The Sponsorship Manual*. Victoria, Australia, Sponsorship Unit.

George, W. and Berry, L. (1981). Guidelines for the advertising of services. *Business Horizons*, July–August, 52–6.

Getz, D. (1991). *Festivals, Special Events and Tourism*. New York, Van Nostrand Reinhold.

Getz, D. (1997). *Event Management and Event Tourism*. New York, Cognizant Communications Corporation.

Giddens, A. (1990). *The Consequences of Modernity*. Cambridge, Polity Press.

Glastonbury Festivals Ltd (2000) *Recycling Crew: Information, Terms and Conditions*. Pilton, Glastonbury Festivals Ltd.

Goldblatt, J. (1997). *Special Events: Best Practices in Modern Event Management*. 2nd edn. New York, John Wiley & Sons.

Goldblatt, J. J. (2000). A future for event management: the analysis of major trends impacting the emerging profession. In *Events beyond 2000 – Setting the Agenda. Proceedings of the Conference on Evaluation, Research and Education, 13–14 July* (J. Allen, R. Harris and L. Jago, eds) Sydney, Australian Centre for Event Management, University of Technology.

Graham, S., Neirotti, L. D. and Goldblatt, J. J. (2001). *The Ultimate Guide to Sports Event Management and Marketing*. 2nd edn. New York, McGraw-Hill.

Greater London Authority (GLA) (2000) *Mayor's Carnival Review Group: Terms of Reference*. London, GLA.

Greater London Authority Carnival Review Group (GLACRE) (2001). *Notting Hill Carnival Review: Interim Report and Public Safety Profile Recommendations for 2001*. London, Greater London Authority.

Greaves, K. (1999). Tailor-made for business. *Marketing Event*, October, 45–50.

Greaves, S. (1996) Post millennium motivation. *Conference and Incentive Travel*, July–August, 46–48.

Guinness World Records (2000). *Most Cash Raised for Charity in a Sporting Event* (Internet). Available from <http://www.guinnessworldrecords.com/record_catagories/recordhome.asp?RecordID=52445> (accessed 12 November 2000).

Hall, C. M. (1989). Hallmark events and the planning process. In *The Planning and Evaluation of Hallmark Events* (G. J. Syme, B. J. Shaw, D. M. Fenton and W. S. Mueller, eds) Aldershot, Avebury.

Hall, C. M. (1997). *Hallmark Tourist Events: Impacts, Management and Planning*. Chichester, John Wiley & Sons.

Hannagan, T. (1998). *Management Concepts and Practices*. 2nd edn. London, *Financial Times*, Pitman Publishing.

Hannam (2000). Sample contract terms and conditions. Kingston upon Thames, Production Services Association.

Hardman, R. (1995). Youth sets the tone for peace in Hyde Park (Internet) *Electronic Telegraph*, 8 May. Available from <http://www.telegraph.co.uk:80/et?ac=004134791906929&rtmo=aspeNpJL&atmo=rrrrrrrq&pg=/et/9/5/5/8/ hyde 0805.html> (accessed 8 April 2001).

Harrison, D. and Hastings, C. (2000). High spirits and bright lights till dawn (Internet) *Electronic Telegraph*, 2 January, issue 1682. Available from <http://www.telegraph.co.uk:80/et?ac=004296952912049&rtmo=kCJ1bACp&atmo= rrrrrrrq&pg=/et/00/1/2/nbri02.html> (accessed 5 February 2001).

Harrowven, J. (1980) *Origins of Festivals and Feasts*. London, Kaye & Ward.

Hemmerling, M. (1997) What makes an event a success for a host city, sponsors and others? Paper delivered to The Big Event New South Wales Tourism Conference, 5–7 November, Wollongong, Australia.

Henderson, P. and Chapman, A. (1997). Thousands are left stranded. *Mail on Sunday*, 6 April, pp. 2–3.

Herzberg, F. (1987). One more time: how do you motivate employees? *Harvard Business Review*, **65**, September–October, 109–120.

Heskett, J., Sasser, W. and Schelesinger, L. (1997). *The Service Profit Chain*. New York, Free Press.

Hicks, H. and Gullet, C. (1976). *The Management of Organisations*. Tokyo, McGraw-Hill Kogakusha Ltd.

Howey, J. (2000). *Outdoor Events Policy – Royal Victoria Park* (Internet) Bath and North East Somerset Council Community, Culture and Leisure Committee, 13 July. Available from <http://www.bathnes.gov.uk/Committee_Papers/CCL/cl000710/13events.htm> (accessed 4 February 2001).

Health and Safety Executive (HSE) (1998). *Five Steps to Risk Management*. London, HSE.

Health and Safety Executive (HSE) (1999). *The Event Safety Guide*. Norwich, HSE Books.

Health and Safety Executive (HSE) (2000). *Managing Crowds Safely*. Norwich, HSE Books.

Home Office (2000). Full reference Home Office (2000). *Dealing with Disaster*. 3rd edn. London, Home Office Communication Directorate. (Internet). Available from: <http://www.homeoffice.gov.uk/epd/publications/dwd.htm> (accessed 8 February 2001).

International Olympic Committee (IOC) (2000). *100 years of Olympic Marketing.* (Internet) Lausanne, International Olympic Committee. Available from <http://www.olympic.org/ioc/e/facts/marketing/> (accessed 10 February 10 2001).

IPSOS RSL (2000). *UK sponsorship statistics* (Internet). Available from <http://www.sponsorshiponline.co.uk> (accessed 31 January 2001).

ITMA (1999). *ITMA2003: here for the first time* (Internet). Available from <http://www.itma2003.com/press/item2.htm > (accessed 4 February 2001).

ITMA (2000). *ITMA2003: people doing business* (Internet). Available from <http://www.itma2003.com/info/index.htm> (accessed 4 February 2001).

Johnson, G. and Scholes, K. (1999). *Exploring Corporate Strategy.* 5th edn. Hemel Hempstead, Prentice-Hall Europe.

Judd, D. (1997). Diamonds are forever? Kipling's Imperialism. *History Today,* January. <http://www.britannica.com/magazine/article?content.id=17875> (accessed 2 January 2001).

Kemp, C. (1995). *Music Industry Management and Promotion.* Kings Ripton, ELM Publications.

Keung, D. (1998). *Management: a Contemporary Approach.* London, Pitman Publishing.

Korman, A. (2000). *Basic Guide to Sponsorship Contracts* (Internet) London, Townleys Solicitors. Available from <http://www.sponsorshiponline.com> (accessed 6 January 2001).

Kotler, P., Armstrong, G., Saunders, J. and Wong, V. (1999). *Principles of Marketing.* 2nd Euro. edn. London, Prentice-Hall Europe.

KRONOS (1997). *The Economic Impact of Sports Events Staged in Sheffield 1990–1997.* Destination Sheffield, Sheffield City Council and Sheffield International Venues Ltd.

Lake District National Park Authority (1999). *Lake District National Park Management Plan.* Cumbria, Lake District National Park Authority.

Levitt, T. (1980). Marketing myopia. In *Marketing Management and Strategy* (K. Kotler and C. Cox, eds) Englewood Cliffs, New Jersey, Prentice-Hall.

Lilley III, W. and DeFranco, L. J. (1999a). *The Economic Impact of Network Q Rally of Great Britain.* Washington, D.C., InContext Inc.

Lilley III, W. and DeFranco, L. J. (1999b). *The Economic Impact of the European Grand Prix.* Washington, D.C., InContext Inc.

Litherland, S. (1997). Expose yourself live. *Marketing Event,* June, 41–42.

Lock, D. (1988). *Project Management.* Aldershot, Gower.

London International Exhibition Centre PLC (2000). *ExCel Rules and Regulation.* Version 14. London, London International Exhibition Centre PLC.

London Marathon (2000). *Runner's Survey Reveals Flora London Marathon as the UK's Number One Annual Fundraising Event* (Internet) London Marathon press release, 3 October. Available from <http://www.london-marathon.co.uk/Media/displayarticle.asp?txtfile=1539582591000.txt&jpgfile=null&template=Sponsor%20%20%20%20%20> (accessed 5 February 2001).

London Mardi Gras (2000). *Statement of Values for the Pride March and Parade* (Internet) London, London Mardi Gras. Available from <http://www.londonmardigras.com/newmaster/pages/statementvalues.htm> (accessed 20 December 2000).

Lord Mayor's Show (2000). *History of the Show* (Internet). Available from <http://www.lordmayorsshow.org/hist.htm> (accessed 11 January 2001).

Lovelock, C., Vandermerwe, S. and Lewis, B. (1999). *Services Marketing: A European Perspective.* Hemel Hempstead, Prentice-Hall Europe.

Lulewicz, S. (1995). Training and development of volunteers. In *The Volunteer Management Handbook* (T. Connors, ed.) New York, John Wiley and Sons.

Machiavelli, N. (1962). *The Prince*. Trans. L. Ricci. Chicago, Mentor Classics.

Manchester 2002 (2000a). *Manchester 2002 Commonwealth Games Corporate Plan*. Manchester, Manchester 2002 Ltd.

Manchester 2002 (2000b). Manchester 2002 the XVII Commonwealth Games. Press release, 6 April. Manchester, Manchester 2002 Limited.

Manchester 2002 (2000c). *Spirit of Friendship Festival Executive Summary*. Manchester, Manchester 2002 Ltd.

Marsh, P. D. V. (1984). *Contract Negotiation Handbook*. 2nd edn. Aldershot, Gower.

Maslow, A. (1954). *Motivation and Personality*. New York, Harper & Row.

McCurley, S. and Lynch, R. (1998). *Essential Volunteer Management*. 2nd edn. London, Directory of Social Change.

McDuff, N. (1995). Volunteer and staff relations. In *The Volunteer Management Handbook* (T. Connors, ed.) New York, John Wiley & Sons.

McKay, G. (2000). *Glastonbury: A Very English Fair*. Gollancz (Internet). Extract available from <http://www.uclan.ac.uk/facs/class/cultstud/staff/glafest.htm> (accessed 20 April 2001).

McLuhan, R. (2000). 20 ways to cut costs. *Marketing Event*, March, 43–44.

Mellor, P. (2000). The core debate. *Access All Areas*, November–December, 16.

Middleton, V. T. C. (1995). *Marketing in Travel and Tourism*. Oxford, Butterworth-Heinemann.

Millennium Commission Press Office (2000). August Bank Holiday Sees High Point for Millennium Festival. Millennium Commission press release, 23 August (Internet) Available from: <http://www.millennium.gov.uk/latest_news/news-room/archive/23-08-00.htm> (accessed 7 February 2001).

Millennium Commission (2000). Celebrating the Millennium. (Internet) Available from: <http://www.millennium.gov.uk/how_to_join/festivals/index.htm> (accessed 7 February 2001).

Mintel (2000). *Music Concerts and Festivals*. London, Mintel International Group Ltd.

Mohr, K., Backman, K., Gahan, L. and Backman, S. (1993). An investigation of festival motivations and event satisfaction by visitor type. *Festival Management and Event Tourism*, **1**(3), 89–97.

Monmonier, M. (1996) *How to Lie with Maps*. 2nd edn. Chicago, University of Chicago Press.

Morgan, M. (1996). *Marketing for Leisure and Tourism*. London, Prentice-Hall.

Motor Sports Association (1999). *MSA Report Reveals Economic Impact of World Rally Championship* (Internet) Slough, Motor Sports Association press release, 19 November. Available from <http://www.msauk.org/dynamic/news/article.html?ArticleId=4> (accessed 29 May 2001).

Mullins, L. J. (1999) *Management and Organisational Behaviour*. 5th edn. London, *Financial Times*, Pitman Publishing.

Neighbourhood Arts Unit (1991). *Community Festival Handbook*. Melbourne, City of Melbourne.

NetAid.org (1999). Netaid.org Web Site Sets World Record for Largest Internet Broadcast; More than One Thousand Organizations Join Initiative to Fight Extreme Poverty. 12 October 1999. (Internet) Available from: <http://app.netaid.org/sponsors/press/worldrecord.html> (accessed 11 March 2001).

New Leisure Markets (1995). *Festivals and Special Events*. New Local Authority Leisure Markets, 4. Headland, Cleveland, Business Information Futures Ltd.

Newham Leisure Services (2000). *Reasons to be Cheerful: Newham's Local Culture Strategy*. London, Newham Leisure Services.

National Outdoor Events Association (NOEA) (1993). *Code of Practice for Outdoor Events: Other than Pop Concerts and Raves*. Wallington, NOEA.

National Outdoor Events Association (NOEA) (1997). *Code of Practice for Outdoor Events: Other than Pop Concerts and Raves: Amendments and Updates*. Wallington, NOEA.

Noise Council (1995). *Code of Practice on Environmental Noise Control at Concerts*. London, Chartered Institute Environmental Health Officers.

North West Arts Board (1999*). No difference, no future! Action for cultural diversity in Greater Mancheste*r (Internet) Manchester, North West Arts Board. Available from <http://www.arts.org.uk/directory/regions/north_west/report_cult_div.html> (accessed 12 July 2000).

Notman, S. (1999). *BEIC Topic Report: The Tourism Sector in Birmingham*. Birmingham, Birmingham Economic Information Centre.

Office for National Statistics (2000). *Table CAS74 Gender and Social Grade by Age*. (Internet) London, Office for National Statistics. Available from <http://www.statistics.gov.uk/census2001/pdfs/ cassocialgrade.pdf> (accessed 4 January 2001).

O'Neill, S. (2000). Geldoff fury as can't-do culture kills new year fireworks (Internet) *Daily Telegraph*, issue 2006, 21 November. Available from <http://www.telegraph.co.uk:80/et?ac=004296952912049&rtmo=psQlBMSe&atmo=rrrrrrrq&pg=/et/00/11/21/nnew21.html> (accessed 6 February 2001).

Owen, J. and Holliday, P. (1993). Confer in Confidence: an Organiser's Dossier. Broadway, Worcester, Meetings Industry Association.

Oxford Interactive Encyclopedia (1997). *Folk Festival*. The Learning Company, Inc.

PA Cambridge Economic Consultants (1990). *An Evaluation of Garden Festivals*. HMSO.

Pagonis, W. G. (1992). *Moving Mountains Lessons in Leadership and Logistics from the Gulf War*. Boston, Harvard Business School Press.

Palmer, G. and Lloyd, N. (1972). *A Year of Festivals: British Calendar Customs*. London, Frederick Warne.

Peach, E. and Murrell, K. (1995). Reward and recognition systems for volunteers. In *The Volunteer Management Handbook* (T. Connors, ed.) New York, John Wiley & Sons.

Perry, M., Foley, P. and Rumpf, P. (1996). Event management: an emerging challenge in Australian education. *Festival Management and Event Tourism*, **4**, 85–93.

Policy Studies Institute (PSI) (1992). Arts festivals. *Cultural Trends*, **15**. London, Policy Studies Institute.

Reid, F. (1995). *Staging Handbook*. 2nd edn. London, A. & C. Black.

Ritchie, J. R. B. (1984). Assessing the impact of hallmark events. *Journal of Travel Research*, **23**(1), 2–11.

Robbins, S. and Coulter, M. (1999). *Management*. International edition, 6th edn. Upper Saddle River, New Jersey, Prentice-Hall.

Robinson, G. (2000). The creative imperative: investing in the arts in the 21st century. *New Statesman* Arts Lecture 2000, Banqueting Hall, Whitehall, 27 June, London, Arts Council of England.

Rogers, T. (1998). *Conferences: A Twenty-First Century Industry*. Harlow, Addison Wesley Longman.

Rolfe, H. (1992). *Arts Festivals in the UK*. London, Policy Studies Institute.

Rose, D. and O'Reilley, K. (1998). *The ESCR Review of Government Social Classifications*. London, Office for National Statistics/Economic and Social Research Council.

Roslow, S. Nicholls, J. and Laskey, H. (1992). Hallmark events and measures of reach and audience characteristics, *Journal of Advertising Research*, July–August, 53–59.

Saleh, F. and Ryan, C. (1993). Jazz and knitwear: factors that attract tourists to festivals. *Tourism Management*, August, 298–297.

Select Committee on Culture, Media and Sport (1999). *Fourth Report: Staging International Sporting Events*. London, The Stationery Office.

Select Committee on Culture, Media and Sport (2001). *Third Report: Staging International Sporting Events*. London, The Stationery Office.

Shone, A. (1998). *The Business of Conferences*. Oxford, Butterworth-Heinemann.

Shone, A. with Parry, B. (2001). *Successful Event Management*. London, Continuum.

Slack, N., Chambers, S. and Johnston, R. (2001). *Operations Management*. 3rd edn. Maidenhead, *Financial Times*, Prentice-Hall.

Sleight, S. (1989). *Sponsorship: What It Is and How to Use It*. Maidenhead, McGraw-Hill.

Slice (2000). Creamfields 2000. (Internet) London, Slice. Available from: <http://www.slice.co.uk/creamfields00_sitemap.html> (accessed 2 February 2001).

Society of Motor Manufacturers and Traders (SMMT) (2000). *British International Motor Show Sets New Records* (Internet) London, Society of Motor Manufacturers and Traders press release. Available from <http://www.prnewswire.co.uk/cgi/release?id=16355> (accessed 5 February 2001).

Sodexho Prestige (2000). *Corporate Hospitality Guide 2000–2001: Best Practice Guide*. Alperton, Sodexho Prestige.

South East Arts (1998). *A Festival's Strategy for the South East*. London, England's Regional Arts Boards.

Stayte, S. and Watt, D. (1998). *Events: From Start to Finish*. Reading, ILAM.

Stoner, J. A. F., Freeman, R. E. and Gilbert D. R. Jr (1995). *Management*. 6th edn. Englewood Cliffs, New Jersey, Prentice-Hall.

Sunshine, K., Backman, K. and Backman, S. (1995). An examination of sponsorship proposals in relation to corporate objectives. *Festival Management and Event Tourism*, **2**(3/4), 159–166.

Tourism Works (1996). *Economic Impact of the European Championships 1996 on the City of Leeds: An Image Volume Value Study*. Leeds, Leeds City Council.

Thompson, J. L. (1997). *Strategic Management: Awareness and Change*. 3rd edn. London, International Thompson Business Press.

The Institute of Logistics and Transport (TILT) (2001) *Glossary of Terms* (Internet) Corby, The Institute of Logistics and Transport. Available from <http://www.iolt.org.uk> (accessed 6 February 2001).

Torkildsen, G. (1999). *Leisure and Recreation Management*. 4th edn. London, E. & F. N. Spon.

Toulmin. V. (1995). National Fairground Archive (Internet) Sheffield, University of Sheffield. Available from <http://www.shef.ac.uk/uni/projects/nfa/history/charter> (accessed 24 April 2001).

Travers, T. (1998). *The Wyndham Report*. London, Society of London Theatre.

Tribe, J. (1997). *Corporate Strategy for Tourism*. London, International Thompson Business Press.

UK Sport (1998). *Public Opinion Survey – Importance and Measure of UK Sporting Success*. London, UK Sport.

UK Sport (1999a). *A UK Strategy: Major Events – A 'Blueprint' For Success*. London, UK Sport.

UK Sport (1999b). Memorandum submitted by the United Kingdom Sports Council. In *Fourth Report: Staging International Sporting Events. Volume II Minutes of Evidence* (Select Committee on Culture, Media and Sport). London, The Stationery Office.

UK Sport (1999c). *Major Events: The Economics – a Guide*. London, UK Sport.

UK Sport (2000a). *UK Bids for World Stage* (Internet) UK Sport press release, 15 June. Available from <http://www.uksport.gov.uk/cgi-bin/read-article.cgi?articleid =52> (accessed 28 December 2000).

UK Sport (2000b). *Major Events Blueprint: Measuring Success*. UK Sport.

Uysal, M., Gahan, L. and Martin, B. (1993). An examination of event motivations. *Festival Management and Event Tourism*, 1(1), 5–10.

Vasey, J. (1998). *Concert Tour Production Management*. Boston, Focal Press.

Veal, A. (1997). *Research Methods for Leisure and Tourism*. 2nd edn. London, Pitman.

Verwey, P. (1999). *Sample Audience Survey Questions*. London, Arts Council of England.

Vroom, V. (1964). *Work and Motivation*. New York, John Wiley & Sons.

Wales Tourist Board (WTB) (2000). *A Tourism Strategy for Wales*. Cardiff, Wales Tourist Board.

Wells, W. D. and Gubar, G. (1966). Lifecycle Concepts in Marketing Research. *Journal of Marketing Research*, 3, 355–63.

Wood, H. (1982). *Festivity and Social Change*. London, Leisure in the Eighties Research Unit, Polytechnic of the South Bank.

Xerox Corporation (1998). *Guide to Waste Reduction and Recycling at Special Events*. New York, Xerox Corporation.

Yorkshire Tourist Board (2000). *Love Parade at Roundhay Park, Leeds: Event Evaluation*. York, Yorkshire Tourist Board Research Services.

Younge, G. (1999). New beat to saving the world from debt (Internet) *Guardian Unlimited*, 15 February. Available from <http://www.guardianunlimited.co.uk> (accessed 15 April 2001).

Zeithaml, V., Parasuraman, A. and Berry, L. (1990). *Delivering Quality Service: Balancing Customer Perceptions and Expectations*. New York, Free Press.

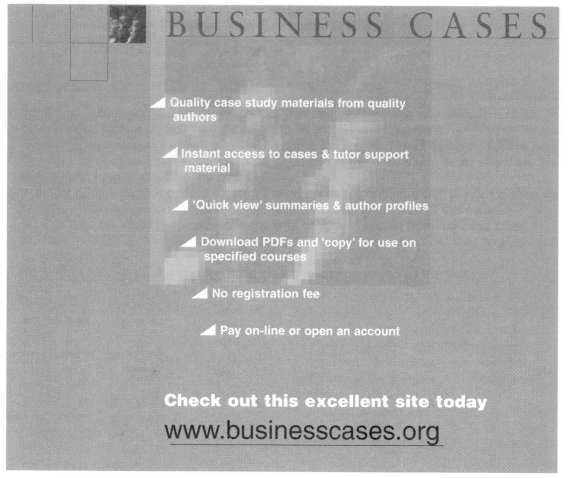

Index

Marketing plan, 145, 146
  sponsorship as integral part of, 153
Marketing research, 143–4, 146
Martell Grand National, *see* Aintree Grand
    National
Maslow's hierarchy of needs, 102–3, 122–3
Master budget, 177
Master of ceremonies (MC), 254, 260
Matrix structures, 81–3
Measurable objectives, 71, 87, 160, 162, 242,
    273
Measuring success, 50, 149
Media:
  role in events, 49, 56–7, 61, 211–14
  role in sponsorship, 154
Media logistics, 230–1
Media monitoring, 165, 283
Media release, 284, 285
Media technology, 57
Meeting Professionals International (MPI), 12
Meetings, 174, 200, 262, 272
  feedback, 275
  multi-agency, 212–13
  risk assessment, 201
Meetings Industry Association (MIA), 12,
    175
Mega-events, 16–17, 287–90
Mela, 26
Mendip District Council, 208, 209
Merchandising, 187, 196
Message(s), promotion, 139
Meteorological factors, 73
MICE (Meetings, Incentives, Conventions
    and Exhibitions), *see* Business events
Milestones, 172, 237, 240
Millennium:
  events, 59–60
  funding, 11
  television coverage, 56
Millennium Commission, 11, 59–60
Millennium Dome, 33, 36, 60
  queuing, 220–1
  ticket distribution, 218
Millennium Experience, 60
Millennium Festival, 11, 12, 17, 30–1, 60,
    209
Millennium Square, Leeds, 12, 26, 41
Misrepresentation, 198
Miss Saigon, 19
Mission, 69–70
Mission statement, 70
Mobile Outdoor Catering Association
    (MOCA), 13

Monarchy, and events, 6
  see also Queen Elizabeth, Queen Victoria,
    Royalty
Monitor (sound systems), 258
Monitoring the event, 272, 286
Motivating staff and volunteers, 101–6
  content theories, 102–4
  process theories, 104–6
Motivations, to attend festivals, 121–2
Motor Sports Association (MSA), 285
Multi-agency group, 203, 212, 213
Multiculturalism, 7, 26, 223, 287–90
Multiplier analysis, 282
Music events, 211–14, 250
Music festivals, 8, 167–9, 208–11
Music, live, market, 20

Naming rights, 160, 165
National Agricultural Centre, *see* Royal
    Show
National Arenas Association (NAA), 13
National Exhibition Centre (NEC), 8, 43
National Exhibitors Association (NEA), 12
National parks, as venues, 227–8
National Outdoor Events Association
    (NOEA), 13
National Society for the Prevention of
    Cruelty to Children (NSPCC), 135
National Statistics Social Economic
    Classification (NS-SEC), 125
National Vocational Qualifications (NVQs),
    13
NEC, *see* National Exhibition Centre (NEC)
Needs, motives and benefits offered by
    events, 122–3
Negative impacts of events, 29–30
Negotiations, 241–2
NetAid 1999, 10
Network analysis, 239–40
Network Q Rally, 29, 42, 284
  economic impact, 285
Network structures, 83–4
Networking, 160
New Year's Eve celebrations, 30–1, 60, 201,
    202, 220
  cancellation of London 2000 event, 31
  television coverage, 56
Newbury and Royal Berkshire Show, 21
Newham Council, cultural strategy, 28
Newsletter, 168
Noise Council, 207
Noise limits, breach, 208
Northern Ireland Events Company, 37

Hospitality, Leisure & Tourism Series

Queen Elizabeth: (cont.)
 Golden Jubilee, 23
 involvement in Beacon Millennium
  Project, 60
 Silver Jubilee, 6
Queen Victoria, Diamond Jubilee, 6
Questionnaires, see Surveys
Queuing, 220–1
Quotation, 182–3

RAC Signs Service, 221
Radio, 57
Radio One, 211–14
Raffles, 187–8
Ratio analysis, 176–7
Reading Festival, 75, 142
Reciprocal relationship, sponsorship, 152–3
Recording the event, 265–6
Recruitment:
 hiring procedure, 96–7
 paid and voluntary staff, 94–5
 procedures, 92
 selection procedure, 96
Recruitment budget, 94
Recycling, 229
Red Nose Day, 9, 56
Reference groups, influence of, 124
Regional Arts Association, see Regional Arts
  Board
Regional Arts Boards, funding, 9, 11
 see also Arts Council
Regulations, 205–7
Rehearsal, 264
Reporting guidelines, 188
Reporting of Injuries, Diseases and
  Dangerous Occurrences Regulations
  1995 (RIDDOR), 201
Reports, 174–5, 188–9
 from security staff, 274
 from stage managers, 274
 to stakeholders, 273
Reserved seating, 252
Retrenchment strategy, 75
Return on capital employed (ROCE), 177
Return on investment (ROI), 177
Revenue, 184, 185–6
Revenue budget, 78
Revenue-oriented pricing strategy, 136
Revenue sources, 184, 185–6
Reward and recognition techniques, 105–6
'Rider' on entertainment contracts, 194–5

Risk assessment, checklist, 204
Risk assessment, meetings, 201
Risk management, 199–203, 254
 and insurance, 205
 five steps to, 200–4
 use of work breakdown structure (WBS),
  237
Risks:
 evaluation, 201–2
 event specific, 202–3
 decision-making, 201
 identification, 200–1
 recording, 203
 review, 203–4
 what is it?, 199
Road Hauliers Association, 222
Roskilde Festival, 30, 209
Rotary International World Convention, 21
Roundhay Park, 212
Rowdyism, 30
Royal & Ancient (R&A), 88–9
Royal Ascot, 4, 9, 30
Royal Bank of Scotland Street Party, see
  Edinburgh's Hogmanay
Royal events, 35
 see also Queen Elizabeth; Queen Victoria
Royal Festival Hall, see Festival of Britain
  1951
Royal Show, 21
 park and ride, 32
Royal Victoria Park, 29
Rugby League World Cup, 10, 19
Rugby Union World Cup, 10, 19, 183, 272
 job creation, 42
 role of Wales Tourism Board, 39
 sponsorship, 56
Rules, 79
Run sheets, 265
Ryder Cup 2001, 10

Sales promotion, 139
Sample contract, 192–3
Scarborough Fayre, 3
Scheduling, 237–8
Seasonality and events, 40
Seating, 89, 252
Secondary reference group, 124
Security alert, see Aintree Grand National
Security arrangements, 218, 231, 232
Security deposit, 195
Security staff, role, 274

Hospitality, Leisure & Tourism Series